CURRICULUM STUDIES IN CANADA

Present Preoccupations

Edited by Anne M. Phelan and William F. Pinar

The largest specialization in faculties of education in Canada is curriculum studies. *Curriculum Studies in Canada* represents the present preoccupations of curriculum scholars in Canada. Set against the backdrop of the COVID-19 pandemic, contributors engage with significant themes, among them ongoing efforts at justice for Indigenous Peoples, the continuing arrival of immigrants and refugees, Canada's complex relationship to the United States, and issues related to the climate crisis.

Addressing such realities through the field of curriculum studies and the school curriculum is critical at this historical conjuncture given the complex and shifting intersections of local and global dynamics restricting education. To this end, contributing scholars serve as intellectual activists to address the critical need for understanding curriculum responsive to the vexed relations among schools, nation-building, social reconstruction, and identity development. Their activism yields more sophisticated understandings of what it means to be educated in Canada. Contributors trace the legacy of their work and reflect on their present scholarly preoccupations in light of their past endeavours. In doing so, *Curriculum Studies in Canada* offers an invitation to readers: to study, remember, dialogue, and navigate an uncertain world with them.

ANNE M. PHELAN is a professor in the Department of Curriculum and Pedagogy at the University of British Columbia and an honorary professor at The Education University of Hong Kong.

WILLIAM F. PINAR is the Tetsuo Aoki Professor in Curriculum Studies at the University of British Columbia.

Curriculum Studies in Canada

Present Preoccupations

EDITED BY ANNE M. PHELAN
AND WILLIAM F. PINAR

UNIVERSITY OF TORONTO PRESS
Toronto Buffalo London

© University of Toronto Press 2024
Toronto Buffalo London
utorontopress.com
Printed in the USA

ISBN 978-1-4875-5169-8 (cloth)
ISBN 978-1-4875-5171-1 (paper)
ISBN 978-1-4875-5173-5 (EPUB)
ISBN 978-1-4875-5172-8 (PDF)

Library and Archives Canada Cataloguing in Publication

Title: Curriculum studies in Canada : present preoccupations / edited by Anne M. Phelan and William F. Pinar.
Names: Phelan, Anne M., editor. | Pinar, William F., editor.
Description: Includes bibliographical references and index.
Identifiers: Canadiana (print) 2024032921X | Canadiana (ebook) 20240329252 | ISBN 9781487551698 (cloth) | ISBN 9781487551711 (paper) | ISBN 9781487551728 (PDF) | ISBN 9781487551735 (EPUB)
Subjects: LCSH: Curriculum planning – Canada. | LCSH: Education – Curricula – Canada. | LCSH: Education – Social aspects – Canada.
Classification: LCC LB2806.15.C87 2024 | DDC 375/.0010971–dc23

Cover design: Val Cooke
Cover image: steeve-x-art/Alamy Stock Photo

We wish to acknowledge the land on which the University of Toronto Press operates. This land is the traditional territory of the Wendat, the Anishnaabeg, the Haudenosaunee, the Métis, and the Mississaugas of the Credit First Nation.

This book has been published with the help of a grant from the Federation for the Humanities and Social Sciences, through the Awards to Scholarly Publications Program, using funds provided by the Social Sciences and Humanities Research Council of Canada.

University of Toronto Press acknowledges the financial support of the Government of Canada, the Canada Council for the Arts, and the Ontario Arts Council, an agency of the Government of Ontario, for its publishing activities.

Canada Council for the Arts | Conseil des Arts du Canada

ONTARIO ARTS COUNCIL
CONSEIL DES ARTS DE L'ONTARIO
an Ontario government agency
un organisme du gouvernement de l'Ontario

Funded by the Government of Canada | Financé par le gouvernement du Canada | Canada

Contents

Preface

The purpose of this project, both as a seminar series (Curriculum Studies in Canada 2020–1: http://curriculumstudies.ca) and as an edited volume, is to register present preoccupations of curriculum studies scholarship in Canada. These range from climate crisis, conflict, history, identity, memory, science, and sexuality to truth and reconciliation, each topic treated in singular fashion, each located in a specific place, at a particular time, in unique circumstances. Because, then, each essay etches in the field a distinctive mark, each resists subsumption into general categories, declines to be positioned in any hierarchy of urgency. To honour this non-reducible distinctiveness, we organized the contents of this collection alphabetically according to the author's last name.

Yet, as co-editors, we very much share the sense that a field of study – *this* field of study – is "always promising and threatening to amount to something" (Stewart, 2010, p. 340). Like all fields of study, curriculum studies in Canada demands some sense of "collective attunement and a more adequate description of how things make sense, fall apart, become something else, and leave their marks" (p. 340), in *this* place and at *this* time. Why these particular preoccupations, and why now? What are the field's hopes, dreams, expectations of itself and its institutions? What are its points of endurance at being challenged or obligation to move on in an era that compels Canadians to reflect upon and reconstruct their visions of democratic, sustainable futures through education?

The COVID-19 pandemic provided an important backdrop to this project, but our choice of invitees was shaped by even more significant realities, among them ongoing efforts at justice for Aboriginal peoples, the continuing arrival of immigrants and refugees, a complex relation to the United States, and issues related to climate crisis. Addressing such realities through the field of curriculum studies and the school curriculum is critical at this historical conjuncture given those complex and shifting intersections of local and global dynamics restricting education. To this end, we identified scholars whose intellectual activism aspires to address the critical need for understanding curriculum responsive to the vexed relations among schools, nation-building, social reconstruction, and identity development, activism that yields more sophisticated understandings of what it means to be educated in Canada. We invited each to trace the legacy of their work and to reflect on their scholarly preoccupations in the present in light of those past endeavours. In their turn, the authors issue an invitation to readers: to study, remember, dialogue, and navigate an uncertain world with them. From these shared responsibilities the future unfolds.

Anne M. Phelan
William F. Pinar

REFERENCE

Stewart, K. (2010). Afterword: Worlding refrain. In M. Gregg & G.J. Seigworth (Eds.), *The affect theory reader* (pp. 339–53). Duke University Press.

Acknowledgments

We wish to acknowledge the contributions of the curriculum scholars who, during challenging times, generously agreed to participate in the on-line Curriculum Studies in Canada seminar series (2020–1), and to contribute thereafter to this volume.

In particular we want to thank Dr. Ying Ma, former post-doctoral fellow at the University of British Columbia, for her assistance in coordinating the seminar series and editing the volume. Thanks also goes to Jill Morris, doctoral candidate at the University of British Columbia, for her assistance in proofreading and formatting the collection.

Finally, we wish to acknowledge the support of the Social Sciences and Humanities Research Council of Canada, the Faculty of Education (a Learning Transformed Grant), and the Centre for the Study of Teacher Education without which this collected volume would not have been possible.

CURRICULUM STUDIES IN CANADA

Introduction: Curriculum Studies in Canada

WILLIAM F. PINAR

The phrase I have used for the chapter's title was chosen deliberately to emphasize the field over the nationality. And "Canadian" is itself too complex a concept to function as a clarifying modifier only. Like the field itself, Canada – Létourneau spells it "Kanada" – is multivariate, in motion, its origin Indigenous, then land occupied by Europeans, now by immigrants from everywhere, all seeking a future freed from the past. But being freed from the past cannot occur unless the past is remembered, worked through, amends made. Truth and reconciliation animate both the field and its present preoccupations.

"Where are we at, in this place and this time, as Canadian curriculum scholars?" Answers to that question – posed by Nicholas Ng-A-Fook (2014, p. 14), the question of this collection – you can glimpse within. The book is, I emphasize, only a glimpse: after all, thirteen essays, however broad their reach, cannot convey everything that curriculum studies scholars in Canada are undertaking as you read. While not a comprehensive representation of the field, then, these essays, I suspect, come close – in topic, tone, intention. I invoke those three interwoven aspects of contemporary curriculum studies to point to features of a field that can sometimes seem scattered and unrelated, even to those of us on the inside. I intend to test Strathausen's assertion that "Each academic discipline comprises a complex system of discursive practice that creates its own dynamics and follows its own laws of structural development" (2017, p. 293). "Laws" does seem an overstatement for a field formed by the humanities and the arts, supplemented by social and political theory. Nomological laws are the province of the natural sciences, and of those social sciences that attempt to copy them, but they convey no aspiration of fields focused on particularity, however embedded in the particular the universal might be. The terms "discursive practice" and "dynamics" and "structural development" may pertain, however, as being focused on the curriculum while contemporaries – even when culturally, generationally, and in gender separated – does encourage confluences of "discursive practice" and "dynamics," confluences that create at least the illusion of specific "structural development."

Sweeping in scope, the topics testify to the problematics of the present, a present informed – often deformed – by the past, obvious in the case of environmental degradation, climate crisis, planetary (in)habitability: the topic with which two of the essays are preoccupied. A present deformed by the past is prominent in the catastrophe of cultural genocide as well; truth and reconciliation are now disciplinary dynamics as well as the challenge of a national commission. One essay is devoted exclusively to this topic, but other essays are also structured by these dynamics, evident when scholars acknowledge the land on which scholars work. (I am writing from my home in what is now northwest Washington State, the ancestral land of the Nooksack People.) Cultural genocide has not been undergone by Indigenous Peoples only; certain settlers have suffered this fate, depicted in the essay devoted to Quebec. All cultures – in their anthropological senses – may be at risk today, if the technologization of everything continues unabated (Pinar 2022). Certainly, the form of the school is threatened, as one essay makes clear. Teaching remains, if understood not only as "instruction" – imparting information, as the internet can – but as "pedagogy," making sense of "information," enabling students and scholars to become knowledgeable, including about themselves. These essays perform "pedagogy," often autobiographically animated, on occasion playfully enacted if always earnest, especially when conflict is concerned, another topic addressed in this collection. These topics are not random nor free-floating in space; each is situated in place, in time, in life history, History, culture, embodied and personified in human subjects, codified in school subjects, at least one – science – in the shadow cast by the behemoth below the 49th parallel.

That I would enlist "tone" to demarcate curriculum studies might strike some as odd given the legacy of neutrality and impartiality in scholarship and academic research, the shadow of a science that positions personality to the side, a prerequisite to finding what the facts reveal. Educators, too, separate themselves from what they teach, but about which they can become impassioned. Many curriculum scholars are former schoolteachers – almost all are now university teachers – and that professional passion is present in the presentation of even scientific research. Professional passion becomes intensified when the topic is timely, when it is something current and compelling, setting off in one instance an alarm, in another a lament, one writer wistful, another reprimanding, another indignant, all contemplative. Tone there is, perhaps part of the "affective turn in the humanities" (Strathausen, 2017, p. 301). Like its musical analogue, the tone of the prose to follow varies, sometimes within the same essay. But the sound of scholarship (Gershon, 2017) is an indelible feature of curriculum studies in Canada.

Careful not to commit the intentional fallacy, I make no claims about the authors' intentions, only about those intentions explicit in the text. Overall, these are pedagogical in character, no surprise given many scholars' prior school-teaching experience, given that almost everyone is teaching now. The essay as pedagogical is committed to clarification, to truth-telling not only in service to advancing knowledge in the discipline – in curriculum studies that is a somewhat uncommon intention about which I have worried (Pinar, 2007) – but also to inform and explain, even to arouse students who, teachers hope, become engaged intellectually and emotionally in what they study and its possible relation to their lives and the world we inhabit. To that intention, tone and topic testify, the two become interrelated, tone in congruence (Shuchat-Shaw, 1980) with topic. That congruence is sounded from the start.

The Essays

"We are writing these papers in the midst of uncertain and difficult times," Kumari Beck starts, citing the COVID-19 pandemic, the Black Lives Matter protests, anti-Asian racism, the ongoing climate emergency, and the 2021 discovery of the remains of 215 children on *Tk'emlúps te Secwépemc*, the site of the former Kamloops Indian residential school in British Columbia. These "impossibilities of keeping hope alive" – for "education generally," for "curriculum more specifically" – constitute "incursions into the attempts I make to carry on work in the academy." This writing is "borne of such vulnerabilities, the expectation that we continue to work as if nothing else was going on." Beck testifies to "a sense of a collective, a collective that is a tapestry of storied strands, connecting one to another," providing her a "feeling of gathering strength, and this gives me hope."

Acknowledging the urgency of the present Beck returns to the past, recalling "key moments in my engagement with, explorations of, and practising with curriculum as international text." The first occurred in a Ceylon (now Sri Lanka) school where she was taught "the best of British literature, art, and theatre, Greek pottery, architecture, and plays," as well as "the histories of ancient Rome, Greece and England." Through such study Beck was "called into existence," indeed "defined by what is now my first language, English," a consequence of a "well-rounded, high-quality education that has enriched my life," adding: "I was internationalized long before I left home." Enlisting in the "army of knowledge conveyers," Beck taught the curriculum she had been taught, "carefully reproducing the classrooms of my own teachers. Taking up the White Man's burden, I taught the English canon with great care, never straying from the script."

The second key moment Beck recounts was comprised of "cracks" in her teaching, cracks that appeared "many years later" while teaching new immigrants – carpenters and mechanics – in a private post-secondary classroom in British Columbia. Facing that class of "all men, I went blank," perhaps due to the "borrowed grey tweed suit that I had forced myself to wear (to appear the part), or a "feeling with" this diverse group of men who, like me, were wondering how we came to be sitting in this grey and gloomy place (it was a rainy November in Vancouver), far from home." Whatever the specific cause, "something snapped, and I slowly pushed aside the teaching manual," starting instead a "conversation about what brought us there." Beck remembers that "what happened next that day and for the rest of the three weeks" was an "opening up" to the creative tension that can occur in between the curriculum-as-plan and the curriculum-as-lived.

The third moment – "entering and occupying the field" – occurred when Beck decided to study international education, a formalization of her childhood and teaching experience that "operated on principles such as relationality, reciprocity, learner-centred and liberatory education (Freire), and constructivism." Again, tensions between curriculum-as-plan and as-lived occurred, in this instance between "the expectations of students and our intentions to be liberatory." Questions arose: "Was constructivism an imposition of Western thought?" Why must students be encouraged to "break with the hierarchical relationships that they were familiar with in schooling in their home countries?" How could these tensions – contradictions – be addressed?

For twelve years Beck taught in a Master of Education program – teaching English as an additional language – designed specifically for international students. Beck taught one of the elective courses, "Current Issues in Curriculum and Pedagogy," to mostly international students. She started her classes by asking: "What would you like to learn?" The answer, Beck reports, was often "silence, not a reflective silence, or a contemplative moment, but a weighty silence," prompting her to wonder: "How I might support the recovery of personal truth among my students, to name and interrogate the many ways in which they are diminished in their journey to get here?" She concluded that "I should extend the time to talk about what brought each of us here, to this point and wait for the curriculum." Here the past migrates into the present and the curriculum can become self-revelation.

The past haunts the present in Kathy Bickmore's essay as well. Despite Canadian commitments to peace, pluralism, and multiculturalism, Bickmore begins, Canadian schools are also shaped by their parent "patriarchal settler state." That painful paradox preoccupies Bickmore; she has focused her curriculum research on "persistent violence, disproportionately affecting marginalized people." She wonders how the curriculum might address "violence and social justice conflicts," thereby enacting those very commitments to peace and pluralism to which Canadians declare allegiance. Such a curriculum of conflict encourages the "continuing expression of difference," as well as ongoing study of "un-peace." Bickmore affirms that violence is "*not* inevitable," that "its underlying conflictual causes can be satisfied, redirected, ended, or mended," that nonviolence can be taught, as Hongyu Wang (2014) knows. Bickmore shows that "meaningful peacebuilding education," while "challenging," is nonetheless "possible in public schools."

How? "Peace*building*," Bickmore explains, "involves multidimensional ongoing efforts" to "transform" the causes of conflict, then "to redress and repair their disproportionate harm to the most vulnerable." That occurs by "helping students to acquire language, concepts, skills, and relationships for recognizing, communicating, and deliberating about the cultural and social-structural causes and consequences of destructive conflicts, and about what people can do collectively about these problems," in so doing demonstrating that the school curriculum can support "youths' development of agency for transformative peacebuilding." What undermines peacebuilding is that the "curriculum tends to be skewed by the unjust social structures and oppressive cultural beliefs and practices," often shifting "responsibilities for achieving just peace onto individuals, instead of enabling and inspiring them to probe social-structural, cultural, and political factors that constrain as well as enable their agency." Even so, Bickmore remains "guardedly optimistic" that the curriculum can be converted so that it "*can* help more young people, more of the time, to develop capabilities and motivating relationships for handling complex contemporary justice conflicts," including economic and racial inequality, the former highlighted during the COVID-19 pandemic, the latter by the Black Lives Matter and Idle No More movements.

Bickmore immigrated to Canada 30 years ago, where she developed a "transnational comparative perspective from a new place." She has conducted "Peace-Building Citizenship Learning research in Mexico, Bangladesh, and Canada …, finding uncanny similarities alongside some differences," namely that the curriculum-in-use in Canadian, Bangladeshi, and Mexican schools included a "range of conflict learning opportunities, from narrow to multidimensional," the most common of which was an "emphasis on negative peace through avoidance or compliance." While she found curricular inclusion of certain "social diversities" in each nation, "intersecting gendered aspects of conflict and violence were often ignored, especially in Canada." Moreover, "political conflicts" were often taught only in the" past tense," in Canada as occurring in "far-away places." Such a "narrow, symptom-focused conflict avoidance" curriculum, Bickmore concludes, "could *block* development of more democratic and multidimensional forms of democratic agency." When "multiple dimensions of conflicts and potential peacebuilding action options" are included in the curriculum, when "teachers find ways to listen and to support their self-expression and action roles," the curriculum can create "space for young people to develop hope and capabilities, to build just peace in their own and others' lives."

As Bickmore knows, sustaining "just peace" is problematic when colonization keeps occurring, shadows cast by the past discolouring the present. School science education in Canada, David Blades begins, lives under the long shadow cast by the American post-Sputnik reforms of the 1960s. Referencing the recently revised British Columbia school science curriculum – he was a member of the development team – Blades describes how "we worked *within* the shadows" created by the light of this influence. To this American science curriculum provinces have, in the past, added "Canadian examples and some reorganization of the order of topics," amounting to "little to no change in purpose, orientation, and topics." This failure to produce an authentically Canadian science curriculum Blades attributes to "the *agenda* of the curriculum reform," namely the determination to produce "scientists and technologists to ensure a national advantage in a global economy."

A "truly Canadian" curriculum, Blades continues, would address "the social and environmental consequences of technological and scientific innovation," a curriculum not designed to produce "rocket scientists but a science literacy that takes seriously our positioning and responsibility to the survival of other species." At first Blades thought the Science-Technology-Society-Environment (STSE) initiative might meet this goal, but he quickly concluded that it "still represented an ethos of social engineering." In 2001 the United States reaffirmed "the direction and intentions of the post-Sputnik reforms in 2001 of a set of science learning standards for science education by the American Association for the Advancement of Science (AAAS)." In 2012 the US National Research Council published *A Framework for K–12 Science Education: Practices, Crosscutting Concepts, and Core Ideas*, making the case, as Blades writes, that "science education is of national importance because, the United States' position in the global economy is declining, in part because US workers lack fundamental knowledge in these fields and so a new curriculum is needed to address the critical issues of US competitiveness." Blades appreciates that this "new" curriculum conception is "parallel to the post-Sputnik reforms in intention," in effect extending "the shadow of the post-Sputnik reforms," now "reset as a fight for economic superiority through the social engineering of science education." This redirection of Sputnik-era curriculum reform from military to economic ends was "entrenched" when STEM – science, technology, engineering, mathematics – replaced STSE. STEM, Blades appreciates, "reflects and continues the agenda of using school science for social engineering to reinforce a neoliberal hegemony of superiority in global competition through a focus on a particular set of skills needed for capitalist expansionism."

The 2016–19 science curriculum reform undertaken in British Columbia focused on "the idea of an *educated citizen*," a focus that meant that students should study "science as a human activity." Those engaged in this reform, Blades continues, were well aware that previous iterations of school science education curriculum had "emphasized science content mastery over the processes of science." Believing that "learning the processes of science lay at the heart of being an educated citizen," reformers repositioned "content" as the "means" by which to learn the "processes" of science, a "radical change from any other approach to science education in the world." The new curriculum continued to emphasize "big ideas in science with content serving as *examples* of these big ideas." Finally, British Columbia curriculum developers "deliberately provided little detail about content," encouraging "teachers" to "decide on how to elaborate the content in a way that would help students learn the processes of science." Moreover, the ministry encouraged teachers to experiment with "new" forms of assessment appropriate to the reform. "[W]e let go of progress as a single, defined movement," Blades concludes, enabling teachers and students to "be open to surprise, to creativity, and to complexity precisely," casting the "curriculum as an on-going dialogue with teachers and students without a specific plan for the outcome of the dialogue." For the moment, it would seem science education in British Columbia has moved outside the shadow of Sputnik, reflecting a specifically Canadian conception of curriculum.

Sidestepping shadows cast by the past is a problematic Susan Dion knows well. "I recognize that there has been some change," Dion begins, acknowledging that "many teachers" are "shifting from the perfect stranger to the not-so-perfect stranger position asking if this has something to do with me, how do I make sense of it, what do I need to know, what am I to do?" In this "post-TRC moment" many "well-intentioned folks" are trying "to help," but the failure of the curriculum to "provide teachers and students with that which they need to engage with and learn from Indigenous people's experiences and perspectives is ongoing." Dion invokes the concept of "double bind" to depict what "teaching decolonizing and Indigenous content creates … for both students and teachers." Indigenous students seek not "settler guilt and pity" nor do they wish to be positioned as the "expert" on "Indigeneity," thereby being reduced to an "object of the settler gaze." Nor do settler teachers "want to have their ignorance exposed," or – worse – be "accused of anti-Indigenous racism." Given the double bind in which the present moment positions both Indigenous students and settler teachers, Dion calls for cultivating "awareness of implication," an insight Teresa Strong-Wilson (2021) shares.

Such awareness means acknowledging that Indigenous students and settler teachers are "differently implicated in colonial structures," obligating settler students and teachers to listen to "Indigenous perspectives," to "work with teachers' resolve to do what is in the best interest of their students and to work with their commitment to having a positive impact." Settler teachers "need to be prepared to feel bad, discomfort, conflict, shame," to acknowledge that "settlers (themselves included) have unearned privileges, and it is not equitable or fair." A "curriculum that can cope with these challenges would support settler Canadians to simultaneously hold that while Canada is a good place for many it was achieved at the expense of Indigenous people." A "Curriculum of Implication needs to be a part of the K–12 program," Dion continues, a curriculum that gives "guidance in how to navigate what it means to be implicated," adding: "While this might feel like a centering the feelings of settlers, identifying and working through emotional response is necessary to create conditions for learning." Such a curriculum will also enable Indigenous students to appreciate that what they don't know – about Indigenous cultures and languages, about the history of cultural genocide in Canada – is "directly tied to colonialism."

Genocide is a subject Claudia Eppert knows as well. Acknowledging her location – Treaty Six Territory – Eppert sees the "skies obscured by wildfire smoke," a human species plagued by pandemic, events reminding us that "we are experiencing the sixth extinction." What does it mean to conduct curriculum studies "in times of extinction"? Such scholarship shadows extinction, requiring us "to grapple with the complexities and possibilities of witnessing as an ethical concept," an "educational imperative of responsivity and responsibility." Eppert wrestles with witnessing in an era that "challenges temporalities, and re-orients remembrance to intertwinements of past, present, and future." She mourns creatures murdered as she remembers her own past, now embedded in – "*textured time-with*" – a present plagued by death and the prospect of catastrophes to come. Witnessing, she explains, is at once historical, contemplative, ecological; witnessing is enacted by the human subject, the very presence of which is now in question. Eppert invokes the Blackfoot concept of *aokakio'ssin* to underscore the significance of attending to what has, what will, happen. This constitutes a curriculum committed to "stay with the trouble rather than look away," to "look toward the skies."

Clermont Gauthier's arc of vision is likewise long, focused on the form of the school, included in which is not only the commanded curriculum but also its conversational accomplishment through the "sensitive and symbolic configuration of the relationship between the teacher and students." He asks: "*Does the school form still have its relevance in the contemporary world?*" Digital technology has the "phenomenal power to change, or even dismantle, the school form." To analyse this threat, Gauthier returns to the "concept of school form," explicating three of its features: (1) the shaping of knowledge, (2) the transmission of knowledge, and (3) the organization that supports its shaping and transmission. It is these very features that twentieth century pedagogy attempted to "overthrow." Gauthier identifies three utopian visions that animated this effort to dissolve the boundary between school-as-institution and life-as-experienced: Thoreau's *Walden or Life in the Woods*, Illich's *Deschooling Society*, and Michel Serres's *Petite Poucette*. It is a boundary now being dissolved as the Internet brings the world outside the school into the school. It is the children of the privileged who enjoy access to this (in Gauthier's fine phrase) "Adamist utopia." Utopic technology is not (only); it also constitutes a "ubiquitous … mode of control." Moreover, in this technologically updated version of Skinner's *Walden II* the teacher is scheduled to disappear, to be replaced by protocol enforced by software. Gauthier shows how central the teacher has always been, always will be, if only to "*ensure an organized functioning, to ensure order, which is the driving principle of the school form.*" Gauthier explains:

> Why is this *order* so fundamental and why does it imply that the space between school and life must be kept separate? If school was life, it would not need to exist, this is what the first utopia reveals. But school doesn't have to be life. It is simply the conscious and articulated recovery of life. The knowledge presented at school simply allows us to understand life, it doesn't have to be life. For its part, digital age does not lead to the disappearance of the school form; on the contrary, it can lead it to its most absolute fulfillment, and to a stern degree.

Gauthier acknowledges that knowledge may now be "everywhere," but knowledge still "requires someone to select it, interpret it to someone else, make it relevant, criticize it, and organize the conduct of actors to function in the real space or at a distance of the class for instruction and education to happen in a collective of students." This is the "fundamental work of the teacher."

Jen Gilbert does such "fundamental work." She explains that what the young need to know about sexuality and gender both progressives and conservatives "reduce … to a knowledge delivery system," focused on "what to include and exclude, the timing of the delivery, and the most efficient platform for the delivery." Such instrumentalism ignores the "volatile, capricious, and elusive nature of a sexuality not bound to categories or identities," resulting in "lists of skills and knowledge" that "arrives too soon and too late, throwing our best laid curricular plans into disarray." Such a curriculum is predicated on the illusion that "we all know what we are talking about when we talk about sex." Gilbert's concern is how "formal sex education defends against sexuality, holds it at bay, cordons it off into particular disciplinary boxes, or transforms it into a sanitized list of activities, feelings, and orientations." Such curriculum can on occasion "both invite students to reflect on their sexual vulnerability and sometimes expose that vulnerability," but too often fail "to capture the emotional experience of learning about sexuality." She continues:

> The unique, lived experiences of sex educators animate the field, give it shape and texture; while the official curriculum – in the form of policy documents and guidelines – tries to make order out of the messy abundance. Sex education, and sex educators, ward off the possibility of controversy by constructing an armour of checklists, guidelines, and standards – weary attempts to solder the curriculum to the legitimizing discourses of health, science, and the law.

Even progressive versions of "sex education-as-checklist," Gilbert points out, "demands compliance." An emphasis on assessment may prove "politically expedient," she adds, "but sex education, even the most progressive kind, is not particularly effective."

Gilbert focuses on a particular progressive argument, namely that "sex education done right saves queer and trans kids' lives," a "framing of sex education as necessary for the health and well-being of LGBTQ+ youth [that] comes at a cost." That cost is a narrowing of "identificatory possibilities for LGBTQ+ youth," explaining that if "progressive sex education invokes depressed, suicidal queer and trans youth as an alibi for promoting an inclusive curriculum, then teachers and students may come to understand queer and trans sexualities and genders as, in large part, sources of risk and danger." Moreover, LGBTQ+ youth "regularly resist their recruitment into the tropes of either victim or resilient hero." Reports of queer and trans lives during the COVID-19 lockdown contradict framings of LGBTQ+ students as "at heightened risk of poor mental health outcomes." Like other students, LGBTQ+ students missed being physically present with their friends and teachers, but they also rediscovered – even reconstructed – themselves during lockdown. "A queer curriculum practice," Gilbert concludes, "sees the messiness of sexuality and gender as itself a place of learning, not something that could be cleaned up through a revised set of guidelines."

Jocelyn Létourneau is also preoccupied with "messiness," with – in his fine phrasing – "the dense matter of the past." He asks: "How do nations – these imaginary communities associated with physical spaces and instituted structures – (re)produce themselves *also* by forging and spreading a historical narrative? How is this historical narrative internalized by "ordinary people" who, in so doing, (un)consciously "nationalize" themselves into matrices of meaning in which their individuality and identity are combined with the reality of a community inscribed over time?" Létourneau reports that "the young students I queried" all knew quite a lot about Quebec history, if a "hodgepodge of statements of all kinds, factual or idealistic, gleaned here and there." He summarizes: "For Francophones, this narrative structure pivots around the following key idea: 'We were had by the Other, who prevented us from accomplishing what we otherwise would have, which led our history into a trajectory of resistance and our collective existence into an experience of powerlessness and bare survival.'" Anglophones tend not to share this narrative as they incorporate Quebec's history into the broader history of Canada; then "they insist on the need to recognize the diverse and pluralistic face of Quebec society over time." They substitute Indigenous peoples for Francophones as the "true victims of History, the only truly oppressed people in Canada."

Embedded in its own historical narrative, each nation has its "own historical *problematic*," a "meta-representation" that conveys a "grand narrative of the Self through which entities grasp themselves as or assemble themselves into a whole and then consolidate and mythistoricize their trajectory through time." For Quebec and French Canada generally, Létourneau suggests, this problematic is "Duality and Victimhood." For English Canada, it is "Diversity and Peace." Each problematic reduces the multiplicity of the past into "something unequivocal, clear, simple, and above all meaningful." The problematic all Canadians share is that all non-Indigenous peoples have "benefited from colonialism," creating for Létourneau a "double bind," given that his "faith in education not to resolve but to contribute to creating the conditions necessary for new and better relationships between Indigenous people and settler Canadians exists alongside my knowledge of the ongoing lack of significant progress." Despite this "double bind I continue to have faith that our combined work is making it possible for more settler teachers to turn toward Indigenous students." That faith – that curricular turn – constitutes Canada as "more of an open question than a conclusive answer, more of a sum of provisional arrangements than a definitive program, more of an unfinished composition than a completed score."

An "open question" is a powerful concept for the country – and for that country's curriculum studies field. What knowledge is of most worth remains the open, ongoing curricular question. But, as Létourneau laments, Canada's is an open question caged inside a "double bind," faith in education alongside the fact of its failure to fix the catastrophes our ancestors have bequeathed us. In contemporary Canada, Anne Phelan writes in the epilogue, "we breathe the air of ongoing colonialism *and* reconciliation, of neo-liberal imperialism *and* public education, of exponential growth *and* sustainability, of freedom *and* responsibility." Keeping Canada's question open may mean inhabiting the conjunction, even if these conjunctions threaten, on occasion, to paralyze the polity.

No paralysis for David Lewkovich, even if he is also wrestling with a double bind, but he, too, keeps the curriculum question open, wondering what it would mean to "slow" the "forward movement" of teacher education – a field focused on the future – and turn to "dilatory, digressive spaces [that] may invite future teachers to play with speculative forms of articulation," to release "what may otherwise remain unexpressed." He has found that comics and graphic novels "appear to use methods of interpretive uncertainty as a means of amplifying the different kinds of readings that readers may pursue." In teacher education, "governing what can and cannot be talked about, what is and is not thinkable, is often maintained at the expense of the kinds of curiosity that distraction, dilatoriness, and dreaming inevitably encourage." Lewkovich asks: "What if, we may add – on the subjects of narrative, desire, and pleasure – education becomes a place to explore the uncertain detours of the middle, rather than a predetermined requirement to shut such exploration down?" Can exploring "the middle" mean inhabiting the conjunction, keeping the question open? Truth is, Lewkovich testifies, educational experience as lived is "unavoidably indeterminate and inconclusive," often "prone to revision, and despite the teacher's best efforts, sometimes never experienced at all." He suggests that "learning to linger in the dilatory may be seen as an important way for preservice teachers to reckon with the emotional challenges of education itself," prompting "alternative forms of speculative articulation." To remind prospective teachers that "adolescence and all it represents is not just something that exists in other people, I often ask my students to engage in autobiographical work that helps to reacquaint them with the emotional qualities of these years, while also recognizing that, as a series of psychic relations, adolescence never actually disappears." He also asks students to tell stories and to then illustrate them, as "the minor details that students use in their comics" nonetheless disclose students' "current concerns, fears, and desires as preservice teachers." One is reminded of Beck's invitation to her students to work from within.

Lewkovich posits adolescence and teacher education as "non-places" wherein lived experience occurs in "close relation to a different world (adulthood and the classroom, respectively) that is simultaneously ultra-real and theoretical." He asks students to compose "literary non-places," what he thinks of as "synthetic experiments that slow the forward movement of learning down, focusing less on teleological, satisfactory conclusions, than on what is speculative, fragmentary, and incomplete." Both "reading and comics creation appear to encourage middling as a verb," enabling prospective teachers to "explore the defenses and anxieties of being in a place where knowledge, both of self and others, is not always secure and dependable." Such assignments constitute "a preparation for classroom life … insert[ing] an element of wonder in teacher education," anticipating processes of "knowledge creation and sense making in schools." Such teacher education allows prospective teachers "to touch what is more transient and elusive about the inner worlds of teachers and students." Lewkovich concludes: "Teaching with the middle is thus equivalent to teaching with and through mystery – excessive, everchanging, persistent, invisible, unavoidable, and if we can bear being honest about not knowing, an important part of what seems to make us human." Teaching in the middle – that bridge Aoki (2005 [1981], p. 228) knew is not a bridge but suspension in-between – and learning because we do not know, imply dwelling in both the "world of the is and not yet" (Aoki 2005 (1987), p. 156).

Nicholas Ng-A-Fook, too, teaches "in the middle," as we see from seven narrative snapshots of curriculum in motion, in time, in place, "struggling while running, to find a pace, one's place, as an uninvited guest along the shores of the Kichi Zibi, on the unceded and unsurrendered traditional territories of the Anishnàbeg." At once literal and symbolic, curriculum constitutes "a confluence of turbulent temporal movements, reactivating, reconstructing, juxtaposing, and restorying (restoring) a subject, subjected, in this chapter, and at this situated moment, to "life writing," "settler colonialism," "truth, and then 'reconciliation.'" Each of these topics and tempos appear in each narrative snapshot, including one of his teaching of EDU 6102: Curriculum Studies Seminar, focused on the "isness" of curriculum studies. Each also appears in the other snapshots: Life Writing Research as *Currere*, Reactivating Settler Colonial Dominions Toward Re/Making an End, A Canadian Curriculum Theory Project, Changing Courses, a Coursing, in Relation to Global Pandemic, Podcasting A Canadian Curriculum Theory Project, and Reconstructing Curriculum Studies in Canada.

Through the "punctum" (Richter 2000, p. 225) these snapshots provide, Ng-A-Fook reactivates key concepts, crucial issues, crushing events, political movements, among them the school-to-prison pipeline, climate crisis, settler colonialism, the ethics of care, treaty education, consciousness, psychic integration, revolt, reparation, genocide, assimilation, tolerance, terror management theory, fetishizing fear, colonial racisms, commemorative monuments, homelessness, empathy, new materialism, Elders' teachings, curriculum policy reforms, Black feminist autobiographical research and living curriculum as nonviolence. And all this during four waves of the COVID-19 pandemic. "Reconstructing curriculum studies," Ng-A-Fook concludes, "calls on us to reactivate and reconstruct our imagination … calls on us to continue troubling and re/making the grammar of settler colonialism," and in so doing, discovering the "isness" of curriculum studies in Canada, what it means to conduct curriculum studies, recalling Eppert's searing phrase, "in times of extinction."

Veronica Pacini-Ketchabaw looks towards the skies too, emphasizing education as "ethico-political," seeking to "redress the instrumentalization of early childhood curriculum at a time when neoliberalism organizes most relations within the field." She theorizes "early education as a possibility for transforming the status quo, for invention of otherwise worlds, for reconfiguration of what humanity might become." To do so, she returned to her past, not solely an "individual journey" she insists: "I have not/do not walk alone." Arranging her autobiographical reflections performatively, Pacini-Ketchabaw begins with Act 1, titled "Pedagogical Commitments at a Time of Ecological Catastrophe," recalling her work this past decade with colleagues in the Common Worlds Research Collective, a collective committed to enabling "early childhood educators and young children to respond to the climate catastrophe." In Act 2, titled "An Education in the Midst of the Horrors of State Dictatorship," Pacini-Ketchabaw returns to her own early education, which took place during dictatorship in Argentina (1976–83). "Becoming a teacher and an early childhood educator following a brutal dictatorship," she tells us, "meant that I was exposed to the strong movement towards community participation and democratization that pervaded education at that time." In Act 3 – "Migration and Engagements with Multicultural Education" – Pacini-Ketchabaw recalls her migration to Canada where she was introduced to a "different mode of neoliberal education," although "not the blatant authoritarian education that I had encountered during my childhood." In Act 4 – "A Curriculum Framework within the Grasps of Neoliberalism" – she recalls her participation, along with other early childhood colleagues, in the development of the "first British Columbia early learning curriculum framework," and recently, in its revision.

This curriculum revision ignores developmentalism to embrace "post foundational theories," even incorporating concepts with which Pacini-Ketchabaw and her colleagues in the Common Worlds Research Collective have been working for the last 10 years. "Despite efforts to promote early education as an ethico-political activity," she judges,

> early childhood centres and other educational institutions continue to prioritise workforce supply for economic growth. Humanist-inspired projects to achieve social justice and freedom have been hijacked by economic development and productivity agendas. Capitalist extraction, production, and consumption continue to be associated with human "progress and development."

Just as progressive ideas were hijacked by Fascists one hundred years ago (McGlazer, 2020, p. 3), it appears that "Common Worlds Pedagogies" have also been usurped to "maintain the status quo … not simply misunderstood but are quickly appropriated with neoliberal aims." Times of extinction, indeed; capitalism incorporates everything.

"We compose ourselves and this piece as settlers in a colonial state," Jackie Seidel and her colleagues begin, naming the place where "we learn together in *Moh'kins'tsis*," the place "where the snow-melt and glacier-fed Bow and Elbow Rivers converge, the place where Treaty 7 was signed in 1877," now known as Calgary. "We commit ourselves to learning about the ongoing colonial history of Canada," Seidel and her colleagues continue, citing their 2019–20 participation – "as teachers" – in the Fridays for Future youth climate strike movement. Their confrontation of "climate change denialism, racism, and misogyny" acknowledges that curriculum is "deeply and historically entangled and implicated in a cultural system that now portends an existential and catastrophic threat to life itself." They document this activism with eight autobiographical pieces prompted by three questions: "*What are we learning from participating in the strikes? What does it mean to be a teacher in this time and place? What are our pedagogical responsibilities to children and the future?*" The climate crisis requires "acting in every way possible, as fast as possible" to provide the young with a livable future, an inhabitable planet: "We strike for all children in the present, for all future generations, and all future time."

Striking for the future requires remembering the past, including that present prosperity – so very unequally distributed – is extracted from the exploitation of others: human, non-human, planetary. Remembering the past makes the present intelligible, including the life-extinguishing impacts of that prosperity upon those who have contributed little to the climate crisis. Seidel and her colleagues' participation in strikes – and their collaboration in the composition of this essay – "signal our commitments to Indigenous-settler reconciliation and decolonization, to moving forward in a good way." Additionally, "our participation signals our commitment to ways of learning and being together that create livable and socially just futures including for our more-than-human kin." Bequeathed calamities, we reactivate the past to problematize the present that forecloses the future: these temporal dynamics structure curriculum studies in times of extinction.

Like her colleagues in this collection – Teresa Strong-Wilson is a "concerned subject" (Strong-Wilson 2021, p. 153) quite conscious of being implicated yet also quite capable of reconstruction – Strong-Wilson experiences deep "disquiet." She returns to a school where she herself had been a student, a school she had not seen in decades, a "disquieting return" as she observes the effects of a teacher's words on students, leaving Strong-Wilson wondering about "the potential violence *of* our words and actions, as teachers." She understands that "Teaching is not always a rational discourse; in fact, there is much going on that lies on and below the surface of what is said and is not said or more appositely, felt." Returning to her former school, to the reprimand she witnessed the teacher issue there, Strong-Wilson writes:

> I remember how shocked I felt when I heard the first reprimand [to the class], which was on the occasion of my first visit ... when I was, again ironically, sitting at the teacher's desk. For it was as if I was an elementary student again. I did not identify with her frustration as a teacher. Instead, I found myself mentally and emotionally back in my student desk, feeling small and insignificant, powerless to escape from this room that suddenly had all the air sucked out of it and where all my fibres were telling me to run, fast.

The event reminds Strong-Wilson that in her own teaching "at a certain point, I stopped trying to be loved by students," focusing instead "on my love of the subject," teaching so that they could "move ... towards what was harder, of their own accord." She noticed that "students began to love me then, when there were no expectations on my part that they would." In times of extinction, "resolve" (Pinar 2015, p. 180) is the rudder that steadies and stears us.

Strong-Wilson fastens less onto "foreshadowing" than on "backshadowing" and, especially, "sideshadowing," this last idea "allow[ing] for grasping what did happen ... along with what else might have happened, thus unsettling the *present* time." Sideshadowing, Strong-Wilson continues, allows us to attend the "significance" of the present moment, its "alternatives," what it spawns, "thus giving the lie to any 'single story,'" fixing "our attention back to contiguity: the placing of a teacher and her students in relation to myself and my claims about myself, herself in relation to her own self and stories, myself in relation to the place where I grew up and the school that I attended as an elementary student, each of us in relation to the counter-stories." And "perhaps most importantly of all, sideshadowing restores to time its processual possibilities, in which choices are ongoing and recursive rather than fixed and unalterable." To avoid foreclosure "on time, and especially on another's time, whose time is their own," Strong Wilson wants to "remain open to what can still happen, even as I have hope in the teacher's preoccupation, her furor," an "internal vortex" that "makes time speed up and confrontation inevitable: with counter-stories, with students and, one hopes, with oneself as teacher." That aspiration seems central to curriculum studies in Canada.

Conclusion

Leslie Armour (1981) construes "national culture" as "both binding us together" and "recognizing the discreteness of our various communities," adding that "through literature and art we can build a world which we can share" (p. 141). If one positions "curriculum studies" as what "bind[s] us together" and "present preoccupations" for "various communities" in Armour's first phrase, and "scholarship" for "literature and art" in the second, the character of this collection becomes clarified. Knowledge of most worth is what we enlist to address the pressing issues of the day; such knowledge both binds us together and acknowledges the "discreteness" of what preoccupies each of us: climate crisis, planetary degradation, species extinction, cultural genocide, conflict, sexuality, truth and reconciliation.

"National culture" – in a conceptual as well as anthropological sense – reminds that curriculum studies, while worldwide, is nationally configured, often organized around national curriculum reforms. Because that is not the case in Canada, this field seems somewhat severed from the agendas of provincial ministries of education, more tethered to teacher education, prompting Anne Phelan (2015) to explicate their "complicating conjunctions." And however focused on the future, as David Lewovich points out, teacher education is structured by its practically-inflected past, a fact Teresa Strong-Wilson's essay emphasizes, if differently. That past is multivariate, multinational, and embodied in specific persons, as Kumari Beck, Kathy Bickmore, and Veronica Pacini-Ketchabaw testify. Haunted by the past we all are, as Blades, Dion, Gauthier, and Létourneau explain (again, if differently). Québécois and Anglophones, Indigenous and non-Indigenous alike grapple with the temporal dynamics of cultures and communities: reactivating the past to understand the present and find the future. Teaching truth towards reconciliation – however Sisyphean that professional obligation might be (Coulthard 2014) – constitutes (in Strathausen's phrasing) the "dynamics" our "discursive practices" create, the "law" of "structural development" the field follows. That truth is knowledge of most worth – knowing that sexuality, like national identity, remains an existential project with which not only the young struggle (as Gilbert so insightfully understands) – is itself a truth entrusted to teachers and scholars who face the challenges of communicating it, participating in complicated conversation not only in classrooms but within the field itself.

What we have here is a photograph, a still shot of a field very much in motion, a collection of essays that provides answers to Nicholas Ng-A-Fook's reverberating question. Where "we are at" in a literal sense is on the unceded, ancestral, traditional lands of Indigenous Peoples, a fact to be acknowledged and its history taught. Susan Dion's essay may be the only one in this collection focused exclusively on this central curriculum issue, but you'll note that other scholars locate themselves on the First Peoples' lands. While threatening – due to its frequency – to become an empty ritual, the land acknowledgement testifies to the ongoing clash of cultures. "When we acknowledge that UBC is located on the 'unceded, ancestral territory of the Musqueam people,' Samuel Rocha (2020) writes,

> the reality of "unceded, ancestral territory" can be understood in more than one way. In the most immediate sense this is a political statement of non-surrender. Concretely, this means that we are not gathered on the Crown Lands; there is no colonial sovereign in possession of this territory. But this can also, on my understanding, be understood as a spiritual statement of non-surrender. We are not gathered on soulless, inanimate ground; there is no modern scientific sovereignty over the metaphysical reality of this place. Unceded, ancestral territory, in this sense of spiritual resistance, is another way to say that the land is always-already sacred, and it will never be surrendered to a worldview where nothing is sacred. The demand is not for tolerance or respect; sacred land demands *reverence*. We must know how to worship. (p. 144)

Witnessing may not be worship, but it is a "discursive practice" that implies reverence for what has been lost in this era of extinction. Witnessing means mourning – as Claudia Eppert testifies – but it also implies outrage, as Seidel and her colleagues make clear.

What is being lost now is life itself, an extinction accompanied – caused? – by a pervasive, predatory, and intensifying technologization that disables humanity from confronting our profane present. As the planet becomes less habitable, the rich devise escapes into "outer space" while the rest of us – if our economic circumstances allow – escape to the Cloud, that virtual also termed "alternative" reality to which many migrate now. Not the actual migration – "experience that is at once traumatic and liberating" (Gordon, 2020, p. 110) – from one place to another to which several scholars testify in this collection. Not present in place – a political, cultural, sacred specificity as Rocha asserts – we become lost in space, that is, no place in particular. Witnessing to this elusive unreal present might be what curriculum studies scholars share in common, not the first time that scholars have been bonded by what they cannot abide or may not survive. "When we consider the fellowship of intellectuals associated with the Frankfurt School," Gordon (2020, p. 104) reminds, "we cannot ignore their shared experience of exile," that "the critical theorists of the first generation were united by trauma." While we too face fascism, our emergency is epitomized by the COVID-19 pandemic, at once a deadly disease and a metaphor for the plague destroying humanity. Testifying to these facts while teaching towards a time afterward remains our resolve.

REFERENCES

Aoki, T. (2005 [1981]). Toward understanding curriculum. In William F. Pinar and Rita L. Irwin (Eds.) *Curriculum in a new key: The collected works of Ted T. Aoki* (219–28). Lawrence Erlbaum.

– (2005 [1987]). Toward understanding computer application. In William F. Pinar and Rita L. Irwin (Eds.), *Curriculum in a new key: The collected works of Ted T. Aoki* (151–8). Mahwah, NJ: Lawrence Erlbaum.

Armour, L. (1981). *The idea of Canada and the crisis of community*. Steel Railing Publishing.

Coulthard, G. (2014). *Red skin, white masks: Rejecting the colonial politics of recognition*. University of Minnesota Press.

Gershon, W. (2017). *Sound curriculum: Sonic studies in educational theory, method, and practice*. Routledge.

Gordon, P. E. (2020). *Migrants in the profane: Critical theory and the question of secularization*. Yale University Press.

McGlazer, R. (2020). *Old schools: Modernism, education, and the critique of progress*. Fordham University Press.

Ng-A-Fook, N. (2014). Provoking the very "idea" of curriculum studies as a counterpoised composition. *Journal of the Canadian Association for Curriculum Studies, 12*(4), 10–68. DOI: https://doi.org/10.25071/1916-4467.37169

Phelan, A. (2015). *Curriculum theorizing and teacher education: Complicating conjunctions*. Routledge.

Pinar, W. F. (2007). *Intellectual advancement through disciplinarity: Verticality and horizontality in curriculum studies*. Sense Publishers.

Pinar, W. (2015). *Educational experience as lived: Knowledge, history, alterity*. Routledge.

– (2022). Indexical traces of the real: Teaching in the techno-nation-state. In D. Tröhler, N. Piattoeva, and W. Pinar (Eds.), *World yearbook of education 2022: Education, schooling and the global universalization of nationalism* (136–49). Routledge.

Richter, G. (2000). *Walter Benjamin and the corpus of autobiography*. Wayne State University Press.

Rocha, S. D. (2020). *The syllabus as curriculum: A reconceptualist approach*. Routledge.
Shuchat-Shaw, F. (1980). The meanings of congruence. *Journal of Curriculum Theorizing*, *2*(1), 178–202.
Strathausen, C. (2017). Thing-politics and science. In G. Edmondson & K. Mladek (Eds.), *Sovereignty in ruins: A politics of crisis* (pp. 292–317). Duke University Press.
Strong-Wilson, Teresa. 2021. *Teachers' ethical self-encounters with counter-stories in the classroom. From Implicated to Concerned Subjects*. Routledge.
Wang, H. (2014). *Nonviolence and education: Cross-cultural pathways*. Routledge.

1 Storying Curriculum as International Text

KUMARI BECK

Introduction

We are writing these papers in the midst of uncertain and difficult times. Over the past months since this project was born, we have witnessed and been part of crises of various kinds: the global pandemic that still rages on in new forms and manifestations, the Black Lives Matter protests that went global, anti-Asian racism, the ongoing climate emergency, and in the past months, the grim news announcing the discovery of the remains of 215 children on Tk'emlúps te Secwépemc, the site of the former Kamloops Indian residential school in British Columbia, and since then, in other former residential school sites across Canada. The impossibilities of keeping hope alive for education generally, and for curriculum more specifically, rear up from time to time, incursions into the attempts I make to carry on work in the academy. This paper is borne of such vulnerabilities, the expectation that we continue to work as if nothing else was going on, and yet, in the telling of the stories, I am also experiencing a sense of a collective, a collective that is a tapestry of storied strands, connecting one to another and reflecting (in Deleuze and Parnet's words) a "multiplicity [that] grows in the middle" (cited in Aoki, 2005b, p. 205). There is a feeling of gathering strength, and this gives me hope.

This chapter seeks to capture key moments in my engagement with, and exploration of, curriculum as international text, as a scholar-teacher. Early in my explorations I was influenced by Janet Miller's (2006) keynote address to the triennial meeting of the International Association for the Advancement of Curriculum Studies, in Tampere, Finland. It is a compelling theorizing, informed by diverse feminist scholarship, of possibilities and tensions that may arise in the enactment of a worldwide field of curriculum studies already impacted by transnational mobilities. Miller's argument that a worldwide field of curriculum studies is always in the making resonated with my personal experience of the internationalization of curriculum. For this paper, it was her methodology that recaptured my attention. In that account she employs the notion of "*working autobiography* as both genre and mode of inquiry … conceptualizing autobiographical practices as spaces of negotiation" (p. 33, emphasis in original). As a genre, a working autobiography challenges notions of unchanging and fixed categories and binaries, "engaging," in Ellsworth and Miller's (2005) phrasing, "with and responding to the fluidity and malleability of identities and difference" (as cited in Miller, 2006, p. 33). As a mode of enquiry, such autobiography, as Grewal (1994) notes, disrupts the idea of a fixed and known "self" and "opens possibilities for syncretic, 'immigrant,' cross-cultural, and plural subjectivities, which can enable a politics through positions that are coalitions, intransigent, in process, contradictory" (cited in Miller, 2006, p. 33). This framework allows me to hold, simultaneously, multiple perspectives that are often in tension with one another, and not seek resolution of those tensions. It frees me from representing myself in habitual ways that maintain a unitary, uncomplicated view of who I am and becoming. What follows is my working autobiography of curriculum in the internationalization of education, through my educational experiences, my teaching, and my research.

I offer this in the form of several preludes. A prelude is an introduction, promising something more important to come. In music, the word originally referred to the practice of warming up the voice or instrument by performing a few notes. A prelude is often an introductory composition for orchestra or a single instrument; it could also be a stand-alone piece (Oxford English Dictionary, n.d.). A prelude usually features a series of recurring themes or motifs, and is considered to be improvisational in style, or exploratory. This present composition is likewise improvisational, and there may be recurring themes sounding across them. Each prelude is an introduction to something more important to come, and that something is still in the making.

Prelude I – Re-membering

I still hear the flat, almost monotone, of T.S. Eliot's voice reading "Preludes" and other poems, the crackle of dust on the surface of the vinyl amplified on the speakers. My father would regularly select an album or two of poetry and plays to bring home from the British Council library that was a few doors down from his photographic studio in Galle Face, Colombo (in what was then called Ceylon). The albums were recordings of famous British actors and actresses reading Chaucer, Shakespeare, Wilde, Wordsworth, Keats, Eliot, G.K. Chesterton, and others. These voices – the enunciation, the tones – set a deep appreciation of not just the English language, but the refinement they represented. At night, our home was filled with the sound of preludes, fugues, nocturns, and sonatas, piano and violin concerti, string quartets, symphonies, and choral music – classical music from our own extensive collection of records.

In school my aesthetic sensibilities were further honed to appreciate the best of British literature, art, and theatre, Greek pottery, architecture, and plays, the classics as they were called; the histories of ancient Rome, Greece, and England; in everything we learned, we had a solid foundation in the canon. I am called into existence and defined by what is now my first language, English. I would not hesitate to say that I had a well-rounded, high-quality education that has enriched my life. I was internationalized long before I left home.

Along the way there were some moments of dissonance.

The time was the 1970s, and the country was in the midst of a wave of nationalism, a political experiment in socialism, and multiple incidents of civil unrest. Early in the decade we had experienced a name change for our country, from Ceylon (a foreign name) to Sri Lanka (the ancient name), and a symbolic breaking with British rule to become a republic. A year previously, an armed insurrection, led by rural youth who were members of a communist political party, disrupted the country. Schools and universities were closed for months, delaying the start of my first year at university where I enrolled in the English Department.

University education in my home country is free, which made access to higher education broad-based. Studying English Lit appealed only to a small number of students, mostly from the capital city and a few other urban centres. I found myself on a campus that better reflected the social groups of the country than I had previously been exposed to in the school I attended for elementary and secondary schooling. As I tried with my fellow English Department students to hide markers of privilege and make new friends from other disciplines, I became aware for the first time of the costs of my education and the implications of the larger histories of colonialism. As the world around me expanded, I was introduced to politics and socialism; and class, gender, and religious differences that were at play. At the same time, I struggled to resolve the contradictions inherent in pursuing an English degree, sitting in a half-walled building with a corrugated metal roof that was the English Department, space shared with stray dogs and broken furniture (we used to call it "the dog house"). Around us we could feel the tensions of social unrest, the undercurrents of student rebellion prevailing from the recent country-wide insurrection, and of ethnic divisions that were to erupt a few years later.

It was a difficult and necessary lesson in unequal relations. I was beginning to see the "inter," the between spaces, and a growing ambivalence about entering those spaces. Ambivalence, as theorized by Homi Bhabha (1994) "produces the colonized as a social reality which is at once an "other" and yet entirely knowable and visible" (p. 70–1), the ""otherness" … at once an object of desire and derision" (p. 67). My own education, and that of others schooled in urban settings and high-status schools, was oriented around the avoidance of derision. We did this by following a British curriculum and the ensuing "O" and "A" level examinations[1] that ranked and sorted students into "successfully educated" and unsuccessful categories. At the time, however, my growing awareness of these social realities was just that – a glimpse into other realities, but nothing disrupted my views of what knowledge was worth knowing.

These sensibilities, the "proper educated way" of doing things, informed my teaching. My first years of being a teacher in my home country illustrated just how successfully I had become one of Lord Macaulay's children.[2] In his now famous (or infamous) Minute on Education, Macaulay argued for the importance of establishing

> a class of persons, Indian in blood and colour, but English in taste, in opinions, in morals, and in intellect. To that class we may leave it to refine the vernacular dialects of the country, to enrich those dialects with terms of science borrowed from the Western nomenclature, and to render them by degrees fit vehicles for conveying knowledge to the great mass of the population. (cited in Thirumalai, 2003)

I joined that army of knowledge conveyors, "teaching the curriculum" and carefully reproducing the classrooms of my own teachers. I taught the English canon with great care, never straying from the script. It was the quintessential "curriculum-as-plan" (Aoki, 2005a, p. 159) not put together by some distant ministry official, but by myself, cementing the plan through mimicry, prompted by some unconscious (or conscious) recognition that I can never be the copy of the original: "*almost the same but not quite ... almost the same but not white*" (Bhabha, 1994, p. 89, emphasis in original). This colonial foundation was an added layering of complex terrain to Aoki's "C & I landscape" (2005b, p. 200). The coercion to mimic maintains control, "mimicry *repeats* rather than *re-presents*" (Bhabha, 1994, p. 88). The recognition that I will never be quite the same maintains the power of the colonial curriculum-as-plan, the colonization of the mind (Nandy, 1983) that informs my becoming.

Prelude II – Resistance

The cracks in my teaching came many years later, in a private postsecondary classroom in British Columbia. My immigrant status and its accompanying lack of Canadian work experience had, until then, denied me work in Canada. In this case, my English degree and the fact that I spoke English without an accent opened the door to a three-week teaching assignment. I was hired in a temporary position to teach English to new immigrants who were following a federal work program in the trades of carpentry and mechanics. I was handed a manual with instructions that I stick to the worksheets, the sequencing, and the lesson plans because they had been carefully designed by someone with a PhD. All I had to do was to ensure that in three weeks, my students could read and follow along in their trades manual when they joined the regular program.

As I faced that first group of carpenters, all men, I went blank. I can't quite point to where and how the cracks first appeared – whether it was the discomfort of a borrowed grey tweed suit that I had forced myself to wear (to appear the part), or a "feeling with" this diverse group of men who, like me, were wondering how we came to be sitting in this grey and gloomy place (it was a rainy November in Vancouver), far from home. Something snapped. I pushed aside the teaching manual authored by someone with a PhD, and I started a conversation about what brought us there. What happened next – that day and for the rest of the three weeks – was an opening up on my part to what Aoki (2005a) identifies as "the fundamental way in which we all experience life" (p. 164), and "a living in tensionality – a tensionality that emerges, in part, from indwelling in the difference between two curricula: the curriculum-as-plan and the lived curriculum" (p. 202). I witnessed the struggles, confusion, and frustration of adult newcomers to Canada as they tried to assimilate into their new community and maintain some sense of their identities. Along with them, I too was learning about the boundaries, positionings, and contradictions encountered through the act of becoming a Canadian. To be here we had to give up parts of ourselves, to be invisible, and to be known only in unitary terms of our newness, our foreign-ness, or our national identity.

As Ashcroft writes, "The successful disruption of the territory of the dominant occurs, not by rejecting or vacating that territory but by inhabiting it differently" (Ashcroft, 2001, p. 53). And inhabit it differently we did! We transformed into a noisy, busy, lively group of 16 men and a woman, connected through our common experiences of being here; we listened to each other's unique life stories, witnessed one another's vulnerabilities without judgement and with empathy, listened to Peter Gzowski on CBC, and took turns to facilitate conversations on such topics as "what I hate about Canada" and "how to defeat stupid English." They wrote, they composed, sang original tunes, taught one another how to read the trades manual, and they laughed. "[M]ultiplicity is not a noun" (Aoki,[3] 2005c, p. 269).

One interpretation of the transformation in the classroom could be read as deviance. As Bhabha (1994) argues, "[m]imicry is at once resemblance and menace" (p. 86) and the uncertainty in whether it is mimicry (following the plan as instructed) or mockery (the noisy classroom) subverts authority, "the sly weapon of anticolonial civility, an ambivalent mixture of deference and disobedience" (Gandhi, 1998, p. 149). The ultimate success of the carpentry students, their deference in the main program (many of them were among the top 5 per cent in the class not just in reading their English manual, but in their becoming as thoughtful and skilled carpenters) excused the disobedience that marked the three-week English class. Thanks to the generous sharing and participation of each of those students in this wild experiment, I grew to appreciate how each of our lived experiences is the curriculum and recognize the complex interconnectedness of the social realities occupied by both teacher and students. The lived lives of both teacher and students understood as what Aoki (2005c) describes as "a language of humility, as the curriculum has to await the invitation of the teacher and students in the classroom" (p. 274).

Prelude III – Entering and Occupying the Field

I don't remember making a conscious decision to be a scholar in international education. There was an assumption that this was a natural fit. When I began graduate school, I was teaching English to new Canadians in an immigrant settlement program and was in a leadership position with an international development NGO. I was also working on contract with the international teacher education office at my university. It was suggested many times that since this was an area of my work, and with my experience of being "from away," international education would be a good fit for my studies, and even for my academic career should I choose to go that route. I acquiesced! In hindsight, I wonder how much of this enthusiasm for this line of scholarship arose out of a sense that I wasn't qualified to take up other areas of study.

International education, as it was known from the 1970s and through to the early 2000s, manifested in educational programs between universities such as ours, and universities from other countries, mostly of the Global South. These activities reflected the orientation of international education in Canada around "humane internationalism" (Trilokekar, 2010) and took the form of development aid such as technical expertise, program and curricular development, and student and faculty exchanges (Pengelly, 1989; Trilokekar, 2010). The critiques of development (Sachs, 1992), and development aid in education (Unterhalter & Carpentier, 2010) established how values and knowledge of the Global North, long established through colonial rule, became further universalized (Dolby & Rahman, 2008), reifying students from the South as objects of development (Schendel and McCowan, 2015).

My work with the international teacher education program in the late 1990s – drafting funding proposals, developing curriculum, and teaching groups of teachers from other countries – was my first experience of the field of international education, so named. The faculty members on our team were very sensitive to how global mobilities and flows further reproduced colonial patterns of North-South relations. Conscious of the prevailing colonial templates for international engagement, we operated on principles such as relationality, reciprocity, learner-centred and liberatory education (Freire, 1968/2000), and constructivism. In our classroom encounters, however, we could not avoid the tensions that arose between the expectations of students and our intentions to be liberatory. Was constructivism an imposition of Western thought? What was to be gained from encouraging students to break with the hierarchical relationships that they were familiar with in schooling in their home countries? In attempting to incorporate curriculum-as-lived, how best do we engage with the contradictions inherent in teacher identities that were schooled in a colonial curriculum and wishing to be even further schooled in traditions that were not their own? We were particularly vulnerable to the dangers of taking on the Canadian identity of "benevolence" (Jefferess, 2008) that was projected onto us. How could we be more invitational and, more importantly, how do we jointly invite the curriculum? We were in the midst of "leading out, an authentic "e(out)/ducere(lead)," from the "is" to new possibilities yet unknown" (Aoki, 2005a, p. 164), and in the process, challenging our own and our students' notions of authenticity.

An echo, or a faint call to take up the White Man's burden sounds as I sit uncomfortably, neither here nor there, in the "inter" of "both this *and* that and more" (Aoki, 2005d, p. 295).

Humane internationalism developed very rapidly from "aid to trade" (Johnstone & Lee 2014; Trilokekar, 2010) around the time the notion of "internationalization of education" became prominent in the early 2000s. Used interchangeably with "international education," and commonly associated (almost singularly) with mobilities, internationalization of education is understood as emerging from the conditions of globalization. Much has been written about the influences of globalization on education, and key among them, the increasing neoliberal orientation of higher education and the internationalization of higher education (Luke, 2010; Marginson, 2006; Ninnes & Hellstén, 2005; Slaughter & Rhoades, 2004; Stein, 2019; Stier, 2004). It is also important to consider globalization as more than a "world market" (Wagner, 2004); and that it is constituted of political, social, cultural dimensions that are complex, multidimensional, and fluid, leading us to understand globalization/s in its plurality (Beck, 2012). David Smith theorizes globalization as being both an imaginary, "a construct of human imagination that serves to organize and mobilize certain forms of action in certain ways" (Smith, 1999, p. 2), and "a facticity" (p. 3) which identifies the multiple dimensions of globalization, the globalizing acts, as well as those acts of resistance and response. Building on these ideas, Smith articulates in another paper the notions of Globalization One, the emergence and influence of neoliberalism; Globalization Two, the response to Globalization One; and Globalization Three, the possibilities for "a new kind of global dialogue regarding sustainable human futures" (Smith, 2006a, p. 81). Smith locates agency in the spaces between imaginary and complex realities, which could lead to resistance and possibility. The complexity, richness, and the possibilities found in this and other theorizings of globalization/s were important influences in my own quest to make sense of the burgeoning economics of internationalization.

The movement to internationalize curriculum studies had a profound impact on my engagement with the field, and I share three early examples of that impact. The very idea of internationalizing curriculum studies caught my attention, as did Pinar's (2005) commitment

> to support this increasing sophistication of curriculum studies scholars, so that, for instance, "domestically" produced North American scholarship is not assumed to be superior (or inferior) to scholarship produced elsewhere, nor scholarship from the "North" automatically dismissed as "hegemonic" or, alternately, uncritically incorporated. (p. 3)

In his vision for the International Association for the Advancement of Curriculum Studies (IAACS) journal, titled *Transnational Curriculum Inquiry* (TCI), Gough (2004) discusses Nancy Fraser's notion of solidarity as shared responsibility, as a way "to rehearse alternative ways to rehabilitate democratic ideals in the wake of their destabilisation by global corporatism" (p. 5). These shared responsibilities can lead to the building of a transnational network of curriculum scholars committed to and willing to enact these solidarities. Miller (2006) considered the impact of global flows and mobilities on curriculum theorizing, and on possibilities for a worldwide curriculum field through "transnational and transcultural collective exchange" (p. 37), arguing that it leads to conceptualizing "a worldwide field of curriculum as always in the making" (p. 34). Miller's ideas prompted me to see the possibilities inherent in the co-existence of contradictory phenomena and situations, and the implications for curriculum construction and theorizing in international education. Curriculum conceived of as always in the making can be open to a plurality of contributions, perspectives, and lived experiences.

I was in the data-collecting stage of my doctoral research when I came across TCI and "discovered" the IAACS network of scholars. Much to my disappointment, none of my graduate-student peers were interested in this body of work, nor in the possibilities for curriculum theory itself. Thanks to the one professor who encouraged me to attend a triennial conference of IAACS, I was able to experience first-hand how conference attendees attended to new forms of collective exchange. Beyond the intellectual stimulation, the papers changed my relationship to the field and my identity as an academic. I had rarely published in the area of curriculum studies but was transformed by the ways in which these scholars validated me, gave me permission to transgress, encouraged me to flourish and seek solidarity as shared identity and shared responsibility.

In contrast to the evolution of the internationalization of curriculum studies and the rich possibilities it afforded for understanding the nature of curriculum as international text, the internationalization of education has been largely undertheorized. The conceptualization of the field has been limited to narrow definitions; for example, Jane Knight's (2004) influential definition describing internationalization as the integration of an international, intercultural, or global dimension into higher education. Regrettably, these conceptualizations foreclose the fluidity, the contradictions and tensions, and the complexities of global flows and processes. The result is an instrumental C&I landscape (Aoki, 2005b) of internationalization, with little theoretical foundations, and instead, a linear, worldwide *and* uniform, simplistic set of practices. The direction was set for universities to take up internationalization as the White Man's burden in a new form of economic expansion, and a mission to recruit and school a new category of "others," the international student.

Internationalization in Canadian universities is thus characterized by the presence of international students, who are recruited by universities, colleges, and even schools, primarily as a source of income. Education in Canada is governed and administered provincially, but international education requires federal involvement given its almost complete focus on inbound mobilities of international students and, to a lesser degree, outbound mobilities of faculty and students engaged in study and research abroad. Provincial governments are enthusiastic supporters of this "sector"; in BC, international education was listed as the fourth highest income generator for the province before the pandemic. It is revealing that federally international education is situated in the Ministry of Trade, explicitly making it a commodity. Canada's federal strategies for international education (Department of Foreign Affairs, Trade and Development-Canada, 2014; GAC, 2019) are rife with the language of competition and have been developed around maximizing economic opportunities for Canada (Trilokekar & Jones, 2020).

These developments have led to a similar approach to internationalizing the curriculum, which is considered to be one of the key strategies of internationalization of higher education. Again, conceptualizations of what constitutes internationalizing the curriculum have resulted in an instrumental approach; for example, an infusion approach, which is based in the assumption that "a curriculum" is already established, and an infusion of international or global content will internationalize it (Mestenhauser, 1998). Multiple workshops are offered in the sector, inviting participants to become skilled in integrating knowledge about the sociocultural contexts of other societies, to develop skills in responding to cultural difference, and to maintain one's cultural identity while understanding and working with others. Leask (2009), widely recognized for her work on internationalizing curriculum, defines it as "the incorporation of an international and intercultural dimension into the content of the curriculum as well as the teaching and learning processes and support services of a program of study" (p. 209). She makes the case that curriculum that is informed by international research and the inclusion of linguistic and cultural diversity will engage students, developing them as global citizens and professionals. Leask (2015) further explains that internationalization of curriculum should be more than just content, and that "students need to develop their ability to think critically, their intercultural competence, and their problem-solving skills" (Leask, 2015, p. 41). Such a model that can be named as "internationalization of curriculum" amounts to a neo-Tylerean approach to curriculum, with lists of skills, competencies, and content that results in freezing the very notions of international-ness, culture, nation, and local-ness. Curriculum and culture itself have become things, and teachers – the curriculum implementers – must take up this heavy harness.

I struggled to maintain the "this *and* "that" (Aoki, 2005d) of growing my curriculum studies self and advancing my program of research in international education, and I often felt that the former is somewhat irrelevant and out of place in the international education community. I'm in the margins of curriculum studies (originally my academic home) because a senior administrator, advising me on preparing for tenure and promotion, indicated that I should choose one or the other. The pursuit of my scholarship in international education meant that I had to leave behind a more serious engagement with curriculum studies. It was either/or, and navigating the "inter" in this case has taken a toll.

Prelude IV – Pedagogic Reaching

For 12 years, I taught in a program that was designated "international." It was a Master of Education program in teaching English as an additional language designed specifically for international students. Students went through the program as a cohort, and most of their required courses were specifically for them, except for one elective where students could enrol in any of the calendar offerings that semester. I taught one of the elective courses, Current Issues in Curriculum and Pedagogy, which was meant to be open to all but typically was filled up by students in the international cohort.

I began the class, as I now do with all my classes, by asking the students: "What would you like to learn?" In many of my classes, the question opens up all kinds of conversations among us and is an important start to building relationships. In this class, however, the question had an unsettling effect. Often there was a silence, not a reflective silence, or a contemplative moment, but a weighty silence. I waited, letting the discomfort of the moment provoke someone to speak up. I then tried to extend the question: "When you chose to take this class, what did you think you would be learning? What were you hoping to learn? What are you curious about?" I then had to prompt students with examples of topics that we might explore together.

I discovered, later, in student reflections and in the course evaluations, the impact of this opening question. For some, it was like this:

> what I want to say is that I did appreciate that I had such a chance to work on what truly interests me. I feel freer and learning becomes more interesting to me …

Or like this:

> I wondered what I would gain from this course – as it covered such a broad range of topics, while other classes seemed so specific. Is it too open, I thought. I quickly learned that this was to my advantage as I was able to use the ideas and apply them specifically to my teaching context, rather than learn a specific concept and then try to see where they fit in my practice. Of particular interest to me has been reading Aoki and thinking about the being-ness of teaching …

Some students felt stuck:

> I am struggling between understanding what it is I should be learning, and what it is I want to be learning.

Through the progression of responses, I could see the onset of judgment:

> I was surprised when the professor asked us what we want to learn. As a teacher I have to know what best to teach my students. I cannot neglect so many important aspects of curriculum when I must do what is my best for my students …

And then, there was anger that the professor was unprepared, disorganized, and wasting their time:

> I just wished she had spent more time imparting her knowledge. A drawback of this teacher is that her attitude toward this course is not serious enough – she did not have a systematical (*sic*) plan for the course, making the classes casual and loose.

These latter judgments, critical of my lack of teaching ability and neglect of my students, were difficult to read, not particularly about the evaluation of my teaching, but more that I had failed to engage this student in what mattered to her. The question posed by Cynthia Chambers, *"What is the significance of inviting people to take up what really matters to them?"* (Chambers, 1998, p. 17) took on new meaning. The invitation that had worked so well, even transformatively, in my class of carpenters did not reach these students. How should I follow up on that invitation, to understand what matters to my students?

My own student experiences taught me to respect the importance of mimicry, to be the same as, to do the same as, and I could see a similar need being expressed by the international students in my classroom. There is a measure of uncertainty and even unpredictability in mimicry that engenders vulnerability – will I be seen? will I measure up? – which discourages experimentation or improvisation. Pratt's (1991; 1992/2008; 1999) notions of autoethnography and transculturation have been useful in making sense of these tensions between mimicry and improvisation. This sense-making involves taking into consideration the power relations of various kinds (recognizing that they are not static) and the diverse forms of negotiation that occur in the contact zone of the internationalizing classroom. Differing from the common understanding of autoethnography as a method of documenting and analysing one's own experience, Pratt (1991) describes it as "representations that the so-defined others construct in response to or in dialogue with those texts" (p. 35). The state of "living in a bifurcated universe of meaning" requires constant negotiation and labour: "On the one hand, one must produce oneself as a self for oneself. That is survival. At the same time the system also requires that you produce yourself as an 'other' for the colonizer" (Pratt, 1999, p. 40). I recall my immigrant experiences of assimilation and I can see how my students live this tension of mimicry and improvisation in both processes.

David Smith (2000) conceptualized teaching in current conditions of neoliberal globalization as responding to issues such as delocalization, the pervasive logic of the market and its discourse of competitiveness, and "a frozen futurism" resulting from the economic dimensions of globalization. He explores the question "What might constitute an appropriate teacherly response to globalization, in the midst of its unfolding complexity?" (Smith, 2000, p. 16). Arguing that teaching must follow a "living in the Now" – that is, paying attention to the present – he proposes three aspects of "teaching in the Now": teaching must be oriented to the recovery of personal truth, truth as shared, and finding truth as finding home (p. 21). The recovery of personal truth counters the disembedding forces and "personal diminishment" (p. 22) resulting from globalization. Truth as shared refers to a relational orientation, and the third aspect, truth as home, is "finding oneself at home in the world" (p. 24). Grounded in the traditions of hermeneutics, teachers are called upon to be "interpreters of culture, rather than merely transmitters or managers" (Smith, 2006b, p. 255), and to use dialogue to facilitate the participation of all learners.

Teaching in this program of international students prompted me to consider how I might support the recovery of personal truth among my students to name and interrogate the many ways in which they are diminished in their journey to get here. My quest to understand more about my own truth sharing, and my role as an interpreter of culture, at first caused some alarm as teacher interpretations, or rather their mis-recognition, of culture and cultural difference are in many cases part of the problem of teaching and learning with/in difference. I think back to my class of carpenters and realize that perhaps rather than asking my international students what they wanted to learn, I should extend the time to talk about what brought each of us here to this point – and wait for the curriculum.

Finding my way through David Smith's question of what might be an appropriate teacherly response to globalization led me to return to Aoki and his recurrent musings on teacher identity. He observes,

> [i]ncreasingly we are called upon to reconsider the privilege of "identity as presence" and to displace it with the notion of "identity as effect" … according to this understanding, our identities as teachers or curriculum supervisors are not so much in our presences; rather, our identities, who we are as teachers, are ongoing effects of our becomings in difference (2005b, p. 205).

Prelude V – A Conversation with Peter

Staying with the question of our becomings in difference, I spotlight the story of Peter, a faculty member who participated in a research study on critical internationalization conducted by my research team a few years ago. Our investigation sought to understand the experiences of students who navigate a globalizing university; faculty who teach a diversity of students in their classrooms; staff who support faculty, students, and administrators; and administrators who create and direct policies and processes in the international portfolio. We hoped to illuminate the complexity of internationalization: the tensions, contradictions, the nuggets, the hidden curriculum, and the curriculum-as-lived in the face of the prevailing simplistic accounts, definitions, rationales, and PR promotions of international education.

Peter was one of the first faculty members who volunteered to participate in the study. When I arrived in his office he was warming up his lunch of soup and apologized for having to eat his lunch throughout our interview. I was even more apologetic in taking up his lunch hour, but he interrupted me to insist that he wanted very much to share his thoughts and experiences.

Peter was an enthusiastic supporter of going elsewhere to learn. He himself had been an international student and had lived in five other countries as a graduate student and postdoc before being hired into his current faculty position in a Canadian university. For someone who had extensive international experience, he did not know the term "internationalization" and reflected that "any activity that involves an international component to it will be part of an internationalization process." He recognized that the boundaries between global and local were blurred, "almost anything that you do will be international at some level." For a university, he observed, "[it is] particularly unavoidable to be international because any knowledge that is being produced is being produced in the context of other knowledge and knowledge today is international."

This latter belief was a common assumption among our faculty participants and is, in a sense, a simplistic view of what is termed "international" and of knowledge creation. In declaring knowledge as international, the distinctive localness, the complex histories, contexts, and identities that make up knowledge are overlooked and even erased. As Western knowledge systems are assigned the highest value, these knowledges are disseminated as a universal standard in what Bourdieu and Wacquant (1999) term "cultural imperialism." This results in the reproduction of hierarchical North-South relations inherent in the so-called neutrality of the knowledge society (Naidoo, 2010).

Peter's idealism extends to his view on internationalization: he believes that if people everywhere have "the experience of travelling to parts of the world where culture, language, etc., are different, then we will have probably a more peaceful world." He expanded on how when people who are very different from one another have time to get to know one another, it leads to better understanding among them. Later in our conversation, however, he appeared to contradict this assertion as he added an important limitation to it. In recalling his own experiences of difference, he described how he found understanding from other international students rather than domestic students: "people like you for who you are and where you don't have to either learn something new or pretend that you are something that you are not." It appears that understanding and peaceful relations occur mostly among international students themselves. He defended the common criticism that international students stick together and don't make friends with local students. He emphasized their constant emotional labour of being different and their need to "seek refuge with each other":

> [T]hey feel isolated and they feel un-understood and they feel under siege most of the time. Their language is a barrier, their humour is a barrier, their behaviour is a barrier. I mean I still remember feeling – I still feel inadequate – culturally inadequate very, very often.

The seeming contradictions expressed by Peter reflect the conditions of globalization and the coexistence of contradictions and tensions.

I asked him how he approached his teaching and he talked at length about the importance of providing opportunities for students to "open up." He explained,

> So, if I wanted people to open up their minds I would try to provide a very diverse group where in some way acceptance for diversity will be encouraged and rewarded and so that people have no choice but to open up and by opening up, then you learn and learning is painful and costly.

Opening up and being vulnerable is the entry point of learning, but this vulnerability is also painful. It is interesting to me that Peter characterizes learning as painful and costly, a point that he made repeatedly in our conversation and no doubt something he learned from his own experience as an international student. But this consideration is not something he includes in his enthusiastic promotion of an international experience for students. When I pressed him about how he provides opportunities for students to open up to different perspectives and whether it was an intentional approach, he confirmed, "Yeah – I'm an educational terrorist!" The words hung in the air between us. It was not a response I was expecting. Peter himself may have been somewhat surprised with his own utterance. He admitted that it was a provocative way of describing his pedagogy; he continued,

> I always tell my students that I would rather make them uncomfortable than make them sleep, so I'm constantly, constantly provoking, and I try to be as respectful as I can. It is not always easy and it is not always … so, for example, I just used the label "an educational terrorist" and that may get some people a little bit concerned. You know, it is intentional – let me shake you up and let's see how you react.

"Terror" for Peter was getting out of one's habitual ways of thinking, of being "terrified" out of one's own frame of reference, a shaking up, perhaps even snapping out of a "frozen future" imaginary, and a living in the Now. Might this go too far, I wondered, and with all the ways in which we are currently threatened by the terror of being erased, discounted and, in the extreme, physically in danger, is this a useful concept? I let him continue:

> I ask questions, I always try to ask questions and I don't answer for them. So, if they have to feel uncomfortable, there is an uncomfortable silence, I let it be and also I give – this is actually a formal approach – I give what I call brownie points to people who will respond to those questions, even if the answer is wrong, my approach is … basically, it's, "you come to university to learn."

Peter makes great effort to create relationships with his students, and this provocation is his way of connecting with them – "I try to be as dynamic as I can, so even though sometimes I have to teach courses with over a hundred students." He encourages risk taking:

> so mistakes are not important, understanding is, and to understand you need to engage, and to engage you need to be thinking about this. So all I want is what you understand and what you see, and if you have an opinion, your opinion then is what we are looking for. And people engage, people engage …

Peter moved into vulnerability by sharing that it was difficult to reach all of his students, including facing the incommensurability of cultural difference.

> Because it is back again to the old situation where I had the right ideology and they have the wrong ideology and that is really – I mean it is the typical cultural productivism …

> But the problem is, if I'm your teacher and you are my student and we need to go through this process, I want to respect you, but on the other hand the only way I know how to do this is the way I know how to do this ...

He paused ...

> The student and the teacher have to crack their own epistemologies.

This journeying together is an integral aspect of what it means to teach. Counter to the actions of terrorists, Peter's version of educational terrorism is based on accompanying the student through the critical thinking process, all the while expecting to change in the process. Vulnerability (or the absence of it) shapes learning experiences for students and for Peter marks his venturing into unpredictable spaces, into teaching in Third Space. Looking more closely at Peter's notions of terror, I come to understand that it is hardly the invocation of fear but a truth sharing and relationality, his own "living in the inter" and the possibilities he offers his students. In Deleuze and Parnet's phrasing, Peter is creating "an open landscape of multiplicity," recognizing that "In a multiplicity, what counts are not ... the elements but what there is between, the between, a site of relations which are not separable from each other. Every multiplicity grows in the middle" (cited in Aoki, 2005d, p. 297).

Preludes Awaiting an Interlude

I offer the preludes in this paper as a warm-up, in the spirit of storied accounts of internationalizing curriculum. As explained in the beginning, the prelude promises something more important to come. There are reprises invoking an open landscape, each note embodying and resonating tonalities that remember past melodies and themes, with hints of something yet to come. The textual interlude that suggests itself is Aokian: "This [open curriculum] landscape [the lived curriculum] is textured by a multiplicity of lines moving from between to between, is ever open, knowing no beginning and no end, resisting enframing" (2005c, p. 207). Mine is not the only voice, and there is a plurality of stories that forms this composition of international education, as the carpenters in my first Canadian teaching job, the international students I taught, and Peter the internationally educated faculty member have illuminated. There is abundance in these notions of "international," and yet I feel little excitement about what is to come.

I am at a point of weariness, and even a hint of cynicism about my engagement with international education in the face of what Aoki might term "a management category" (2005c, p. 271) in a "C & I landscape" (Aoki, 2005b) of internationalizing the curriculum and its frozen futures (Smith, 2000). The programs in which I taught contemporary issues in curriculum, both the international designated program and a foundations program in curriculum and instruction, have folded. The general direction of the internationalization of higher education continues to be neocolonial and market-driven in spite of critiques generated in critical internationalization studies. In this context, scholarship that is critical of the status quo is not taken seriously, and I fear that I am in the margins yet again. Workshops continue to be delivered and scholarship offered on the whats and hows of internationalizing curriculum. I recently wrote about reimagining internationalization through an exploration of a new commons in internationalization, refocusing on educational principles and values, while recognizing the complexities and contradictions inherent in doing so (Beck, 2021). This reimagining, however, remains a lonely task and in isolation from the field.

I referred earlier to a feeling of growing strength in a collective, in the gathering that has come together for this volume. The writing of this paper has highlighted possibilities for my work as a scholar that had not surfaced before, and in directions that are somewhat unexpected. The classroom is where these directions will emerge, and where I seek the next interlude.

NOTES

1 The Ordinary Level examination at grade 10 and the Advanced Level examination at grade 12/13 are direct imports from the British system.

2 Lord Macaulay was a member of British Parliament and a member of the Board of Control, which supervised the administration of India by the East India Company. Macauley, on behalf of the British government, inaugurated a national system of education.

3 Aoki references Deleuze (1987) in *Dialogues.*

REFERENCES

Aoki, T. (2005a). Teaching as indwelling between two curriculum worlds (1986/1991). In W. F. Pinar & R. L. Irwin (Eds.), *Curriculum in a new key: The collected works of Ted Aoki* (pp. 159–65). Lawrence Erlbaum Associates.

– (2005b). Legitimating lived curriculum. Toward a curricular landscape of multiplicity. In W. F. Pinar & R. L. Irwin (Eds.), *Curriculum in a new key: The collected works of Ted Aoki* (pp. 199–215). Lawrence Erlbaum Associates.

– (2005c). In the midst of slippery theme-words: Living as designers of Japanese Canadian curriculum (1992). In W. F. Pinar & R. L. Irwin (Eds.), *Curriculum in a new key: The collected works of Ted Aoki* (pp. 263–78). Lawrence Erlbaum Associates.

– (2005d). Humiliating the Cartesian ego (1993). In W. F. Pinar & R. L. Irwin (Eds.), *Curriculum in a new key: The collected works of Ted Aoki* (pp. 291–301). Lawrence Erlbaum Associates.

Ashcroft, B. (2001). *Postcolonial transformations.* Routledge.
Beck, K. (2012). Globalization/s: Reproduction and resistance in the internationalization of higher education. *Canadian Journal of Education, 35*(3), 9– 23.
– (2021). Beyond internationalization: Lessons from post-development. *Journal of International Students, 11*(S1), 133–51. https://doi.org/10.32674/jis.v11iS1.3847
Bhabha, H. (1994). *The location of culture.* Routledge.
Bourdieu, P., & Wacqaunt, L. (1999). On the cunning of imperialist reason. *Theory, Culture and Society, 16*(1), 41–58. https://doi.org/10.1177/026327699016001003
Chambers, C. (1998). On taking my own (love) medicine: Memory work in writing and pedagogy. *Journal of Curriculum Theorizing, 14*(4), 14–20. https://www.researchgate.net/publication/242439736_On_Taking_My_Own_Love_Medicine_Memory_Work_in_Writing_and_Pedagogy
Dolby, M., & Rahman, A. (2008). Research in international education. *Review of Educational Research, 78*(3), 676–726. https://doi.org/10.3102/0034654308320291
Ellsworth, E., & Miller, J. L. (2005). Working difference in education. In J. Miller, *Sounds of silence breaking: Women, autobiography, curriculum* (pp. 179–96). Peter Lang.
Freire, P. (1968/2000). *Pedagogy of the oppressed* (30th anniversary ed.). Bloomsbury.
Gandhi, L. (1998). *Postcolonial theory: A critical introduction.* Columbia University Press.
Gough, N. (2004). Editorial: A vision for transnational curriculum inquiry. *Transnational Curriculum Inquiry, 1*(1). https://doi.org/10.14288/tci.v1i1.6
Grewal, I. (1994). Autobiographic subjects and diaspora locations: Meatless Days and Borderlands. In I. Grewal & C. Kaplan (Eds.), *Scattered hegemonies: Postmodernity and transnational feminist practice* (pp. 231–4). University of Minnesota Press
Jefferess, D. (2008). Global citizenship and the cultural politics of benevolence. *Critical Literacy: Theories and Practices, 2*(1), 27–36.
Johnstone, M., & Lee, E. (2014). Branded: International education, 21st century Canadian immigration, education policy, and the welfare state. *International Social Work, 57*(3), 209–21. https://doi.org/10.1177/0020872813508572
Knight, J. (2004). Internationalization remodeled: Definition, approaches, and rationales. *Journal of Studies in International Education, 8*(1), 5–31. https://doi.org/10.1177/1028315303260832
Leask, B. (2009). Using formal and informal curricula to improve interactions between home and international students. *Journal of Studies in International Education, 13*(2), 205–21. https://doi.org/10.1177/1028315308329786
– (2015). *Internationalizing the curriculum.* Routledge, Taylor & Francis Group.
Luke, A. (2010). Educating the other: Standpoint and theory in the "Internationalization" of higher education. In E. Unterhalter & V. Carpentier (Eds.), *Global inequalities and higher education: Whose interests are we serving?* (pp. 43–65). Palgrave Macmillan.
Marginson, S. (2006). Dynamics of national and global competition in higher education. *Higher Education: The International Journal of Higher Education and Educational Planning, 52*(1), 1–39. https://doi.org/10.1007/s10734-004-7649-x

Mestenhauser, J. (1998). Introduction. In J. Mestenhauser & B. Ellingboe (Eds.), *Reforming the higher education curriculum: Internationalizing the campus* (pp. xi–xxvii). American Council on Education & Oryx Press.
Miller, J. L. (2006). Curriculum studies and transnational flows and mobilities: Feminist autobiographical perspectives. *Transnational Curriculum Inquiry, 3*(2), 31–50. https://ojs.library.ubc.ca/index.php/tci/article/view/30
Naidoo, R. (2010). Global learning in a neoliberal age: Implications for development. In E. Unterhalter & V. Carpentier (Eds.), *Global inequalities in higher education: Whose interests are we serving?* (pp. 66–90). Palgrave Macmillan.
Nandy, A. (1983). *The intimate enemy: Loss and recovery of self under colonialism.* Oxford University Press.
Ninnes, P., & Hellstén. M. (Eds.) (2005). *Internationalizing higher education: Critical explorations of pedagogy and policy*. Springer
Oxford English Dictionary (n.d.). Prelude. Retrieved August 20, 2021, from https://www-oed-com.proxy.lib.sfu.ca/view/Entry/150227?rskey=MbVRqz&result=1&isAdvanced=false#eid
Pengelly, B. (1989). *The development of international education activities in British Columbia Colleges 1978–1988* [Unpublished master's thesis]. University of British Columbia.
Pinar, W. F. (2005). Complicated conversation: Occasions for "intellectual breakthrough" in the internationalization of curriculum studies. *Journal of Curriculum Studies, 1*(1), 2–26.
Pratt, M. L. (1991). Arts of the contact zone. *Profession*, 33–40. https://www.jstor.org/stable/25595469
– (1999). Apocalypse in the Andes. *Américas, 51*(4), 38–47.
– (2008). *Imperial eyes: Travel writing and transculturation* (2nd ed.). Routledge. (Original work published 1992).
Sachs, W. (1992). *The development dictionary: A guide to power as knowledge.* Zed Books.
Schendel, R., & McCowan, T. (2015). Higher education and development: Critical issues and debates. In T. McCowan & E. Unterhalter (Eds.), *Education and international development: An introduction* (pp. 275–93). Bloomsbury Academic.
Slaughter, S., & Rhoades, G. (2004). *Academic capitalism and the new economy: Markets, state, and the new economy.* Johns Hopkins University Press.
Smith, D. G. (1999). Economic fundamentalism, globalization and the public remains of education. *Interchange, 30*, 93–117. https://doi.org/10.1023/A:1007577616645
– (2000). The specific challenges of globalization for teaching and vice versa. *The Alberta Journal of Educational Research, XLVI*(1), 7–26. https://www.researchgate.net/publication/234655734_The_Specific_Challenges_of_Globalization_for_Teaching_and_Vice_Versa
– (2006a). Globalization and curriculum studies. In *Trying to teach in a season of great untruth: Globalization, empire and the crises of pedagogy* (pp. 81–98). Sense Publishers.

– (2006b). Postcolonialism and globalization: Thoughts towards a new hermeneutic pedagogy. In Kanu, Y. (Ed.) *Curriculum as cultural practice*. (pp. 215–59). University of Toronto Press.

Stein, S. (2019). Critical internationalization studies at an impasse: Making space for complexity, uncertainty, and complicity in a time of global challenges. *Studies in Higher Education*, *46*(9), 1771–84. https://doi.org/10.1080/03075079.2019.1704722

Stier, J. (2004). Taking a critical stance toward internationalization ideologies in higher education: Idealism, instrumentalism, and educationalism. *Globalisation, Societies and Education*, *2*(1), 1–28. https://doi.org/10.1080/1476772042000177069

Thirumalai, M. S. (2003). Lord Macaulay: The man who started it all and his Minute. *Language in India*, (3), http://www.languageinindia.com/april2003/macaulay.html

Trilokekar, R. D. (2010). International education as soft power? The contributions and challenges of Canadian foreign policy to the internationalization of higher education. *Higher Education*, *59*(2), 131–47. https://doi.org/10.1007/s10734-009-9240-y

Trilokekar, R. D. & Jones, G. A. (2020). Federalism and internationalization. In M. Tamtik, R. D. Trilokekar & G. A. Jones (Eds.), *International education as public policy in Canada* (pp. 29–49), McGill-Queen's Press.

Unterhalter, E., & Carpentier, V. (2010). Introduction: Whose interests are we serving? Global inequalities and higher education. In *Global inequalities in higher education: Whose interests are we serving?* (pp. 1–39). Palgrave Macmillan.

Wagner, P. (2004). Higher education in an era of globalization: What is at stake? In J. K. Odin & P. T. Manicas (Eds.), *Globalization and higher education* (pp. 7–23). University of Hawaii Press.

2 Schooling for Building Just Peace: Comparative and Canadian Perspectives on Facing Difference, Conflict, and Violence in Education

KATHY BICKMORE

Canadian curriculum and social policies are known for commitment to peace, pluralism, and multiculturalism – inclusive approaches to difference. Yet, Canadian school institutions are also shaped by a patriarchal settler state, in the interest of preserving hegemony. Persistent violence, disproportionately affecting marginalized people, has not been a priority concern in curriculum scholarship. The paradox worth studying is that while aspects of schooling may ignore or reinforce violence and injustice, other aspects of schooling may contribute to students' opportunities and capabilities to build just peace (Lopes Cardozo, Higgins, & Le Mat, 2016). In this chapter, drawing primarily upon my own Canadian and transnational comparative research, I explore this puzzle: *How could publicly funded schools offer multi-vocal education for handling violence and social justice conflicts, thereby symbolizing and helping to materialize people's hopes for just peace*? In a nutshell, I argue that education for just (sustainable) peace is conflict education: encouraging continuing expression of difference, surfacing, and facing contrasting perspectives on the causes and consequences of un-peace. I will show how such meaningful peacebuilding education is challenging but demonstrably possible in public schools.

Difference is a social asset – it does not necessarily imply conflict. Conflict occurs when a particular difference becomes a problem for somebody: disagreement, hostile bias, competing needs and desires (interests), broken social ties, or plain misunderstanding. Conflicts are inevitable. Violence, however, is *not* inevitable: its underlying conflictual causes can be satisfied, redirected, ended, or mended.

Violence may be *direct* – intentional personal-physical harm – or *indirect* harm resulting from systemic injustice. Two intertwined forms of indirect systemic violence are *cultural* norms and beliefs legitimizing social exclusion and harm towards others, and *social-structural* hierarchies of resource inequity (Galtung, 1990). Intimate gender-based and criminal violence may be so normalized as to seem inevitable (Bourgois, 2009). Incremental "slow violence" to ecological environments also disproportionately harms marginalized people (Nixon, 2011). Intimate, gendered, and ecological systemic violence are often ignored, even in peace-conflict and democratic citizenship education scholarship (exceptions include Brown & McCowan, 2018; Call-Cummings & Hook, 2015; Howarth, 2014; IEP, 2021; Kovinthan Levi, 2019; Quaynor, 2014). Each form of harm encourages or reinforces the other forms. So it is important to study the social conflicts that underlie indirect and normalized violence, and what school-based education can do about them – especially in contexts where these are not hidden by the fog of war.

Political theorist Nancy Fraser (2004, 2005) articulates how the social conflict problems that underlie violence may be redressed and transformed into justice. Fraser's first two dimensions of social justice parallel Galtung, Bourgois, and Nixon's dimensions of social conflict: *social-structural* transformation facilitating redistribution of resources and status, and *cultural* transformation towards recognition and inclusion of diverse social identity groups. Fraser also articulates a third dimension of justice, *political* representation: *processes* through which all parties gain voice and participate in nonviolent efforts to remedy social justice conflicts within, but also beyond, the purview of nation-states because many injustice conflicts transcend borders. Fraser's theory addresses both "what" social conflicts are about (substantive: cultural recognition and social-economic redistribution) and "how" people and groups may participate in transforming systemic violence into justice (procedural: political representation in decision-making). All three intersecting dimensions imply an important role for learning, in building a strong foundation for just (thus, sustainable) peace. This chapter applies these theories of justice and peacebuilding to education.

The outer points of the triangle in figure 2.1 represent the three dimensions of violence: (1) participation and non-representation or mis-representation in handling conflicts (such as direct physical-personal harm, political oppression, corruption and tyranny), (2) cultural exclusion or misrecognition (such as sexism/misogyny, racism and classism), and (3) social-economic inequity (such as exploitation causing poverty, or destructive monopolization of ecological environments). The *nonviolent* ends of the same axes are the three dimensions of *just peace*. The shading inside the triangle represent three types of responses to conflict: peace*keeping*, peace*making*, and peace*building* (Galtung, 1976). Peace*keeping* and peace*making* respond to current episodes or escalations of conflict (disputes, human rights atrocities, wars). The next ring inward represents peace*keeping* initiatives that rely upon force – securitization – to control or stop violence. Peace*keeping* strategies (such as child abuse protection, or separating warring factions) can be essential,

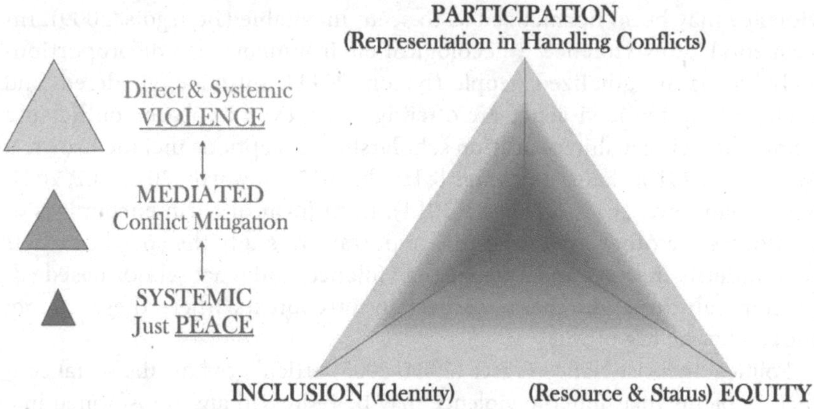

2.1. Dimensions of conflict, from violence to just peace

but are incomplete and temporary peace measures because they focus on controlling symptoms (behaviour), not addressing causes, of violent conflict. Peace*making*, represented by the darker shading intersection closer to the middle, means participatory processes of negotiation, problem-solving, and restorative justice dialogue to help participants understand and address immediate needs and causes of conflicts in order to prevent or resolve episodes of escalation. Larger-scale democratic processes (legislative and court decision-making), designed to mitigate some causes and consequences of conflicts, also fall into this category. Fraser (2004) calls such peacemaking and regulated conflict mitigation decisions "affirmative" remedies: they mitigate particular harms without redressing the roots of injustice conflicts, thereby affirming the existing social system. Examples include anti-discrimination laws, minimum wage regulations, domestic violence shelters. Finally, peace*building*, represented by the darkest central triangle, includes but transcends episodic peacemaking processes. Peace*building* involves multidimensional ongoing efforts to "transform" the systemic political-participatory, economic-equity, and cultural-inclusion factors that cause and exacerbate destructive conflicts, to redress and repair their disproportionate harm to the most vulnerable. Peacemaking and peacebuilding require citizen actors to develop knowledge, understandings, and procedural capabilities in all three dimensions of just peace, at local and wider scales. Below I apply this framework to the peacemaking and peacebuilding learning opportunities (both substantive understandings and procedural capabilities) that may be included (or not) in school curriculum-pedagogy – including the implicit curriculum of organizational and human relations practices and the ways

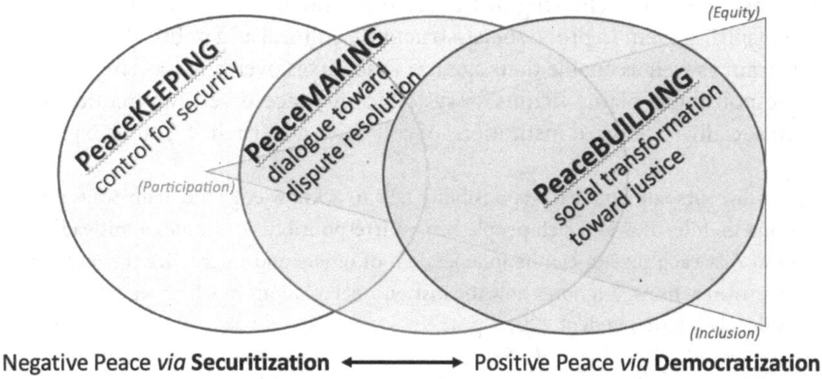

2.2. Alternate goals for handling conflict: Peacekeeping, peacemaking, peacebuilding. © K. Bickmore, 2021

these may (or not) build upon young people's informal learning from home and community experience.

Democratic agency for peacebuilding relies on conflict communication and negotiation, understanding of conflict issues, familiarity with possible social conflict actors and actions, and a sense of capability and motivation to engage in conflict resolution and transformation. By helping students to acquire language, concepts, skills, and relationships for recognizing, communicating, and deliberating about the cultural and social-structural causes and consequences of destructive conflicts, and about what people can do collectively about these problems, school curriculum may enable youths' development of agency for transformative peacebuilding. By challenging (or legitimating) chauvinism and inequality, and through (ir)relevance to particular communities' histories of relative deprivation, institutional structures and enacted curriculum in schools may contribute to, or impede, building just peace (Davies, 2017). Young people who grow up in contested or relatively peaceful contexts presumably develop different conflict capabilities through life experience, and so need different curriculum in school (Merelman, 1990). Unfortunately, schooling in many contexts has often reinforced enmity, colonial oppression, and other violence (Bush & Saltarelli, 2000; Matsunaga, 2016; Novelli & Higgins, 2017; Paulson, 2008). Contributing to just peacebuilding through school-based education requires transformation of schooling-as-usual.

The difficulty is that curriculum tends to be skewed by the unjust social structures and oppressive cultural beliefs and practices that permeate schooling: by teaching few ingredients of potentially democratic peacebuilding, while assuming individual deficits rather than systemic causes, schooling may shift responsibilities for achieving just peace onto individuals, instead of enabling and inspiring them to probe social-structural, cultural and political factors that constrain as well as enable their agency. Discourses over-emphasizing individual responsibility blame victims for systemic un-peace, diverting attention away from socially structured institutions of collective governance. Young explains:

> The discourse of personal responsibility fails to acknowledge the many ways that some middle-class and rich people behave irresponsibly. It assumes a misleading ideal that each person can be independent of others and internalize the costs of their own actions. It ignores how the institutional relations in which we act render us deeply interdependent. (2011, p. 4)

Applied to schools, Young's insight highlights the risk of gentle peacekeeping through curriculum – implicit and explicit conflict lessons that enhance the stability of existing hegemonies by guiding students to internalize self-regulation (governmentality) and to comply with adult domination (also Foucault, 2003). Like overt peacekeeping, gentle peacekeeping emphasizes compliance without examining conflicts' causes or transformative remedies. For instance, Canadian textbook multiculturalism has often presented racism, settler colonialism, gender oppression, and other systemic violence as past and resolved, found only among others (Bromley, 2011; Meyer et al., 2010; St. Denis, 2011): this denies the continuing concerns of oppressed social identity groups, discouraging dissent. Justice-based peacebuilding citizenship education, in contrast, requires critical recognition of social conflicts' indirect and collective dimensions, in addition to interpersonal conflict handling skills (Bickmore, 2017; Haste et al., 2017). In particular, showing how people may organize for state and transnational change, to alleviate the systemic causes of harm, would nurture young people's sense of being protagonists.

This chapter examines the puzzle of what all this means, in practical human terms, for school curriculum: Which feasible learning opportunities may constitute building blocks towards – or, may block – students' opportunities to develop and express transformative peacebuilding agency? I remain guardedly optimistic that schooling *can* help more young people, more of the time, to develop capabilities and motivate relationships for handling complex contemporary justice conflicts, notably the global mal-distribution of health factors exposed by the COVID-19 pandemic, and the racist and colonial mis-recognition brought to light by the Black Lives Matter and Idle No More movements.

Schooling for Building Just Peace: Starting with Canada

I immigrated to Treaty 13 territory in Canada 30 years ago, after growing up on the Haudenosaunee Six Nations Confederacy territory (across Lake Ontario) and eventually completing a PhD in international comparative education in the United States. My concern with violence, gender, injustice, and kids in trouble is rooted in my early life experience. I decided to learn about Canada before re-developing a transnational comparative perspective from a new place.

My first major research effort in Canada, Safe and Inclusive Schools, examined school and school board policy environments and cultures to identify the dilemmas and possibilities educators face in handling conflict, direct violence, and systemic violence towards creating safe(r) and (relatively) inclusive schools. The project focused on three big-city districts with students from ethnoculturally, racially, and economically diverse backgrounds, each in a different Canadian province. The 89 purposively sampled interviewees included centrally assigned and school-based educators who were involved with any aspect of conflict intervention (safe schools peacekeeping and peacemaking), or prevention (peacebuilding, including explicit education, equity work, and inclusive governance). The research also analysed curriculum guidelines and other policy in each province and board (Bickmore, 2006, 2011a). In one district, we also studied five focus schools, in areas with comparable low social-economic status and high proportions of newcomer and racialized students, but contrasting violence and suspension rates. In each of those two high schools and three elementary schools, we interviewed adults involved with peacebuilding, peacemaking, or safe-schools peacekeeping control activities.

One interesting finding was how broad or narrow sets of students were enabled to perform a wide range of peacekeeping, peacemaking, and peacebuilding "leadership" roles. Among the three school boards and provincial regimes, opportunities for active student peacemaking or peacebuilding engagement were not available at all schools, despite the project's purposive sampling to identify such activities. High-status, academically successful, compliant students were most often selected for leadership opportunities. Peer social skills facilitators and mediators were disproportionately female and white-Anglo in some schools, but much more diverse (representative and inclusive) in others. The peacemaking initiatives that did *not* maintain gender, academic status, and ethnocultural diversity among student leaders (through adult mentors' support and advocacy for assertive or struggling students) tended not to touch all populations in their schools: inclusive leadership teams, in contrast, generally had broader positive influence on peace in their schools. Some democratic representation exercises like student councils became mechanisms for sharing power across diversities, while others became popularity contexts that reinforced existing social hierarchies. Funding for adult mentorship and programming, in all three school boards, apparently had been reduced and reallocated from relatively democratic student leader roles (peacemaking such as peer mediation, and peacebuilding such as equity advocacy), towards more emphasis on high-status students contributing to peacekeeping control of lower-status peers (Bickmore, 2004, 2011b), whereas, the focus schools with the lower violence and suspension rates had the broadest diversity of student leaders acting agentically to address conflicts they considered important. Allocation of

Peacekeeping

- Peer playground monitors (boards A & B)
- Student helpers in various forms (all 3 boards)

Peacemaking

- Social skills leaders, such as playground games leaders, and anti-'bullying' peer educators (board B), mixing peacekeeping and peacemaking
- Peer mediators facilitated dispute resolution, on playgrounds or by referral (all 3 boards, but very few schools).
- Adult-facilitated mediation, restorative justice circles, and conflict resolution education were somewhat more common (primarily boards B & C)

Peacebuilding

- Co-curricular anti-bias leadership courses, camps & conferences (all 3 boards, reduced frequency due to budget constraints)
- Student councils and other student participation in school governance (all 3 boards, but playing an active part in few schools)
- Affinity, advocacy & equity action groups: identity-based groups such as Muslim Students Associations or Gay-Straight Alliances, or more general Equity Clubs, self-organized co-curricular activity (all 3 boards, not many schools).

2.3. Differing student "peace' leadership for safe and inclusive schools

regular work responsibilities (resources) and professional development for school and board staff was required to sustain and develop peacemaking and peacebuilding programming.

Because the Safe and Inclusive Schools research showed that many students of low social-economic status did not get much access to co-curricular (especially after-school) peacebuilding learning opportunities, my subsequent research focused on learning opportunities that are accessible over time to whole student populations. Implicit curricula of human relations, conflict management, and discipline tend to focus energy on perceived *disruptors*, *after* episodes of interpersonal conflict escalation, and to risk reinforcing racial and other inequities (Dunning-Lozano, 2019; Jull, 2000; Lustick, 2021; Welsh & Little, 2018). In contrast, explicit curriculum (classroom lesson pedagogies, especially in mandatory subject areas) could (try to) engage *all* students in facing multiple points of view on a broader range of conflictual questions – *before, during, and after* episodes of visible conflict, in the *world* as well as in school relations. Paradoxically, conflict dialogue pedagogies may open political space by inviting contrasting viewpoints and constructive disagreement yet be especially risky for participants with minoritized experiences or beliefs (Parker, 2016; Parker & Bickmore, 2020; Schultz, 2009; Zúñiga et al., 2012). Much of the scholarship on "controversial issues" pedagogies frames power-imbalanced justice conflicts as problematic for democratic citizenship education dialogue: a position may be founded upon indefensible evidence, as in climate change denial (Ho & Seow, 2015), or may refuse to dignify the basic human rights of one social identity group (Hess & McAvoy, 2015). Yet, it is feasible and crucial to accept and mitigate risks, to crack open hegemonic knowledge systems embedded in mainstream curriculum practice (also Pace, 2019). In response, the Peace-Building Dialogue project investigated students' opportunities to encounter, engage, and express contrasting and conflicting perspectives through discussion of conflicts in classrooms (Bickmore & Kovalchuk, 2012; Bickmore & Parker, 2014).

Fieldwork began with participant observation in three purposively selected teacher professional development initiatives, presenting different approaches to peace-building dialogue pedagogy: a prescriptive restorative justice conferencing approach designed to facilitate relationship-repair dialogue between "offenders," "victims," and affected communities after incidents of harm; an Indigenous-led talking-piece peace circle approach used in both post-incident restorative peacemaking and proactive pedagogies for building rapport and understanding; a genocide history citizenship education program linked with contemporary challenges of social exclusion (Bickmore, 2015). My team then conducted interviews and classroom observations with three to five K-12 classroom teachers from each of these teacher development initiatives (total 11), committed practitioners of conflict dialogue pedagogies.

Participating teachers each found ways to use discussion about conflicts – built into the ways they conducted their classrooms, into language-literacy work, or within the conflicts meaningful in particular subject areas – as learning opportunities. For example, as a culminating activity in a grade 12 general science unit on pathogens and disease, Ms. Parisi[1] conducted a restorative dialogue circle on health care policy in relation to a scenario of HIV-AIDS transmission. Ms. Parisi had taught her students a peace circle process: passing a talking piece around to give each person an opportunity to voice their perspective (and listen to peers) on each question, or to pass without speaking when they wished. She asked the group: "Should HIV-infected individuals who don't take the necessary precautions and are out there doing risky behaviours that expose them to infectious agents have the right to the same publicly funded medical insurance as others who don't have HIV?" Mid-way through the session, Ms. Parisi temporarily sped up the dialogue by allowing back-and-forth rebuttals (in practice, dominated by the most confident voices), then returned to passing the talking-piece to include all in a final deliberation. Ms. Georgalis included in her grade 10 history unit on genocide conflicts (Nazi Germany, Armenia, Rwanda) students' own experiences of identity-based exclusion. Late in the unit, Ms. Georgalis showed a social media video clip in which an elderly Holocaust survivor and his grandchildren danced to the song "I will survive" on the grounds of the Auschwitz death camp. Like Ms. Parisi, she had already taught norms for thoughtful, mutually respectful discussion. She asked the class: "Was this an appropriate memorial?" Many students expressed passionate and divergent viewpoints, and explained when they changed their minds. In these curricular episodes students practised expressing their own perspectives and peacebuilding citizenship commitments in contexts of injustice, using reasoning and evidence learned in subject area curriculum.

Among primary grades in the same research project, Ms. Brown facilitated a peace circle to guide her students' creative resolution of a conflict that had emerged between girls and boys over their use of playground space. First, she invited each child to "Share something about recess today and how it went." Then, circulating the talking piece each time to each child, Ms. Brown asked questions to help students interpret the conflict and to suggest ways for girls and boys to share the playground space fairly. After the circle, students acted out their preferred ways of solving the problem. In kindergarten, Ms. Holly read aloud a story about a child considering whether to step on an ant. After engaging the class in role play and talk to interpret the feelings and preferences of each character, she arranged them in a circle and invited each to share: "If you were the child in this situation, what would you do and why?" These vignettes show how some forms of perspective-taking and dialogue about inequity conflicts can model and teach inclusion, as well as communication capacity-building. Together, these case studies demonstrate the feasibility (as well as the complexity and apparent rarity) of justice-oriented conflict dialogue pedagogies in public classrooms.

Transnational Research: Opportunities for Just-Peacebuilding Learning in Regular Schools

Finally, the transnational comparative Peace-Building Citizenship Learning research examined the relationships among social conflict, violence, citizenship, peacebuilding, and learning opportunities in schools and life experience, in contrasting national contexts of Canada, Bangladesh and México. To inhibit prevailing ethnocentric and Global North-centric assumptions about who experiences violent conflict (and how schools respond), this transnational comparative work critically examines "our" education in Canada, in parallel with the ways the team studied others' educations in Bangladesh and Mexico, finding uncanny similarities alongside some differences. What these sites had in common was the pervasiveness of social conflict including direct violence – thus, the need for peacebuilding education perceived by the participants – and the fact that these are regular curricula in ordinary public-school classrooms, accessible to all, not specialized peace or citizenship education initiatives. The three countries have different cultural and historical contexts and widely varying overall levels of violence indicated by differing positions on the Global Peace Index, a composite measure of conflict/peace indicators such as safety and security, militarization, and domestic and international violent conflict (IEP, 2016). In contrast to most published research about education and conflict, none of these communities were war zones or divided societies; yet all suffered pervasive direct and systemic violence. The cases are sets of purposively selected schools in high-poverty, big-city neighborhoods where direct violence was pervasive – in one Canadian city (three schools in the province of Ontario – 81 youth and 17 teachers), two Bangladesh cities (four schools in different parts of the country – 36 youth and 16 teachers), and one Mexican city (four schools in the state of Guanajuato – 81 youth and 21 teachers). Dialogic workshops involving multiple focus groups of students in each school, and (separately) a series of sessions with one focus group of their teachers, elicited reciprocal reflection and discussion on the social conflicts experienced by marginalized youth in each context, and on the ways their daily schooling did and did not build on their experience to develop their sense of agency for transforming those conflicts. The research compared the youths' expressed understandings and worries with the curriculum-in-use described by the students and their teachers. Beyond location in marginalized communities experiencing violence, the main criterion for inclusion was participants' interest in discussing how their education did and could address problems of violence and citizenship.

Canada is the most peaceful national context included in the Peace-Building Citizenship study (IEP, 2016). However, violence remains very evident, especially in some economically marginalized areas (Doob & Cesaroni, 2004; Eizadirad, 2016). Multiculturally oriented active citizenship goals have been prominent throughout Canada's (provincially regulated) public education curricula, including Ontario's. However, students from different social identity and status locations may have unequal citizenship learning experiences in school, disconnected from their lived experiences and concerns (Farmer, et al., 2015; Tupper & Cappello, 2012). While curriculum policy discourse emphasizes student-centred and critical thinking pedagogies, institutional factors and standardized testing reinforce teacher-centred transmission (Bickmore, 2014). All the schools in this research (elementary grades 5–8) had predominantly racialized first- and second-generation immigrant student populations with a variety of home languages. Especially in two of the schools, most students described their school and neighbourhood climates as violent and insecure.

Canada (1 city in Ontario)	Mexico (1 city in Guanajuato)	Bangladesh (2 cities – central mixed-income & peripheral poorer)
Global Peace Index: 8 (peaceful)	Global Peace Index: 140 (violent)	Global Peace Index: 83 (medium)
Conflicts: Quebec/ francophone Canada vs. English Canada; emerging Indigenous rights voice; some "terrorism"	**Conflicts:** blended Spanish colonial & Indigenous origins; contemporary Indigenous resistance; major criminal gang violence	**Conflicts:** w/colonial British Raj India & since 1947 w/ (West) Pakistan; internal political rivalry & violence
Poverty ~1/7, big gaps; ~67% Christian (most Catholic), ~25% no religion, urban Ontario: many religious minorities; schools secular	Poverty ~1/3, big gaps; ~75% Catholic; schools secular	Poverty ~1/4, big gaps; 90+% Muslim, religious education required in own religion; schools gender segregated

2.4. Contexts for peacebuilding citizenship learning research. © K. Bickmore, 2021

Participating Canadian teachers taught some capabilities for peacemaking and just peacebuilding embedded in subject area lessons, and led class discussions. However, some focus group students and teachers lamented the aggression and exclusion in their class discussion experiences. All participating teachers led oral and written language lessons that included elements of conflict analysis and resolution – such as discerning alternate points of view – applied to conflicts in fiction stories, news articles, or NGO and UN-related websites. Classes practised creative and communicative expression through arts, graphic representation, mapping, media literacy, and multi-media productions. These building-block lessons for peacemaking participation often did not explicitly address cultural (bias and inclusion), or especially social-economic, dimensions of conflicts.

Teachers and students did describe a few learning activities examining complex justice conflicts, sometimes organized around narratives about exemplary leaders such as Nelson Mandela, Malala Yousafzai, and Terry Fox, who confronted conflicts far away in time or place. Another common strategy, enabling teachers to include conflictual issues and (yet, paradoxically) avoid guiding conflict education, was student-selected independent enquiry projects. Virtually all student participants demonstrated good conflict communication and conflict analysis skills in the (research) focus groups – listening attentively, participating readily, responding constructively to peers' alternate viewpoints, articulating emotions and perspectives on justice issues. However, many said that they did not feel confident and wanted more opportunity to learn and practise conflict analysis, dialogue, resolution, and justice-building processes in school.

Bangladesh experiences a medium level of violence compared to other countries (IEP, 2016). Bangladesh's dense population is 98 per cent of Bengali ethnicity, mostly Sunni Muslim. Its constitution promises integration and religious freedom. Conflicting approaches to Islam's relationship with government, and Hindu-Muslim conflict exacerbated by British colonizers, are key axes of tension (Siddiqi, 2011). Violence and insecurity escalate in large cities during election campaigns and anti-government protests (ibid.). The Bangladesh public school system is national, delivered in single-sex schools. Religious education is required; minority religions have alternate approved courses such as Hinduism and Moral Education. As in Canada, official curriculum encourages participatory pedagogies, including student opportunities to speak about their experiences in class; however, pressures to cover content for high-stakes standardized exams often impede such opportunities. Our sample in Bangladesh includes one boys' school and one girls' school, grades 6–10, in each of two cities – a large city with economically mixed populations and a high level of criminal and political violence, and a smaller, less affluent city experiencing somewhat less direct violence. Focus groups were facilitated by Bangladeshi research team member A. Salehin Kaderi (2018). Bangladeshi students in both communities endured pervasive normalized cultural, direct, and social-structural violence; in particular, gender-based aggression and some corporal punishment in school, political corruption, and poverty. Student focus group participants clearly articulated structural, political, and cultural constraints on their agency, yet many declared their commitment to contributing to just peace.

The prevailing curriculum enacted in the participating Bangladesh schools, implicitly in patterns of conflict management and explicitly in classroom lessons, reflected a moral code and steep hierarchies in which those with less power (including students) were often denied opportunities to present their points of view or participate in problem solving. At the same time, the curriculum-in-use included some potential justice-sensitive peacebuilding citizenship education. One Bangladeshi teacher explained a typical view in participating schools: "The purpose of education is to bring discipline, stability, and peace in social and national lives. We all want peace. … Indeed, the curriculum policy makers have tried to include peace-relevant elements in the curriculum. … indirectly, with different names than peacebuilding … but they are there." Perhaps more frequently than in the Canadian and Mexican schools, there were explicit lessons about the consequences of some systemic injustice conflicts, for instance in the immorality of gender-based aggression and the value of sharing material aids with the poor. Overlapping curricular space included analysis of (neo-)colonial relations, and of particular social-structural inequities such as dowry abuse and discrimination against Indigenous hill tribes. As in Canada, these lessons were often animated by narratives about individual leaders helping to mitigate particular kinds of social harm. Curriculum tasks invited students to explain conflict symptoms and to take a stand against perpetuation of such inequalities – which, in research focus groups, they demonstrated clear capability to do. There were opportunities for students to voice, even occasionally to debate, their own perspectives on some issues – although they usually (implicitly or explicitly) required students to articulate points of view considered acceptable by the powerful in the school and the society, at times blaming victims or legitimizing violence towards perceived enemies. The least common curricular opportunity in these schools, as in the other jurisdictions, was to autonomously deliberate about options for actually taking nonviolent collective or citizen action to help transform specific systemic conflicts. In sum, participating Bangladesh students showed in focus group conversations considerable capability and commitment to democratic peacebuilding citizenship. Their curriculum-in-use offered several infrequent and constrained, but tangible, opportunities for students to expand their horizons of social conflict analysis and capabilities for some forms of peacebuilding engagement.

Mexico was the most violent national context included in the Peace-Building Citizenship study (IEP, 2016). Drug cartel and gang aggression, and associated armed "security" activity, have killed tens of thousands in recent decades (also Leenen & Cervantes-Trejo, 2014). In this context of intensified systemic inequality (IEP, 2015), less affluent young adolescents have generally received (and achieved) less quality citizenship education, compared to affluent peers (Diazgranados-Ferráns & Sandoval-Hernández, 2017). Although historically the Spanish concept of *convivencia* meant differing ethnocultural groups living peacefully and cooperatively together, the term has been reinterpreted and appropriated as a core value in Mexico emphasizing individual non-aggression (Carbajal Padilla, 2013; Nieto & Bickmore, 2016). Many Mexican state school regulations, including in Guanajuato, recently have adopted "*Convivencia*" laws focused on punishing individual students and their parents for infractions, rather than addressing their perspectives on the causes of conflicts (Perales Franco, 2018; Zurita Rivera, 2012). At about the same time, however, Mexico's national education reform created a civics-ethics curriculum with a new emphasis on democratic participation, critical thinking, and human rights (Bascopé, et al., 2015). Associated initiatives have shown promise to instill nonviolent and democratic attitudes and competencies, and even to mitigate some inequality in such learning (Cárdenas, 2017; Reimers et al., 2014). Our sample in Mexico includes two intermediate schools (grades 7–9) and grades 5–6 in two primary schools, all in high-poverty neighborhoods in one large city in Guanajuato state. In addition to poverty and social marginalization, the young participants in all these schools reported substantial experience with direct physical violence – including gender-based violence in their homes, fighting and bullying among peers, and violent competition among criminal gangs in the community.

All the participating Mexican teachers emphasized explicit values education, especially the importance of respectful *convivencia* (peaceful coexistence). All of them frequently implemented teamwork pedagogies, sometimes guiding heterogeneous groups to recognize one another's strengths and work together inclusively. Many also used arts-based pedagogies including role play. Teachers described a typical conflict analysis pedagogy, especially in civics-ethics lessons: the class would read or view "cases" of conflict (from textbooks, poetry, news, videos, comic strips, or images); identify the motives, feelings, and concerns of each character about the problem; then express their own opinions about, "what would you have done in this situation?"

As in the other jurisdictions, a few curricular episodes examined contrasting viewpoints in systemic conflict examples in some depth. Orally or in letter-writing assignments, students occasionally were invited to explain their perspectives about conflicts experienced in the community, especially the pros and cons of family members' frequent decisions to migrate away to work in North America. A rare history unit examined the roles of various people (including displaced Indigenous people and workers) in founding their city, examining how they handled problems and disagreements. Another teacher's unique history lesson engaged students in comparing a pre-Revolution leader (President Porfirio Diaz) to an insurgent leader (Zapatista Comandante Marcos) in contemporary news. One science lesson investigated the economic and ecological advantages and disadvantages of (polluting) leather tanneries in the neighbourhood. In these activities students would have had experiences encountering conflicting perspectives, thinking for themselves, and engaging dialogically with others with whom they agreed and disagreed. As in the other jurisdictions, virtually all students in the Mexican focus groups demonstrated clear conflict communication capability – articulating and explaining various actors' and their own points of view, listening and engaging respectfully with peers' contrasting ideas – and enthusiastic interest in studying and discussing conflict issues in more depth in school.

Discussion and Conclusion

The curriculum-in-use described by participants in the Canadian, Bangladeshi, and Mexican schools in the Peace-Building Citizenship project included a whole range of conflict learning opportunities, from narrow to multi-dimensional. The most common "peace" curriculum-in-use described by participants in all participating contexts was an emphasis on negative peace through avoidance or compliance. While accommodation of some social diversities was often absorbed into each national narrative, intersecting gendered aspects of conflict and violence were often ignored, especially in Canada. Political conflicts were often described in the past tense (plus, in Canada, in faraway places). Under conditions of violence and social exclusion – as in these research contexts – this narrow, symptom-focused conflict avoidance could *block* development of more democratic and multidimensional forms of democratic agency.

Curriculum episodes described in all three contexts included some potentially democratic building blocks for just-peacebuilding. Juxtaposing the curriculum emphases within and across these contexts makes visible alternative approaches to conflict-peacebuilding education; for instance, focusing on conflict communication skills, values, and/or analysis of viewpoints and injustices. In Canada, the teachers taught multicultural awareness and individual character education to "make a difference," narrating a peaceful "nation of immigrants." In Bangladesh, participating teachers taught moral precepts and exemplary narratives of Islam, alongside a national enmity narrative in relation to Pakistan. In Mexico, participating teachers taught values for interpersonal behaviour such as respect and cooperation, and a national narrative of *mestizaje* (seamlessly blended Indigenous and European origins). Most of the teachers participating in this study believed that such cautious, pacifying, and unifying versions of peace education were prerequisites – *building blocks* – for development of actively democratic, even transformative, peacebuilding citizenship inclinations, identities, and capabilities.

The above approaches to social conflict and violence, and especially the rarer curriculum episodes in each setting that probed multiple dimensions of conflicts and potential peacebuilding action options, demonstrate the feasibility of (some) justice-oriented peacebuilding education in these ordinary public schools in non-affluent, violence-plagued contexts. The curricular and co-curricular student peacebuilding leadership and agency opportunities reviewed in the earlier Canadian studies offer further evidence of the significant ways in which young people can contribute multi-vocally and multi-dimensionally to their own and each other's peacebuilding learning and agency when their teachers find ways to listen and to support their self-expression and action roles. Examples to complement the transnational cases include peer-facilitated dispute resolution, affinity group and equity work, and inclusive conflict dialogue infused in core subject matter lessons. Just-peacebuilding requires critical attention to the indirect as well as direct personally experienced dimensions of violence, and to contrasting perspectives on the social conflicts underlying and reinforcing that violence. Unidimensional peacekeeping-oriented practices, in contrast, repress the expression of diversity, creativity, and agency dampening to change. Multidimensional learning opportunities – engaging diverse students in encountering and expressing themselves about social-structural equity, cultural inclusion, and political participation action options – can happen in ordinary public schools. Such curriculum practices can widen space for young people to develop hope and capabilities, to build just peace in their own and others' lives.

NOTE

1 All proper names in research finding summaries are pseudonyms.

REFERENCES

Bascopé, M., Bonhomme, M., Cox, C., Castillo, J., & Miranda, D. (2015). Curricular guidelines and citizenship attitudes in Latin American students: a comparative analysis. *Revista Latinoamericana de Ciencias Sociales, Niñez y Juventud, 13*(2), 1169–90. http://www.redalyc.org/articulo.oa?id=77340728043

Bickmore, K. (2004). Discipline for democracy? School districts' management of conflict and social exclusion. *Theory and Research in Social Education, 32*(1), 75–97. https://doi.org/10.1080/00933104.2004.10473244

– (2006). Democratic social cohesion? Assimilation? Representations of social conflict in Canadian public school curricula. *Canadian Journal of Education, 29*(2), 359–86. https://doi.org/10.2307/20054168

– (2011a). Education for "peace" in urban Canadian schools: Gender, culture, conflict, and opportunities to learn. In P. P. Trifonas & B. Wright (Eds.), *Critical issues in peace and education* (pp. 88–103). Routledge.

– (2011b). Policies and programming for safer schools: Are "anti-bullying" approaches impeding education for peacebuilding? *Educational Policy, 25*(4), 648–87. https://doi.org/10.1177/0895904810374849

– (2014). Peacebuilding dialogue pedagogies in Canadian classrooms. *Curriculum Inquiry, 44*(4), 553–82. https://doi.org/10.1111/curi.12056

– (2015). Incorporating peace-building citizenship dialogue in classroom curricula: Contrasting cases of Canadian teacher development. In R. Malet & S. Majhanovich (Eds.), *Building democracy in education on diversity* (pp. 17–39). Sense Publishers.

– (2017). Conflict, peace-building, and education: Rethinking pedagogies in divided societies, Latin America, and around the world. In K. Bickmore, R. Hayhoe, C. Manion, K. Mundy & R. Read (Eds.), *Comparative and international education: Issues for teachers* (2nd ed.) (pp. 268–99). Canadian Scholars Press.

Bickmore, K., & Kovalchuk, S. (2012). Diverse ways of creating classroom communities for constructive discussions of conflict: Cases from Canadian secondary schools. In P. Cunningham & N. Fretwell (Eds.), *Creating communities: Local, national, and global* (pp. 590–605). CiCe.

Bickmore, K., & Parker, C. A. (2014). Constructive conflict talk in classrooms: Divergent approaches to addressing divergent perspectives. *Theory and Research in Social Education, 42*(4), 291–335. https://doi:10.1080/00933104.2014.901199

Bourgois, P. (2009). Recognizing invisible violence: A 30-year ethnographic retrospective. In B. Rylko-Bauer, L. Whiteford, & P. Farmer (Eds.), *Global health in times of violence* (pp. 17–40). School for Advanced Research Press.

Bromley, P. (2011). Multiculturalism and human rights in civic education: The case of British Columbia, Canada. *Educational Research*, *53*(2), 151–64. https://doi.org/10.1080/00131881.2011.572363

Brown, E., & McCowan, T. (2018). Buen vivir: Reimagining education and shifting paradigms (Forum). *Compare*, *48*(2), 317–23. https://doi:10.1080/03057925.2018.1427342

Bush, K., & Saltarelli, D. (Eds.). (2000). *The two faces of education in ethnic conflict: Towards a peacebuilding education for children*. United Nations Children's Fund Innocenti Research Center. https://www.unicef-irc.org/publications/pdf/insight4.pdf

Call-Cummings, M., & Hook, M. R. (2015). Endorsing empowerment? A critical comparative study of peace education in Jamaica and Peru. *Journal of Peace Education*, *12*(1), 92–108. https://doi:10.1080/17400201.2014.970616

Carbajal Padilla, M. P. (2013). Convivencia democrática en las escuelas. Apuntes para una reconceptualización. *Revista Iberoamericana de Evaluación Educativa*, *6*(2), 13–35. https://doi.org/10.15366/riee2013.6.2.001

Cárdenas, M. (2017). Developing pedagogical and democratic citizenship competencies: 'Learning by Participating' program. In B. García-Cabrero (Ed.), *Civics and citizenship: Theoretical models and experiences in Latin America* (pp. 207–39). Sense Publishers.

Davies, L. (2017). Justice-sensitive education: The implications of transitional justice mechanisms for teaching and learning. *Comparative Education*, *53*(3), 333–50. https://doi:10.1080/03050068.2017.1317999

Diazgranados-Ferráns, S., & Sandoval-Hernández, A. (2017). The civic competence gaps in Chile, Colombia, and Mexico and the factors that account for the civic knowledge gap: Evidence from the 2009 international civic and citizenship education study (ICCS). In B. García-Cabrero, A. Sandoval-Hernández, E. Treviño-Villareal, S. Diazgranados-Ferráns & M. G. Pérez Martínez (Eds.), *Civics and citizenship: Theoretical models and experiences in Latin America* (pp. 155–92). Sense Publishers.

Doob, A., & Cesaroni, C. (2004). *Responding to youth crime in Canada*. University of Toronto Press.

Dunning-Lozano, J. (2019). School discipline, race, and the discursive construction of the "deficient" student. *Sociological Spectrum*, *38*(5), 328–45. https://doi:10.1080/02732173.2018.1532364

Eizadirad, A. (2016). Is it "bad" kids or "bad" places? Where is all the violence originating from? Youth violence in the City of Toronto. *Review of Education, Pedagogy, and Cultural Studies*, *38*(2), 162–88. https://doi.org/10.1080/10714413.2016.1155956

Farmer, D., Cepin, J., & Breton-Carbonneau, G. (2015). Students' pathways across local, national, and supra-national borders: Representations of a globalized world in a francophone minority school in Ontario, Canada. *Journal of Social Science Education*, *14*(3), 75–83. DOI 10.2390/jsse-v14-i3-1398

Foucault, M. (2003). Technologies of the self. In P. Rabinow & N. Rose (Eds.), *The essential Foucault: Selections from the essential works of Foucault 1954–1984* (pp. 145–69). The New Press.

Fraser, N. (2004). Recognition, redistribution, and representation in capitalist global society [Nancy Fraser interviewed by H. Dahl, P. Stoltz, & R. Willig]. *Acta Sociologica*, *47*(4), 374–82. https://doi:10.1177/0001699304048671

– (2005, Nov./Dec.). Reframing justice in a globalizing world. *New Left Review*, *36*, 1–19. https://newleftreview.org/issues/ii36/articles/nancy-fraser-reframing-justice-in-a-globalizing-world

Galtung, J. (1976). Three approaches to peace: Peacekeeping, peacemaking, peacebuilding. In J. Galtung (Ed.), *Essays in peace research: Peace, war, and defense (Vol. 2)* (pp. 297–8). Christian Ejlers.

– (1990). Cultural violence. *Journal of Peace Research*, *27*(3), 291–305. https://doi.org/10.1177/0022343390027003005

Haste, H., Bermudez, A., & Carretaro, M. (2017). Culture and civic competence: Widening the scope of the civic domain. In B. García-Cabrero, A. Sandoval-Hernández, E. Treviño-Villareal, S. Díazgranados Ferrans & G. Pérez-Martínez (Eds.), *Civics and citizenship: Theoretical models and experiences in Latin America* (pp. 3–15). Sense Publishers.

Hess, D., & McAvoy, P. (2015). *The political classroom: Evidence and ethics in democratic education*. Routledge.

Ho, L. C., & Seow, T. (2015). Teaching controversial issues in geography: Climate change education in Singaporean schools. *Theory & Research in Social Education*, *43*, 314–44. https://doi:10.1080/00933104.2015.1064842

Howarth, K. (2014). Connecting the dots: Liberal peace and post-conflict violence and crime. *Progress in Development Studies*, *14*(3), 261–73. https://doi:10.1177/1464993414521336

IEP, Institute for Economics and Peace. (2015). *Mexico peace index 2015: Analyzing the changing dynamics of peace in Mexico*. https://www.files.ethz.ch/isn/191426/Mexico%20Peace%20Index%20Report%202015_1.pdf

– (2016). *Global peace index 2016: Ten years of measuring peace*. www.economicsandpeace.org

– (2021). *Ecological Threat Report 2021: Understanding Ecological Threats, Resilience and Peace*. http://visionofhumanity.org/resources

Jull, S. (2000). Youth violence, schools, and the management question: A discussion of zero tolerance and equity in public schooling. *Canadian Journal of Educational Administration and Policy*, (17). https://journalhosting.ucalgary.ca/index.php/cjeap/article/view/42680

Kaderi, A. S. (2018). *Peacebuilding citizenship education in a Muslim-majority context: Challenges and opportunities in Bangladeshi public schools*. [Doctoral dissertation, University of Toronto]. http://hdl.handle.net/1807/92009

Kovinthan Levi, T. (2019). Incremental Transformations: Education for Resiliency in Post-War Sri Lanka. *Education sciences*, *9*(1), 11. https://doi:10.3390/educsci9010011

Leenen, I., & Cervantes-Trejo, A. (2014). Temporal and geographic trends in homicide and suicide rates in Mexico, from 1998 through 2012. *Aggression and Violent Behavior*, *19*(6), 699–707. https://doi.org/10.1016/j.avb.2014.09.004

Lopes Cardozo, M, Higgins, S., & Le Mat, M. (2016). *Youth agency and peacebuilding: An analysis of the role of formal and non-formal education Synthesis report on findings from Myanmar, Pakistan, South Africa, and Uganda*. University of Amsterdam. https://educationanddevelopment.files.wordpress.com/2016/06/youth-agency-synthesis-report-final16.pdf

Lustick, H. (2021). "Restorative justice" or restoring order? Restorative school discipline practices in urban public schools. *Urban Education*, *56*(8), 1269–96. https://doi:10.1177/0042085917741725

Matsunaga, J. (2016). Two faces of transitional justice: Theorizing the incommensurability of transitional justice and decolonization in Canada. *Decolonization: Indigeneity, Education & Society*, *5*(1), 24–44. https://jps.library.utoronto.ca/index.php/des/article/view/26530

Merelman, R. (1990). The role of conflict in children's political learning. In O. Ichilov (Ed.), *Political socialization, citizenship education, and democracy* (pp. 47–65). Teachers College Press.

Meyer, J. W., Bromley, P., & Ramirez, F. O. (2010). Human rights in social science textbooks: Cross-national analysis, 1970–2008. *Sociology of Education*, *83*(4), 111–34. https://doi.org/10.1177/0038040710367936

Nieto, D., & Bickmore, K. (2016). Citizenship and Convivencia Education in Contexts of Violence: Transnational challenges to peacebuilding education in Mexican schools (Educación Ciudadana Y Convivencia En Contextos De Violencia: Desafíos Transnacionales A La Construcción De Paz En Escuelas De México – in English). *Revista Española de Educación Comparada*, (28), 109–34. https://doi:10.5944/reec.28.2016.17087

Nixon, R. (2011). *Slow violence and the environmentalism of the poor*. Harvard University Press.

Novelli, M., & Higgins, S. (2017). The violence of peace and the role of education: Insights from Sierra Leone. *Compare: A Journal of Comparative and International Education*, *47*(1), 32–45. https://doi.org/10.1080/03057925.2015.1119650

Pace, J. (2019). Contained risk-taking: Preparing preservice teachers to teach controversial issues in three countries. *Theory & Research in Social Education*, *47*(2), 228–60. https://doi:10.1080/00933104.2019.1595240

Parker, C. (2016). Pedagogical tools for peacebuilding education: Engaging and empathizing with diverse perspectives in multicultural elementary classrooms. *Theory & Research in Social Education*, *44*(1), 104–40. https://doi:10.1080/00933104.2015.1100150

Parker, C., & Bickmore, K. (2020). Complexity in restorative justice education circles: Power and privilege in voicing perspectives about sexual health, identities, and relationships. *Journal of Moral Education*, *50*(4), 471–93. https://doi.10.1080/03057240.2020.1832451

Paulson, J. (2008). The "two faces" today? *Research in Comparative and International Education*, *3*(1), 1–4. https://doi:10.2304/rcie.2008.3.1.1

Perales Franco, C. (2018). *School-community relationships and convivencia: An ethnographic study of conflict management, inclusion, and participation in two Mexican primary schools*. [Doctoral Dissertation, University College London].

Quaynor, L. (2014). "I do not have the means to speak": Educating youth for citizenship in post-conflict Liberia. *Journal of Peace Education, 12*(1), 15–36. https://doi:10.1080/17400201.2014.931277

Reimers, F., Ortega, M. E., Cardenas, M., Estrada, A., & Garza, E. (2014). Empowering teaching for participatory citizenship: Evaluating the impact of alternative civic education pedagogies on civic attitudes, knowledge, and skills of eight-grade students in Mexico. *Journal of Social Science Education, 13*(4), 41–55. https://doi:10.2390/jsse-v13-i4-1357

Schultz, K. (2009). *Rethinking classroom participation: Listening to silent voices*. Teachers College Press.

Siddiqi, D. M. (2011). Political culture in contemporary Bangladesh: Histories, ruptures and contradictions. In A. Riaz & C. C. Fair (Eds.), *Political Islam and governance in Bangladesh* (pp. 7–26). Routledge.

St. Denis, V. (2011). Silencing Aboriginal curricular content and perspectives through multiculturalism: "There are other children here." *Review of Education, Pedagogy & Cultural Studies, 33*(4), 306–17. https://doi.org/10.1080/10714413.2011.597638

Tupper, J., & Cappello, M. (2012). (Re)Creating citizenship: Saskatchewan high school students' understandings of the "good" citizen. *Journal of Curriculum Studies, 44*(1), 37–59. https://doi.org/10.1080/00220272.2011.618951

Welsh, R. O., & Little, S. (2018). The school discipline dilemma: A comprehensive review of disparities and alternative approaches. *Review of Educational Research, 88*(5), 752–94. https://doi:10.3102/0034654318791582

Zúñiga, X., Mildred, J., Varghese, R., DeJong, K., & Keehn, M. (2012). Engaged listening in race/ethnicity and gender intergroup dialogue courses. *Equity & Excellence in Education, 45*(1), 80–99. https://doi:10.1080/10665684.2012.644962

Zurita Rivera, Ú. (2012). Las Escuelas Mexicanas y la legislación sobre la convivencia, la seguridad y la violencia escolar. *Educación y Territorio, 2*(1), 19–36.

3 Beauty in the Shadows: Curriculum Change and the New BC School Science Curriculum

DAVID BLADES

Introduction: Shadow as Metaphor

The metaphor of a shadow is a common rhetorical device in English (Shilperoord & Weelden, 2018). Shadows can represent fear or danger: we are frightened by our shadow, things lurk in shadows, possibly evil things. The metaphor of a shadow indicates a sense of ruin; something or someone can become a shadow of their former glory or self. Shadows can rhetorically indicate a sense of the incomplete, the not fully formed, "mere shadows" indicating the unclear, the ill-informed, with the opposite being completely informed beyond "a shadow of a doubt."

Shadows can refer to where we can live and stand, as in a shadow or under a shadow. In this sense, shadows are something to *escape* from, shadows can "stalk our lives," they are cast on us, events cast a "long shadow" of influence. Yet in the shadows lie hope that we can leave the shadows-as-influence, we "come out from under a shadow or out of the shadows" into the light; we live in the hope that there is "light at the end of the tunnel." In this way, shadows are a rhetorical device used to represent a movement *away*: from fear, from doubt, a stepping away; *progress* towards the better from the shadows as we move from darkness into the light.

This metaphor of shadows – one of progress as escape from an influence into the light of illumination – provides an opportunity to make sense of recent changes to the school science curriculum, particularly the secondary school curriculum, in the province of British Columbia (BC), Canada. These recent changes can be seen as part of a history of attempting to escape the long shadow cast by major reforms in science education following the Second World War. However, this chapter challenges this viewpoint, arguing that the most recent change effort in BC reflects lingering *within* shadows of curriculum reforms in ways that reveal creativity, complexity, and the beauty of possibilities.

The Long Shadow of Post-Sputnik Reforms on Canadian Science Education

School science education curricula were under revision across the United States when the former Soviet Union launched the first human-made satellite, *Sputnik*, in October 1957. As I have documented (Blades, 1997), awareness that these technologies demonstrated Soviet nuclear intercontinental ballistic missile capability fueled incriminations in the United States that the country was not producing enough scientists and technologists to match Soviet technological achievements. The result, well documented in curriculum history, was the US National Defense Education Act (1958), which gave educational institutions unprecedented access to the large military budget at the time, resulting in millions of dollars devoted to the cooperative involvement of scientists, educators, and learning theorists in the development of science education curriculum materials (Helgeson et al., 1977, p. 1). By 1960, 93 per cent of all post-war US government funds for education came from the US Department of Defense National Science Foundation, and NASA; the goal of this investment was "the production of top-notch, career scientists through the studies of the traditional disciplines of biology, chemistry, and physics" (Blades, 1997, p. 15). As science education historian Michael Matthews (1989) notes, the result was new curricula for schools with the intention of creating a new pool of scientists in order to catch up and then beat the Soviet Union in technological innovation.

These new science programs for schools included new textbooks, lesson plans, films, and kits of materials so complete that most countries, including Canada, aligned with American political ideologies and capitalism and simply imported the materials directly to their school systems. In this sense, the American curriculum changes to their school science programs, especially those for secondary schools, cast a long shadow on curriculum development in Canada.

As a high school student, I remember when these new programs came to our school. The programs contained large kits, film strips, and new textbooks. Our teachers were excited to use these materials and shared their enthusiasm with us; we all felt part of something innovative and exciting, embracing the illumination of the new materials.

In 1979, I graduated from university, certified to teach in the public schools in British Columbia. I tried faithfully to implement the post-Sputnik reforms in my teaching career but immediately noticed an issue: the post-Sputnik reforms did not contain any Canadian examples. I was not alone in this concern; many Canadian science educators felt similar frustrations with the American materials. Worse, the new programs were laden with concepts embedded in a system of mandatory provincially designed final exams that left little time for student enquiry. The result was that many teachers fell to lecturing to prepare students for tests, a pedagogy that students found irrelevant and boring and largely responsible for the subsequent drop in the number of students considering a career in a science-related field.

Canadian nationalism also affected attitudes towards the US science programs. In science education, the Science Council of Canada engaged in a four-year study of science education in Canada (1980–4), one of the most comprehensive studies of school curriculum conducted by any nation. One result of this study was the recommendation that provinces develop their own school science programs that reflected their history, geography, and environments; in essence, escaping the shadow of the American post-Sputnik reforms by creating the bright light of a uniquely Canadian science curriculum.

This proved difficult. By the 1990s all provinces in Canada, including BC, were engaged in revisions to their school science curricula.[1] The first province to attempt full revision of their school science materials was Alberta. In my analysis of this massive effort at curriculum change, I note that despite considerable effort and expense "*nothing had changed*" (Blades, 1997, p. 83; emphasis in text) except the order of the topics in the curriculum. In fact, every province found that when it came to escaping the shadow of the post-Sputnik reforms, what seemed to result was more Canadian examples and some reorganization of the order of topics. In essence, there was little to no change in purpose, orientation, and topics in the school science programs. One possible reason for this lack of illumination could be that the agenda of the curriculum reform stayed the same: the topics and direction of the curriculum still reflected an effort at producing scientists and technologists to ensure a national advantage in a global economy. It would take a new perspective on why we teach students science to offer a pathway out from the shadow of the post-Sputnik reforms and into the light of a new approach to science education.

Creating a New Light: STS Science Education and the Pan-Canadian Framework

During my struggles to teach students science using the American science education curriculum and materials, I discovered a new approach to teaching high school science. In a keynote address, Hurd (1975) argued instead for a *citizenship* approach to science that focuses on the interdisciplinary relationships between science, technology, and society (STS). During my master's degree studies I discovered that by the end of the 1990s there were several programs around the world attempting to adopt an STS approach to science education.

I found the STS approach (later "STSE" with the addition of "environment" to the initialism) an exciting new direction towards a science curriculum that could be truly Canadian, a move out of the shadow of the post-Sputnik reforms based on international competition towards the light of a science education that was for all students, a science education that could help students develop the attitudes and skills to deal with the social and environmental consequences of technological and scientific innovation. This was science education not for producing rocket scientists but a science literacy that takes seriously our positioning and responsibility to the survival of other species. I did not realize at the time, however, that STSE science education still represented an ethos of social engineering, this time using school science education to develop an early start on solving societal issues, such as global environmental degradation.

Adopting an STSE approach to science education in Canada was encouraged when the Council of Ministers of Education in Canada, an affiliation for provincial cooperation in curriculum development, published in 1997 the *Common Framework of Science Learning Outcomes, K to 12: Pan-Canadian Protocol for Collaboration on School Curriculum for Use by Curriculum Developers*. This document represents a significant attempt to become a new light, one that casts out the shadows of the post-Sputnik reforms. While not mandated as Canadian law, the *Framework* did provide the learning outcomes for a national science curriculum based on four key foundations. One of these foundations was the adoption of an STSE approach to science education curriculum development.

The principle of an STSE approach was a new direction for science education in Canada, but the *Common Framework* document revealed that coming out from the shadow of the post-Sputnik reforms is a particularly difficult challenge. As I noted in a speech to the Alberta Teachers' Association (Blades, 2000), the *Common Framework* continues the post-Sputnik reforms' perspective towards science as a "culturally neutral subject with special access to truth about the natural world" (p. 1). In my address I also observe that when it came to actually adopting the STSE approach, provincially "changes were limited in effect" (p. 1), because teachers did not have sufficient background in an STSE approach, a consequence of the post-Sputnik science programs they studied as students and teacher candidates.

As the adoption of an STSE approach faltered in Canada, the United States continued to reinforce the direction and intentions of the post-Sputnik reforms in 2001 with the generation of a set of science learning standards for science education by the American Association for the Advancement of Science (AAAS). As Marx and Harris (2006) note, these documents "emphasize[d] the importance of high-quality instruction that focuses on substantive science content" (p. 468); while Canada was grappling with STSE approaches to science education, the United States was further entrenching the content of the post-Sputnik curriculum reforms. While the AAAS standards did not link achievement standards to learning content, the publication that same year of the Federal *No Child Left Behind* initiative encouraged states to develop achievement standards for content, including science, in the format of high-stakes testing. At this time many Canadian provinces also introduced or reintroduced mandatory testing in their school systems, which further continued the influence of the shadow of the post-Sputnik reforms in Canada and threatened the adoption of the Pan-Canadian Framework recommendations.

This shadow was destined to grow as the United States continued to elaborate and refine "accountability" measures for students learning science content. In 2012 the US National Research Council published, *A Framework for K-12 Science Education: Practices, Crosscutting Concepts, and Core Ideas*. This document argues that science, engineering, and technology "permeate nearly every facet of modern life and hold the key to solving many of humanity's most pressing current and future challenges" (p. 1). The document also argues that science education is of national importance because the United States' position in the global economy is declining, in part because US workers lack fundamental knowledge in these fields, and so a new curriculum is needed to address the critical issues of US competitiveness. Effectively, this new framework is parallel to the post-Sputnik reforms in intention, replacing competition with the Soviet Union with gaining advantage in a globalized economy, albeit with a more pedagogically sound approach to science education. In this way, the shadow of the post-Sputnik reforms continued, reset as a fight for economic superiority through the social engineering of science education.

This redirection of the post-Sputnik agenda towards economic leadership was further entrenched with the introduction of a new orientation to science education, one that emphasized science, technology, mathematics, and engineering (STEM). STEM science education has effectively replaced STSE approaches to science education in the United States and many locations in Canada, casting a long and current shadow on school science curriculum development. As I observe in an article on curriculum reform in science education, the rationale for STEM over all other approaches to science education,

> has parallels with the post-Sputnik reforms: In a globalized world, increasing participation in STEM careers is advanced by nation-states as a way to win the assumed race for economic advantage through leadership in technological innovation. In this way, STEM becomes a vehicle for social engineering in parallel to the agenda of the post-Sputnik reforms, only in the case of STEM the cause of national security is relocated in gaining economic advantage in a globalized economy. (Blades, 2020, p. 21)

In his thorough review of STEM approaches to science education, Zeidler (2014) notes that there does not seem to be any single approach characterized as STEM, and the only unifying agenda seems to be the intention of making careers in STEM fields more appealing to students. In this way, STEM reflects and continues the agenda of using school science for social engineering to reinforce a neoliberal hegemony of superiority in global competition through a focus on a particular set of skills needed for capitalist expansionism.

The long shadow of the post-Sputnik reforms is thus given new impetus in STEM and many Canadian provinces have moved to adopt STEM approaches. In British Columbia, however, a new science education curriculum emerged that does not reflect STEM, the approaches and content of the post-Sputnik reforms, or even particularly embrace an STSE approach to science education. This new science curriculum seems to be unique, a seemingly impossible development given the ubiquity of STEM and the powerful influence of post-Sputnik curriculum developments in science education.

The New BC Curriculum: Lingering in the Shadows

From 2016 to 2019 the province of British Columbia developed a "radically different approach to science education" (Blades, 2019, p. 24). Appreciating the unique nature of this new approach begins with the previous science education curriculum for students in BC. Between 1995 and 2015 science education in the province was mandated legally through documents called "Integrated Resource Packages" (IRPs). These IRPs were ponderous documents, some in excess of 400 pages. Each document provided information on the "prescribed learning objectives" (PLOs) for science education and associated assessment strategies. As I note in my review of science education in British Columbia, the content knowledge of each course reflected "the science courses originally developed as part of the post-Sputnik US curriculum reforms" (Blades, 2019, p. 21). These IRPs were popular; "teachers and preservice teachers appeared to appreciate the science IRPs for their comprehensive, sound advice on what and how to teach" (p. 24). Assessment strategies were also reflected on high-stakes, mandatory government-administered final exams for senior grade level science courses, which invariably reflected science content knowledge. Also recommended to be included in instruction were the skills and attitudes associated with science enquiry at various grade levels – which we call the process skills of science education – but the sheer size of the documents caused some teachers to ignore the preliminary pages and move directly to the list of PLOs for a particular grade or subject. As a result, teachers could essentially miss important aspects of the IRPs, such as the emphasis on process skills.

In 2001, the province published the *Science Curriculum Review Report* (Monkman, 2001) that outlined the status of science education in BC with an emphasis on how students in BC compared to peers on international tests of science education. The report also makes several key recommendations for revising science education in the province. This included aligning science education more towards science and technology studies by incorporating the vision and the foundational statements of the *Common Framework of Science Learning Outcomes* (1997) as well as developing a "more cohesive framework of K-12 standards, benchmarks, and learning outcomes based on the generally accepted major themes of Science" (p. 18).

This brief history reveals that BC existed in the shadow of influence of the US post-Sputnik reforms in science education. Later, the BC Ministry of Education tried to escape this shadow by adopting the bright illumination of an STSE focus to science education and the scope and sequence of science topics as presented in the *Common Framework of Science Learning Outcomes.* The attempted escape was unsuccessful; instead, BC moved in a new direction in 2011 with the announcement of the *BC Education Plan.* This plan summarized months of community consultation and extensive discussions with parents, teachers, and university teacher educators. I was involved in these consultations and was surprised by government openness to suggestions. What was needed, the plan argued, was "a new approach to curriculum, one in which it would be easier for teachers to use their professional knowledge to guide students in developing the skills and understanding that would help them become successful citizens" (British Columbia Ministry of Education, 2011).

This plan included a new approach to curriculum development. While most provinces tended to use a systematic step-by-step approach to curriculum change that reflected a technical-linear research-design-implement-evaluate approach, BC adopted the following principles for curriculum redesign (Walt, 2015):

- Ensure core competencies are explicit in redesign.
- Limit the amount of prescription while ensuring a solid focus on essential learning.
- Allow for flexibility and choice for teachers and students.
- Focus on the important concepts and big ideas in each area of learning.
- Emphasize higher order learning and deeper learning.
- Respect the inherent logic and unique nature of the disciplines while supporting efforts to develop cross-curricular units.
- Integrate and embed First Peoples Principles of Learning and Aboriginal knowledge and world views.
- Align assessment and evaluation with the redesign of the curriculum.

Of particular note are the "core competencies," which instead of being content knowledge were redefined as the qualities of educated citizens. BC thus moved from specifying what students should particularly know towards a curriculum that helps students develop the intellectual, personal, and social skills for success in and beyond schooling through the foundational competencies of communication, thinking, and personal and social competency.

I was involved in the earliest stages of the development of the new BC curriculum, and it was challenging to figure out a curriculum that limited "the amount of prescription while ensuring a solid focus on essential learning" and that also allowed "for flexibility and choice for teachers and students." Discussions about realizing this directive ranged widely and forced our small committee of ministry officials and myself to consider exactly what it means for students to learn science as educated citizens in a world where information (and misinformation) on practically any topic is available to students through digital media. We came up with the notion that there are some "big ideas" in science, and perhaps these should be the focus of the new curriculum. At this point we were trying to come out from the shadow of the post-Sputnik reforms reflected in the IRPs and the *Common Framework of Science Learning Outcomes* (1997) as well. We were searching for something new, a uniquely made-in-BC science curriculum that would truly prepare students for the challenge of citizenship in the twenty-first century. Our conversations, while not preserved in print, centred around finding a new way that science education might promote the development of an educated citizen.

Our development process did not reflect at all a technical-linear approach; in fact, as one member of the team described it, our free exploration of ideas was almost a kind of curriculum anarchy fully supported by the Ministry of Education. We met with teachers over several days and came up with an approach to science education that would emphasize the interconnections of science, the environment, and technology – which was close to reflecting the STSE approach of the *Common Framework of Science Learning Outcomes* (1997). In this way, we came under the shadow of that document, no doubt partially due to my personal involvement with the *Common Framework of Science Learning Outcomes* as well as playing a leadership role on the development committee of the new curriculum. In retrospect, I believe that I was still motivated by an attitude of progress: we were going to develop the best new curriculum yet for school science education, one suited and developed for the twenty-first century!

The idea of a science-environment-technology focus did not materialize, however. Wider consultation revealed that the proposed science curriculum was too vague. Teachers did like the big ideas of science, however, so development continued to expand on what these meant. When this happened, the development of the new science curriculum ceased striving to escape the shadows of previous curricula in science education and especially the influence of standards-based assessment. It was as if those previous influences were no longer relevant, or even considered. Instead, the development *lingered in the shadows* of influence, not trying any longer to have the best, newest, most ideal curriculum. Instead, developers returned to focus on the idea of an *educated citizen.*

In science education, a focus on being an educated citizen meant that students would need to understand the processes of science, the skills, attitudes, and limitations of science as a human activity. The committee rightly believed that previous school science education curricula emphasized science content mastery over the processes of science; we believed that learning the processes of science lay at the heart of being an educated citizen. This led to a remarkable and unique shift in the BC curriculum to focus on the processes of science with content as a *way or means to learn these processes.* This was a radical change from any other approach to science education in the world. The focus of the new curriculum continued to be on the big ideas in science, with content serving as *examples* of these big ideas. Finally, the developers deliberately provided little detail about content aside from a brief listing for each grade level so that teachers could decide on how to elaborate the content in a way that would help students learn the processes of science. In effect, the new curriculum shifted from a static document to a living, dynamic negotiation of science education between teachers and students and the outline provided by the Ministry of Education. At the same time, the Ministry encouraged teachers to experiment with new forms of assessment, further engaging teachers in what was to become a continual form of curriculum implementation.

I struggled to make sense of this change and predicted that teachers would find the new curriculum vague, unsupportive, and even a bit unnerving in how they were now expected to teach science process skills and interpret the rather sketchy content suggestions. I was wrong. Surprisingly, the curriculum has been received well and teachers seem relieved to finally have the freedom to teach students science the way that they believe it should be taught and to develop lessons that reflect their pedagogical content knowledge. Of course, some teachers found the curriculum far too loose in organization and content and wanted more clarity, especially around the details of content. Initially those in the Ministry of Education directly responsible for developing the new curriculum, which was the majority of the committee I served on, did not make the content more specific. They did, however, provide examples to help define what the content, often just a word or phrase, *might* mean, emphasizing that defining the meaning of the content was up to teachers. The group likely most unnerved by the new curriculum were the pre-service teachers I taught as a university professor, who found the curriculum sketchy. It *is* sketchy, that's the point – anything more prescriptive would inevitably become another version of STEM or its parent curriculum in the post-Sputnik reforms.

There was nothing linear in the approach to curriculum reform; it was more of a creative generation of ideas and then seeing what teachers think, remaining completely open to their ideas. Given that school curriculum change is almost always a return to the status quo (Blades, 1997), how was BC able to make such a radical shift from the long shadows of influence that threatened to define the direction of the new changes? Rather than trying to escape from these shadows, I believe inspiration and possibilities were able to emerge because the development lingered *in* the shadows.

The New BC Science Curriculum: Beauty in Shadows

Were it not for shadows, there would be no beauty (Tanizaki, 1977, p. 28).

While involved in a research project on the role of beauty in science education I discovered *In Praise of Shadow* by Japanese artist Jun´ichirō Tanizaki (1977). As we have seen, in English shadows are almost always considered negative rhetorical metaphors. But Tanizaki argues that this view of shadows reflects a particularly Euro-centric perspective and that, in fact, shadows reveal great beauty.

This perspective is reflected in the Japanese Kanji symbol for shadow or shade:

影

The Kanji is made of two parts. The left side indicates "scene" as in a scene of play or show and the right side, three dashes, indicates "hair." This sense of shadow involves stopping to see a scene before you, but the scene is partially blocked by your hair, suggesting caution or even some playfulness. In no way, however, is there a suggestion that shadows should be eliminated. Tanizaki (1977) explains this perspective:

> The progressive Westerner is determined always to better his [sic] lot. From candle to oil lamp, oil lamp to gaslight, gaslight to electric light – his quest for a brighter light never ceases, he spares no pains to eradicate even the minutest shadow. (p. 30)

He notes that, "light is not used for reading or writing or sewing but for dispelling the shadows in the farthest corners, and this runs against the basic idea of the Japanese room" (p. 37), adding, "but perhaps we may be allowed at least one mansion where we can turn off the electric lights and see what it is like without them" (p. 42). And when you do, he argues, what you discover is great beauty.

Using the example of a Japanese tatami room, Tanizaki (1977) explains that these rooms form beautiful patterns in the shadows created by the paper (or often now thin plastic) walls:

> The beauty of a Japanese room depends on a variation of shadows, heavy shadows against light shadows – it has nothing else. Westerners are amazed at the simplicity of Japanese rooms, perceiving in them no more than ashen walls bereft of ornament. Their reaction is understandable, but it betrays a failure to comprehend the mystery of shadows. (p. 17)

It is this very return to basics, to simplicity, that presents an aesthetic appreciation. Tanizaki tells us that the Japanese, "never tire of the sight, for to us this pale glow and these dim shadows far surpass any ornament" (p. 17).

Rather than try to modify or somehow achieve greater light than the previous science curriculum, in the early stages of our development team we worked *within* these shadows, appreciating how their patterns encouraged us to return to a basic, direct, and seemingly simple question: What is essential for students to know about science? There is beauty in returning to fundamental questions and wrestling with the answers as this exposes the particular biases about science that we each brought to the question. What we realized is that learning science is an important part of being an educated citizen, but we struggled to comprehend what would be important for students to know about science. This struggle led us to a second form of beauty made present in shadows: creativity.

In his novel, *Mirror Mirror*, Maguire (2009) writes that, "the eye is always caught by light, but shadows have more to say" (p. 2). The particular beauty of subtle creation is revealed in the way shadows highlight that which is hidden by darkness or, more often, bright light. Tanizaki (1977) explains how this creativity is revealed by shadows with the example of Japanese lacquerware. Speaking of new, glittery objects to be held in light, he writes that for many Japanese, "we do not dislike everything that shines, but we do prefer a pensive luster to a shallow brilliance, a murky light that, whether in a stone or an artifact, bespeaks a sheen of antiquity" (p. 10). He then provides an example of this sheen:

> I realized then that only in the dim half-light is the true beauty of Japanese lacquerware revealed. As I gazed at the trays and bowls standing in the shadows cast by that flickering point of flame, I discovered in the gloss of this lacquerware a depth and richness like that of a still, dark pond, a beauty I had not before seen. (pp. 11–12)

In this way, shadows are *necessary* to reveal the subtle aspects of the creative decorations of Japanese lacquerware, or are, more appropriately, *part* of the decoration, to be appreciated only in the faint light of shadows. In the same way, lingering in the shadows of national and international efforts to reform school science, we were able to engage in a creative exploration that led us to consider the "big ideas" of science as perhaps a starting point for developing a new school science curriculum. We did not feel the burden of having to step into the light of the post-Sputnik reforms nor the continuing darkness of using science education for social engineering for military or economic advantage. Freed from either obligation, we could create and decorate. This freedom led us to consider the importance of the big ideas in the light of being an educated citizen and the subsequent, startling realization that, for BC, perhaps it was more important to teach students about how science works and the skills associated with science than emphasize science content knowledge. I believe that we would not have reached this viewpoint had we adopted a version of STEM, revised post-Sputnik program, or even STSE science education. Instead, in the shadow of these major reform efforts, we lingered, playing with ideas and creating new ways of thinking about science education that opened up possibilities we all found beautiful. For example, we realized that we could release teachers from the burden of teaching massive amounts of science concepts by calling instead on their expertise to help students understand how science works, and when it does not work, *through* the use of concepts *as examples*. It is this approach that opens possibilities for teachers to deeply investigate science-based issues and ideas with students and in turn create a science education beautiful in relevancy.

This curriculum development was not easy, however. Part of the development of the new BC science program meant developers, including teacher consultants, had to give up trying to steer the development in any particular direction. For me, I was initially disappointed that the new programs did not directly reflect an STSE approach to science education or infuse environmental perspectives into the content. As Julie Exline (2013) observes in *Gifts of the Shadow*,

> There's also a certain beauty to be found in shadow experiences – those in which we suffer painful losses or question our beliefs, for example. In their subtle and intricate forms, blends of light and shadow add a sense of texture and depth. They press us toward nuance and complexity. (p. 4)

Tanizaki (1977), drawing from the Japanese Kanji for shadow, uses the example of Japanese Kabuki Nō theatre to explain the important of blending light and shadow:

> The darkness in which the Nō is shrouded and the beauty that emerges from it make a distinct world of shadows which today can be seen only on the stage ... The Bunraku puppet theatre was for long lit by lamplight, even after the introduction of electricity in the Meiji era, and that this method was far more rightly suggestive than modern lighting. (pp. 25, 27)

We found this complexity as the developers tried to knit together big ideas, an emphasis on science processes and suggested content all squeezed into the existing framework of grades and courses. It would have been easy to slip into the seductive light of control, to produce another IRP that would "guide" teachers into how to teach students science the way we envisioned, but this moment slipped by as the developers continued to linger in the shadows, unresolved by modern lighting. What emerged instead seemed almost like a reckless abdication of responsibility: Developers decided to let teachers figure out how the parts would all work together. What this actually accomplished is the invention of a curriculum complicated by individual teacher expertise and student experience. In this decentering of curriculum, teachers became liberated to make sense of a sketchy, Kabuki-like curriculum, one where only the outline of ideas is present, inviting teachers to make sense of ideas and directions for themselves.

Tanizaki (1977) points out that "we Orientals, as I have suggested before, create a kind of beauty of the shadows we have made in out-of-the-way places" (p. 28). He continues: "We find beauty not in the thing itself but in the patterns of shadows, the light and the darkness, that one thing against the other creates" (p. 28). In this sense, shadows are not only protection from strong illumination but beautiful in themselves, when ideas and topics are shadowy enough to allow for the types of conversations that liberate curriculum from top-down, instrumental approaches, creating new possibilities by inviting teachers to join curriculum developers creating in the shadows, drawing inspiration from the complex patterns only possible because of the interplay of light and darkness.

Curriculum Change as Lingering in Shadows

Curriculum theorist Ted Aoki challenged a technical-linear approach to curriculum change by inviting us to consider the translation of curriculum from plan to practice. Aoki (2004) notes that teachers tend to dwell within and between two worlds: "the world of curriculum-as-plan and the world of curriculum-as-lived experiences" (p. 163), what he calls the "Zone of Between" (p. 163). He envisions this Zone as a place of openness and possibility as a teacher makes sense of what has been mandated to teach but has not yet actualized this plan with students.

Curriculum change as lingering in shadows has parallels with Aoki's Zone of Between, but with one key difference. While lingering in shadows can be a place of creativity and insight, there is not movement from one place to another; instead, lingering in shadows is productive precisely by avoiding the temptation to move out of the shadows or destroy the shadows by creating a new, bright light.

In these places of dappled light and shifting shadows formed by bright light, our vision is less distinct. This lack of clarity encourages the revelation of new patterns or creativities that are otherwise overtaken by bright illumination. We can appreciate the light and that which blocks the light forming shadows but not be defined by this light. In curriculum change, this means letting go of the desire to be the best, brightest, newest way to solve the problems of humankind through school science education. In the shadows, we let go of progress as a single, defined movement. Without this defining principle of science education curriculum development, we can be open to surprise, to creativity, and to complexity precisely because we can't see the way forward. We leave the game of progress towards the next, bright illumination and thus open up curriculum as an on-going dialogue with teachers and students without a specific plan for the outcome of the dialogue. This "post-modern" approach to curriculum recasts the notion of "development" into a continual, circular conversation of suggestion and advice by those charged with coming up with ideas and those realizing these ideas with students.

This approach has resonated with teachers in BC. A 2015 presentation by the BC Ministry of Education Director of Curriculum and Instruction (Walt, 2015) shared the following quotes by teachers:

- *Overall, we fully support the new directions taken . . . recognizing change is needed to prepare students better for a future in a vastly more complicated and less predictable world.*
- *These changes are long overdue. The biggest strength is, by shortening that enormous list of learning outcomes, we can now focus on thinking and learning and the big ideas. Now there is some flexibility to help us better personalize learning and to find ways to use areas of student interest to facilitate learning.*

This general sense of acceptance and even praise for the new curriculum suggests a successful development, one that teachers can personalize and use. Yet comments from the field also reveal that few teachers discuss the processes of science as a curriculum focus, indicating perhaps that the intention of the new curriculum is still being overshadowed by the content-focus of the post-Sputnik reforms.

It is too early to say if the curriculum dynamic established in BC will continue in its present forms. A dual aspect to this curriculum – processes and content – has evolved from the original plan. Concerns by teachers that the curriculum is too vague proved too tempting to Ministry developers, who then focused on elaborating content but not the process skills. The other important change is that the new curricula in science in the province now prefaces the list of topics under content with the legally binding phrase, "students are expected to know." This reemphasis on the knowledge component of science education represents a return to the light of the post-Sputnik reforms; in the case of BC, it will be tempting for teachers to return to the old IRPs for guidance on how to teach and assess the topics listed in the new curriculum. If this were to happen, curriculum development in BC will have slipped out from lingering in the shadows and become a light itself, joining at least in part the expressions of the post-Sputnik reforms in the modern incarnation of STEM.

To escape the blinding light of an ideology of progress, that we can somehow "improve" curriculum, we need to remain in the shadows and not try to define everything, and let *teachers do their job* by providing, perhaps, an outline of topics *for their professional consideration.* Already we see that the temptation to clarify, elaborate, and mandate is seeping into the curriculum change in BC. This should not be discouraging but expected, since *change is difficult.* But, as Foucault (1988) reminds us, "as soon as one can no longer think things as one formerly thought then, transformation becomes both very urgent, very difficult, and quite possible" (p. 155). It is this hope, that lingering in shadows presents an opportunity to see things in new ways, that we might even for a moment avoid the seduction of previous illuminations and in the beauty of shadows find the inspiration, creativity, and complexity of new curriculum possibilities.

NOTE

1 In Canada, each province has jurisdiction for education; there is no national educational system, although remarkable similarities exist in school curriculum among provinces.

REFERENCES

Aoki, T. (2004). Teaching as in-dwelling between two curriculum worlds. In W. F. Pinar and R. L. Irwin (Eds.), *Curriculum in a new key* (pp. 159–66). Laurence Erlbaum.

Blades, D. (1997). *Procedures of power and curriculum change: Foucault and the quest for change in science education*. Peter Lang.

– (2000). The problem with snakes: Critical reflections on the Pan-Canadian Common Framework of Science Learning Outcomes. *ATA Magazine, 81*(1). https://www.teachers.ab.ca/News%20Room/ata%20magazine/Volume%2081/Number%201/Articles/Pages/The%20Problem%20with%20Snakes.aspx.

– (2019). Science education in Canada: British Columbia. In C. D. Tippett & T. M. Milford (Eds.), *Science education in Canada: Consistencies, commonalities, and distinctions* (pp. 13–37). Springer.

– (2020). The curriculum of science education reform. In W. Shubert & M. Fang (Eds.), *Oxford Encyclopedia of Curriculum Studies*. https://doi.org/10.1093/acrefore/9780190264093.013.1057

British Columbia Ministry of Education (2011). *BC's education plan*. http://buildingpublicunderstanding.org › bc_edu_. plan

Exline, J. (2013). Gifts of the shadow. *Psychology Today*. https://www.psychologytoday.com/ca/blog/light-and-shadow/201302/gifts-the-shadow.

Foucault, M. (1988). *Michel Foucault: Politics, philosophy, and culture* (L. Kritzman, Ed.). Routledge.

Helgeson, S., Blosser, P., & Howe, R. (1977). *The status of pre-college science, mathematics, and social science education: 1955–1975. Science Education, 1*, Ohio State University Center for Science and Mathematics Education.

Hurd, P. (1975). Science, technology, and society: New goals for interdisciplinary science teaching. *Science Teacher, 42*(2), 27–30.

Maguire, G. (2009). *Mirror mirror: A novel*. Harper Collins.

Marx, R. W. and Harris, C. J. (2006). No Child Left Behind and science education: Opportunities, challenges, and risks. *The Elementary School Journal, 106*(5), 467–78. https://doi.org/10.1086/505441

Matthews, M. (1989). A role for history and philosophy in science teaching. *Interchange, 20*(2), 3–15. https://doi.org/10.1007/BF01807043

Monkman, D. (2001). *Science curriculum review report. British Columbia Ministry of Education. U.S. Federal Legislation.* (1958). *National defense education Act of 1958.* https://www.govinfo.gov/content/pkg/STATUTE-72/pdf/STATUTE-72-Pg1580.pdf

Shilperoord, J., & Weelden, L. (2018). Rhetorical shadows: The conceptual representation of incongruent shadows. *Spatial Cognition & Computation, 18*(2), 97–114. https://doi.org/10.1080/13875868.2017.1298113.

Tanizaki, J. (1977). *In praise of shadows* (T. J. Harper, Trans.). Leete's Island Books.US Department of Education (2001). No Child Left Behind Elementary and Secondary Education Act. https://www2.ed.gov/nclb/overview/intro/execsumm.pdf

Walt, N. (2015). *Education transformation: Curriculum redesign.* PowerPoint Presentation to the University of Victoria, January 20, 2015, by the B.C. Ministry of Education.

Zeidler, D. (2014). STEM education: A deficit framework for the twenty first century? A sociocultural socioscientific response. *Cultural Studies of Science Education, 11*(1), 11–26. https://doi.org/10.1007/s11422-014-9578-z

4 Indigenous Students and Settler Teachers Caught in the Double Bind of Settler Schooling

SUSAN DION

Introduction

Nii ellongoomahtiik. K'winga-newulohmow. Nii Ndushiinzi Sheshkoohaaluwees Dion.

Noonjiiyayii naahii waak Takaronto. Nii Ndulaapeewi / potwatomay. Niiha nish minito. Anushiik

My engagement with curriculum studies started more than thirty years ago with concerns about representations of Indigenous people in the history and social studies curriculum. At that time, I wrote about the perfect stranger (Dion, 2009) explaining how resistance on the part of most Canadians to engage with Indigenous people's experiences and perspectives was rooted in their need to uphold an understanding of themselves as good, caring people who earn their success through hard work, defend equity, and protect human rights. While this identity position has been repeatedly challenged by Indigenous people's activism, scholarship, art, and literature, through state sanctioned inquiries and commissions, and most recently by the unearthing of the bodies of children hidden in unmarked graves on Indian Residential School sites, the struggle on the part of curriculum studies to respond continues (Miles, 2021; Wotherspoon, & Milne, 2020; KAIROS Canada, 2018). Despite promises for reform, even recently revised curriculum guidelines fail to adequately address Indigenous topics or to provide serious engagement with settler colonialism and its ongoing significance in structuring the relationship between Indigenous and non-Indigenous people (Schaefli et al., 2018; Lamb & Godlewska, 2021; Wilson, 2020).

I recognize that there has been some change. Many teachers, like many Canadians, are shifting from the perfect stranger to the not-so-perfect stranger position, asking, If this has something to do with me, how do I make sense of it, what do I need to know, what am I to do? While in this post-TRC moment education is crowded with well-intentioned folks wanting to help, what Indigenous people need and want from education continues to challenge most educators' capacities to engage with and learn from the history of settler colonialism and its ongoing significance in structuring the relationship between us. The failure within curriculum studies to provide teachers and students with what they need to engage with and learn from Indigenous people's experiences and perspectives is ongoing.

Even so, the desire to do things differently creates potential and interests me a great deal. Drawing on my teaching, research, and public lectures, in this chapter I bring together the voices of Indigenous students with the voices of educators to identify and tease out the ways in which teaching decolonizing and Indigenous content creates a double bind for both students and teachers. While students want access to a curriculum that reflects Indigenous people's experiences and perspectives, they do not want to be on the receiving end of settler guilt and pity, they do not want to be made to perform as if always experts, nor do they want their indigeneity to be the object of the settler gaze. Settler teachers do not want to have their ignorance exposed, their commitment to national narratives challenged, their fear of making mistakes and being accused of anti-Indigenous racism made visible. Reflecting on these double binds for Indigenous students and settler teachers, I argue that hope lies in an approach that cultivates awareness of implication, creates space for investment in hearing Indigenous perspectives, works with teachers' resolve to do what is in the best interest of their students and to work with their commitment to having a positive impact.

Positioning Myself

In my introduction I say *Noonjiiyayii naahii* – I am from down river. Occupied and named the Delaware River Valley, in our language the territory is Lenapehoking – Land of the Lenape. Although we were forcibly removed from our territories during the mid-1700s, our teachings, ontologies, and epistemologies are rooted in life lived in relationship with the river and the land. We carry our language, our stories, our ceremonies, and traditions with us wherever we go and, as Brock Pitawanakwat (2008) explains, "As urban Nishnaabeg, our ancestral legacy is to reconnect with the landscape and live honourably and sustainably wherever we reside" (p. 171). I spent my childhood in a small city in southwestern Ontario where the St. Clair River meets Lake Huron and have spent most of my adult life living on the shores of Lake Ontario in relationship with the city, the urban Indigenous communities, and the diversity of people who call Tkaronto home.

My five siblings and I were in many ways fortunate: the poverty and violence of settler colonialism were a part of our lives, but so was the warmth of our parents' love for each other. Still, the shadow of colonialism eclipsed that warmth. While our father shared stories of his childhood, stories of an Irish-Catholic family leaving home and arriving in Quebec City, our mother was almost silent about her childhood experiences growing up at Moraviantown Reserve Number 47. When I finally found a way to talk with my mother about her life, my strongest memory was her sense of insult. Her words stay with me: "They judged us incapable as if we did not know how to take care of ourselves and our children." The disdain she expressed reflected a deep sense of pride in her own and her family's capacities to care for themselves and each other. When I was an elementary school teacher, I was reminded of experiences from my own childhood, and concerns rooted in those experiences returned and propelled my life's work investigating questions about Indigenous people and the public school curriculum.

Caught in the Double Bind

A group of high school students are on a 12-day canoe trip in Algonquin Park. The students attend a private school, and most are from upper-middle-class families, and they are almost exclusively white. It is early in the term, but the students have been together long enough to have learned a little bit about each other. In particular, they know that one of their classmates is First Nations. It is day five of the trip and it is the fifth straight day of rain. The 16 students and their two teachers have stopped for lunch. They have paddled to shore and are sitting huddled together on the riverbank, eating lunch and trying to stay warm. Brenda turns to Niki and asks, "Niki, don't you know how to do a rain dance or something to make it stop raining?" At that very moment Niki turns towards her teachers, they turn away. Niki responds with a deep sigh of exasperation and the moment passes. However, for Niki and for her teachers, the question, the asking, and the turn away never pass.

Brenda's question, premised on stereotypical ways of knowing, exposes her lack of knowledge, creates discomfort and, while likely unintentional, causes harm. It imposes an expectation and a responsibility on Niki as if, by virtue of her status as a First Nations person, she was in some way responsible for providing a solution to the class's less than pleasant experience in the natural environment. When Niki turns to her teachers for assistance, they – who know enough to know that the question is problematic – turn away, pretending that they didn't hear. In turning away, they abandon their responsibilities to both Niki and Brenda.

Brenda's question draws attention to Niki's difference with no consideration for her difference. This exchange exposes the double bind for both students and teachers.

Asking what students know and don't know about the history of Indigenous people in Canada – what stories they have heard and what stories they tell – requires a willingness to risk being exposed. Specifically, on a canoe trip, amidst the northern Ontario landscape, with her Indigenous classmate alongside her, what story does Brenda hear and in what ways is it different from the story that Niki is experiencing? And this is key: Brenda's question draws attention to a significant difference, and ignoring it causes harm. Reflecting on and questioning the question opens possibilities for learning. For example, Brenda may have known full well that Niki did not know a rain dance; her question might have been an attempt to add humour to a miserable situation. While Brenda can afford to find humour in asking Niki if she knows a dance, for Niki there is nothing funny about her lack of access to ancestral knowledge.

What might Niki have been able to learn about herself from this question had her teachers supported further enquiry? What might she have wanted to say and teach others?

- I want you to know how much I wish that I did know about the dances, songs, and ceremonies of my ancestors.
- I want you to appreciate my sense of loss, how deeply I mourn for the loss of Indigenous knowledge.
- I want *you* to know the stories of *our* ancestors – that brought us to this place where I, an Anishinaabe student, sat with you and the rest of our class and listened to our white teachers teach me how to paddle a canoe.
- And I want you to know that I have a right to learn my language and to access Indigenous knowledge.

What is at stake for the teachers, and what would they say in defence of turning away? More importantly, what would they identify as necessary to make turning *toward* possible?

- We did not want to accuse a student of racism; that would create more tensions. How do we teach students about our own implications in racism?
- In part the canoe trip was intended for students to feel pride in the beauty of Canada; this was part of the history curriculum we would be teaching. How do we navigate teaching about both pride and shame in our country?
- We do not know what Niki knows or how she feels; we do not know how to make this better for her.
- It is our job to teach our students, but we do not know what to teach; it makes us feel inadequate, so we avoid it.

Attending to the questions illustrates how something that appears innocent may be complicated for students and their teachers. As much as the teachers know that they ought to respond, their fear of not knowing what to say, of making it worse, prompts their turn away. Caught off guard by the casual asking of an offensive question, Niki is unable to speak back to the lack of knowledge and understanding that informs it. Both the teachers and students are trapped, unable to navigate their way through to an engagement with settler colonialism. Revisions to curriculum must prepare and support teachers and students in navigating the double binds of settler schooling.

A Curriculum of Implication

I was speaking with a group of teachers in eastern Ontario about treaty rights and why it is necessary for all Canadians to learn how our government failed to follow through on treaty promises when I was interrupted by a familiar question. I was explaining how broken treaties contribute to the barriers Indigenous people confront in establishing economic security when an audience member asked, *"But isn't that what we all want? We all want economic security. Why should Indigenous people get special status?"*

This question surfaces two critical considerations many Canadians struggle to comprehend. First, Indigenous people occupy a distinctive place on this land and, second, Indigenous people have not been treated the same as every other Canadian. Canada was established on Indigenous land, and much of that land was acquired through treaty negotiations. Boundaries were determined, access to resources, rights, and responsibilities were recorded in treaty agreements. Understanding the story of Canada requires knowledge of treaty history, including the ways in which broken treaties benefitted some and devastated others.

While many teachers wrestle with recognizing the significance of settler colonialism, Indigenous students do not have that luxury. They cope with the implications in their everyday lives. I was doing research in northern Ontario, interviewing Anishnaabe youth about their lives, when a student interrupted, asking:

> But miss, why do we even have reserves? City kids can get up at 8:30 and still get to school on time. If I want to go to school, I have to catch the bus at 7:00 AM. Why do we have to live on reserves? (Cited in Dion, 2013)

Indigenous students and settler teachers are differently implicated in colonial structures. Indigenous students need and want access to the history of settler colonialism. They, like all students, have a right to curriculum that will allow them to make sense of their lives. Conversely, these topics challenge settler teachers by disrupting their narrative frames, creating questions they are unprepared to answer. Their reliance on dominant discourses, including multiculturalism, to support their resistance is well documented. Teachers rely on well-developed strategies to maintain their position as knowers, provide answers, and maintain certainty.

When being a teacher and covering the curriculum are expected to make one feel good and capable, it creates limitations on what can be taught. What teachers and students need is not only permission to be uncomfortable but also a curriculum that identifies and engages with their discomfort. Acknowledging the impact of broken treaties, interrogating the reserve system, the Indian Act and the whole of settler colonialism is unsettling (Regan, 2010). Teachers need to be prepared to feel bad, discomfort, conflict, shame. They need to be able to comfortably acknowledge that settlers (themselves included) have unearned privileges, and it is not equitable or fair. Supporting settler teachers and students "to reflect on, and rethink, how their identities, both individual and collective, are connected to Canada's history of colonialism is essential, not to promote a sense of guilt but to understand how they benefit" (Miles, 2018, p. 303). Even if they know they ought to teach the material, teachers can get caught in a web of emotions that complicates their decisions about what and how to teach.

A curriculum that can cope with these challenges would support settler Canadians to simultaneously hold that – while Canada is a good place for many – it was achieved at the expense of Indigenous people. "How might teachers and students ethically reflect on their individual and collective identities and how they are implicated in the colonial project?" (Miles, 2018, p. 303). It is possible for these questions to become a part of the curriculum. It is not enough to include Indigenous content; a Curriculum of Implication needs to be a part of the K-12 program. Indigenous educators, artists, and activists are bringing this content to the attention of teachers who need a curriculum that will provide guidance on how to navigate what it means to be implicated. While this might feel like a centring of the feelings of settlers, identifying and working through emotional responses is necessary to create conditions for learning.

Curriculum to Bridge the Chasm

> White settler violence directed at those imagined as threats lives just beneath the surface of everyday settler life, and importantly, flows through institutions such as policing, [schooling] embedding itself in everyday professional routines. (Razack, 2020, p. 2)

The lack of Indigenous content in their classes is one of the primary concerns identified by students. It is, as Razack identifies, an everyday professional routine, and, for Indigenous students, an act of violence. Students are aware of their teachers' lack of knowledge and understanding of Indigenous experiences, perspectives, histories, and cultures and describe the different ways teachers respond to their requests for the inclusion of Indigenous content.

> LILLY: They never really bring up the fact about, like, the residential schools and the history about that, and that's really important too.
> ELY: Same with the White Paper, that's never touched.
> JOE: Not in my history class.
> KEN: Not much. [cross talk] Even if there is, it's a lot of one-sided – it's a lot from the white perspective. Like, there's a lot missing. In our history classes, they never talk about issues with Aboriginals. (Dion, 2018, p. 29)

Students' requests for inclusion of this content constitute a threat to teachers' understanding of Canadian history, the students themselves become a threat.

While it is encouraging to hear students advocating for the inclusion of Indigenous peoples' histories, experiences, and perspectives, the ongoing exclusion reflects deeply held beliefs. Refusing to teach the history of settler colonialism sustains the colonial order. It sustains the teachers' coherence as the subject of history and control of the curriculum is secured. The comment shared with me by a high school student – *"They'd scoot past the residential schools like really quick"*– reflects the ease with which teachers avoid addressing Indigenous topics in their classes (Dion, 2018, p. 29).

Students' descriptions reflect the ways in which their teachers rely on the hierarchy of the classroom, their power as teachers and, furthermore, use the students' own bodies against them, stating, "Oh, wait okay, Liz, you come and teach it then because you're Native" (p. 33). Creating fear is a familiar strategy used to keep Indigenous students in line, reassuring themselves that white entitlement is protected and the Indigenous threat is contained (Razack, 2020).

Working on a research project with the Ontario Ministry of Education brought me into conversation with students from across the province. I was engaged in conversations with a group of secondary school students when one young man explained: "We don't even know what we want because we never had it" (Dion, 2018, p. 33). Many students expressed frustration with teachers who expected them to know their histories, languages, and teachings. They felt judged by both teachers and classmates who asked questions such as: Do you speak your language? How Indigenous are you? And, what's your clan?

Students are particularly uncomfortable in classes where they rightfully expect the inclusion of Indigenous content and the topics are absent. They also talked about their experiences of discomfort when Indigenous topics are introduced and their classroom teachers turn to the students themselves to act as experts and to take on the role of teacher.

> "Oh, wait okay, Liz, you come and teach it then because you're Native." I was, like, oh, but I don't actually know that much either, which just shows – but yeah. I don't know, it just bothers me because we're hearing so much about other histories. And it's just, like, okay, but what about Canada's – a big part of Canada's history is First Nations people, but yet we don't hear anything about it. (Dion, 2018, p. 99)

Classrooms can be dangerous places for Indigenous students to be. On the one hand, they want the content to be taught, but they do not want to be made responsible for teaching the material themselves.

In these discussions students describe their confrontation with the *Double Bind of Settler Schooling*. When students assert their Indigenous identity and ask that their histories be included they open themselves up to scrutiny and expectation. They run the risk of having their identities challenged with questions such as, How Indigenous are you? They risk being made responsible for representing all Indigenous people, and they risk being asked to take up the position of the teacher, expected to know and to teach. Or they stay silent and become implicated in their own erasure. The history of colonialism and policies of forced assimilation have created conditions in which many Indigenous students have limited knowledge of their history and culture. As these students explain, teachers are supposed to be the ones doing the teaching. When students are unable to respond to their teachers' demands, they are made to feel like failures – failures as students and failures in their Indigenous identities.

While Canadians are starting to learn about the impacts of cultural genocide perpetrated through residential schools, most do not know that in Canada laws were passed making it a crime to speak our languages, practice our culture, and pass on stories and ceremonies to our children and grandchildren. Indigenous students are made to feel ashamed of their own lack of knowledge and/or judged by outsiders as less authentically Indigenous because of what they don't know. Most people do not understand that not knowing was the goal of Canadian policies of forced assimilation, as was the chasm that exists between Indigenous peoples and settler Canadians. The success of settler colonialism required fear of the Indigenous *other*, a fear that continues to be experienced by Indigenous students when their requests for the inclusion of Indigenous content is received as a threat by their teachers.

In recent years, my teaching has been in classes where most of the students are Indigenous. At the beginning of class, many students tentatively express concern stating, "I'm Indigenous but I don't really know anything about it." As the course proceeds and they begin to learn about the policies and practices aimed at forced assimilation, they begin to understand that their ignorance is directly tied to colonialism. First they get angry and then they proceed to work hard at learning the specifics of both settler colonialism and their own nation's, community's, and family's stories.

Some settler educators experience their own angry response when they come to learn the truths of settler colonialism. They begin to appreciate how the chasm between Indigenous and non-Indigenous people was purposefully constructed. Listening to and learning from the voices of First Nations, Métis, and Inuit have the potential to provide settler teachers with what they need to be able to act in response to their own ignorance. In my recent research, educators consistently reported what they most appreciated about the project was how much they were learning from Indigenous people, and what most surprised them was the depth of their own ignorance. In response to the depth of ignorance, the curriculum needs to be flooded with Indigenous content. Teachers and students need time to engage with a broad range of resources from which they can learn. They need curriculum that addresses the chasm and creates space for understanding its significance.

Curriculum Serving Shared Best Interest

After a talk for teacher candidates at the University of British Columbia, a small group gathered to speak with me one-on-one. I was not immediately surprised by the student who explained how as a settler she particularly appreciated the space I offered her for learning from Indigenous voices. She asked, "Can settlers participate in reconciliation if we are relegated to a place of guilty, greedy, violent oppressor?"

For me, this question surfaces a serious challenge – how to teach about colonialism without reproducing dominant narratives centring violence and oppression that requires Indigenous people to be perpetual, pitiful victims and settler Canadians to be limited to guilty oppressors. We cannot erase the violence of colonialism *and* the curriculum cannot focus exclusively on the violence. We can invest in learning and commit to actions that remediate harm and contribute to relationships rooted in respectful acknowledgment of Indigenous peoples' rights to self-determination.

Understanding that the relationship between Indigenous people and settlers was and, in many ways, continues to be premised on greed, power, and control over our bodies and land does not mean that settler Canadians today want the current relationship to continue. The path to creating new and better relationships requires knowledge and understanding of existing relationships, how we came to occupy these places in relationship with each other and, importantly, how new and better relationships serve our shared best interests. If settler Canadians are locked into positions of the guilty perpetrator of violent oppression and Indigenous people are perpetually required to be victims, new and better relationships are impossible. Historically our relationships have been defined by judgments about the inferiority and incapacities of Indigenous people and the refusal to recognize and respect difference. The relationship premised on judgments of "less than" that justified the theft of land and resources needs to be identified, investigated, and reconciled.

Curriculum that starts from the position that most teachers are committed to acting in service of their students' best interests can be useful in addressing the complicated perpetrator–victim entanglement that serves to reproduce resistance from both settler teachers and Indigenous students.

Curriculum That Draws on Teachers' Desire to Have a Positive Impact

My teaching and research bring me into contact with many educators who are willing and wanting to engage with learning the history of settler colonialism. My questions to them are: Why are you doing this work? What motivates you to engage with this difficult history? In response, I am told: I do it because I want to make a difference, I want to have an impact.

The desire to have an impact is a positive motivating force that inspires people to take action and do the work of learning so as to contribute to creating equity and justice. As much as this desire to make things better is good, it can derive from a problematic place. When the desire to have an impact comes from an un-interrogated place of privilege it can reproduce the saviour–victim relationship. When an audience member tells me, "I want to help, what can I do to help?", my response is a gentle reminder to take responsibility and investigate the ways in which Canadians have benefited from colonialism.

Settler teachers need a curriculum that will engage both themselves and their students in learning about the land on which they live, work, and learn: Whose traditional territory is it? When were Indigenous people removed from the land? How was the land used before and after contact? And who became wealthy from the land? In my years of experience working in the field of Indigenous education, I find most teachers want to have a positive impact in the world. Learning to work with consciousness of their own place in the relationship shifts the "how can I help you?" approach to "how can I take responsibility and work to establish/re-establish respectful relationships with you?" Curriculum that engages settler teachers and their students in learning how to address settler colonialism can result in positive impacts.

Conclusion

Writing this chapter has been a chore. I changed my focus and approach too many times to count, and I am grateful to the editors for their patience. Pushing the submission deadline to the absolute limit and having written something that was admissible, I sat down to write the conclusion, and only then did I recognize my own double bind. My faith in education not to resolve but to contribute to creating the conditions necessary for new and better relationships between Indigenous people and settler Canadians exists alongside my knowledge of the ongoing lack of significant progress.

In part, the constant shift in my approach to the chapter is rooted in my feeling that I am not saying anything new. Even now, as I reread this chapter, my sense is that I have said this all before. Many of my colleagues in the academic world have said this all before. As early as 1832 Chief Shingwaukonse (1773–1854) said it. He advocated for the creation of *Teaching Wigwams* where

Anishinaabe and settlers could learn together. He was committed to establishing a curriculum that would teach students skills necessary for living in respectful relationship, maintaining Indigenous rights, and ensuring self-determination for his people.

As much as I and others argue in support of a curriculum that will make a difference, what I experience is ongoing inadequacies. We know that fear of what it will mean to make the changes continues to constrain. I agree with Simpson et al. (2011) who wrote:

> We will need to repeatedly turn toward difficult questions: Who is a settler? Who is Indigenous? Who is responsible, for what, and in what ways? What do equity and justice look like and require? What do anti-colonial ways of living, with each other and with the land, look like? How can we imagine an anti-colonial public and Canada when we are so entrenched in a colonial system and way of life?

Indigenous educators, artists, academics, and activists will continue to keep these questions on the national agenda. Increased awareness on the part of the public makes it less scary for teachers and curriculum writers to do what is necessary and, in spite of the double bind, I continue to have faith that our combined work is making it possible for more settler teachers to turn toward Indigenous students.

REFERENCES

Dion, S. D. (2009). *Braiding histories: Learning from Aboriginal peoples' experiences and perspectives*. UBC Press.

– (2013). Webs of strength and resistance: Hearing Aboriginal adolescent girls telling their stories. In D. Pepler & B. Ferguson (Eds.), *Understanding and addressing girls' aggressive behaviour problems: A focus on relationships* (pp. 73–92). Wilfred Laurier University Press.

– (2018). *The Listening Stone Project Year Four: Investments in teaching and Learning Lessons from the Indigenous Education Focused Collaborative Inquiry*. For the Council of Ontario Directors of Education. Toronto, Canada. https://www.ontariodirectors.ca/downloads/Listening_Stone/LSPY4_Report_August_3_2018.pdf

Kairos Canada. (2018). *2018 Annual Report / Rapport Annuel 2018*. https://www.kairoscanada.org/product/annual-report-2018

Lamb, C., & Godlewska, A. (2021). On the peripheries of education: (Not) learning about Indigenous peoples in the 1995–2010 British Columbia curriculum. *Journal of Curriculum Studies*, *53*(1), 103–23. https://doi.org/10.1080/00220272.2020.1774806

Miles, J. (2018). Teaching history for truth and reconciliation: The challenges and opportunities of narrativity, temporality, and identity. *McGill Journal of Education/ Revue des sciences de l'éducation de McGill*, *53*(2), 294–311. https://doi.org/10.7202/1058399ar

– (2021). Curriculum reform in a culture of redress: How social and political pressures are shaping social studies curriculum in Canada. *Journal of Curriculum Studies, 53*(1), 47–64. https://doi.org/10.1080/00220272.2020.1822920

Pitawanakwat, B. (2008). Bimaadziwin oodenaang: A pathway to urban Nishnaabe resurgence. In L. B. Simpson (Ed.), *Lighting the eighth fire: The liberation, resurgence, and protection of Indigenous Nations* (pp. 161–73). Arbeiter Ring Pub.

Razack, S. H. (2020). Settler colonialism, policing and racial terror: The police shooting of Loreal Tsingine. *Feminist Legal Studies, 28*(1), 1–20. https://doi.org/10.1007/s10691-020-09426-2

Regan, P. (2010). *Unsettling the settler within: Indian residential schools, truth telling, and reconciliation in Canada*. UBC Press.

Schaefli, L., Godlewska, A., Korteweg, L., Coombs, A., Morcom, L., & Rose, J. (2018). What do first-year university students in Ontario, Canada, know about First Nations, Métis, and Inuit peoples and topics? *Canadian Journal of Education/Revue canadienne de l'éducation, 41*(3), 688–725. https://journals.sfu.ca/cje/index.php/cje-rce/article/view/3247

Simpson, J. S., James, C. E., & Mack, J. (2011). Multiculturalism, colonialism, and racialization: Conceptual starting points. *Review of Education, Pedagogy, and Cultural Studies, 33*(4), 285–305. https://doi.org/10.1080/10714413.2011.597637

Wilson, P. (2020). Indigenous content in curriculum: The challenge. *BU Journal of Graduate Studies in Education, 12*(1), 26–32.

Wotherspoon, T., & Milne, E. (2020). What do Indigenous education policy frameworks reveal about commitments to reconciliation in Canadian school systems? *The International Indigenous Policy Journal, 11*(1), 1–29. https://doi.org/10.18584/iipj.2020.11.1.10215

5 Questions of Witnessing: Historical, Contemplative/Nondual, and Ecological

CLAUDIA EPPERT

Introduction

I begin this chapter in gratitude to prairie skies. I have resided in Edmonton, Alberta – located on Treaty Six Territory – since 2007. Living under these beloved skies reminds me of the expansiveness possible in Life. However, in the summer of 2021 as in recent summers, these skies were obscured by wildfire smoke from Alberta and British Columbia. Indeed, approximately 900 wildfires blazed across Canada. The smoke had me dwelling on complicated dynamics between illumination and obscuration – between what is in view and what is hidden. I contemplate Ng-A-Fook's (2014) question: "Where we are at, in this place and this time, as Canadian curriculum scholars" (p. 1)? Clearly, we remain in the midst of a global pandemic, but still invisible to many, despite wildfires and other climate change indicators, is that we are experiencing what Kolbert (2014) identifies as the sixth mass extinction. The 2020 World Wildlife Fund "Living Planet Report Canada: Wildlife at Risk," confirms that COVID-19 has "at its roots ... deep connections to the degradation of habitat" (p. 4).[1] During the pandemic, I read Camus's (1948) *The Plague* for the undergraduate English language arts education methods course I teach. Set in the French Algerian town of Oran in the 1940s, the novel explores the town people's responses to an outbreak of the plague. Its protagonist, medical doctor Bernard Rieux, and other key characters – among them, a journalist, wanderer, town clerk, and Jesuit priest – struggle differently with questions of ethical responsibility during quarantine. *The Plague* has been regarded as an allegory for the French resistance to Nazi occupation during the Second World War. My reading is preoccupied with questions of extinct, extirpated, endangered, threatened, and vulnerable species of special concern. In Canada, I map and dwell with the following, in very rough geographical terms. *In the north, Polar Bears, the Atlantic Walrus, Barren Ground Caribou, the Bowhead Whale, the Narwhal. In the east, the North Atlantic Right Whale, Eastern Wood Pewee, Mainland Moose, and the Atlantic Puffin. In the west, the Vancouver Island Marmot, Red Legged Frog, Townsend's Mole. And, in the south, the American Badger, Small-Mouthed Salamander, and Bobolink. To name only a few species, among so many others.* I purposely capitalize their names and write in italics.

To think curriculum studies and English language arts today, I propose, is to think these fields in extinction, in times of extinction; with relation both to the rapid decline of species and also the potential of human species extinction. As Jean-Pierre Dupuy (2015) contends, "We are living today in the shadow cast by the prospect of catastrophes that, separately or in combination, threaten to bring about the disappearance of the human race from the earth" (p. 1). The provocation – indeed, in my view, obligation – to think in extinction, both other species and our own, extends beyond socially constructed national borders. As the 2019 Intergovernmental Science-Policy Platform on Biodiversity and Ecosystem Services (IPBES) reports, approximately one million plant and animal species in the world are currently threatened with extinction.[2] In this chapter, I contemplate species extinction through a life-writing (Hasebe-Ludt et al., 2009; Chambers et al., 2012) and care-writing lens in keeping with curriculum studies' commitments to *currere* – to self-study and self-expressivity of individually lived educational experience oriented to and informed by the world (Pinar, 1975, 2011, 2019; Pinar & Grumet, 1976). Rephrasing Ng-A-Fook's question to Where am *I* at in this place and this time as a Canadian curriculum scholar, my response is one of despair at species losses as well as hope (a complicated hope) for pathways of ethical responsivity/responsibility to be realized.

Currere returns me to autobiographical reflections on past, present, and future scholarly interests and pursuits. In the process, I find myself challenged by entanglements of illumination/obscuration, absence/presence, knowledge/ignorance, and by obligations to enact a "*difficult return*, a psychic and social responsibility to bring the dead into presence, a responsibility that currently involves learning to live with, and in relation to loss" (Simon et al., 2001, p. 2). Regarding species extinction, the responsibility is not only for the dead but also for current species' suffering due to habitat losses and other human-made factors. It is also for anticipated losses. Extinction challenges temporalities, and re-orients remembrance to intertwinements of past, present, and future. I *study*, my generational ends and species' ends in question (Simon et al., 2001; Pinar, 2011, 2015). For example, I learn that *in 1914, the last remaining passenger pigeon, named Martha, died in a Cincinnati Zoo. Once numbering in the billions, these orange-brown birds that were once summer residers in Canada, became extinct in only a few decades due, it is believed, to natural selection and also extensive hunting enabled by commercial pigeon industries arising from buildings of the national telegraph and railroad.* In a March 2021 email exchange, William F. Pinar shared that he has had a long fascination with this bird. The name, passenger pigeon, derives from the French *passage*, which translates to "passing by." To pass by something generally refers to something happening without being noticed. In what follows, I compose a *currere* of my *Bildung* (self-formation) that, despite its grounding in questions of ethical living, has passed by species extinction and now seeks to bring this absence into presence. I trace past research preoccupations first with historical witnessing and then with contemplative, nondual witnessing for what they might lend to current questions and "complicated conversations" (Pinar, 2019) regarding exigencies of ecological witnessing. I do so in exegetical and subjective engagement with Albert Camus's (1948) novel *The Plague*. I conclude with a reading of this novel that directs curriculum in extinction towards the skies.

Questions of Ethical Living and Engagement

I begin, then, learning that around my birth year, *the Argentinian Red-Bellied Gracile Opossum was last seen, its believed extinction due to habitat loss from agriculture and industry development. It was also the last recording of the Hawaiian bird, the St. Helena Darter, and the Moloka'i Creeper.* Born in Germany to German parents, my mother an artist (lapsed Catholic), my father a professor (atheist), our family travelled considerably. We lived in Myanmar, roughly about the time the *South Island Snipe was last reported on Big South Cape Island, and the freshwater Turgid Blossom was last recorded in the southern Appalachians. It may also have been the time of the extinction of the Mexican Grizzly Bear.* After Myanmar, we returned to Germany and subsequently moved to the United States around when, I learn, *the Saint Helena Earwig and the New Zealand Greater Short-Tailed Bat became extinct.* We then moved to New Brunswick, Canada, where I began first grade and found my BFF in reading literature. This move coincided approximately with the last recordings of the *Amistad Gambusia, Kaua'i 'akialoa, and Blackfin Cisco.* My burgeoning love for stories soon competed with childhood hours, days, months, and years spent in the several-hundred-acre woodland park that bordered our home (this *Bildung*, in part, motivating current concerns of ecological witnessing). We frequently travelled back and forth to Germany to be with relatives. My grandmother immigrated to Canada sometime in my late childhood or early adolescence, upon remarrying, my grandfather having died years before. My step-grandfather was a post-war Polish Jewish immigrant. My grandmother and step-grandfather resided on a farm outside of Montreal. In my teenage years, my family moved to Iran, but the Iranian revolution demanded an early return. *I learn that during this time the White-eyed River Martin in Central Thailand and the San Felipe Hutia in Cuba were last recorded, their believed extinction due to hunting and other causes. In the 1970s, the Caspian Tiger, named so because one of its habitats was by the Caspian Sea in Iran, was declared extinct, as was the Japanese Sea Lion. Thailand's Siamese Flat-Barbelled Catfish was last sighted, along with the*

Yunnan Lake Newt. Not long after returning from Iran, we moved to Singapore, where I attended an International Baccalaureate school and volunteered at a Vietnamese refugee camp. A year later, I returned to my Canadian home town in order to begin undergraduate studies in English literature. *During these formative decades, under the Wikipedia heading "Timeline of Extinctions in the Holocene," I count approximately 73 species last recorded (although I debate the accuracy of this timeline). In my searches for additional information, I learn that in 1964, the International Union for Conservation of Nature and Natural (IUCN) first established its Red List of Threatened Species* (2022–2).[3]

Graduate studies in English literature followed, which were in turn followed by studies in teaching English as a second language and, then, undergraduate and graduate studies in literature education, with intersecting interests in philosophy, history, and curriculum. At some point during graduate studies, I realized an *underlying* and, now, *enduring* preoccupation with "social suffering" (Kleinman et al., 1997) and with questions of ethical living and engagement, so aptly voiced by Derrida (1994) in his *Specters of Marx* as questions of "learning to live" (p. xviii), alone and with others. I came to recognize I had two long-held and ongoing beliefs: capacities for human and nonhuman flourishing depend upon generative sociopolitical conditions, and self, society, and story inextricably link. Indeed, consequentially, I continue to experience dismay when educators (thankfully few) tell me sociopolitical questioning should not be part of the English language arts classroom, or upon encountering research projects invested in schools but devoid of societal enquiry, as if school, subject, and society are somehow isolable. In "What are the Language Arts for?" Maxine Greene (1988) reminds readers that while the twentieth century saw significant scientific and technological advances, it also witnessed fanaticism and genocide. Greene opens her article with reference to Holocaust survivor Elie Wiesel's observation that "we are all on a train that is running toward a precipice," and she admonishes educators to hear Wiesel's call for human senses of responsibility to steer "events toward the sun and not toward the abyss" (p. 475). She contends that if we do not hear Wiesel's address for ethical responsibility, then we "are likely to become like the citizens of Oran in Camus's *The Plague* … people caught in the habitual, preoccupied with doing business" (p. 475). *I did not know that in the1990s the Splendid Poison Frog, the Chiriqui Harlequin Frog, and the Alvarez's Dwarf Crayfish and the Baolan were last recorded. The 1990 IUCN Red List reported "698 mammals, 1047 birds, 191 reptiles, 63 amphibians, 762 fishes and 2250 invertebrates" (p. ix) as threatened.*[4] *The 1996 IUCN Red List reported 5,205 animal species threatened with extinction.*[5]

Lived experiences, my own and others, indelibly invested me with deep wariness of certainties, and contrasting commitments to interminable questioning, which includes critically questioning the question (Eppert,1999, 2000). Further, I discovered loyalties to what philosopher Simone Weil (1909–43) described as a "gymnastics of attention" (Weil, 1947; Eppert, 2004). I have long valued the term *engagement,* which to me gestures to *textured time-with* – to attention, dwellings, intimacies, relationships, and commitments to "dialogic questioning engagement" (Eppert, 2000, p. 215), dialogic in recognition that learning takes place in relationships with the unconscious, others, and environment, and with both the tangible/material and intangible/immaterial. Literature has personally always been characterized by experiences of engagement more than reading, which, although I deploy the word, I have long felt encompasses senses of disembodied *techne.*

Finally, in graduate studies, I realized preoccupations with questions of witnessing, particularly in contexts of educational engagements with literature, life story, testimony, and the arts. So compelling for me in the language of witnessing, for example, is its embeddedness in deep complexities of speech/silence, remembering/forgetting, knowing/not knowing, understanding/not understanding, engagement/disengagement, attention/inattention, absence/presence, representable/unrepresentable, and so on (Eppert, 2024) – complexities that underlie this chapter. According to the *Oxford English Dictionary,* witnessing derives from the Old English root *wit,* variably meaning the seat of consciousness, and also thought, memory, attention, understanding. As I discuss elsewhere (Eppert, 2024), witnessing, for me, constitutes an "ethical concept" (Simon & Eppert, 1997, p.178; see also, Eppert 2023b) that calls us to participate in "complicated conversation among self, society, history, and culture" (Pinar, 2011, p. xv). For me, not only knowledge/power, remembrance/pedagogy (Simon et al., 2000, p. 2) but also witnessing/transformation constitutes an indissoluble couplet. In Greene's (1988) eyes, the citizens of Oran "lack imagination, the capacity to look at things as if they could be otherwise" (p. 475). Informed by my own lived experience, I believe one cannot bear ethical and pedagogical witness without, in some way, being transformed.[6]

Longtime questions of ethical living and engagement have prompted *three* inter-related and overlapping movements regarding educational complexities of witnessing. Pinar (1975) identifies *currere* as movement and what is "conceptualized through time" (p. 19). In what follows, I briefly outline each of these three movements, as their interweaving sets the stage for discussion of current ecological preoccupations with species losses and extinction.

Movement #1: Historical Witnessing

The first movement spanning the 1990s and early 2000s focused on dynamics and challenges of "historical witnessing" (Eppert, 1999, 2000). I first encountered the term witnessing in my readings and re-readings of Felman and Laub's (1992) *Testimony: Crisis of Witnessing in Literature, Psychoanalysis, and History* soon after its publication. Their text delves into Shoah remembrance and counts as one of my all-time beloved scholarly works. Indeed, it so engulfed me that decades later select chapters still pepper the syllabi of my graduate classes.

I first studied literary/literature education and feminist pedagogy with Professor Deanne Bogdan, and then remembrance pedagogies with Roger I. Simon (my doctoral supervisor) and a cohort of graduate students who comprised the Testimony and Historical Memory Project in the 1990s (e.g. Eppert et al., 1996, Simon et al., 2001). We wrestled with educational complexities of remembrance and witnessing with regard to historical events of human initiated mass violence in recognition of the insufficiencies of remembrance defined simply as learning the lessons of history so as to avoid repeating historic mistakes (Simon et al., 2000). Extended time before a single shared keyboard, the cohort, in my view, truly embodied notions of study (Simon et al., 2001, Pinar, 2011, 2015), dialogic questioning engagement, and complicated conversations with "difficult knowledge" (Britzman, 1998). My own research interests at the time lay principally with Holocaust remembrance and with postcolonial novels authored by women who bore witness to, for example, the internment of Japanese Canadians during the Second World War, legacies of slavery, and the colonization and cultural genocide of Indigenous peoples in North America. I observed that these novels powerfully contested conventional *Bildungsromane*, conservative onto-epistemological paradigms of *Bildung*, as well as challenged modern hegemonic traditions of reading. In the face of a post-traumatic century, Felman and Laub's (1992) theorization of complex relations between history and consciousness, literature and testimony, trauma and pedagogy, witnessing and testifying (p. xiii) compelled me. I contemplated these relations with respect to literature education, in light also of the scholarly turn to ethics in the 1990s and 2000s (Garber et al., 2000), and recognition that the phallogocentric paradigm defining learning as *maieutics* – as the transmission of ready-made information through processes of recollection, memorization, and repetition was deemed ethically and educationally insufficient (Eppert, 1999). I wondered (and still wonder) about the implications for English language arts classrooms and teacher education – for ELA education's six strands of reading, writing, listening, speaking, viewing, and representing (strands, in my view, that bear on all subject areas). My studies were propelled by Felman and Laub's (1992) concerns and also by literary theorist Susan Handelman who posed, "What does it mean to say a text 'teaches us something'? Can the idea of the 'literary' incorporate the notion of 'teaching'? Does a text 'teach' us how to teach it?" (as cited in Eppert, 1999, p. 15). They further followed from Adam Zachary Newton's insight that "to read a text … means bearing some burden of responsibility, believing oneself addressed, and thus answerable – to the text itself, or to one's reading of it" (as cited in Eppert, 1999, p. 45).

I look back upon these years, now searching for threading concerns – given wide-ranging scholarship on witnessing, what haunted? I recall and identify this: maturing in the darkness of my parents, grandparents, uncles, aunts, and step-grandfather's war-time tellings, hesitancies, stammers, and silences, ever unable to fathom their experiences, my preoccupations centred on responsivity and responsibility to alterity, which to me meant that which "exceeds the resources of [I] consciousness" (Eppert, 2000, p. 222), that which "I" cannot fully know, let alone represent (Eppert, 1999, 2000). Theoretically inspired by Felman and Laub, forays into psychoanalysis, and continental philosophy, particularly the philosophy of Emmanuel Levinas, I explored notions of "witness-learning," as a memorial practice that emanates from and is directed towards a "radical learning ethic" that breaks with normative traditions of epistemology and ontology (Eppert, 1999, p. 22) and delves into pedagogical and curricular "interruption [and] attempts to open spaces for a potential awakening to exteriority" (p. 175). I eschewed the "solipsistically performative" (p. 146) and enquired, through literature as case studies, into cognitive and emotional obstructions and capacities for being "one-for-the other" (p. 152) – for witnessing as "anagnorisis," that is, embodied and critical insight that disrupts certitudes, unsettles narrow worldviews, and opens us more fully to responsibilities we bear for each other and the world (Eppert, 1999, p. 187; Eppert, 2000; Simon et al., 2001). While cognizant of critiques of the term *learning* for its limited associations as one-to-one transactional products of instruction (Pinar, 2015, p. 16), for me, learning encompasses surprise and what Levinas (1969, p. 73) names "traumatism[s] of astonishment" – encounters with alterity that unsettle conservative paradigms of *Bildung*, and call learners into question and obligation (Eppert, 1999, 2000). Levinas identifies ethics as "first philosophy" (Peperzak, 1995): the saying within and beyond the enclosures of the said addresses me to ethical response and responsibility prior to Western ontology/metaphysics and epistemology (Simon & Eppert, 1997; Eppert 1999, 2000). Rather than dialectic methodology (Eppert, 1999, p. 175), or, for that matter, didactic methodology that risks foreclosing learning through prescriptive replies to "how to" questions, my preference was for the language of "approach … interminably oriented toward shifting the terms of (readerly) answerability from ontology/epistemology to ethics and a radical learning (*Bildung*)" (p. 175). I was compelled by witnessing enquiry as "ap/proximal" (p. 176), as vulnerability to alterity's touch, and as remaining dynamically open – "a movement rather than an entity, an activity rather than a statement" (p. 175).

Finally, the postcolonial novels I studied powerfully storied characters on pathways to healing and transformation in the face of trauma and injustice. I explored what I called characters' "remembrance-learning" as not only their learning to live with loss but also their working through of traumatic experience in ways that initiated a marked transformation in their lives (Eppert, 1999, 2000). These novels furthered interests in transformation, not as the "narrowly therapeutic" (Simon & Eppert, 1997, p. 180), not as strategic or reductive consolatory or moralizing pedagogies (Simon et al., 2000, p. 4), and not as intervention, but rather as diversely lived, as an interminable open question, and as embedded in "exigencies of justice, compassion, and hope" (Simon & Eppert, 1997, p. 177).

Although perhaps I had heard about Camus's *The Plague* in prior years, Felman's interpretation of it sparked my own longing to read it, a longing finally realized decades later. Like Greene, Felman references the novel because it exemplifies challenges of human conscience in contemporary times (Felman & Laub, 1992, p. 96). She engages it as a metaphor for the Holocaust and observes how the novel's townspeople did not want to admit the event of the plague because it "does not enter, and cannot be framed by, an existing frame of reference (be it of knowledge or belief)" (p. 103). Felman quotes from Camus: "In this respect our townsfolk were like everybody else, wrapped up in themselves: in other words, they were humanists, they disbelieved in pestilences" (p. 103). She consequently explores "problems of a radical and necessary transformation" (p. 96) with regard to historical and ethical categories. I now consider her reading in the context of plant and animal extinction and the as yet insufficiently discussed imbrication of genocide-ecocide. *February 2021 headlines announce that populations of the Monarch Butterfly (butterflies, longtime symbols of metamorphosis) have declined over 80 per cent in the last two decades, due to climate change, pesticides, and deforestation, among other causes.*

Movement #2: Contemplative/Nondual Witnessing

The second movement has spanned the close of the 1990s to now, fuelled by persistent questions of "mindful attentiveness" (Simon et al., 2000, p. 3) and the "modernist project of the consolidation of self and the maintenance and perpetuation of subject-object binaries" (p. 8). Questions of historical witnessing gave way to questions of why human-initiated mass destruction in the first place. I pondered seeds of human greed, aggression, indifference, and dynamics of an ethics of empathy, care, and compassion. Psychoanalysis was compelling but, at the time, not landing in certain ways. In the spring-summer of 1999 (or was it 1998), inspired by a Buddhist text recommended by a friend and another text I happened across at my local bookstore on Taoism/Daoism, I embarked on what would become a longtime study of Taoist/Daoist, Buddhist, Hindu, Sufi, and other wisdom texts (Eppert 2023a).

It remains difficult to convey why this wisdom literature so significantly affected me; the closest I come is as a child learning from my mother about negative or empty space in art. Most of my formal schooling, it seemed, had focused on the subject before me – a positive, substantive *Bildung,* from *Bild,* meaning "picture or image," with few remembered exceptions. As my mother taught me, empty space around the image is, in effect, the real subject. It gives shape and life to *Bild,* as does the interminable interplay between negative and positive embedded within the whole of space/time. In my view, the sages Lao Tzu,

Chuang Tzu, Confucius, Mencius, Vyasa, Buddha, Rumi, Gurdjieff, and others variously recognized this and much more, and conceived their ethics and aesthetics from it. In differing ways and degrees, theirs are philosophies giving voice to emptiness and nonduality. As I began studying their texts, it seemed some-thing – the tangible/material was coming into somewhat more moving balance with no-thing – the intangible/immaterial in ways I had not previously encountered – that had not been part of a long school inheritance informed by the legacies of educational reformer Ramus and Descartes, Bacon, and other contributors to the scientific revolution, the latter which, while profoundly and beneficially heralding medical and technological insights, also contributed to divisions of knowing.

I became interested in questions of consciousness. In 1999, upon arrival in Baton Rouge to take up a position at Louisiana State University, I joined a Taoist/Daoist study group for some years, which included Tai Chi/Taiji yang-style practice (Eppert 2023a). I additionally learned meditation at a local Vietnamese Buddhist monastery and continued yoga. Those were definitive years of grieving the dearth of access to Asian and other wisdom in my decades of schooling. *Approximately in those years, of plants, the Saint Helena Olive became extinct. Of animals, the Chinese Paddlefish, The Po'ouli, and Western Black Rhinoceros were last recorded. The last Pyrenean Ibex, named Celia, died, and the South Island Kokako and Chinese River Dolphin (Baiji) of the Yangtze River were declared extinct. I learn that the Baiji was the first dolphin species to become extinct due to human activity.*

I began to explore nondual witnessing as supporting a contemplative inward/outward-turned gymnastics of attention in recognition of nonduality between inner and outer. While nonduality is diversely defined, it generally references the interdependence or interconnectedness of all Life, writ large. In Buddhism, more specifically, dependent origination (*paticcasamuppāda*, in Pali) denotes the conditionality of all arising existence. Nonduality is embedded in lived human experience but tends to be concealed therefrom. To extrapolate, one can observe one's thoughts, emotions, sensations ever arising and waning, which often begets the question of who is doing the observing. The *Katha Upanishad*, composed circa 6000 BCE, observes two being seated at "life's fountain" in the "secret cave of the heart" (Easwaren, 1987, p. 88). One of the seated two is ever anxiously *selfing* preoccupied, in other words, habitually seeking solidification and separation in time-space in, for example, discriminating likes and dislikes and other compositions leading to a bifurcated consciousness. I wonder if perhaps selfing processes are the consequence of existential anxieties of separation, loss, chaos, and death. The *Upanishad* describes the other of the seated two as perennial awareness, which impartially observes the minutiae of the ceaseless rudimentary, dualistic machinations of preoccupied and attached selfing. The contemplative seated observer – perennial awareness – goes by different names, including the nondual *Witness,* although perhaps witness/ing is a better term, so as not to impute substantiality, "I'ing" to it. It is said that behind witnessing is more witnessing, possibly ad infinitum. Because the busy chasings, aversion, and delusion that comprise selfing are so loud and centre stage, so replete with clinging, presence of abiding awareness, of witness/ing capacities often remains obscured: witness/ing bears a hidden nondual curriculum, brought to light commonly although not exclusively through meditative and other contemplative practices. "All the world's a stage/And all the men and women merely players" the Bard philosophized (*As You Like It,* Act II, Scene 7). Elsewhere, he describes the tale of the human, (the "poor player") as "full of sound and fury, signifying nothing" (*Macbeth,* Act V, Scene 5), herewith poeticizing dualistic selfing while additionally gesturing to witness/ing nothing/emptiness. Nothing/emptiness is often regarded as referencing and encompassing sources of indivisible Life. Indivisible Life, it should be noted, does not mean uniformity and the disavowal of difference but rather diversity-in-unity (Eppert et al., 2015).

Contemplative nondual witnessing constitutes a neglected core of human experience in contemporary mainstream North American schooling and culture. I remember co-writing "what implicates me in bearing [historical] witness … is my inexperience in hearing the testimony that addresses me. Encountered is … the experience of my inexperience to hear and learn" (Simon et al., 2001, p. 310). Witnessing brings awareness of nuances in my inexperience to hear and learn, for example, nuances of dualistic mental, emotional, perceptual activities and subtleties of distortions, prejudices, projections, and fantasies. Psychiatrist Dori Laub details "hazards of listening" when engaging Shoah testimonies: these include overwhelm, paralysis, anger and outrage, numbness, withdrawal, fear, awe, fact-finding obsession, and hyperemotionality (Felman & Laub, 1992, p. 72–3). Nondual witnessing introduces potential additional hazards; for example, attachments to opinion, judgment (in contrast to discerning wisdom), and self-aggrandizement arising from dualistic thinking and being generally. Being *hooked* on either/ors, agreement/disagreement, assumptions, on the self's assured rightness and others' wrongness, not to mention grasping, greed, and other symptoms of what Joanna Macy (2003) describes as a "battlefield" way of seeing and engaging the world (p. 19) can foreclose on relational ethics, on justice, care, and compassion.

Attunement to dualisms' conceptual boundaries is not to therewith disavow dualisms, but rather to recognize them as interminably permeable rather than solid, as waxing and waning, ever shot through with each other and in interplay. Nondual witnessing attends to insight into energetics and motions of life/death, and the unlearning of discursive ruminations of I versus you essentialized discourses diminishing generative relations and solidarity. It bears potential to inform historical witnessing, insofar as historical witnessing encompasses "vigilance to … the particular and multiple ways in which practices [of reading and learning] obstruct one's abilities to be vulnerable to others, to hear others on complex non-thematizable terms (Eppert, 1999, p. 142). With reference to Camus's *The Plague*, Greene (1995) describes vigilance as essential to combating "indifference, abstractness and complicity" (p. 50). By no means easy or once and for all, witnessing involves ongoing vigilance regarding subtle attachments of contemplative materialism ensconced in separation, divisions, hierarchies, and other displacements.

In my view, nondual witnessing seems a more radical "radical learning ethics" than all academic radicalities I have encountered to-date. (Radical, I note, derives from the Latin word *radix*, meaning "root"). As Ergas (2013) describes, mindfulness turns Descartes's dictum, "I think, therefore I am," entirely on its head. First, it puts intellect back into balance and returns attention to the body so feared and marginalized in Cartesian grammars, naïve in the belief that intellect is the sole engine of consciousness. Bodies require historical witnessing in and through time: past, present, and future. Felman (1992) maintains the artist's role is to "demolish the deceptive image of history as an abstraction … by bearing witness to the body … the body's otherness to theory" (p. 108). Abstractions can risk dematerializing and forgetting the "body in pain" (Scarry, 1985), and Levinas (1999) stresses that "one must refuse to be caught up in [their] tangle" in recognition of their criminal potential (p. 88). Wisdom texts resonantly deconstruct hegemonies of abstraction. As the *Katha Upanishad* observes, "the Self [awareness/witness] cannot be known through study/Of the scriptures, nor through the intellect (Easwaren, 1987 p, 87). Only through revelation. Such lines reposition study not as imposition but as yielding rather than mastery, as surprise. Regarding marginalization of the body, including species bodies and the earth-body rooted in Life, I am reminded of Camus's description in *The Plague* of one character as "a man of learning, a scholar. He hasn't come in contact with death; that's why he can speak with such assurance of the truth – with a capital T" (p. 116).

That said, restoring the body from its historical Eurocentric disavowal (and/or romanticism) is not to simply reverse hierarchies and deny thought's significance (indeed, critical thinking is vitally important, particularly in today's fake era), but rather to recognize interdependence/interconnection, therewith not only a "democracy of species" (Kimmerer, 2013, p. 112), but also a *democracy of experience*, attentive to dual and nondual, human and nonhuman. Democratizing experience, supported by nondual witnessing and including inexperience, opens up the question: What constitutes the entire field of consciousness in which thinking is situated? (Rumi would answer, the field "beyond ideas of wrongdoing and rightdoing" (Barks, trans., 2004, p. 36). In my view, nondual witnessing invites questions with the potential to deconstruct not only hegemonies of thought (and philosophy) but also hegemonies of "I am," creating space for possible realities and resources of no separate and sovereign self. It unsettles self-centeredness without, at the same time, denying the significance of lived experiences. Finally, as already indicated, it deconstructs hegemonies of "either/or" – armies of me/you, body/mind, thought/emotion, inner/outer, self/no-self, self/society, and interminably so on. I often catch my dualistic mind at work, particularly when I theorize a term – even a term like "witnessing," which like all else calls for a modest approach and has limits (as I will introduce shortly). While valuing theory, I also observe, like Terdiman (2000), "theory is always constructed" (p. 31) and "chooses aspects of the world to emphasize and veils or ignores others" (p. 32). Along resonate lines, I note William Blake's (1906/2022) observation of how the "doors of perception" (p. 14) can occlude sight of the infinite.

At Louisiana State University, I was introduced to curriculum theory – its emphasis on lived experience, intertwinements of inner/outer, self/society, critiques of instrumentalism, embrace of interdisciplinarity, *currere*, and much more. As noted elsewhere (Eppert, 2023a), The Curriculum Theory Project welcomed Asian philosophy in education in a climate still resistant to it. Hongyu Wang and I co-edited *Cross-Cultural Studies in Curriculum: Eastern Thought, Educational Insights*, in which I introduced the term "witnessing curriculum" (Eppert, 2008b), contesting curricula embedded in fear/anxiety, control, and separateness, pointing to "fictions of character" in musings on divisive selfing, and endeavouring to bring Asian wisdom to bear upon pressing social issues. Thereafter, I began reading other wisdom texts from numerous different traditions, non-Western and Western. And I began pondering what truths, meanings, and wisdom if any, and however incomplete, really, do my dual and nondual lived experiences (and experiences of my inexperience) tell – apart from what I read – an unsettling and unsettled question. In the process, I noticed my teaching commitments shifting, still committed to questions of social (and, by now, environmental) suffering but more respectful of the partiality of knowledge that makes complicated conversations necessary, generative, exciting, and ever inconclusive. Along these lines, Salcel (2020) references Suzuki's Zen teaching: "When we think we know something, there is something we do not know" (p. 21). Interests in wholistic, nondual education attuned to rhythms of Life sprouted. *I search websites again, for information on species in Louisiana. I count 21 endangered species, and 17 threatened animal species, among them numerous turtles (Green Sea, Hawksbill Sea, Leatherback Sea, Loggerhead Sea, and more), both the Red-Cockaded and Ivory-Billed Woodpecker, the Gopher Tortoise, and the Piping Plover – also endangered in Alberta.*[7]

Movement #3: Current Preoccupations with Ecological Witnessing

In Louisiana, I encountered a stunning humid southern landscape of mockingbirds, cypress trees, azaleas, and alligators while also being confronted with the injustices of Cancer Alley, an 85-mile tract along the Mississippi River lined with petrochemical facilities that has polluted air and ground water and impacted the health of the St. James Parish African American community. According to the 2000

Toxic Release Inventory, during my first full year there, Louisiana, a population of 4,468,976 people then, produced 9,416,598,055 pounds of waste, ranking number 1 in the country for production related waste.[8] When Hurricane Katrina ravaged New Orleans in 2005, questions of ecological suffering/trauma and witnessing moved indelibly to the forefront (Eppert 2023a). I distinctly remember then noting a call for edited book chapters on a campus bulletin board and ruminating on how marginalized environmental education seemed in educational scholarship.

Interest arose regarding ways in which wisdom texts might contribute to questions of ecological witnessing and transformation, revealing, for example, possibilities for understanding transformation as not only direct but also indirect, not only perceptible but also imperceptible (Eppert, 2009). Marilyn Doerr (2004), in her *currere*-informed work on an environmental autobiography project, invites her students to engage in inner, implicated critical questioning: "How does my personal life, how do my personal choices in that life, impinge on the rest of the world?" (p. 135). For a long time, my diet became pescatarian. *From worldwildlife.org, I now learn that "Freshwater fish populations are collapsing. Nearly one-third of all freshwater fish are threatened with extinction" and "[i]n 2020 alone 16 freshwater fish species were declared extinct."*[9] If before I had been concerned with the past, and then with a hermeneutics and phenomenology of presence, I was becoming increasingly despairing of the future. I since observe that Hurricane Katrina has *"damaged 16 federal wildlife refuges and altered habitat for at least three endangered or threatened species, including the endangered Alabama Beach Mouse, Kemp's Ridley Sea Turtle, and some species of Wading birds"* (Sheikh, 2005, p. 4).

Completion of my "Witnessing the Integrity of Water" chapter (Eppert, 2009) accompanied my return to Canada in 2007. While transitioning from a hot, humid climate to a cold, dry one, from mockingbirds to magpies, gas and oil dominance remained constant as did environmental racism, in northeast Alberta, the site of the tar sands (the world's second largest oil deposit). Approximately 23,000 Indigenous people reside in the region. While ecological issues became part of teaching and presentations (e.g., Eppert, 2008c, 2010, 2014, 2017), I still felt internally pressed with puzzles of nonduality. However, increasing scientific reports of ecological destruction made it all too obvious that "[t]o continue with economic and educational business as usual is absurd, and we could justifiably say that this is mental illness in the extreme. What is the sense of learning algorithms or alliteration if all of sentient existence is at stake?" (Eppert et al, 2015, p. 289). Questions of transformation have since become rather desperate for me, concurrent with faith in educational possibilities, because "the nondual ground of wisdom and compassion is always available" (Eppert et. al, 2015). Thinking curriculum in extinction across subject areas cannot be an add-on, a past-time, but rather, I believe, constitutes a ground and path imperative.

And so, "here I am" (Levinas, 1985, p. 106) in the present, invariably in/sufficiently so, and variably keen to unpack the "here," "I," and "am" of this phrase. That said, concurrently, I am cognizant of Levinas's Abrahamic reference to "Here I am" as ethical obligation to the address of alterity, an "I" intactness shattered in facts of species extinction and a subjectivity reconstituted in a responsive/responsible, relational, and intersubjective rather than individual me and mine sociopolitics, so constitutive of the "Capitalocene" (Moore, 2015, p. 176). My *witnessing currere* now looks both back and forward, seeking to challenge linear temporalities, and immersed in catastrophe and contradictions – cognizant that a curriculum in extinction is situated in a societal past and present marked with what Haraway (2016) identifies as an "unprecedented looking away" (p. 35). Yet, it also invests in a *Jetztzeit*, a now time Walter Benjamin (1968) identifies as pregnant with revolutionary potential. As he contends, "In every era, the attempt must be made anew to wrest tradition away from a conformism that is about to overpower it" (p. 255). I return to Ng-A-Fook's (2014) question: "Where we are at, in this place and this time, as Canadian curriculum scholars" (p. 1)?

Here I am: It is believed that the last Eastern Elk, which once populated southern Canada and the US may have been shot in Pennsylvania on 1 September 1877. The Labrador Duck, once found breeding in Labrador and northern Quebec, was last sighted in New York in 1878, its extinction possibly due, among other reasons, to the overharvesting of its eggs, or the decline of its shellfish food sources due to industrialization. It is believed that the Newfoundland Wolf had been hunted to extinction in 1930s, although it was found again in 2019. It is believed that habitat destruction may have caused the extinction of the Queen Charlotte Islands Caribou (also known as Dawson Caribou) in Western Canada, the last three having been killed by local hunters in Haida Gwaii in 1908 (their pelts and bones on display at the Royal British Columbia Museum). The Sea Mink, inhabiting the Maritime provinces, became extinct in the late 1800s, due to an unregulated fur trade. The Cascade Mountain Wolf lived in the Pacific northwest, and was declared extinct in 1940, due to excessive hunting.

Here I am: In Alberta, the Swift Fox, Bison, Sage Grouse, Piping Plover, Ord's Kangaroo Rat, Whooping Crane, Mountain Plover, and 10 other animal species are endangered. The 2022 Alberta Conservation Committee lists not only 16 endangered species but also 17 threatened species, and 17 species of special concern.[10] According to the David Suzuki Foundation, across Canada, currently, "521 plant and animal species are considered at risk under Canada's Species at Risk Act."[11] Between 2010 and 2019, the IUCN declared the extinction of 160 species on Earth. In 2020, it declared 15 extinct species. In December 2022, it cited 10,739 vertebrates, 6,161 invertebrates, 24,914 plants, and 294 fungi and protists as threatened species – a total of 42,108 threatened species.[12]

Here I am: Canada is home to 80,000 known species, excluding viruses and bacteria, and including the protozoa, chromist, fungi, plant and animal kingdoms.[13] According to the 2020 "Living Planet Report Canada: Wildlife at Risk," since 1970, "populations of Canadian species assessed as at risk have plunged by an average of 59 per cent and species assessed as globally at risk have seen their Canadian populations fall by an average of 42 per cent."[14] The report cites that threats are multiple and include overexploitation, invasion, disease, pollution, climate change, urban development, transport, human disturbance, agricultural activity, energy production, system modifications to improve human welfare, and geological events.

I cannot help but note that 1970, the beginning of this plunge, closely coincides with my move to Canada and my elementary school beginnings. The Living Planet report further states that "[d]espite conservation efforts to date, global goals and trajectories for biodiversity conservation, sustainable use of resources and climate change mitigation are unlikely to be achieved without vigorous, urgent and transformative action from all sectors of society" (p. 63). It points out that Canada "is the steward of one quarter of the world's remaining areas of high ecological integrity" (p. 66). According to the report, "the next decade will be critical in reversing catastrophic wildlife loss and climate breakdown." I ask myself, what does/might "high ecological integrity" look like, in curriculum studies and ELA, not to mention other subject fields?

Here I am: Sitting on my front doorsteps, in lonely seasons of COVID-19, bird book and binoculars in hand, seeking to learn the birds in this neighbourhood.

Here I am: Teaching the Secondary Alberta ELA Program of Studies, conceived in 2003. While emphasizing the importance of reflecting on "fundamentals of human existence," and grappling "with the intricacies of the human condition,"[15] mentions of climate change and ecological issues are absent. McClanahan (2013) remarks, "according to Glotfelty (1996), upon reading the current [literature education] canon, 'you would never suspect that the earth's life support systems were under stress. Indeed, you might never know that there was an earth at all (p. xvi)'." McClanahan further notes that "in secondary literature classrooms, where students study how ethics impact their moral and spiritual lives, 'we have fairly well ignored our impact on the natural world or our relationships with it (Bruce, 2011, p. 13)'." She concludes, what such an omission "implicitly tells our English Language Arts students" is that "'our ecological relationship with our habitat is either a matter of little importance or something only relevant to 'science geeks' (Bruce, 2011, p. 13)" (McClanahan, Overview Section, paras. 1–3).

Here I am: Rereading *The Plague*. Camus's narrator describes Oran as a town focused on commerce, a town "without pigeons, without any trees, or gardens, where you never hear the beat of winds or the rustle of leaves" (p. 3). I am reminded that Mary Aswell Doll already in 2000 identified the "greening of the imagination" as a curricular and ELA necessity (Doll, 2000). Greene (1988) provokes teachers to "see beyond and move beyond the classroom" (p. 475) and bear witness to widespread pestilences, other injustices and abuses, the earth's desertification and the commodification of children and the turning of their education into economic competitiveness. Referencing Camus, she writes, "it may be extreme to compare all this with the pestilence or plague; but we know well that children and young people suffer in the thousands from the separation or the exile Camus' narrator saw as the most fearful consequence of plague. They may experience it through abandonment, through the absence of community, through a felt erosion of concern" (p. 476). Greene urges an education in which ELA teachers, rather than being seduced by business-as-usual preoccupations debate "their own being in the world" (p. 476) and enable the young to "summon up (or invent, or imagine) alternative possibilities for themselves" (p. 476). She implores language arts educators to teach in ways that challenge technocratic hegemonies, that "release the imagination" and cultivate "wide awakeness." Defining wide awakeness, she quotes Alfred Schutz who describes it as "originating in an attitude of full attention to life and its requirements" (as cited by Greene, 1977, p. 121).

Here I am: Learning of a complicated relationship between environmental educator Chet Bowers (1935–2017) and Greene. Bowers (1991) published "An Open Letter to Greene titled 'The Problem of Freedom in an Era of Ecological Interdependence,'" in which he challenges Greene for her lack of attention to "community as an ecology where humans are understood as living in an interdependent relationship with natural systems – plants, animals, soil, and other parts of the natural world that make up the information and food chains that sustain life" (p. 326). He asserts that "ecological survival is now the overriding issue we face" (p. 327). Bowers argues that what we need now is an understanding not of a "dialectic of freedom" but a "dialectic of interdependence" (p. 330). I wonder if and how Greene replied to his letter, and, resistant to either/ors, I wonder if these times call for an interdependent freedom, emerging from dialogue with Greene's "dialectic of freedom," Levinas's "difficult freedom," Buddha's liberation, Foucault's freedom, and Bower's interdependence, among others.

Here I am: Preparing to offer a graduate course on life writing research, and reading about Indigenous *Métissage,* I learn of the Blackfoot wisdom of *aokakio'ssin,* which Donald (2012) describes as "a pedagogic call to *pay attention* to what is going on around us, interpret these insights in relational ways, and bring the understandings gained from the interpretative process to expression through language and ceremony – to share them with others" (p. 550, italics in original).

Here I am: As per usual, one and a half feet in Canada and half a foot in Germany. I have begun reading Heise (2016), who contends that "biodiversity, endangered species, and extinction are primarily cultural issues, questions of what we value and what stories we tell" (p. 5). She writes that national environmental legalization in Germany was passed when the National Socialists obtained power. Goering "sought to bring the extinct aurochs back to the forests of Lithuania and

Poland" (p. 98). Goering, Hitler's associate, was responsible for the passing of the animal protection act, the hunting act, and the nature protection act in the early 1930s: "these constituted the first unified, nationwide legislation of its kind in German history" (p. 98). How to process this information?

And, here I am, indefinitely so on …

"Staying with the Trouble": Notes Towards Past, Present, and Future Ecological Witnessing

In the face of unparalleled looking away in times of anthropogenic climate change, rather than ongoing turning away or giving up, Haraway (2016) emphasizes the interdisciplinary imperative of "staying with the trouble" (p. 1). She writes that in these times, "the task is to become capable, with each other … *of response*" (p. 1). To become capable of response, in other words, to meet the disproportionate responsibility for ecological integrity we as Canadians bear, as the Living Planet Report states, entails a staying with the trouble that "requires learning to be truly present" (2020, p. 1). Reading these words, following from Greene's regarding a "full attention to life," I am reminded again of the significance of witnessing, this time, however, both *historical and contemplative nondual witnessing in the service of ecological witnessing.* This is what I question and am moved/moving to explore for the time being. By way of conclusion, I sketch some fragmentary notes of questions, thoughts, insights, inspirations, and orientations, informed by recent readings.

Fragment #1: Historical Ecological Witnessing

Inasmuch as events and experiences of human-initiated singular and mass violence call for ethical remembrance, so too does human-initiated destruction of land, sky, and nonhuman species. Yet, commemorative practices regarding the nonhuman are not (yet) commonly found in mainstream North American culture. I wonder, what might remembrance pedagogies and ecological witnessing of species extinction look like, in the public sphere and in educational sites? This question itself seems to call for a radical learning ethic, one that interrupts histories of anthropocentric ontologies, ethics, methodologies, and epistemologies. Not only the breadth and depth of extinction but also the diversities and alterities of multispecies "requires something more than an egoism which predefines remembrance as that which confirms who one is and what one knows" (Simon & Eppert, 1997, p. 177). As Rose, Van Dooren, and Chrulew (2017) state in their remarkable edited collection titled *Extinction Studies: Stories of Time, Death, and Generations,* "extinction is one of the gravest challenges to ethics and action confronting all of us today, even if it does so in varied and diverse ways. The reverberations of our inadequacies are everywhere apparent"

(p. 7). Species extinction compels me to return again to a quote from Felman, so beloved that I repeatedly cite it (e.g., Eppert, 2024), namely,

> the question of the witness, and of witnessing, as nonhabitual, estranged conceptual prisms through which we attempt to apprehend – and to make tangible to the imagination – the ways in which our cultural frames of reference and our preexisting categories which delimit and determine our perception of reality have failed, essentially, both to contain, and to account for, the scale of what has happened in contemporary history. (Felman and Laub, 1992, p. xv)

Felman identifies an unprecedented "radical historical crisis of witnessing" (p. xvii) in that the atrocity of the Shoah "does not enter, and cannot be framed by, any existing frame of reference (be it of knowledge or belief)" (p. 103). She observes that just like for Camus's victims of the plague, many did not believe the news about the Final Solution, because, according to Felman, we can only witness "that which is within reach of the conceptual frame of reference we inhabit" (p. 104). Hence, the *Shoah* was an event without a witness, in the sense also that the true witness is the one who died. Species extinction also constitutes an atrocity that "*cannot, historically, be witnessed*" (p.104, italics hers) within historical anthropocentric frames of reference. Whereas Greene calls educators to be wide awake, Felman resonantly but in a more qualified way gestures to a curriculum situated in the "urgency of waking up into a history and a reality with respect to which we are not and perhaps cannot be, fully and sufficiently awake" (p. 271). On such terms, a curriculum of witnessing is lodged not only in breakages of anthropogenic frames but also in troubling dualisms of attention/inattention, knowing/not knowing, understanding/not understanding, presence/erasure, and so on implicit in witnessing's etymology.

Wolfe (2017) maintains that "extinction is never a generic event and is always a multi-contextual phenomenon requiring multidisciplinary modes of encounter and understanding" (p. viii). Following from Felman, cognizance of the limits of witnessing also situates a multidisciplinary praxis of witnessing in *lack* of understanding and action, missed encounters, past and anticipated loss represented in traces, fragments, remnants, splitting, and failures of translation, melancholia, among other challenges. The provocative essays in Rose, Van Dooren, and Chrulew's (2017) collection speak to the necessity of "witnessing the multifaceted ... unraveling of forms of life that is occurring around us" (p. 8) and the importance of questioning which species are mourned when, why, and how. Each essay traces a particular extinct species. Cary Wolfe (2017), in his foreword to this collection, states that we need to attend deeply to "what goes out of the world" and "what is lost to the world" (p. viii) with every loss of a being. He quotes from James Hatley's beautifully written chapter in this collection, about the 1905 extinction of the Japanese Honshu wolf (wolf is

Ōkami, in Japanese): "Something like Ōkami should not disappear in our time without its departure having been noticed, without its loss mattering" (Hatley, as cited by Wolfe, 2017, p. viii). I wonder, might we not say the same of species in Canada? *While Pinar experiences affinity with the Passenger Pigeon, and Anne Phelan with the Atlantic Grey Whale (informed by her experiences teaching grade six in Ireland), I note the flightless Great Auk and its tragic vulnerability. Once in the millions, the Auk (deeply valued in Indigenous cultures) was easily exploited for its down feathers and eggs as it lacked fear of human predators. A slow walker, it possessed no readily available means of land escape. Found along the coasts of Canada, the bird became extinct in the mid-1800s, the last confirmed two killed off the Iceland coast in the 1840s.*

Fragment #2: Contemplative Nondual Ecological Witnessing

From what I have gleaned to date, ecological scholarship is abundant with discussion of gymnastics of attention. While Rose, Van Dooren, and Chrulew (2017) draw upon the language of witnessing in the context of extinction studies, Tsing (2015), for example, introduces an "arts of noticing" with reference to the lives and commerce of the Matsutake mushroom. She challenges narratives of progress and "techniques of alienation that turn both human beings and other beings into resources" (p. 19), disavowing these in favour of indeterminancy and multidirectionality. She draws attention to the modern human conceit of human world-making, when life is everywhere suffused also with nonhuman world-making projects. Her arts of noticing reorient attention to multispecies world making, to "interrupting geographies and tempos" (p. 38), and to transformation through indeterminate encounters.

Eco-literary theorist Morton (2017) emphasizes "ecological awareness" (p. 186), which he discusses in conversation about Buddhist thought. He distinguishes himself from Žižek who disavows Buddhism on the basis that it supports practitioners' passivity. Instead, Morton's critique, directed more against neoliberal mindfulness, or McMindfulness it seems, claims that it "turns the practitioner into a maniacally active worker who now has a whole new job to do … namely to remain calm" (p. 185). He reminds practitioners that meditation means "awareness," as "something effortless, something the practitioner is not 'doing' at all" (p. 185). My own meditative experience tells me something different than Žižek's generalized critique allows.

While, like Morton, I am equally critical of neoliberal instrumentalization and commodification of mindfulness, I recognize value to mindfulness not only in one-pointed concentration trainings but also, for example, in Buddhist ethical emphasis on non-harming. Based on his discussion of effortless awareness, perhaps Morton would criticize my interest in vigilance, which connotes certain effort, but I find both awareness and vigilance meritorious, both with their uses and potential abuses, like all else. That said, akin to Morton, I connect with meditation not as chasings after, but rather letting go, dropping storylines, yielding to surprise and insight, and profound experiences, both difficult and easy, of "just this." To me, this contemplative dimension also yields a different understanding of transformation – as "what happens to us over and above our wanting and doing" (Gadamer, 1994, p. xxviii). Morton importantly asserts, "one doesn't act awareness, it happens to one. It seems to have its own kind of existence, from its own side" (p. 186). On such terms, as he wonderfully states, "awareness *rocks*" (p. 186). Like geologist Jill S. Schneiderman (2013), who brings both contemplative practices into her teaching and also vast geological time to, in turn, bear upon contemplation – indeed, it needs to be remembered that the earth is 4.57 billion years old – Morton infuses his description of ecological awareness with vital geological considerations. Ecological awareness, he asserts, "is knowing that there are a bewildering variety of scales, temporal and spatial, and that the human ones are only a very narrow region" (p. 186). It is this humbling work that intrigues me most currently (see, also, Eppert, 2024); that is, in what ways might knowledge from geology, botany, biology, physics, and other sciences be able to inform ecological witnessing and a curriculum in extinction? How might these and other fields delve into deeper commensurable and incommensurable conversation with nondual and ecological witnessing informed by learning from many wisdom traditions and texts? And, in what ways might such dialogue inform not only curriculum but also English language arts education? Additionally, in what ways might ELA, teacher education, philosophy of education, and literary, poetic, and aesthetic engagement participate in and contribute to intercultural/cross-cultural/transcultural and interdisciplinary/multidisciplinary/transdisciplinary complicated curricular converations and transformational exigencies (Eppert, 2020, 2021, 2023b)? And, finally, in what ways might a curriculum in extinction be enmeshed in care and lifeworld possibilities?

Future Ecological Witnessing: Shadow Questions and Exegetical Textual Engagement

Species extinction challenges conventional linear temporalities, bringing questions of remembrance and historical witnessing into the present and future. In past writing (Eppert, 2000) I described witnessing as "an interminable learning practice, a learning of what it means to be answerable to the address of past and present others" (p. 215). I now wish I had written past, present and *future* others. I ponder, what might it mean to ethically remember the future in contexts of species extinction and existence? English language arts education, in my view, benefits from an exegetic reading stance (Eppert, 2008a) that regards the text not as object for masterful critique but rather, as previously indicated, as a teaching. I believe such an engaged reading stance invites arisings of troublesome questions that admit of no resolute answers. Simon and Armitage-Simon (1995) introduce the notion of "shadow texts," namely, "secondary narratives constructed in response to the unresolved questions a primary narrative elicits" (p. 269; see also, Simon & Eppert, 1997). More specifically, "shadow texts" are engagements with "unresolved questions" (p. 269) that arise in encounters with testimonies of mass destruction, questions such as "why did people let these events happen" (p. 269). Their focus is on historical testimonies, namely, testimonies regarding the Nazi genocide of European Jewry and the bombings of Hiroshima and Nagasaki, and such picture books as Yukio Tsuchiya's (1997) *Faithful Elephants* or such young adult literature as Carol Matas's (1993) *Daniel's Story*. However, in my view, difficult and unresolved questions – what I would like resonantly to call "shadow questions" – also pertain to the present *and* the future, indeed, in the context of species extinction, the very question of *a* future. In my classes, young people are asking: Why is climate change happening? Why is more not being done? What will be my and my children's future?

Clearly one way to address climate change in curriculum and English language arts education is to introduce literature that grapples with species extinction and allows for such questions to be asked. Yet, I believe, certain texts elicit shadow questions and exegetical engagements more than others. For example, children's picture books that address species extinction include Alexandra Wright and Marshall Peck III's (1992) *Will We Miss Them? Endangered Species*, or Chelsea Clinton and Gianna Marino's (2019) *Don't Let Them Disappear: 12 Endangered Species Across the Globe.* Whereas the latter text assumes a conventional linear temporality – situating itself in the present and imploring young readers not to let species disappear in the future – the former text is a bit more evocative. It can be read dually, first as the shadow question of will we miss extinct species in some undetermined future. Yet, it can also be read as asking readers, in some ways, to imagine themselves into the future and consider, from within that future, whether they are missing endangered species. In other words, within this novel question of remembrance – of mourning (perhaps mourning, or perhaps melancholia) – from within the future, is another unresolved question, a shadow question from a potentially spectral-ghostly future, if humans are also no more, directed to the past that is our present; namely, did people let these events happen? And, also, what are the consequences if they didn't?

In another text, Felman (1987) draws on Lacan, who in turn, according to Renata Salcel (2020), was inspired by Buddhist lectures on ignorance as one of the three fires or poisons in order to consider educations implicated in "passions of ignorance" (p. 79). Felman describes ignorance not as "a passive state of absence, a simple lack of information" (p. 79) but rather as an "active dynamic of negation, an active refusal of information" (p. 79). The question of will we miss them is not only a question of melancholia or mourning but also the question of missing as in passing by, not seeing, not being present to, thus a question of witnessing in recognition of its interplay of attention/inattention, and so on, returning me to the underlying theme of this chapter. It implicates the present precisely in complexities of knowledge/ignorance, that is, in pedagogies and curricula of gymnastics of in/attention. Felman (1987) maintains that while traditional pedagogy postulates desires for knowledge, what she terms "revolutionary pedagogies" require attending to performative desires to ignore, to "resistances to knowledge" (p. 79). Attending to these resistances, I contemplate, might open to a holding open of the future, a radical remembered future. This returns me to the prairie skies with which I began this chapter.

Conclusion: Reading *The Plague*, Reading the Skies

Passions of ignorance call for inclusions of literature regarding species extinction as well as climate change more generally into curriculum studies that persistently challenge unprecedented looking away and provoke questions of witnessing implicated in complicated dynamics of attention/inattention as well as nondual dynamics of imagination and failures of imagination. For Felman, the "failure to imagine" (Felman & Laub, 1992, p. 103) is precisely why literature like *The Plague* is needed – because it gives insight into both the historical reality of the event and also the "historicity of its unimaginability" (p. 105).

Recently, I came across Gourley's (2020) brilliant Dupuy-informed reading of *The Plague*. Citing Dupuy, Gourley details the importance of "speaking of the unpalatable truth so as to resist 'our ability not to see when faced with the obvious-ness of suffering and atrocities'" (p. 747). He reads the novel's changing representation of weather and illustrates how the novel's townspeople at first ignore the climate and nonhuman world, but then, as the novel progresses, they begin to relate differently. At the novel's outset, Camus's representations of the sky – and, one might add, "violent extremes of temperature" (Camus, 1948, p. 5) – reveal Oran as a town "trapped by climate change" (Gourley, 2020, p. 738). The skies forewarn of a plague to come but the residents of Oran, including the novel's protagonist and narrator Rieux, are unable to "read the premonitory signs of the grave events to follow" (Camus, 1948, p. 6) because this would mean reckoning with the consequences. The town largely remains passive, turning its back on the weather. Quarantine and increasing devastation, however, prompts the townspeople – as they become more subject to the nonhuman world, via the rats and fleas transmitting the plague, for example – to become more conscious of sky, sun, and rain. They become increasingly distressed by their vulnerability to the weather. Gourley (2020) observes that as the novel continues, although the townspeople begin to feel more threatened by the climate, they largely continue on with their lack of understanding (p. 743). Gourley further writes,

> perception of their sudden powerlessness overlooks their historical disinterest in anything but the human world and their rigid separation of human and nonhuman worlds.... The Oranais seek to reassert their primacy over the nonhuman world, a model of relation that clearly does not fully understand the reality of the plague epidemic, nor does it approach harmony or equilibrium, which would promote a possible long-term coexistence (p. 743).

Although the townspeople are beginning to develop awareness of their connection to the nonhuman world, their "passion for ignorance" persists, as too does their lack of attention to the future. Camus states, "This drastic, clean-cut deprivation and our complete ignorance of what the future held in store had taken us unawares" (1948, p. 64). As Gourley (2020) observes, the plague rules out any possible futures (p. 743). The townspeople continue with a business-as-usual present that obviates the future.

Yet, Gourley (2020) then brings attention to the ways in which, as the plague more fully grips the townspeople, their relationship to the nonhuman world finally transforms. They become observant – noting the smells of the soil, the changing seasons, the nature of the sky: "The Oranais' experience of the plague epidemic serves as a prompt for the townsfolk to re-engage with the nonhuman world; to understand themselves as part of an ecosystem that extends beyond their own small city and its mundane aspirations" (p. 744). Following their being quarantined the townspeople search the skies "for a sign" (p. 736). Slowly, and in the face of much ambivalence, the townspeople learn, albeit it is not until the end of the novel that lessons are fully realized, with the arrival of a change of weather. Gourley beautifully shows how the novel comes to make evident human dependence upon the nonhuman world, and the interdependence between human and nonhuman. The townspeople transform, become attuned to ethical obligation to attend to the nonhuman world, to stay with the trouble rather than look away. Like the townspeople, we might together begin to look towards the skies.

ACKNOWLEDGMENTS

My thanks to Bill and Anne for inviting me to contribute to this edited book. My chapter was first submitted to them in December 2021. Since then, among other happenings, I learn on the news that there has been a grey whale sighting in the Atlantic for the first time in 200 years.

NOTES

1 WWF Canada. (2020). Living planet report Canada: Wildlife at risk. Currie, J., Snider, J., Giles, E., World Wildlife Fund Canada. Toronto, Canada. https://wwf.ca.

2 Intergovernmental Science-Policy Platform on Biodiversity and Ecosystem Services (IPBES). (2019, May 05). Media release: Nature's dangerous decline

'unprecedented; species extinction rates accelerating'. http://ipbes.net/news/Media-Release-Global-Assessment#:

3 The IUCN Red List of Threatened Species (2022–2). *Background and history.* http://iucnredlist.org/.

4 World Conservation Monitoring Centre (1990). *The 1990 IUCN Red List of Threatened Animals.* International Union for Conservation of Nature and Natural Resources: Cambridge, UK. https://portals.iucn.org/library/sites/library/files/documents/RL-1990-001.pdf

5 Baille, J.E.M. & Groombridge, B. (Compilers and editors). (1996). *IUCN Red List of Threatened Animals.* International Union for Conservation of Nature and Natural Resources. Cambridge, UK.

6 That said, transformation is a complex term, an individual, communal, collective experience that is often used in educational contexts and calls for critical unpacking and careful, nuanced attention.

7 US Fish and Wildlife Service. (2020). *Louisiana's threatened and endangered species by parish.* Louisiana Ecological Field Services Office. www.fwe.gov.

8 United States Environmental Protection Agency. (2002, May). *2000 Toxics Release Inventory (TRI) Public Data Release Report: Executive Summary.* Office of Environmental Information, Washington, DC. www.epa.gov.

9 World Wildlife Fund. (February 23, 2021). One-third of freshwater fish face extinction and other freshwater fish facts. Worldwildlife.org.

10 Environment and Pars, Environment and Sustainable Resource Development. (2022) *Species at risk assessed in Alberta: Fish and wildlife stewardship.* Environment and Parks. https://open.alberta.ca.

11 David Suzuki Foundation. *Species at risk.* https://davidsuzuki.org/project/species-at-risk.

12 IUCN Global Species Programme Red List Unit (2022). *IUCN red list version 202-202: Table 1A.* International Union for Conservation of Nature and Natural Resources (IUCN). Cambridge, UK. www.iucnredlist.org.

13 Canadian Endangered Species Conservation Council (2016). *Wild species 2015: The general status of species in Canada.* National General Status Working Group. www.wildlife-species.canada.ca.

14 WWF Canada. (2020). *Living Planet Report Canada: Wildlife at risk.* Currie, J., Snider J., and Giles E. World Wildlife Fund Canada. Toronto, Canada. https://wwf.ca.

15 Alberta Education (2003). *English Language Arts Program of Studies (Senior High).* Alberta Learning. https://education.alberta.ca.

REFERENCES

Barks, C. (Trans.) (2004). *The essential Rumi.* Harper/San Francisco.

Benjamin, W. (1968). Theses on the philosophy of history. In H. Arendt (Ed.) *Illuminations, Walter Benjamin, essays, and reflections.* (pp. 253–64). Harcourt Brace Jovanovich.

Blake, W. (1906/2022). *The marriage of heaven and hell.* Moncreiffe Press. https//www.amazon.ca/Marriage-Heaven-Hell-William-Blake-ebook/dp/149592386X

Bowers, C. A. (1991). An open letter to Maxine Greene on "The problem of freedom in an era of ecological interdependence." *Educational Theory*, *41*(3), 325–30. https://doi.org/10.1111/j.1741-5446.1991.00325.x

Britzman, D. (1998). *Lost subjects, contested objects: Toward a psychoanalytic inquiry of learning*. SUNY press.

Bruce, H. E. (2011). Green(ing) English: Voices howling in the wilderness? *English Journal*, 100(3), 12–26.

Camus, A. (1948). *The plague*. Modern Library Edition.

Chambers, C.M., Hasebe-Ludt, E., Leggo, C., & Sinner, A. (Eds.). (2012). *A heart of wisdom: Life writing as empathetic inquiry*. Peter Lang.

Clinton, C. & Marino, G. (2019). *Don't let them disappear: 12 endangered species across the globe*. Philomel Books.

Derrida, J. (1994). *Specters of Marx: The state of the debt, the work of mourning, & the new international* (P. Kamuf, Trans.). Routledge.

Doerr, M. (2004). *Currere and the environmental autobiography: A phenomenological approach to the teaching of ecology*. Peter Lang.

Doll, M, A. (2000). *Like letters in running water: A mythopoetics of curriculum*. Lawrence Erlbaum Associates.

Donald, D. (2012). Indigenous Métissage: A decolonizing research sensibility. *International Journal of Qualitative Studies in Education*, *25*(5), 533–55. https://doi.org/10.1080/09518398.2011.554449

Dupuy, J. (2015). *A short treatise on the metaphysics of tsunamis*. Michigan State University.

Easwaren, E., (Trans.). (1987). *The Upanishads*. Nilgiri Press.

Eppert, C. (1999). *Learning responsivity/responsibility: Reading the literature of historical witness*. Doctoral dissertation. University of Toronto.

– (2000). Re-learning questions: Responding to the address of past and present others. In R. Simon, S. Rosenberg, & C. Eppert (Eds.), *Between hope and despair: Pedagogy and the remembrance of historical trauma* (pp. 213–30). Rowman and Littlefield.

– (2004). Altering habits of attention and inattention in education: Simone Weil and Emmanuel Levinas. In H. A. Alexander (Ed.), *Spirituality and ethics in education: Philosophical, theological, and radical perspectives* (pp. 42–54). Sussex Academic Press.

– (2008a). Emmanuel Levinas, literary engagement, and literature education. In D. Egea-Kuehne (Ed.), *Levinas and education: At the intersection of faith and reason* (pp. 67–84). Taylor & Francis.

– (2008b). Fear, (educational) fictions of character, and Buddhist insights for a witnessing curriculum. In C. Eppert & H. Wang (Eds.), *Cross-cultural studies in curriculum: Eastern thought, educational insights* (1st ed., pp. 55–108). Lawrence Erlbaum, Taylor and Francis.

– (2008c). *Remembering our (re)source: Eastern meditations on witnessing the integrity of water*. [Paper presentation]. The American Educational Research Association (AERA). New York, USA.

– (2009). Remembering our (re)source: Eastern meditations on witnessing the integrity of water. In M. McKenzie, H. Bai, P. Hart, & B. Jickling (Eds.), *Fields of green: Restorying culture, environment, and education* (pp. 191–210). Hampton Press.
– (2010, November). *Rethinking social and environmental healing through Asian wisdom.* [Paper presentation]. Apres Vous: Ethics, pedagogy, memory, and justice, a symposium for Dr. Roger I. Simon. Ontario Institute for Studies in Education, University of Toronto, Toronto, Canada.
– (2014, October). Intercultural wisdom: Questions of loss, ethics, & hope. Paper presented in B. Pinar, W. Doll, & D. Trueit (Chairs), 2014–2015 Seminar Series on *International perspectives in curriculum and pedagogy*. University of British Columbia, Vancouver, BC, Canada.
– (2017, May). Introduction to witnessing. Paper presented at plenary session on *Complexities of environmental witnessing through theatre: Engaging Soutar's Watershed.* Presented at the Canadian Association for Theatre Research (CATR) at Congress. Toronto, Canada.
– (2020). Forest walks in the Anthropocene: Meditations on grief, joy, and a restorative politics. In M. Bussey & C. Mozzini-Alister (Eds.), *Phenomenologies of grace: The body, embodiment and transformative futures* (pp. 65–84). Cham, Switzerland: Palgrave MacMillan.
– (2021). Contemplating educations of ecological well-becoming, with gratitude to (mother) earth, wildlife, and women. In C. Eppert & J. Bach (Guest Eds.) *Questions of gratitude: Storying transformative and curricular relationships with women's experiences and lives* [Special symposium]. *Curriculum Inquiry*, *51*(3), 307–31. https://doi.org/10.1080/03626784.2021.1941797
– (2023a). Lingerings. In P. Hendry, M. Quinn, R.W. Mitchell, J. Bach (Eds). *Curriculum histories in place, in person, in practice: The LSU curriculum theory project*, (pp. 166–8.) Routledge.
– (2023b). After hope: Empire, ecocide, & Sebald's Steller's *Bildung*. In T. Strong-Wilson, R. L. Castro, W. Crichlow, & A. Yoder (Eds.). *Curricular and architectural encounters with W.G. Sebald: Unsettling complacency, reconstructing subjectivity*, (pp. 272–91). Routledge.

Eppert, C. (2024). Ruminations on rocks: Ethical and ecological turns in witnessing. In P. P. Trifonas and S. Jagger (Eds.), *Handbook of curriculum theory, research, and practice*, (pp. 199–215). Springer.

Eppert, C. Hiller, C., Rosenberg, S., Salverson, J., & Simon, R. (1996). Historical memory, violence, and civic education. *Orbit*, *27*(2), 19–21. https://inclusion.com/site/wp-content/uploads/2017/12/1996-Students-with-Disabilities-and-Global-Education.pdf

Eppert, C., Vokey, D., Nguyen, T. T. A., & Bai, H. (2015). Intercultural philosophy and the nondual wisdom of "basic goodness": Implications for contemplative and transformative education. *Journal of Philosophy of Education*, *49*(2), 274–93. https://doi.org/10.1111/1467-9752.12141

Ergas, O. (2013). Descartes in a "headstand": Introducing "body-oriented pedagogy." *Paideusis, 21*(1), 4–12. https://doi.org/10.7202/1071570

Felman, S. (1987). *Jacques Lacan and the adventure of insight: Psychoanalysis in contemporary culture*. Harvard University Press.

Felman, S. & Laub, D. (1992). *Testimony: Crisis of witnessing in literature, psychoanalysis, and history*. Routledge.

Gadamer, H. G. (1994). *Truth and method* (2nd edition). Continuum Publishing Company.

Garber, M., Hanssen, B., & Walkowitz, R.L. (Eds.). (2000). *The turn to ethics*. Routlege.

Glotfelty, C. (1996). Introduction: Literary studies in an age of environmental crisis. In Glotfelty, C. & Fromm, H. (Eds.), *The ecocriticism reader* (xv–xxxvii). Athens, GA: University of Georgia Press.

Gourley, J. (2020). "Trapped by the climate": Reading Camus's *The Plague* in light of anthropogenic climate change. *Interdisciplinary Studies in Literature and Environment, 27*(4), 732–52. https://doi.org/10.1093/isle/isaa112

Greene, M. (1977). Towards wide-awakeness: An argument for the arts and humanities in education. *Teachers College Press, 79*(1), 119–25. https://doi.org/10.1177/016146817707900105

– (1988). What are the language arts for? *Language Arts, 65*(5), 474–81. https://www.jstor.org/stable/41411412

– (1995). *Releasing the imagination: Essays on education, the arts, and social change*. Jossey-Bass.

Haraway, D. (2016). *Staying with the trouble: Making kin in the Chthulucene*. Duke University Press.

Hasebe-Ludt, E., Chambers, C. M., & Leggo, C. (2009). *Life writing and literary métissage as an ethos for our times*. Peter Lang.

Heise, U. K. (2016). *Imagining extinction: The cultural meanings of endangered species*. University of Chicago Press.

Kimmerer, R.W. (2013). *Braiding sweetgrass: Indigenous wisdom, scientific knowledge, and the teachings of plants*. Milkweed Editions.

Kleinman, A., Das V., Lock, M. (Eds.) (1997). *Social suffering*. University of California Press.

Kolbert, E. (2014). *The sixth extinction: An unnatural history*. Picador.

Levinas, E. (1969). *Totality and infinity*. (A. Lingis, Trans.). Duquense University.

– (1985). *Ethics and infinity: Conversations with Philippe Nemo*. (R.A. Cohen, Trans.). Duquesne University.

– (1999). *Alterity and transcendence*. Columbia University Press.

Macy, J. (2003). *World as lover, world as self: Courage for global justice and planetary renewal*. Parallax Press.

Matas, C. (1993). *Daniel's story*. Scholastic.

McClanahan, L. (2013, January). The greening of the language arts: Considering sustainability outside of the science classroom. *Journal of Sustainability Education*,

4. http://www.jsedimensions.org/wordpress/wp-content/uploads/2013/01/LauraMcClanahanWinter2013.pdf

Moore, J. W. (2015). *Capitalism in the web of life*. Verso.

Morton, T. (2017). *Humankind: Solidarity with nonhuman people*. Verso.

Ng-A-Fook, N. (2014). Provoking the very "idea" of curriculum studies as counterpoised composition. *Journal of the Canadian Association for Curriculum Studies, 12*(1), 10–16. DOI: https://doi.org/10.25071/1916-4467.37169

Peperzak, A. T. (Ed.) (1995). *Ethics as first philosophy: The significance of Emmanuel Levinas for philosophy, literature and religion*. Routledge.

Pinar, W. F. (1975). *The method of "currere". Autobiography, politics, and sexuality: Essays in curriculum theory*. Peter Lang.

– (2011). *The character of curriculum studies: Bildung, currere, and the recurring question of the subject*. Palgrave MacMillan.

– (2015). *Educational experience as lived: Knowledge, history, alterity: The selected works of W. F. Pinar*. Routledge, Taylor & Francis.

– (2019). *What is curriculum theory* (3rd ed.). Routledge, Taylor and Francis.

Pinar, W. F. & Grumet, M. R. (1976). *Toward a poor curriculum*. Kendall/Hunt.

Rose, D.V., Van Dooren, T., & Chrulew, M. (Eds). (2017). *Extinction studies: Stories of time, death, and generations*. Columbia University Press.

Salcel, R. (2020). *A passion for ignorance: What we choose not to know and why*. Princeton University Press.

Scarry, E. (1985). *The body in pain: The making and unmaking of the world*. Oxford University Press.

Schneiderman, J. (2013). Ground truth: Investigations of Earth simultaneously spiritual and scientific. In J. Lin, R. L. Oxford, & E. J. Brantmeier (Eds.), *Re-envisioning higher education: Embodied pathways to wisdom and social transformation* (pp. 249–64). Information Age Publishing.

Sheikh, P. A. (2005). The impact of hurricane Katrina on biological resources. *CRS Report for Congress*. Congressional Research Service: The Library of Congress.

Simon, R. I. and Armitage-Simon, W. (1995). Teaching risky stories: Remembering mass destruction through children's literature. *The English Quarterly, 28*(1), 27–31.

Simon, R. I. & Eppert, C. (1997). Remembering obligation: Pedagogy and the witnessing of testimony of historical trauma. *Canadian Journal of Education/Revue canadienne de l'éducation, 22*(2), 175–91. https://doi.org/10.2307/1585906

Simon, R. I., Rosenberg, S., & Eppert, C. (2000). Introduction: The pedagogical encounter of historical remembrance. In R. Simon, S. Rosenberg, & C. Eppert (Eds.), *Between hope and despair: Pedagogy and the remembrance of historical trauma* (pp. 1–8). Rowman and Littlefield.

Simon, R. I., Eppert, C., Clamen, M., & Beres, L. (2001). Witness as study: The difficult inheritance of testimony. *The Review of Education/Pedagogy/Cultural Studies, 22*(4), 285–322. https://doi.org/10.1080/1071441000220402

Terdiman, R. (2000). The subject of the other: From alterity to heterology. *Comparative Literature: East & West*, *2*(1), 27–47. https://doi.org/10.1080/25723618.2000.12015280

The IUCN Red List of Threatened Species (2022). *Background and history.* http://iucnredlist.org

Tsing, A. L. (2015). *The mushroom at the end of the world: On the possibility of life in capitalist ruins.* Princeton University Press.

Tsuchiya, Y. (1997). *Faithful elephants: A true story of animals, people, and war.* Clarion Books.

Weil, S. (1947). *Gravity and grace* (E. Craufurd, Trans.). Routledge.

Wolfe, C. (2017). Foreword. In D.B. Rose, T. van Dooren, and M. Chrulew (Eds.), *Extinction studies: Stories of time, death, and generations.* Columbia University Press.

World Wildlife Fund. (2020). Living planet report Canada: Wildlife at risk. Currie, J., Snider, J., Giles, E., World Wildlife Fund Canada. Toronto, Canada. https://wwf.ca.

Wright, A. & Peck III, M. (1992). *Will we miss them? Endangered species.* Charlesbridge.

6 From Goose Feather Pen to Keyboard: Does the School Form Still Have Its Relevance in the Contemporary World?

CLERMONT GAUTHIER

Introduction

This text highlights a particular theme that has preoccupied me for a long time, namely the school form. This could be summarily defined as a sensitive and symbolic configuration of the relationship between the teacher and students at school, relations that not only concern the curriculum, but also go beyond. We'll see about it later.

It is not a question of presenting here the results of empirical research in the usual sense of scholarly colloquia, but rather of conducting a reflection on the future of the school, a reflection that I will articulate around the following question: Does the school form still have its relevance in the contemporary world?

Why this question? Because the development of digital technologies today challenges the school more than ever before. As an illustration, in her recent report to the minister of National Education entitled *Repenser la forme scolaire à l'heure du numérique* [Rethinking School Form in the Digital Age], Ms. Becchetti-Bizot, Inspector General of National Education in France, pointed out that

> Much more than the introduction of digital tools and how to use them in the classroom, the ambition from the outset has been to **comprehensively rethink the school form** – e.g., the ways of teaching and learning, the organization and layout of learning spaces and times, teaching content and resources, the methods of monitoring and piloting evaluation, teacher training and the relationship of the school to its environment and to the actors of education, and in particular to parents. (2017, p. 10)

Digital technology would now, it seems, have this phenomenal power to change, or even dismantle, the school form. It is this project that we intend to analyse.

In order to do this, we will first define the concept of school form according to three characteristics: (1) the shaping of knowledge; (2) the transmission of knowledge; (3) the organization that supports this shaping and transmission. Next, we will see how in the twentieth century the new pedagogy was formed as an attempt to overthrow the school form. Three utopias will then serve us as benchmarks to reveal directions of the new pedagogy: Thoreau's *Walden or Life in the Woods*, Illich's *Une société sans école* [Deschooling Society], and finally, Michel Serres's *Petite Poucette*. In the present case, the idea of utopia is to demonstrate something, to make it exist by words and, therefore, to help us to elaborate our argument. Third, we will examine what the future of the school form could be, and this from two considerations: first, that which could be called *adamist utopia* and then, that of the dematerialization of the school form through expert systems of which Skinner's *Walden II* (1948) was a kind of utopian foreshadowing.

The Concept of School Form

The concept of "school form" was introduced almost 40 years ago by sociologist Guy Vincent in his book *L'école primaire française* [The French elementary school]. According to him, the school form appears throughout the Western world, between the sixteenth and eighteenth centuries. He expresses it very well in the following excerpt:

> Unlike this ancient mode by hearsay, seeing doing and doing with, the school form of transmission of knowledge and know-how, put the emphasis on the written form, leads to the separation of the "schoolboy" from the adult life, as well as the knowledge from doing.
>
> Furthermore, it requires submission to rules and to a specific discipline that replaces the old personal relationship tinged with affectivity, which therefore creates a new social relationship. The child can no longer wander the streets; he is subject to the order that characterizes the classic city and is "locked" in the walls of the school, a place apart from his own place. He must move in a row, has a strict schedule and must obey the rules displayed on the walls of the class, the first of which is the rule of silence.
>
> The teacher must limit himself to play the role of monitoring, directing the reading and exercises done with books, applying without anger the penalties carefully provided for in the regulations for each offense. (Vincent, 2008, p. 49)

Why would the school form have appeared at that time? It is linked, according to the author, to the establishment of a new urban order. This generally

6.1. Adriaen van Ostade, (1610–85). *The School Master,* 1662.

corresponds to a hypothesis that we formulated several years ago, which states that pedagogy appeared due to the increase in the number of students attending the class and that forced the teachers of the seventeenth century to radically change their way of teaching the class (Gauthier, 1993). This is a hypothesis that I would describe as "quantitative" to explain the genesis of the school form. Indeed, at this time in urban areas the number of students was becoming more and more significant. Four factors can explain this phenomenon: the Protestant Reformation, the Catholic Counter-Reformation, the new negative vision of childhood (Ariès, 1960), and the problems of delinquency in the cities. The combined effect of these factors led to an increase in students attending school and to the establishment of schools. This will force the teacher to otherwise organize his class and its functioning. Due to larger

6.2. Jean-Baptiste de la Salle, (1651–1719). *Showing a Classroom.* (Undated work).

numbers of students, he will no longer be able to teach in the "individualized" mode modelled on the preceptorship. Neither will he be able to teach in an improvised way in the most complete disorder, as illustrated by Van Ostade's famous painting below (figure 6.1).

He will have to radically change his way of doing things, so that he can better control what is happening in his workspace, that is, his class. The Brothers of the Christian schools are the example par excellence, as shown in figure 6.2.

They formalized, that is, they gave form to what was until then improvised, more or less organized, unstructured, and not yet institutionalized. From the informal, from the lack of form, we went to the formalized: we introduced a boundary, a separation from the confusion. Ordering, in the sense of putting in order, is the active principle of this pedagogical transformation. In his masterful study, *Discipline and Punish*, Foucault (1975) spoke of the same system that affected prisons, hospitals, armies, factories, and schools, namely, that of transforming confused multitudes into ordered multiplicities (p. 172). It is a question of organizing the multiple, of giving oneself an instrument to go through it and master it. It is a question of imposing an "order" on it.

With regard to the school, three types of formalization of confused multitudes are deployed: those that concern (a) knowledge, (b) its transmission, and (c) the organization of the classroom environment so that transmission can take place. Let's look at them one by one.

Shaping Knowledge

As Vincent and his collaborators (1994) point out, "the invention of the school form is accomplished in the production of school disciplines" (p. 17). It is the constitution of the fields of school knowledge, strictly speaking. For example, religion is not studied in the Bible, but rather in the catechism, which now becomes the scholarly knowledge of religion. Similarly, civilities are considered the school knowledge of obedience to rules (work in silence, take ranks, raise the hand before asking a question, and the like). The same applies to the formatting of syllabaries – tables for reading, writing, arithmetic, and so on. In addition, each field of knowledge is divided by degrees; for example, among the Brothers of the Christian schools there are nine orders (levels) in reading, six in writing, six in arithmetic.

The Shaping of the Transmission

To the shaping of the knowledge to be taught corresponds the codification of the method of teaching this knowledge. This is how knowledge and its transmission are recorded in writings: "a pedagogy of drawing, music, physical activity is not done without a writing of drawing, a musical writing [...]" (Vincent, 2008, p. 31). These writings are, so to speak, the first treatises of pedagogy that abound in detail on how to teach these school knowledges.

More generally, there is also a shift from *individual* to *simultaneous teaching*. Having more students in urban classrooms prevents the practice of the most commonly used form of teaching until now, singular pedagogy (see figure 6.1). Simultaneous teaching now allows the teacher to address all students at the same time and makes it possible for them to do the same exercises at the same time (see figure 6.2). The invention of the printing press made this pedagogical transformation possible.

The Formatting of the Class Organization

Larger numbers of students require, in addition to shaping knowledge and its transmission, shaping the organization of the classroom. It refers to several dimensions: space, time, student behaviour, and even the teacher.

For example, it is recommended that the school be located in a rather quiet *space*, set back, cut off from the world. Windows placed in height out of the reach of the students' eyes are also valued so that they are not tempted to constantly look at what is happening on the street. In addition, the space of the class is the subject of a very precise formalization: it is methodically gridded. Student places are thus meticulously determined: places for the poor, places allocated according to the level of progress of the students, places related to succeeding or failing academically (the bench of infamy), and so on.

Similarly, educators of old felt the obligation to fill time. Idleness being the mother of all vices, as the saying goes, there will be no downtime in the classroom. There is a real obsession with filling time: from morning to night, from arrival to exit, students will be constantly busy.

Additionally, the behaviour of students is controlled in terms of body, movement, and conduct. The body is now subject to a code of postures: posture for prayer, posture for sitting, posture for standing, posture for holding a goose feather, posture for writing. Also, the movement of students must be done in an orderly manner; that is why the ranks were instituted. Finally, rewards and punishments were formalized. The old process of the impulsive teacher who unceremoniously strikes his pupils or embraces them has been replaced by that of a graduated scale of punishments and rewards administered by a serious master, who intervenes in full control of his emotions. Finally, we must not forget that the master himself is also part of this system of subjugation characterized by obedience to impersonal rules (Vincent, 2008), an anonymous control system in which one no longer obeys a specific person, but rather rules which are imposed on students as well as teachers, in all schools or colleges in the community (Lahire, 2008). From Vincent's point of view, it is precisely on this aspect that we find the principle of intelligibility of the school form. We'll get back to it.

This school form continues over the centuries. It undergoes relatively significant transformations: from the simultaneous mode in the seventeenth century, then the mutual mode in the nineteenth, then to mass education which explodes in the twentieth century under the effect of the school laws prescribing compulsory school. But its profound nature will be little changed.

One may think that this transformation of the confused multitudes into ordered multiplicities has been, in short, of formidable efficacy over time since it has succeeded in educating the masses – which is not negligible, it must be agreed.

New Pedagogy as an Attempt to Overthrow the School Form

With the advent of new pedagogy, the entire twentieth century will become a vast attempt to overthrow the school form or what might be called the pedagogical tradition. The dominant argument most often used is the following: the traditional school is separated from life, so it is necessary to unify this space and abolish this border that isolates the school from life.

Let us examine this attempt to overthrow the school form through three scenarios that express this desire well: *Walden or Life in the Woods* of Thoreau, *Une société sans école* [Deschooling Society] of Illich, and finally, *Petite Poucette* of Michel Serres.

A First Case

Thoreau's *Walden or Life in the Woods* (1854/1990) is in a way the archetype of new pedagogy:

> If I wanted a boy to know something about the arts and sciences, for example, I would not follow the ordinary walk, which is simply to send him to the neighborhood of some teacher, where everything is professed and practiced, except the art of life. (1854/1990, p. 17)

A flagship book of American literature, *Walden* remains one of the reference books of libertarian thought of the '60s. The *Beat Generation*, Jack Kerouac, the hippie movement, May '68 have found in it a source of inspiration. In fact, this is a kind of revival of *Émile*, Rousseau's famous utopia: "living is the job I want to teach him" (1762/1951, p. 12).

This attempt to overturn traditional pedagogy pursues the project of establishing a different foundation for teaching; that is, in the very extension of the natural learning of life – that which Geary (2005) calls primary learning – children learn a little bit randomly from the events of life during the evolution such as that involved in learning of speech or walking. As Dewey (1976) pointed out: "What can be done to break down the barriers which have unfortunately come to separate the school life from the rest of everyday life of the child" (p. 59)? In this sense, this author tells us: "learning to read, write, draw when the need arises, quite naturally, as he (student) learned to speak when he had something to ask or say" (Snyders, 1971, p. 72).

A Second Case

Decades later, with Illich (1970/1971) and his famous book *Une société sans école* [Deschooling Society], launched in the heart of the bubbling '70s, we still observe the same project of removing the separation between school and life. In it he presents a radical critique of the school system. For Illich, compulsory school is an obstacle to education and instruction.

Where have we learned most of the things we know, he wonders? Outside school: "It is out of school, or outside, that everyone learns to live, learns to speak, to think, to love, to feel, to play, to swear, to manage, to work" (Illich, 1970/1971, p. 57). That is why the school must, according to him, reconnect with life: "In the classroom, children are kept away from the everyday reality of Western culture" (1970/1971, p. 62).

For Illich, a society without school would need certain types of resources that would be made available and accessible to all. For example, all objects of knowledge (libraries, museums, factories, airports, farms, everyday objects, etc.) should be made available to the public. There should also be a knowledge exchange service – for example, in lists of people offering their skills to others. An organization should also be set up to facilitate meetings and exchanges, networking and matching of equal peers who have the same knowledge needs.

A Third Case

Then in the twenty-first century we encounter *Petite Poucette* by Michel Serres (2012). In the interval between the 1970s and now, a new human was born, solemnly declares the philosopher Michel Serres. He (this new human) no longer has the same head or inhabits the same space, he says (p. 15). Serres asks three fundamental questions: First, what content to pass on? Second, to whom to pass it on? Third, how to transmit it?

To these questions he answers as follow: What to transmit? Knowledge is already there, everywhere on the web. To whom to pass it on? Knowledge is already accessible to all. How to transmit it? Access to knowledge is open, distributed. "Now distributed everywhere, knowledge spreads in a homogeneous, decentralized space, free of movement. The old [classroom] is dead" (Serres, 2012, p. 42), he says.

In the same sense, and as we saw in our brief introduction, the idea of uniting school and life is therefore still very much present today, this time with the internet and IT: "The school can no longer remain a sanctuary away from the world" (Becchetti-Bizot, 2017, p. 4).

The Future of School Form

Adamist Utopia

In the first case, resulting from the extension of the ideas of Rousseau, Thoreau, and Dewey, opening the school on life implies subordinating education to life. In fact, it amounts to trusting the chance of life, according to encounters, but in the end, it is giving decisive weight to the privileged, to those who are well born, to the "happy few" already filled by life who can replace without too many problems the shortcomings of bad luck. At the same time, it also amounts to letting the multitudes, those with a less "naturally" endowed life, fend for themselves, not to say leave them *confused*.

The Illichian Utopia Accomplished by Technology with Petite Poucette

Furthermore – we saw it briefly with *Petite Poucette* – technology can actually, in many ways, replace the teacher in the sense proposed by the utopia of Illich. Indeed, (1) knowledge is everywhere on the internet; (2) its transmission can be done by networking through collaboration between students; and (3) the organization of transmission can be realized remotely and in an open time – synchronous or a-synchronous.

However, this technological relay not only opens up a possibility; it also frames, it gives a form; it "formats" – to use a contemporary term. This relay formats (1) *knowledge*. Indeed, search engines are not neutral, they are programed by algorithms. One has access to databases with keywords, and sponsors pay to be spotted first by search engines. In addition, this relay formats (2) the *transmission*. For example, the PowerPoint tool compels the content to be expressed in a certain way, it offers great potential, but organizes the transmission. Finally, this relay formats (3) *the organization of the transmission* in the sense that, for example, in distance training (FAD), a-synchronous or synchronous, it is necessary to obey the pre-established exchange system conditioned by the options of a menu.

It is a fourth utopia, Skinner's *Walden II* (1948), that serves as a revelation for this problematic in the posture of Illich and Serres. In his book, Skinner's idea is precisely to eliminate the political reference and to establish the government of the expert, not to say the robot!

By bringing together the three utopias *Walden II, Une société sans école* [Deschooling Society] and *Petite Poucette*, we see that, in the abolition of the boundaries between school and life, it is now the expert system that will take over and organize human relations through technology.

If we follow the logic of Vincent (1980), creator of the concept of school form, indicating that it is understood from the system of subjugation that it puts in place and, particularly, from obedience to impersonal rules, then far from disappearing with the digital, we can think that the school form will unfold even more in the reign of digital. And in the continuation of the utopias of *Une société sans école* [Deschooling Society], *Petite Poucette*, and *Walden II*, this obedience to impersonal rules also becomes a subjection to rules of operation that are more and more ubiquitous, but also more and more imperceptible. Perhaps, in the end, we are witnessing the completion of the transition from a disciplinary society to a control society as Foucault (1975) and Deleuze (1990) so aptly pointed out. The control societies are replacing the disciplinary societies (Deleuze, 1990, p. 242). Even now, the control is going further with the emergence of algorithmic societies with the Big Data (Paquette, 2018).

In Conclusion

Our thesis is threefold.

1. First, in the wake of the first Rousseauist utopia, to unite school and life is to make the school disappear for the benefit of life and, in this case, it will be the privileged class – whose life is itself more endowed than the school – which will undoubtedly have the means to overcome the inadequacies of life and benefit fully from this Adamism.
2. Second, in the wake of the utopias of *Une société sans école* [Deschooling Society], *Petite Poucette*, and *Walden II*, the school form does not necessarily disappear with technologies. On the contrary, it flourishes more. Indeed, the change of the school form exists in its disappearance only in appearance from the sensitive field, all becoming ubiquitous but imperceptible as a mechanism through the new modes of control made possible by technology.
3. But something, or especially someone, may have really disappeared in these two utopian processes, and this is the *teacher*.

Indeed, the project to unite school and life either leads directly to the end of the school form, in which case the master is replaced by life that is transmuted by teaching, or, paradoxically, to a school form driven by the digital in a robotic spiral where the master is no longer considered really necessary. In this second case, by situating the principle of generation – that is, intelligibility – of the school form in this relation to impersonal rules, Vincent (2008) gives an exaggerated importance, in our opinion, to this *impersonal* dimension, as if the teacher were a puppet at the very beginning of the constitution of the school form.

But now, the teacher is absolutely present; he is indeed there from the beginning and he has always been, as is clearly seen, for example, in the writings of the *Conduct of Christian Schools* in the seventeenth century. We even see him in these old texts enunciate his suffering in the face of difficulties in exercising his profession. It is even better seen in Brother Agathon's 1834 book, *Les douze vertus d'un bon maître* [The twelve virtues of a good teacher], who, beyond the impersonal method imposed by his community, seeks the way to intervene with finesse with the students. There is a "neither too much nor too little" in his prescriptions everywhere in his book. The *right* moment, the *necessary* intensity, the *appropriate* gesture, the *right* speech, the *reasonable* action, the *sufficient* proximity or distance, the *appropriate* firmness or flexibility do not refer to statistical averages or coded gestures. These terms rather express the singular, central, and fundamental place that the teacher's pedagogical tact occupies (Gauthier, 2019).

In fact, the teacher, encountering difficulties in exercising his profession due to the number of students, is led to look for a way to take control before the disorder settles in his classroom. It is rather, in my opinion, this need for teachers to ensure an organized functioning, to ensure order, which is the driving principle of the school form and not the relation to impersonal rules as Vincent suggests. The relationship to impersonal rules seems to us only one element among a set of strategies deployed to turn these confused multitudes of students into ordered multiplicities (Foucault, 1975, p. 174).

It is undoubtedly this presence of the teacher that ensured the American school would not, according to Cuban (2013), really change between 1880 and 1990. Indeed, he points out, for more than a century in the United States the many pedagogical innovations have not changed the fundamental portrait of the school. True, new has been added to the old, but without fundamentally transforming the school form. The school has somehow digested innovations (Durampart, 2016) through a mechanism that Cuban (2013) calls "dynamic conservatism." The teacher is undoubtedly part of this process of dynamic conservatism because in his class he takes some and then leaves some. Certainly, he can integrate what suits him in his operation, but he does not hesitate to not use what risks becoming a pellet in the execution of his work.

For the teacher, *order* is fundamental to being able to practise his profession with an increasing number of students. This is why it was necessary to establish and maintain a separation, a fence, a boundary, a delimitation of space, between school and life: to ensure this transformation of confused multitudes into ordered multiplicities.

Why is this *order* so fundamental, and why does it imply that the space between school and life must be kept separate? If school was life, it would not need to exist; this is what the first utopia reveals. But school doesn't have to be life. It is simply the conscious and articulated recovery of life. The knowledge presented at school simply allows students to understand life; it doesn't have to be life. For its part, the digital age does not lead to the disappearance of the school form; on the contrary, it can lead it to its most absolute fulfillment, and to a stern degree. Indeed, the ways in which mutual teaching works (one teacher for 1,000 students!) are, for example, only a pale foretaste of the modes of control exercised by the digital spectrum: *impersonal, imperceptible,* and *omnipresent* control.

Knowledge may be there, everywhere. Its networking simplified, it nevertheless requires someone to select it, interpret it to someone else, make it relevant, criticize it, and organize the conduct of actors to function in the real space – or at a distance from the class – for instruction and education to happen in a collective of students. This task is first and foremost the fundamental work of the teacher in relation to his students. Heir, critic, and cultural interpreter, this is precisely where his fundamental role lies. In failing to maintain the essential place of the teacher, and therefore of the school form that is essential to him, *either the multitudes will remain confused or they will be duped!*

Epilogue: What Does the Pandemic Tell Us about the School Form?

Since March 2020, the pandemic has turned the school world upside down, from kindergarten to university. The vast majority of countries have closed their schools, either totally or partially, in long or short waves, because of the dangers posed by COVID-19. According to UNESCO, nearly two billion students and approximately 60 million teachers have been directly affected by this measure, which is unique in its scope in the modern history of education (Borges and Tardif, 2020).

As a result, the pandemic has forced states to put forward several alternatives to face-to-face teaching, such as remote learning for several days or weeks using various synchronous tools (TEAMS, ZOOM, Google Meet, Google Classroom, etc.) or asynchronous activities.

There are obviously many different scenarios, but one thing is clear: technology has spread rapidly to a level never before seen in the school world. Moreover, it has also given rise to strong hopes among some distance education proponents that it will completely transform the current conventional education system.[1] Are we witnessing, as we pointed out in the introduction, the emergence of a new form of schooling like the one desired by Mrs. Becchetti-Bizot, the general inspector of French national education?

In our opinion, this is far from certain. Let us briefly examine some aspects of the question.

1. First, let us ask what was the impact of virtual schools on learning before the pandemic?

   In this regard, Bissonnette and Boyer (2021) reviewed several studies on the impact of distance learning on student performance in virtual schools. In particular, they mention the work of Ahn and McEachin (2017) who found negative effects of virtual schools on learning in elementary and secondary mathematics and reading. In a nutshell, their results show that in virtual schools both weak and strong students became even weaker!

   Bueno (2020) analysed the performance of over 100,000 students attending virtual schools in Georgia between 2007 and 2020. He found that attending a full-time virtual school resulted in statistically significant declines in performance in English, science, and social studies among elementary and middle school students. This phenomenon even lowered the likelihood of graduating from high school.

Finally, in their review of research on the effectiveness of virtual learning in elementary and secondary schools, Prettyman and Sass (2020) are led to the conclusion that in overall terms, the results of virtual learning in comparison to face-to-face learning hold little promise. Schools that operate totally online, as a rule, present gains in learning clearly below those of physical schools.

2. Next, let us ask what the measured impacts have been of technology usage during the pandemic in schools.

   In this regard, Bissonnette and Boyer (2021) report that they identified 19 studies on the effects of seclusion and virtual teaching on the academic progress of primary and secondary students in different countries (UK, Australia, Belgium, USA, France, and the Netherlands). They found a trend towards negative results for reading but with a greater negative impact on mathematics among students who received distance learning classes during the first confinement, especially in primary schooling. It was estimated in June 2021 that the learning delay among students was between five and nine months. This is enormous, to say the least. To the credit of the education systems, they were certainly caught off guard and reacted in a hurry to this unprecedented phenomenon, but that is not enough to be satisfied with the near-zero impact of virtual education in the context of confined environment.
3. In fact, let's try to highlight what this experience of teaching in virtual mode reveals precisely with regard to the question of the school form.

First of all, the pandemic has also made it possible to see that school is a formidable place of socialization for young people. Face-to-face school brings something that the virtual cannot replace: the direct contact of students with their friends at school, the pleasure of being with them, of playing, of exchanging, of doing activities together. The school seems to have been greatly missed by young people, and this from the kindergarten to the university. The virtual has been at best a poultice in times of crisis, but has not proved to be a real remedy that would have allowed young people to live their youth while learning and educating themselves normally.

Moreover, from the point of view of the teacher, as we know, teaching is a job of relationship. The teacher enters into a relationship with his or her students both to make them learn given cultural content, but also to educate them in the sense of instilling in them values that are essential for functioning in society. It is through direct, repeated, and prolonged contact with his students that the teacher can fully interact with them. From a distance, they obviously lose much of their ability to do so. Anyone who uses TEAM, ZOOM, or other platforms in their teaching is constantly frustrated by the frozen faces of their audience, if not by the sight of avatars! The teacher cannot check at a glance, as he or she normally does in the classroom, how well his or her students are listening and engaging in the task. Just as the student needs his friends, the teacher needs the proximity of a face-to-face audience in order to do his job fully and with satisfaction.

It is also important to mention that it is not the role of parents to do school. During the pandemic, many of them had to take time off work to adequately support their children. In the context of synchronous virtual school, it is practically impossible for them to reconcile their professional life with virtual school, especially with young children in primary school (Carignan and Rodriguez, 2021). This reconciliation is even more difficult when the virtual school adopts a schedule that is similar or almost similar to the face-to-face one. In this case, the virtual school is transformed into a home school, a training modality that is not chosen by the parents and for which they are, for the most part, not competent. In addition to the elements of the curriculum, they also need to learn the basics of the software and applications used in the classroom. Like most teachers who have received no training – or at best minimal and emergency training with several tools – they found themselves, with only a few days notice, having to deal with the emergency of the teaching situation with all the technical and logistical challenges that entails (connection problems, inaudible microphones, freezing of the images, difficulty in using the software proficiently in real time, switching from one application to another, etc.).

On 25 March 2021, Radio-Canada published an article entitled "Ontario could make online courses a permanent option," referring to Ontario Premier Doug Ford's desire to make this second learning system permanent – to which parents and teachers' unions resolutely responded: No thanks! (Carignan and Bissonnette, 2021). These disturbing signals from the Ford government confirmed this desire to shift the focus, including some of the funding, from face-to-face public education to distance education modalities.

Ultimately, it must be recognized that bringing school closer to life is an old idea that is still very relevant. In this respect, the pandemic will have played a revealing role, but in a different sense from that of our utopians described earlier. It will have revealed the necessity of the face-to-face relationship in the sense that the mass school cannot be cut off from the world, from its world in flesh and blood. It is true that we can even use technological tools that are part of life (telephones, tablets, computers), but this does not mean that the school (for example, the school form) will have to change its nature fundamentally and that it will become virtual. Some, like Dubet (2021), assert that a return to the identical after the pandemic, that is, to the old world, will probably no longer be possible. Nothing is less certain in our opinion. The virtual school cannot become a long-term solution, neither for the students and their parents, nor for the teachers, nor for society. Even in higher education, young adults need their peers. What the pandemic will have revealed in the context of mass education as we have been living it for a century is that online education has been only an emergency solution allowing teachers and classmates to maintain some contact with the school. It is a solution whose positive impact on learning is unfortunately diluted and fortunately can only be temporary. On the contrary, what is fundamental in the school form is its capacity to instruct and educate a mass of students. To do this, the face-to-face meeting between the teacher and his or her students is still essential.

In conclusion, I would like to paraphrase the words of a journalist I was reading this morning (Côté, November 2, 2021): real life, true life, bodily life, life with its rough edges, its smells and its curves, the life of the human condition since the dawn of time, will seem increasingly bland to the techno-lovers. They will judge it archaic, but this need to meet the other, face to face, is the essence of the school form and is absolutely necessary to a quality mass education.

NOTE

1 This is also what high-tech companies are eager to do, as seen in a recent advertisement posted in the magazine University *Affairs*, November–December 2021: Education is changing. Are you ready? You don't need lecture halls or campuses for collaboration. With Cisco's video conferencing and security solutions, securely enable teaching and learning anywhere and at any time while protecting your institution with a secure foundation for distance learning. Chat, polling, Q&A, secure file sharing, and digital whiteboarding. The possibilities are endless. (p. 9)

REFERENCES

Agathon, (Frère). (1834). *Les Douze vertus d'un bon maître, par M. de La Salle, instituteur des Frères des écoles chrétiennes; expliquées par le Frère Agathon, Supérieur-Général*. Séguin Aîné, Imprimeur-Libraire.

Ahn, J., & McEachin, A. (2017). Student enrollment patterns and achievement in Ohio's online charter schools. *Educational Researcher*, *46*(1), 44–57. https://journals.sagepub.com/doi/full/10.3102/0013189X17692999

Ariès, P. (1960). *L'enfant et la vie familiale sous l'ancien régime*. Seuil.

Beccheti-Bizot, C. (2017). *Repenser la forme scolaire à l'ère du numérique. Vers de nouvelles manières d'apprendre et d'enseigner. Rapport à monsieur le ministre de l'éducation nationale*. Inspection générale de l'éducation nationale. https://www.education.gouv.fr/repenser-la-forme-scolaire-l-heure-du-numerique-vers-de-nouvelles-manieres-d-apprendre-et-d-2678.

Bissonnette, S. & Boyer, C. (2021). The effects of remote learning on the progress of students before and during the pandemic. Iniciativa Educação. https://www

.iniciativaeducacao.org/en/ed-on/ed-on-articles/the-effects-of-remote-learning-on-the-progress-of-students-before-and-during-the-pandemic.

Borges, C. & Tardif, M. (2020). Introduction au dossier - Faire école en contexte de pandémie. *Formation et profession*, *28*(4), 1–2. http://dx.doi.org/10.18162/fp.2020.684

Bueno, C. (2020). *Bricks and mortar vs. computers and modems: The impacts of enrollment in K-12 virtual schools*. (EdWorkingPaper: 20–250). Annenberg Institute at Brown University. https://doi.org/10.26300/kahb-5v62.

Carignan, I., & Bissonnette, S. (2021). *Faire des cours en ligne une option permanente pour les élèves? Jamais de la vie*. La voix du Nord. https://www.lavoixdunord.ca/actualites/education/faire-des-cours-en-ligne-une-option-permanente-pour-les-eleves-jamais-de-la-vie-a6ad4be601ef8c51d876fc9aa6a6d10f?sourceOrganizationKey=le-voyageur

Carignan, I., & Rodriguez, J. (2021). L'école virtuelle: donner une voix aux parents ... et aux parents-enseignants. *Journal Le Voyageur*. https://tinyurl.com/4fz56w9x

Côté, M.-B. (2021). Un monde parallèle, l'enfer sur terre. *Le Journal de Québec*. https://www.journaldequebec.com/2021/11/02/un-monde-parallele-lenfer-sur-terre.

Cuban, L. (2013). *Inside the black box of classroom practice. Change without reform in American education*. Harvard Education Press.

Deleuze, G. (1990). *Pourparlers*, Minuit.

Dewey, J. (1976). *The school and society*. University of Chicago Press. (Original work published 1900)

Dubet, F. (2021). La pandémie a-t-elle changé l'école? *Sciences Humaines, 341*, 28–30. https://doi.org/10.3917/sh.341.0003

Durampart, M. (2016). La forme scolaire en action traversée par l'école numérique. *Revue française des sciences de l'information et de la communication*, No. 9. http://journals.openedition.org/rfsic/2492

Foucault, M. (1975). *Surveiller et punir. Naissance de la prison*. Gallimard

Gauthier, C. (1993). *Tranches de savoir: l'insoutenable légèreté de la pédagogie*. Logiques.

– (2019). Le tact pédagogique. *Formation et profession*, *27*(3), 121–4. http://dx.doi.org/10.18162/fp.2019.a187.

Geary, D. C. (2005). *The origin of mind: Evolution of brain, cognition, and general intelligence*. American Psychological Association.

Illich, I. (1971). *Une société sans école* [Deschooling Society]. Seuil. (Original work published 1970)

Lahire, B. (2008). The individual and the mixing of genres: Cultural dissonance and self-distinction. *Poetics* 36 (2–3), 166–88. https://doi.org/10.1016/j.poetic.2008.02.001

Paquette, J. (2018). De la société disciplinaire à la société algorithmique: considérations éthiques autour de l'enjeu du Big data. *French Journal for Media Research*. http://frenchjournalformediaresearch.com/lodel-1.0/main/index.php?id=1439.

Prettyman, A., & Sass, T. R. (2020). *The efficacy of virtual instruction in K-12 education: A review of the literature*. Georgia Policy Labs, Metro Atlanta Policy Lab for Education.

https://gpl.gsu.edu/download/virtual-learning-in-k-12-education-literature-review/?wpdmdl=1952&refresh=603bfaae9bed31614543534.

Rousseau, J.-J. (1951). *Émile ou de l'éducation*. Garnier. (Original work published 1762)

Serres, M. (2012). *Petite poucette*. Le pommier.

Skinner, B. F. (1948). *Walden Two*. Hackett.

Snyders, G. (1971). *Pédagogie progressiste*. Presses universitaires de France.

Thoreau, H. D. (1990). Walden, ou la vie dans les bois [Walden or Life in the Woods]. Gallimard. (Original work published 1854)

Vincent, G. (1980). *L'école primaire française. Étude sociologique*. Presses universitaires de Lyon.

– (2008). La socialisation démocratique contre la forme scolaire. *Éducation et francophonie*, *36*(2), 47–62. https://doi.org/10.7202/029479ar

Vincent, G., Lahire, B., & Thin, D. (1994). Sur l'histoire et la théorie de la forme scolaire. In G. Vincent (Ed.), *L'éducation prisonnière de la forme scolaire? Scolarisation et socialisation dans les sociétés industrielles* (pp. 11–48). Presses universitaires de Lyon. https://doi.org/10.4000/books.pul.9522.

7 The Curricular Landscapes of Sex Education: Curriculum-as-Checklist Meets the Queer Curriculum Practices of LGBTQ+ Youth

JEN GILBERT

Year after year, sex education returns to the news. The controversies, predictable and perennial, often centre on curriculum – what and when children should learn about sexuality and gender in school. Consider some recent examples from North America: parents protest when kindergarten students read books about gay families during circle time; conservative activists worry that if children learn about gender identity in grade 3 they will become confused about their own gender; or progressive advocates insist that affirming language about sexual orientation and gender identity in the sex education curriculum will make LGBTQ+ youth feel more welcome at school. These examples have, at their heart, an optimistic theory of curriculum – optimistic because both conservative and progressive parents and advocates have confidence that students learn what they believe the sex education curriculum teaches. Learning about gender identity can either cause confusion (according to conservative parents) or prevent bullying (according to progressive advocates).

I am on the progressive side of this conflict and believe that young people need access to information about their sexualities and genders. However, I am troubled when both progressive and conservative advocates reduce the curriculum to a knowledge delivery system: we concentrate on what to include and exclude, the timing of the delivery, and the most efficient platform for the delivery. Our concerns are largely instrumental – how can we get this information into these students? And yet, the instrumental concerns bump up against the volatile, capricious, and elusive nature of a sexuality not bound to categories or identities. The sex education curriculum may outline a comprehensive list of skills and knowledge we want young people to receive, but this unruly sexuality escapes our containment and skirts the edges of learning outcomes, glossaries of technical terms, and grade level expectations. Beneath and beside the dry language of official curricula and policy, sexuality disrupts adults' desire to shape the sexual and gender futures of children and youth – sexuality arrives too soon and too late, throwing our best laid curricular plans into disarray.

I have been interested in the relationship between sexuality and sex education curriculum for some time. My research spans several shifts in the curricular landscape – the move from a focus on disease and risk in the HIV/AIDS era of the late '80s and early '90s to the abstinence-only battles of the late '90s; from the inclusion of LGBTQ+ material in the 2000s to the rise of consent in the 2010s. Across these overlapping eras, sex education curriculum and policy attempts to foreclose questions of sexuality by proceeding as if we all know what we are talking about when we talk about sex. Even in the current expansion of sex education to include material on LGBTQ+ sexualities and genders as well as models of affirmative consent, questions of what sexuality is for, or where it comes from, or how it is implicated in violence and aggression, or how it ties us to – and estranges us from – each other, remain unexamined. In this chapter, I stay in these questions. I ask how the official, formal sex education defends against sexuality, holds it at bay, cordons it off into particular disciplinary boxes, or transforms it into a sanitized list of activities, feelings, and orientations. This is one version of Ted Aoki's (1993) description of "curriculum-as-plan" (p. 257) – or, as it might be called in sex education, "curriculum-as-checklist." Sex education, especially when structured through the defensive logics of controversy, risks becoming a prosaic, abstract list of knowledge, skills, and attitudes divorced from the contexts in which young people negotiate their sexual lives. Running alongside this checklist is something closer to Aoki's "lived curriculum" (p. 257) or what Janet Miller (1998) calls a "queer curriculum practice" (p. 301). This orientation allows us to notice encounters between the planned curriculum and the messy contexts in which that curriculum is lived. Aoki invokes "multiplicity" (p. 258) as a trope to capture the movement across different curriculum landscapes. Miller puts queerness at the centre of her theory of curriculum. Queerness, for Miller, is not synonymous with identity; instead, it registers uncertainty, disidentification, and implication to expose how curriculum produces the very subjects it wants to educate. Both Aoki and Miller open up space to consider how sexuality puts a version of sex education "curriculum-as-checklist" in jeopardy. In this chapter, I follow Aoki's lead and move across multiple curricular landscapes: from the dream of a plan that could hold sexuality in its proper place to the messy, queer realities that throw those plans into disarray; from the proliferation of lists and guidelines in sex ed policy to the contradictory narratives of LGBTQ+ youth experimenting with identity during a pandemic. I begin, though, with a story about teaching a novel.

Too Much and Not Enough; Too Soon and Too Late

A few years ago, I was teaching a course on the social foundations of education. I assigned the novel, *Another Brooklyn*, by Jacqueline Woodson (2017). Woodson is a well-known young adult author, and many students read the novel with that audience in mind. *Another Brooklyn* is both straightforward and wispy – four girls, best friends, grow up in Brooklyn and yearn for other places. Like so many girls' lives, the novel includes scenes of sexual violence. During class, students raised the question of whether this novel would be appropriate for young people to read. The conversation was heated and went in two directions. One group got stuck on parsing out the exact age at which this novel could be introduced to young people, and particularly young women. Grade 8? Grade 9? Grade 11? Another group of racialized women students, responding to the strangely concrete nature of that conversation, insisted that if girls were not too young to be victims of sexual violence, then they were not too young to read about it. The whole discussion felt risky and exposed some of the contradictions that sex education curriculum glosses over. Young women's sexuality is understood as perpetually violable and in need of protection even from stories that might help them make sense of their violability; and meanwhile, in that discussion, all the teacher candidates in the room were having to imagine the conditions under which they would have conversations with young people about sexuality and violence. One woman disclosed that she would have appreciated this novel as a young person dealing with the aftermath of sexual violence, while another teacher candidate worried that asking students to read the novel would be itself a form of sexual violence.

I offer this rather circuitous account as a way of pointing to the contradictions that crowd the sex education curriculum. Like teaching *Another Brooklyn*, the sex education curriculum can both invite students to reflect on their sexual vulnerability and sometimes expose that vulnerability. The field of sex education has been shaped by these contradictions. Curriculum developers, educators, and researchers recognize the double bind sex education must operate within. The curriculum must offer to students and teachers a "plan" for discussing the range of issues that gather underneath the umbrella of "sex education" – puberty, sexually transmitted infections, reproductive and sexual health, gender and sexual identities, consent and sexual violence, healthy relationships, and so on. And yet, the plan to discuss these issues – including the order in which they should arrive, the manner in which they should be spoken of, the strategies for assessing students' learning – inevitably arouses complaints that it is both too much and not enough, too soon and too late.

Ted Aoki (1993), in his meditation on curriculum-as-plan, imagines a group of faceless bureaucrats, sitting in an office far from the lived realities of students, devising curricula that are organized around instrumental measures of student learning and littered with abstract concepts like objectives, aims, and goals. Aoki contrasts the curriculum-as-plan with the lived curriculum that emerges from the face-to-face encounters between teacher and students as they figure out how to live together in the space of the school. Aoki describes the difference as one of language: the "curriculum-as-plan" (p. 258) is written by "external curriculum planners, whose techni-scientific language of planning is the striated language of ends-means … this prosaic language is abstract, written for faceless people in a homogenous realm" (p. 261). In contrast, the language of lived curricula is "the more poetic, phenomenological, and hermeneutic discourse in which life is embodied in the very stories and languages people speak and live" (p. 261). With this contrast, Aoki tempts his reader to side, perhaps self-righteously, with the lived curriculum. Who wouldn't want to be on the side of the poetic? I too long for a poetic sex education curriculum that emerges from the embodied stories that young people bring to school. To illustrate, Aoki invokes Ms. O's classroom where Andrew is struggling to learn to read and Margaret is eager to help others and Tom stares out the window daydreaming. Ms. O responds to these and the other 20 unique students, "in-dwelling" (p. 261) with them and transforming the abstract language of curriculum plans into a responsive pedagogy. I can imagine an analogous classroom where Andrew, Margaret, and Tom each bring their struggles, eagerness, and daydreaming to their study of sexuality and gender.

But just as Aoki floats the promise of a lived curriculum, he insists on "multiplicity," a "cumbersome sounding word" (p. 259), he admits, that pushes the curriculum scholar and the teacher to the middle – we are in between the discourses of science and the novel, between plans and lived experience. It is a place the teacher candidates reading *Another Brooklyn* found themselves in. They were moved by the story of August, a Black girl, growing up under the watchful eye of her father, who finds freedom in her friendships with three other girls. They understood, I think, that the texture of the novel matches the texture of classroom life – filled with yearning, betrayals, curiosity, and risk. But they also felt responsible to the language of standards and age-appropriateness that form much of the plans for sex education. What should 13-year-old girls know about sexuality – both their own and others? What might be the outcome of reading a novel with frank discussions of sexuality and violence? The novel, with its retrospective structure and precocious girls, mocks the possibility of age appropriateness and refuses standardization. It was an uncomfortable place – the students were stuck in the middle, like Ms. O, caught between curriculum-as-plan and the lived curriculum. Part of becoming a teacher, and perhaps a sex educator, means learning to dwell in those middle spaces.

Checklists, Evidence, Health

Critical, qualitative sex education research is filled with stories of conflict between the official sex education curriculum and the complex and contradictory space of teaching and learning. For instance, in her ethnography of a sex educators' training program, Kaye Hare (2021b) supplied participants with a range of sex education texts and asked them to create "erasure poems" – a "form of found poetry composed by selectively eliminating or obscuring material components of a text (e.g., letters, punctuation, words, sentences, or paragraphs) to convey ideas, meanings, and feelings" (p. 418). From the dry, abstract language of policy documents, syllabi, and professional handbooks, participants rearranged words and phrases to express their experience of learning to become sex educators and thus responsible for the content of those texts. One poem created by Hare (2021b), "Institutionalized States of Information Abstinence," captures the "technical and officious" (p. 424) language of sex education – three pillars, each representing the tools, knowledge, and communication that make up official sex education, sit on a solid base and are topped by a pitched roof that gives the poem the shape of a pantheon. The pantheon enshrines and guards the "institutionalized states" (p. 415) of knowledge. Off to the side, in the lower right corner, a messy coda pulls together salvaged letters – "affirm bodies sex." The poem illustrates one of the major conflicts novice sex educators (and teacher candidates) navigate – they each had entered into their training because of deeply felt commitments to young people's sexuality but now, as beginning educators, they are bombarded with national guidelines, provincial curricula, and other educational and social policy (Hare, 2021a). The language of policy may have political and educational purchase and provide cover for sex educators to enter schools as "experts," but it nevertheless fails to capture the emotional experience of learning about sexuality.

This example maps the contested curricular landscape of sex education. The unique, lived experiences of sex educators animate the field, give it shape and texture; while the official curriculum – in the form of policy documents and guidelines – tries to make order out of the messy abundance. Sex education, and sex educators, ward off the possibility of controversy by constructing an armour of checklists, guidelines, and standards – weary attempts to solder the curriculum to the legitimizing discourses of health, science, and the law. A brief scan of sex education curricula and policies reveals a whole typology of lists that serve similar functions. *The Canadian Guidelines for Sexual Health Education* – handed to the novice sex educators on the first day of their training in Hare's study – are the gold standard for sex education across Canada. The guidelines are filled with lists – goals and objectives, key concepts, principles, a glossary in the appendix; even "A Checklist for Assessing Programs in Relation to the Philosophy of Sexual Health Education Reflected in the Guidelines" (Public Health Agency of Canada, 2008, p. 13), complete with checkboxes and a graphic image of a pencil. I have no doubt that the information contained in these guidelines is important and helps expand the national conversation on sex ed – the guidelines offer a resource for both policy makers and educators as they try to develop the most ambitious and comprehensive sex education programs their political and social contexts will allow. However, even the graphic layout of the checklist hints at the impossibility of this task. Armed with a pencil, the imagined reader can check off all the ways their ideal sex education curriculum complies with the philosophy reflected in the guidelines. The philosophy is founded on commitments I share – an acknowledgment of cultural diversity, a non-judgmental approach, and an understanding of sexuality across the life span, for instance. And yet, the checklist reduces those commitments to pro forma obligations; it does not invite the reader, or service provider, or educator to reflect on the relationship between sexuality and culture or the differences between sexuality in childhood and old age. Sex education-as-checklist, even the progressive version offered in the guidelines, demands compliance.

The checklists are part of an on-going history. Since the 1990s, sex education controversies have taken the form of a Sisyphean battle: conservative parents and activists protest against inclusive and expansive sex education (often called "comprehensive sex education," especially in the US) on moral and religious grounds; progressive advocates retort with empirical evidence that the inclusive sex education has important health benefits. The '90s fight was aimed at the inclusion of information about contraception and any tacit acceptance of sex outside of heterosexual, monogamous marriage (Irvine, 2004; Luker, 2007; Fields, 2008). Conservative parents and activists felt that if schools taught students how to use condoms, then schools were essentially inviting young people to have sex with each other. Since then, the debate has shifted towards the inclusion of lesbian, gay, bisexual, and transgender content (Greteman, 2018; Quinlivan, 2018; Gilbert, 2021). Conservative activists believe that affirming LGBTQ+ lives in the curriculum "promotes" the premature adoption of queer and trans identities. For instance, in the epic fight (2010–19) over the Ontario Health and Physical Education (HPE) curriculum, conservative groups seized on the inclusion of "gender identity" in a parenthetical list of "invisible differences" that were part of a set of expectations for grade 3. Conservative parents worried that the mention of gender identity in grade 3 could do harm to their children. As Janice Irvine (2004) chronicles, in sex education debates, talk about sex is itself sexual and potentially assaultive. This concrete theory of language imbues the HPE curriculum – even with its drab, lifeless descriptions of bodies – with enormous power. To talk about gender as potentially mutable has the potential to mutate children's bodies. In response, and caught within the paranoid logic of conservatives, progressive advocates must operate from a similar confidence in the power of curriculum. They counter the rhetoric of eight-year-olds being turned trans by a radical curriculum with a turn to empirical evidence, rooted in discourses of science, health, and rights. Marshalling studies and experts, progressive advocates seek to prove that an LGBTQ+-inclusive curriculum protects children from bullying by educating students into acceptance (Gilbert, 2021). To talk about gender identity – to include it on the checklist of topics to be covered – is to affirm the experiences of transgender children and educate cisgender children into tolerance.

This strategy dovetails with the rise of discourses of accountability and the audit culture in education (Taubman, 2010). Caught up in the rage for measurement, outcomes, and impact that affected the entire educational landscape, sex education researchers in the '90s focused on documenting the ways progressive sex education curricula can lower a number of "poor health outcomes," including delaying first intercourse, reducing number of sexual partners, decreasing STI rates, increasing use of condoms during penetrative sexual intercourse, and reducing unplanned pregnancies (Kirby, 2008). In other words, researchers went looking for evidence that talk about sex does not cause young people to have more sex. Researchers have adopted a similar strategy when responding to the current opposition to LGBTQ+-inclusive sex education curricula. Researchers have expanded the scope of "poor health outcomes" to include empirical measures of mental health and well-being to show how inclusive sex education can have a positive impact on LGBTQ+ youths' sense of belonging in school and increase well-being (Snapp et al., 2015). Now, researchers look for evidence that talk about gender identity does not cause children to become transgender, instead, that talk protects trans children from bullying and associated mental health problems.

The commitment to measuring the effects of sex education may be politically expedient but sex education, even the most progressive kind, is not particularly effective. As Jonathan Zimmerman (2016) notes in his global history of sex education: "scholars around the world have struggled in vain to show any significant effect of sex education upon youth sexual behaviour" (p. 124). The field of sex education research is caught in the logic mobilized by conservative activists – if conservative parents believe their children will be damaged by learning about gender identity in grade 3, then the progressive response must be to show that those lessons are not damaging and instead have a protective factor. If parents think access to condoms will inspire young people to have more sex, sex education researchers will mollify parents with reassurances that condoms do not lead to more sex, only more protected sex.

The language of evidence and empiricism has so saturated progressive sex education that O'Quinn and Fields (2020) begin their critique of US national standards for comprehensive sex education with the observation that "'evidence' has replaced 'abstinence' as the idea with foundational cultural authority in sexuality education debates, policy, and practice" (p. 175). When conservative critics draw on discourses of religion, morality, and the family, progressive advocates respond with "evidence-based curriculum" and turn to discourses of science (health) and the law (rights). Here is how one national Canadian sex education advocacy organization describes the task of sex education: "When sex-ed is done right, it can be life changing for people and have significant positive impacts on public health, STI rates, negative health outcomes, gender equality, instances of gender-based violence, including sexual violence, and bullying." (Action Canada for Sexual

Health & Rights, 2020). When sex education is "done right" it saves lives and promotes health and equality; when it's done wrong, we are left to imagine a trail of devastation.

Why should progressive sex education be so closely tied to the legitimizing discourses of health and well-being? We might imagine all sorts of other outcomes from a progressive sex education curriculum – more pleasurable sexual experiences, an expanded – and perhaps poetic! – vocabulary for talking about one's desires, or an analysis of how sexuality is shaped by social inequalities, for instance – but health and well-being name a safe ground that, ironically, distances sex education from sexuality. Epstein and Mamo (2017) describe the rise of "healthism" in discussions of sexuality. Discourses of health "sanitize or legitimize courses of action related to sexual matters, containing or cancelling the stigma that so often adheres to sexuality and extinguishing the flames of political and moral controversy that so frequently threaten to engulf it" (p. 177). Sex education, wrapped in the language of health, ordered neatly in a checklist, defends against the messiness of sexuality.

This focus on health and well-being has become central to the push for including LGBTQ+ content in sex education curriculum. The Ontario controversy offers an example: when the newly elected Conservative government revoked the updated and LGBTQ+-inclusive curriculum in 2015, progressive advocates framed the removal as an attack on the health and well-being of young people, and LGBTQ+ youth in particular. As one activist declared at a rally outside the provincial legislature, "If gay kids don't know it's OK to be gay, they are stressed, depressed, and that can destroy their relationships." This list of bad outcomes, the activist added, meant queer youth are more likely to commit suicide (Ogilvie, 2018). According to this activist, the stakes couldn't be higher: sex education done right saves queer and trans kids' lives. This framing of sex education as necessary for the health and well-being of LGBTQ+ youth comes at a cost. As I argue with colleagues, justifying a progressive sex education curriculum as a way to save suicidal queer and trans youth narrows the identificatory possibilities for LGBTQ+ youth:

> Much like the "damage-centered research" on Indigenous, urban, and disenfranchised communities that Eve Tuck (2009) critiques, this scholarship often "operates, even benevolently, from a theory of change that establishes harm or injury in order to achieve reparation" (413). As much as such a theory might achieve, it also risks conflating LGBTQ+ identities, desires, and communities with depression, harassment, substance abuse, and even suicide. (Gilbert et al., 2018, p. 167)

The lesson here is that the terms on which young people are imagined in the curriculum shape what is possible to imagine in schools. If progressive sex education invokes depressed, suicidal queer and trans youth as an alibi for promoting an inclusive curriculum, then teachers and students may come to understand queer and trans sexualities and genders as, in large part, sources of risk and danger. Bettina Love makes a similar argument – representations of struggling Black queer youth in schools risk repeating the racist and colonial ideas that cause their suffering in the first place. Love (2019) cuts to the quick: "Educational research is crowded with studies that acknowledge dark children's pain but never the source of their pain" (p. 13). Payne and Smith (2019), across their collaborative scholarship, call out anti-bullying programs for focusing on the actions of individual students (and their pain) while neglecting to confront the source of their pain – the homophobia, transphobia, systemic racism, and settler colonialism that pervades schools. If LGBTQ+ youth are intelligible in schools only through concerns about negative health outcomes, then the curriculum becomes structured by those concerns; LGBTQ+ students can only be recognized and affirmed through that frame, and the goal of the curriculum becomes to improve health and protect students' well-being.

Towards a Queer Curriculum Practice

Just as the curriculum-as-checklist cannot capture the messiness of sexuality, LGBTQ+ young people regularly resist their recruitment into the tropes of either victim or resilient hero. Over the past 10 years, I've been part of *The Beyond Bullying Project*, an on-going ethnographic research project that collects stories of LGBTQ+ sexualities and genders in schools (Gilbert et al., 2018). Working with high schools, we install a private booth, equipped with a video-camera and microphone, in a well-travelled part of the school and invite students, teachers, and community members to enter and share any story (it doesn't even have to be true!) of LGBTQ+ sexuality or gender. During the installation, we collect fieldnotes and conduct interviews with teachers, administrators, and students to chart how *Beyond Bullying* is shaping school conversations. In May 2021, in the midst of the COVID-19 pandemic, we worked with two Toronto high schools to design an online version of *Beyond Bullying*. Instead of a storytelling booth, we worked with a web designer to create a storytelling portal where students and teachers could log in to private Zoom rooms and share stories about sexuality and gender.

When we began collecting stories and interviewing students and teachers in May 2021, we expected to hear experiences of waning mental health, struggles with family, boredom, and loneliness. At the time of our research, Toronto was under yet another strict stay-at-home order, students had been in virtual or disrupted school for over a year, and vaccinations were just starting to reach the general public. Social media, news outlets, and public conversations all seemed to emphasize the ways teens, and especially queer and trans youth, were struggling under quarantine. We did hear some of those stories – delayed access to healthcare, unsupportive parents, lack of privacy, the monotony of online school. But we also heard from a surprising number of students that life in quarantine had offered them the emotional and physical space to examine their friendships and explore their sexual and gender identities outside what some named the "toxic" atmosphere of high school. In the absence of face-to-face schooling, in the midst of pandemic losses, and isolated in their homes with their families, young people's sexual and gender identities came under scrutiny. What do I want? Who do I want to be? How can I feel at home in this body? These questions form the heart of a queer curriculum practice of sex education and, surprisingly, they found new space to breathe for some young people living under lockdown. The loss of school as usual, with its curriculum-as-checklists and the ordinary gendered and sexualized practices of school life, made room for genuinely philosophical questions about sexuality and gender.

Interviews with and stories by young people capture both the pain and loneliness of living in isolation and the relief of being with oneself, outside many of the normative pressures of high school, what one student described as "not having to have toxic people around us." For some students, the relief of not having to deal with "toxic people" made room for other kinds of interactions. For instance, Bashita, an 18-year-old queer South Asian student, talked about the ways leaving her camera off during online class makes it possible to flirt without anyone seeing her blush:

> Before going virtual, it was like they can watch me melt so easily, but it's like afterwards I have that screen, so I have 10 seconds to like, breathe a little, pull myself together, and then reply, and I feel like that's happened like a lot of people, especially with, like, um-, a few of my friends, they get very nervous when it comes to flirting, but it's like suddenly they're so good, it's like "no," I know you have like a few minutes to like let yourself calm down and cool down before you get back to it.

The delight that online classes would facilitate flirting – in this case between shy girls – came as a surprise to the research team, as did the report from members of one school's Queer Straight Alliance, that certain, seemingly random, blasts of keyboard typing posted in the class or breakout room chat were coded queer.

Not only did LGBTQ+ students find covert ways of queering the online class, left on their own, in their homes, students used their solitude to ask questions about themselves that previously had felt too risky. Bashita claims that among her friends, "we've all had, like, this whole awakening where we all explored our sexualities, explored our genders, explored like everything, everything, like we have this whole spiritual awakening." Estelle, a queer Latinx senior, chronicles the questions she has been asking herself while in quarantine:

> one of the few things has been, like, my gender identity. Like it's one of those things that I pushed aside, (laughs), I was like, I will get around this one day but not today. And then like, with the whole quarantine stuff I'm like, well I guess I have to solve a couple of issues before I could, like, you know, go forward with my life and live, you know, authentically.

Gender, for Estelle, is tied to a sense of being "authentic," while high school, and its attendant pressures, stands in the way of these asking questions about "issues" and going forward with life. Similarly, Lee, a white queer and trans student, agrees:

> over this pandemic, not only at my school but like generally, so many more kids have come out as something. Because you're no longer like crushed by social pressures of cis-heteronormative high school. You, like, you sit at home … So you think and you're like: maybe I like girls, or maybe I like guys, or maybe I'm not a guy, or maybe I'm not a girl. So, it's … you're always thinking. And so many people over this pandemic came out as trans, (whispers) myself included. … And it's so good to see people become themselves, once they are no longer exposed to like a cesspool of toxicity.

Many of the students articulated some version of high school as "a cesspool of toxicity." The pressures of showing up each day made it difficult for students to take risks. For some, like Sarah, a queer Asian student in grade 12, being away from in-person school allowed her to create a new relationship both to her own self and to school: "when the pandemic started and everything, I don't know why but I just like, really stopped caring about what people like thought, and I just like, really I just like cut off all my hair and I was like, you know what I don't care, and then I joined [the] Pink Day [LGBTQ+ advocacy committee]." Sarah's account captures something of the complexity of young people's lives under COVID. The freedom to study from home, with her camera turned off, meant that she could let go of her long hair, a normative expectation for girls in the high schools we studied, and sign up to participate in a LGBTQ+ school event. The lockdown helped her navigate a new relationship to school as a short-haired, queer student.

These stories of queer and trans lives during lockdown contrast with the framing of LGBTQ+ students as at heightened risk of poor mental health outcomes. These students did miss their friends and teachers, they missed touching and being touched, but they also found and created new versions of themselves under lockdown conditions. Their experience of sexuality and gender was more complicated than any checklist or glossary definition of "transgender." And the school was both a major source of support for their sexual and gender adventures, and the source of much of their suffering. Under the conditions of pandemic schooling, some young people were able to articulate new questions about sexuality and gender for themselves. What will come of these questions as young people negotiate a post-pandemic landscape? How might a lived sex education curriculum receive these questions? Like the teacher candidates who struggle to know what to make of *Another Brooklyn*, perhaps they will learn to live in the uncomfortable middle, curious about how the pandemic has shaped their sexuality. Indeed, if the teacher candidates could imagine that their students will be as adventurous and brave as Bashita, Lee, and Sarah, then what questions would they ask about how to bring *Another Brooklyn* into their classrooms? What conversations about sexuality, gender, violence, pleasure, justice, and danger might they risk having?

Janet Miller (2005), in her essay, "Autobiography as a Queer Curriculum Practice," offers a caution to those – including me – who might be tempted to read these queer and trans youth's stories as a rebuke of the "curriculum-as-checklist" model of identity. Before we turn these young people into truth-tellers or harbingers for some better, more progressive queer future (a more comprehensive checklist!), Miller reminds us that a queering of autobiography seeks out difference and the unfamiliar. A queer curriculum practice sees the messiness of sexuality and gender as itself a place of learning, not something that could be cleaned up through a revised set of guidelines. And crucially for myself, for the teacher candidates stuck in the middle with *Another Brooklyn*, and for the novice sex educators, Miller insists that our thinking about curriculum needs to link us to our own ambivalent desires towards sexuality and gender – that is, the curriculum doesn't just outline what we want children to learn, it also archives the adult's desires for the child: "A queer curriculum practice compels us to consider … how we are implicated in our desires for and enactments of, as well as our fear and revulsions toward, those identities and practices that exceed the norm" (p. 223). That is, our investments in the sex education curriculum – in that checklist – return us to our own histories of desire. This is what Miller, borrowing from Britzman, calls "the tangles of implication" (p. 223). The novel, the poem, the guidelines, and the stories all point not to some established set of knowledge, skills, and attitudes (no matter how exhaustive) we want to impart to youth, but to our own hope and fears for ourselves and for young people.

REFERENCES

Action Canada for Sexual Health & Rights. (2020). *Together for sex-ed: What's next?* https://www.actioncanadashr.org/together-sex-ed-whats-next

Aoki, T. T. (1993). Legitimating lived curriculum: Towards a curricular landscape of multiplicity. *Journal of curriculum and supervision*, *8*(3), 255–68. https://

acurriculumjourney.files.wordpress.com/2014/04/aoki-1993-legitimating-lived-curriculum-towards-a-curricular-landscape-of-multiplicity.pdf

Epstein, S., & Mamo, L. (2017, September). The proliferation of sexual health: Diverse social problems and the legitimation of sexuality. *Social Science & Medicine, 188*, 176–90. https://doi.org/10.1016/j.socscimed.2017.06.033

Fields, J. (2008). *Risky lessons: Sex education and social inequality*. Rutgers University Press.

Gilbert, J. (2021). Getting dirty and coming clean: Sex education and the problem of expertise. *Curriculum Inquiry, 51*(4), 455–72. https://doi.org/10.1080/03626784.2021.1947732

Gilbert, J., Fields, J., Mamo, L., & Lesko, N. (2018). Intimate possibilities: The beyond bullying project and stories of LGBTQ+ sexuality and gender in US schools. *Harvard Educational Review, 88*(2), 163–83. https://doi.org/10.17763/1943-5045-88.2.163

Greteman, A. J. (2018). *Sexualities and genders in education: Towards queer thriving*. Springer.

Hare, K. (2021a). *'All the feels' - Exploring educators' embodied experiences of sex education* [Doctoral dissertation, University of British Columbia].

– (2021b). Institutionalized states of information abstinence. *Art/Research International: A Transdisciplinary Journal, 6*(2), 415–41. https://doi.org/10.18432/ari29540

Irvine, J. M. (2004). *Talk about sex: The battles over sex education in the United States*. University of California Press.

Kirby, D. B. (2008). The impact of abstinence and comprehensive sex and STD/HIV education programs on adolescent sexual behavior. *Sexuality Research & Social Policy, 5*(3), 18–27. https://doi.org/10.1525/srsp.2008.5.3.18

Love, B. L. (2019). *We want to do more than survive: Abolitionist teaching and the pursuit of educational freedom*. Beacon Press.

Luker, K. (2007). *When sex goes to school: Warring views on sex – and sex education – since the sixties*. WW Norton & Company.

Miller, J. L. (1998). Autobiography as a queer curriculum practice. In W. F. Pinar (Ed.), *Queer theory in education* (pp. 301–8). Routledge.

– (2005). *Sounds of silence breaking: Women, autobiography, curriculum*. Peter Lang.

Ogilvie, M. (2018, July 21) 'We can't go back': Students, parents, and activists rally against sex ed curriculum rollback. *Toronto Star*. https://www.thestar.com/news/queenspark/2018/07/21/we-cant-go-back-students-parents-and-activists-rally-against-sex-ed-curriculum-rollback.html

O'Quinn, J., & Fields, J. (2020). The future of evidence: Queerness in progressive visions of sexuality education. *Sexuality Research and Social Policy, 17*(2), 175–87. https://doi.org/10.1007/s13178-019-00395-z

Payne, E., & Smith, M. (2019). Insider stories: Tensions, resistances, and missed opportunities in state LGBT-inclusive anti-bullying policy. *International journal of bullying prevention, 1*(4), 231–45.

Public Health Agency of Canada. (2008). *Canadian guidelines for sexual health education*. http://www.sieccan.org/pdf/guidelines-eng.pdf.

Quinlivan, K. (2018). *Exploring contemporary issues in sexuality education with young people: Theories in practice*. Springer.

Snapp, S. D., McGuire, J. K., Sinclair, K. O., Gabrion, K., & Russell, S. T. (2015). LGBTQ+-inclusive curricula: Why supportive curricula matter. *Sex Education, 15*(6), 580–96. https://doi.org/10.1080/14681811.2015.1042573

Taubman, P. M. (2010). *Teaching by numbers: Deconstructing the discourse of standards and accountability in education*. Routledge.

Tuck, E. (2009). Suspending damage: A letter to communities. *Harvard Educational Review, 79*(3), 409–28. https://doi.org/10.17763/haer.79.3.n0016675661t3n15

Woodson, J. (2017). *Another Brooklyn*. Simon and Schuster.

Zimmerman, J. (2016). *Too hot to handle: A global history of sex education*. Princeton University Press.

8 Which Story of the Canadian Experience Should We Tell Our Young People?

JOCELYN LÉTOURNEAU

I am not a specialist in educational sciences.[1] In fact, I have no training in the field. My interest in grand collective representations has led me, however, into territories also visited by educational scientists. As a historian, I have always been primarily interested, unsurprisingly, in *historic* representations. How do Canadians or Quebecers write themselves, collectively, into the scripts of the past? Through which stories do they internalize their experience in time? How does this narrative of the Self spread in a society? How is the history of We Canadians or We Quebecers, for example, told to children, who are perceived to be the heirs of a national experience and therefore the trustees of a history that must be known and carried into the present in order to colonize the future in the wake of the past?

Inevitably, these initial questions led me to others, some shared by educators and pedagogues, as well as psychologists, neurologists, and memory specialists: How does a person construct their historical representations? How does a person assimilate the historical information that they encounter and use it to make sense of the world, to insert their individuality into the trajectory of time, comfortably and contentedly?

I will not try to distill the many works I have written chasing these questions. Since my interests lay in the production of collective identity, the creation of historical consciousness, and the dissemination of historical knowledge in the community, and also in the importance of the social contexts of learning and the articulation of empirical and ideological knowledge in the construction of meaning on the personal or collective scale, it follows that I found myself in the domain of some important architects of educational science.

An important role was played in this partial shift into the waters of curricular studies by Jörn Rüsen, who invited me to take part in the work of the *Historische Sinnbildung Forschungsgruppe,* a multidisciplinary team that he created in Bielefeld in the mid-1990s. This extraordinarily inspiring man introduced me to Seixas, Wineburg, Von Borries, Ankersmit, Ahonen, and the list goes on. Needless to say that at the time, I was taking and absorbing more than I was giving and contributing. Like other colleagues who have inspired me by their intellectual attitude – I am thinking specifically of Jean Hamelin and Bogumil Jewsiwicki – Rüsen, instead of pulling me back within the boundaries of a canon, encouraged me to expand on my intuitions. He urged me to observe my four children, then aged nine, six, four, and one and a half, to discover how they were crafting themselves into human beings, incorporating the notion of time in their Self and mastering the principles of narration, leading them to conceive of and perceive themselves as stories enmeshed in other, larger and more complex stories. "Papa, tell me about when I was a baby," my four-year-old daughter said to me one day, unleashing a flood of extensively elaborated hypotheses in a long text published in German (Létourneau, 2000).

The next segment of my journey nevertheless veered me back into the production and assimilation of *collective* representations. How do nations – these imaginary communities associated with physical spaces and instituted structures – (re)produce themselves *also* by forging and spreading a historical narrative?[2] How is this historical narrative internalized by "ordinary people" who, in so doing, (un)consciously "nationalize" themselves into matrices of meaning in which their individuality and identity are combined with the reality of a community inscribed over time?

Instead of approaching this issue in the usual way, that is, from the position of the proclaimers – the ones who produce meaning they hope will be espoused wholesale by the destinees – I planned to examine it from the position of the audience, those who receive the finished meaning and make something of it, rather than, as it is usually asserted, simply reacting to what is flung at them. This reversal of perspective, I thought, would open up new prospects about what intrigued me: the probably highly complex marshalling of what is presented (encoded message), on one hand, and what is received (decoded message), on the other. Ergo my empirical studies on the understanding[3] that Quebecers foster and cultivate about the history of their society.

Rather than interrogate my subjects – thousands of young students – about the trivia of Quebec's past – such as "In which year was Montréal founded?" or "Who was the premier of Quebec in 1867?" – I intended, following to some extent in the footsteps of James Wertsch with young Russians (Wertsch, 2002), to ask them to tell or present the (hi)story of Quebec as they saw it, imagined it or understood it. Of course, I reassured my subjects about my intentions: I did not expect any particular history of Quebec from them. They were free to structure their words – narratives, mostly, but also lists, chronologies, drawings, and comic strips – as best they saw fit, as long as their offerings were anonymous, which gave them plenty of narrative latitude.

There is no room here to elucidate the outcome of those investigations, which can be found in a number of other articles (see Létourneau, 2017; 2015), as well as a monograph (Létourneau, 2014). I would, however, like to present some of the findings that stem from my research.

Contrary to popular opinion, "ordinary people" – specifically here the young students I queried, but the finding holds true in older people as well – are not completely ignorant of Quebec history. They know something about it, even a lot about it, a hodgepodge of statements of all kinds, factual or idealistic, gleaned here and there from the "real curriculum" and from what was offered to them as a cultural dowry of sorts, which they do their best to attach to a simple, but powerful narrative structure.[4] For Francophones, this narrative structure pivots around the following key idea: "We were had by the Other, who prevented us from accomplishing what we otherwise would have, which led our history into a trajectory of resistance and our collective existence into an experience of powerlessness and bare survival." Unsurprisingly, Anglophones, young and old, do not have the same knowledge or representation of Quebec history. First, they largely incorporate it into the broader history of Canada. Second, undoubtedly to carve out a legitimate space for their "group" in Quebec's history, they insist on the need to recognize the diverse and pluralistic face of Quebec society over time. Finally, while they may acknowledge the tensions that have historically marked the relationship between Francophones and Anglophones, they reverse the roles of the villains and the victims. They also point out that the Indigenous peoples have ever been, yesterday and today, the ones who suffered the physical, ideological, and political furor of the settlers, be they of French, English, or other descent. Clearly, Francos and Anglos are on the same side against the "unfortunate natives," the only oppressed people on the national stage.

I did not conduct a similar investigation among Canadians in other provinces, nor am I aware of any such studies,[5] other than among Francophone youth in Ontario (Lévesque & Croteau, 2020) and New Brunswick (Robichaud, 2011; Cormier & Savoie, 2011). That is a field ripe for the picking. Some indirect research I undertook has made me think, however, that if one were to ask English-speaking Canadians living outside of Quebec to recount the history of Canada, they would structure it around a set of historical themes and keywords that would include the following: pacifism, diversity, multiculturalism, compromise, agreement, unity, harmony, immigration, English, French and First Nations (Létourneau, 2024). It is important to understand that in the eyes of many Canadians, Canada has become, for all intents and purposes, a moral ideal for the planet. "The world needs more Canada," proclaimed Barack Obama in 2016 before the members of the House of Common in Ottawa.[6] The only blemish on the national portrait: the treatment of Indigenous people, eternal victims of their pitiless European invaders, English and French, equally abusive in their treatment of the First Peoples.

All societies, all nations of the world, have their own historical *problematic*, a sort of meta-representation that coalesces into a powerful image of what they were and continue to be, from the years of yore to the present. Developed and honed by influential prognosticators – not necessarily historians, by the way[7] – these problematics articulate a grand narrative of the Self through which entities grasp themselves as or assemble themselves into a whole and then consolidate and mythistoricize their trajectory through time (Létourneau, 2004). In the case of Quebec and French Canada, this problematic, which has the status of an emblematic, revolves around the ideas of duality and victimhood. In the case of English Canada, it is diversity and peace that fulfill the roles of collective ensign and driveshaft of the national narrative. In both cases, these are historical representations that, while not completely disconnected from a certain factual reality, twist the dense matter of the past into something unequivocal, clear, simple, and above all meaningful.

We would be mistaken to view these representations as mere fabrications. For example, it is entirely possible to recount the history of Quebec from the angle of adversity and struggle between two collective subjects, one of whom, the (French) Canadian, seeking national affirmation, is tripped up by the other, the Anglo, who beats them back into "survival mode," a kind of pathetic provincial subsistence. Likewise, it is possible to recount the history of Canada from the angle of cooperation, mutual respect, related communities, and unity in diversity, where each party making up the country, preferring compassion over force, is driven by the desire to found and build something good and lasting with the other. "Canada has a drive toward mutual accommodation," wrote William A. Macdonald in a recent book with the pompous title *Might Nature Be Canadian?* (Macdonald, 2020). This idea also brings to mind the long-winded speech pronounced by Justin Trudeau in the opening of the television series *Canada: The Story of Us*, broadcast on public television in 2017,[8] in which the prime minister lists the fundamental traits of Canadianness: acceptance, respect, cooperation, unity, togetherness, and so on.

Between a *possible history* and an *accurate history* of an entity, say, a country or a nation, there are, however, disconnects of greater or lesser degree. And this raises a difficult question: If, going no further than these examples, the existing histories of Quebec and Canada – or at least those circulating in the public space that are internalized by "ordinary people," including youth – are revealed, from the perspective of the accuracy of their problematics and the narratives they generate, to be out of sync with the complexity of the past, what problematics or narratives should replace them? In other words, what history can be told about Canada and Quebec that is accurate in terms of facts and historical processes and faithful to the complex matter of the *once-was*?

That is the challenge of curricular studies: not simply transmitting to pupils and students, through the study of history, decisive intellectual skills (criticism, verification, analysis, interpretation),[9] but also offering them a historical narrative that allows them to construct an idea about what was. Based on the investigations I conducted, of which one of the principal conclusions was that the constancy and strength of method struggle to overcome the resistance and pre-eminence of memory,[10] I posit that only a structured, cohesive narrative can effectively overturn a prevailing organized narrative. Abandoning "ordinary people" to multiple perspectives by exposing them to interpretive diversity and initiating them into the logic of narrative construction in order to raise the level of their historical consciousness and enhance the depth of their critical competency generally produces disappointing outcomes. Giddied by the complexity of the reflective processes demanded by historical thinking and disoriented by the plethora of possible narratives about the past, people who lack the reference points and means to confront this intricacy when left to their own devices, which is their customary condition, are loath to abandon the narratives they know, narratives that offer them effective schemes for understanding and that are handy for making sense of something that is not easy to master but that they want to understand and convey simply: the past. It is hard – "unnatural" in Sam Wineburg's words (Wineburg, 2001) – to approach the past using the principles of historical thinking, which rejects and indeed refutes the categories through which people instinctively approach reality in order to strip away its complexity and take hold of it. Once they are out of controlled learning environments, such as classrooms, where the teacher is there to guide them and soothe troubled minds, young people, to focus just on this age group, are pleased to encounter reassuring stories that allow them to align their personal historical consciousness with the historical representations put forward by their community of belonging and through which they connect with or are incorporated into a society. Contrary to one common opinion, which may underestimate the global social environment in which human beings evolve, learn, socialize, join, and become,[11] leaving a historical space is far from a meaningless, painless process for a subject. It is no more or less than exiling oneself from a shared, identity-based territory. It is easy to understand the hardship and reluctance some people might feel about cutting off the narrative moorings that attach them to the quay of their community, a place that represents self-affirmation and well-being.[12] This triggers another question: Could the historical thinking method be viable primarily for the trepidatious among us who yearn to veer away from familiar shores, for bright lights who enjoy surfing complexity and for the erudite equipped to face the unknown? The definitive answer remains to be seen. I, for one, tend to answer in the affirmative to this conundrum, which so many educational experts dread.[13]

Whatever the case, as only a new historical narrative can, in my opinion, overthrow an existing historical narrative and open the subject to a new continent of understanding and intellectual emancipation, which story should be proposed about Canada, to take this example?[14]

My intention is clearly not to offer a panorama of Canadian history in such a short text, nor to discuss the narrative form that the desired story of the

Canadian past could take, except to say that it would be a kind of polythetic history similar to the one I recently developed for Quebec (Létourneau, 2020), focused on intermingled, ambivalent, dissonant, divergent, endo- and exogenous, singular and universal processes through which a community advances through time in a kind of indetermination that leaves the future open to the plurivocal plans of its inhabitants and the multiple possibilities of their interdependence.[15]

In these next pages I plan, instead, to grasp at the essential aspects of the Canadian historical experience but stop myself from identifying an essence in it, imprinting a *telos* on it, or imbuing it with mystique. The challenge I have set down for myself is as follows: how to problematize the Canadian trajectory without emblematizing it, without imposing a retrospective teleology or prospective destiny on it, without subjecting it to either the rectitude of our era or the historical expectations of particular identity groups; how to raise questions about it rather than incite judgment, denounce the moral ideal it projects without rejecting the hopes it contains, avoid looking for lessons in it without fearing to uncover observations that are also its constants. And as if this order were not tall enough, I – ever in thrall to the deniable yet relentless social and political duties of the interpreter – also plan to place my historical problematic at the intersection of the concern for rigour (principle of truth) and the concern for relevance (principle of responsibility). That is, at the crossroads of accurate prehension of what was and a wholesome desire to move forward.

I want to come back to the expression "Canadian historical experience," which is capital in my vision of things. With this expression I mean that Canada is not an atemporal given and a natural framework but rather a historical construct and a progressive reality. Canadian is not an a priori fixed reality or one that is definitively entrenched, but the broadly unpredictable product of human action, the outcome of the actions of men and women acting individually and in groups and who have the desire to establish a physical location and an economic and political field of action that reflects their outlook, ambitions, and specific interests, which tend more towards competition, dissonance, and divergence than towards concordance. From this perspective, Canada is not a completed or closed whole. It is a work in progress, a project in a continual state of incompletion because of the tensions generated by its (in)determinate evolution. In fact, Canada is more of an open question than a conclusive answer, more of a sum of provisional arrangements than a definitive program, more of an unfinished composition than a completed score. Canada is not a moving poem or an exalting novel; it is a perennial draft. It is not a rational ideal that must be concretized at all costs by crushing dissent, but an approximated idea that we are trying to articulate through experimentation and contention.[16] While this state of incompletion creates angst or frustration for some people who would prefer for everything to be determined, established, and firmly cemented, it is, for everyone, a means of freedom that allows us to build on what can still be erected, if such a thing is possible and worthwhile, which it likely is.[17]

The spelling of the word Canada eschews the history that the term claims to embody. Changing the first letter to a K would make the very label of the country reflect the Indigenous primacy effect in the Kanadian experience.[18] While Kanada developed historically as a society that was European in nature, the Kanadian experience is rooted in Indigeneity, which has never ceased to influence the nature of the country, despite being built by physically pushing the Indigenous peoples away and rejecting their cultural heritage.

But the term "Kanada" does not reduce the Kanadian experience to solely its Indigenous component, which has not, indeed, been its most preponderant element for a long time. Two other fundamental components of the Kanadian experience – the French fact and the English fact, generic ensembles that harbour considerable cultural diversity – are also expressed in the name Kanada, which can be pronounced in the French way or the English way (let alone the German way!) without changing the spelling, corresponding well to the reality of the country, whose two dominant linguistic communities coexist, with the third, *separately together*.

The Quebec question is interesting to examine in the framework of a history of Canada seeking to escape from the usual problematics (or emblematics) of duality and victimhood, on one side, and diversity and peace, on the other.

Let us begin by saying that there is no history of Quebec that can be put forward outside the narrative of the Kanadian experience.[19] Not for ideological or political reasons, but for historical ones. Quebec is consubstantial with Kanadianity, which, in return, defines Quebec's core identity. This could be denied, but there is evidence to support it. There is, of course, a desire for nationhood in French Quebec, but in its very broadly dominant form, that has never been directed against Kanada. It has always been, rather, a means to accentuate one of the country's fundamentals, the constitutive duality of Kanada – which has never been simple to live by, given (a) the minority nature of the French fact in Canada, (b) Quebec's relative political isolation, and (c) the inexorable tendency of culturally diversified national spaces, of any sort, to massify, homogenize or crush their constituent, surrounding, or competing cultures. For the Québécois, the ideal of duality does not mean *separated* States, but *reunited* nations (Létourneau, 2006). It is easy to understand how, in 1980 and 1995, the expressions "sovereignty association" and "sovereignty partnership" convinced millions of Quebecers to vote Yes on the question of a new Kanadian alliance.

Historically, the label Canada, which relates back to the reality of a *plan* for the political, economic, ideological, and even nominative domination of a geographic space to colonize and then nationalize, somewhat naively obscures what it could never fully be: the effective achievement of the intended program. This is what led Peter Russell, in a recent work, to speak of Canada as a country based on a series of "incomplete conquests" (Russell, 2017). For him, the Canadian experience is the history of the *abortive* reduction of the Indigenous peoples, the *unsuccessful* provincialization of the Francophones and the *failed* nationalization of English Canada, as well as the outcome of this threefold situation: a country mired in continual tension – irritating and unequal, but creative and performative – among its three founding pillars.

The consequence of this vision is not meaningless, especially for those attached to the prevalent representation, a sort of popular vulgate for a highly complex legislative framework, of Canada as a multicultural community. Presented as an ideology fully adapted to the Canadian diversity and magnified by its proponents as a refounding of the country, Canadian multiculturalism, in the context put forward by Russell's thesis, is precisely the opposite of what it claims to be. Although rehabilitated as a success by a few wily spin doctors, it is, at heart, an admission of the defeat of the dominant powers in the face of the persistence, resistance, and resilience of minority entities, which have refused to cede to their resolutions, pretensions, and impositions. In a sense, Canadian multiculturalism, associated as it must be (though this is often overlooked) with the concepts of federalism, bilingualism, provincialism, regionalism, democratic individualism, and even nationalism,[20] all expressions of the dazzling Kanadian complexity and its irreducibility, is the acknowledgment that there is no way to smelt the country in a die in which the whole can subsume, swallow, or finally and fully dissolve its parts.[21] Spelt this way by French explorers on their arrival and later validated in that form by the English, the term Canada is, at heart, the residual variable of the Kanadian equation, its least common denominator, rather than its grand integrating concept.

There is an interesting point here. If we accept it, Kanada appears, in effect, to be the relatively fortunate accident resulting from a failed plan of nationalist reduction and identity construction, which differentiates it from established models and typical cases.[22] (Concerning this shortcoming, Marshall McLuhan himself declared that "Canada is the only country in the world that knows how to live without an identity.") A source of vexation for *Canadian* nationalists, which include eminent historians worried about the eventual denationalization of the country from a want of historicization,[23] the inherent *shortcoming* in the Canadian experience could in fact be a *sufficiency* or even a *surfeit*. If so, we should rejoice that Kanada is a failed act (or a series of failed acts), particularly because the minority and dominated positions, despite the ordeals experienced and battles lost by those bearing or leading them, succeeded, ultimately, in asserting their presence, and sometimes their program, on the majority and dominant positions. Fundamentally, and paradoxically, Kanada is a country of "beautiful losers," to borrow Leonard Cohen's impressionist metaphor (Cohen, 1966). "Beautiful losers" not in the sense that Kanadians, whatever their primary culture of belonging or allegiance (Anglophone, Francophone, or Indigenous), are a bunch of defeated fools, vanquished milquetoasts, or trounced second-raters – the opposite of Americans, for example, whose national novel and narrative canon proclaims them to be superb winners. "Beautiful losers" in the sense that, in the wake of the unexpected outcomes of history and the limited strength of the powers articulating the Kanadian experience, and also because of the visionary ideas of some players in the Kanadian theatre, there was no chance for any group or culture to completely dominate or fully control the national order, despite the lopsided nature of the relationship among the parties that make up the country.[24]

As such, and for historical reasons – let's not delude ourselves – the Kanadian reality *became* one of obliged measure, forced compromise, and inevitable adjustments among the instituted powers and constituent parties: these three characteristics or dynamics of the collective experience hardening over time into a kind of political culture in which conversation and continual negotiation,[25] underpinned by the differences and divergences that mark the reciprocal relationships of the three Canadian pillars, form the basis of their reconcilement, sometimes within reach, sometimes delayed, sometimes bungled, but never entirely (dis)satisfactory to anyone. While the Kanadian historical experience is, on the surface and *primarily*, one of discord, dissension, strife, friction, disagreement, and conflict related to the vague conquering impulses of the dominant groups that have succeeded each other over the history of the country, it is, at a deeper level and *fundamentally*, at least so far, one of constrained interdependence, detached convergence, separated association, random intersection, asymmetrical compromise, disjointed collaboration, provisional arrangement, and uncertain adjustment stemming from the failure of those conquistadorial urges.

On the basis of this problematic, what history should be taught about Canada to the contemporary heirs of the Canadian historical experience?

We cannot do as we please with what once was. The principle of rigour must be at the centre of the historical enterprise. There is no option, for example, of presenting the Canadian historical experience from the candid angle of perpetual compromise, continual concession, and mutual accommodation. While Peter Russell is accurate in asserting that the history of Canada is based on a series of "incomplete conquests," the idea underlying his thesis is that powers did effectively and ardently seek to model the Canadian experience on their *particular* ambitions and interests.[26]

And, in fact, there was, historically, an intention – a plan – to reduce or eliminate or in any event exclude the Indigenous peoples of Kanada established as Canada. There was an intention – a plan – to marginalize or assimilate or in any event provincialize the French fact in the country. And there was an intention – a plan – to acculturate or merge or in any event to homogenize the inhabitants of Kanada into a uniform, imposed vision of Canada and Canadian. Although, for all sorts of reasons, it turned out to be impossible to achieve these intentions and bring about these plans, the efforts undertaken – and sometimes carried quite far[27] – had major, structuring effects on the construction of Canada, effects that are impossible to undo or redeem in the present. A history of the future of Kanada cannot be built by trivializing, gold-plating, or overlooking these foundational processes.

That said, while the Canadian experience is the story of failed, spoiled, or unaccomplished intentions and plans for assimilation, provincialization, and uniformization, which Russell associates with desired and affirmed attempts at conquest, other elements – players, factors, contingencies, processes, episodes, events, and phenomena – worked to reorient the intended designs or ended up thwarting the imagined, expected, or hoped-for directions.

And, in fact, the Canadian experience is *also* a history of determined resistance and opinionated battles, headstrong protests and inspired visions, progressive actions and generous decisions. To make this capital one of the axles of Kanadianity and its narrative does not make the narrator a cheerleader for the nation. It is more a matter of recognizing that Canada, from which the Kanadian root has never been successfully bowdlerized, established itself amid an interlacing of powers, an ambiguity of systems, and a succession of ambivalent political crannies, which it continues to do today. In a sense, the Kanadian experience is the confirmation that power does not always manage to crush prospects, that the rationale of systems does not always quash the potential of lifeworlds, and that the omnipotence of conformity does not always suppress the possibilities of interstices from which arise discreet movements and slender vitalities, vectors of emergence, crucibles of thought, and action, and even potentialities of transformation and progress.

Without denying the presence and importance of power, systems and conformity in the construction of the country, the history that is taught should also emphasize – in fair measure, of course, and within the framework of a polythetic historical narrative – the prospects, the potentialities arising from lifeworlds, and the opportunities deriving from interstices that have marked the Canadian experience and in the nooks of which have sprouted certain unexpected but attractive, or at least appealing, directions, from the perspective of the possibilities for a heteroclitic and complicated entity – a multinational federation? – to move into the future.

This double insistence on powers *and* prospects, systems *and* lifeworlds, conformity *and* asperity is a reminder of the place of dominance in the configuration of Canada. But it is also a reminder of the possibility for people to change the order of things through their faculty of thinking and capacity of action in view, perhaps, of (re)building the Canadian horizon from a Kanadian perspective.

Critical lucidity and political hope are assuredly two values – two cognitive and reflective horizons that harken back to two central concepts of the model of historical thinking: that of the *methodical* study of the past and that of the *ethical* aspect appropriate to historical questioning and reasoning – that the teaching of history must or ought to inculcate in young minds.

NOTES

1 This text must be read as an exercise in scholarly exploration. Funds for translation, done by Wendi Petersen, have been provided by CELAT (Centre de recherche Cultures-Arts-Sociétés).

2 Let us agree that there are always, in a society, at any given time, several competing historical narratives. There is also always one narrative that is dominant and that, within the community, holds sway in variants ranging from the simplistic to the convoluted.

3 To designate the enunciative magma that comprises what most ordinary people *know* about their society, country, nation, or community, *understanding* is perhaps more apposite than *knowledge*, which relates to the more traditional fact-based litanies.

4 The same conclusion could be drawn about French, Swiss, Spanish or German youth. See Lantheaume and Létourneau (2016). For Americans, see Wineburg *et al.* (2007).

5 Nevertheless, see Peck, Poyntz & Seixas (2011). Note that our colleagues' investigation, conducted with 11 high-school students, did not share the same objectives as ours.

6 U2 frontman and activist Bono had said the same at the Air Canada Center, Toronto, in 2003.

7 It is not necessarily certified historians who develop the overall framework through which societies view themselves across time, although historians contribute to it as well, directly or indirectly. These frameworks are often forged by history-tellers of middling talent and somewhat ideologized. Instrumentalizing the past, they create exuberant and complex historical meta-narratives that offer to a society a historical path that is unequivocal and obvious, or even inspiring and exalting.

8 Available online at https://www.cbc.ca/2017/canadathestoryofus/pm-trudeau-invited-you-to-watch-canada-the-story-of-us-1.4030311/. I analysed the series in Létourneau (2017).

9 See Seixas & Morton, 2012.

10 Lévesque & Croteau (2020) came to the same conclusion after their study. They believe, though, that a subject's sense of identity also decisively influences their historical representations and constitutes an additional obstacle to the triumph of reason (method) over emotion (memory).

11 It is here, no doubt, that I stray from the adherents of historical thinking, despite being one, albeit one who holds reservations about the claim that method alone

can vanquish all-powerful memory. Education experts acknowledge, of course, that the classroom is not the only place of learning for young people, especially for a subject like history. They also know that students are not all disciples of Clio, far from it, that they forget much of what they are taught, that they prefer clarity to ambiguity and simplicity to complexity, and that the emotional memory bequeathed by a grandmother, to cite the personal and classic example of Henri Brunschwig, ravages the reasoned expertise transmitted by the teacher. As specialists in the modes and techniques of learning, education experts trust in their methods – it would be absurd if they did not – to elude the weight of social contexts and ensure the triumph of their processes. Based on my work on the development of historical consciousness in youth and what I have observed about the process of personal socialization, my confidence in the method is not as firm as that of my esteemed colleagues. For a lucid evaluation of the uncertainties and limits of the historical thinking method, see Pollock (2014).

12 Works inspired by social psychology are fairly eloquent on the influence of cultural narratives on collective representations and stagings of the Self from the perspective of social connection and individual completeness. See Bougie (2005).

13 Many, but not all. Peter Lee and Denis Shemilt, for example, but also Bruce VanSeldright, S. G. Grant, and Stéphane Lévesque, have acknowledged in their work the power of cultural knowledge and schemas, including a group's identity-based narrations, in the creation of the historical consciousness of youth and also insisted on the need to take this into account in students' historical education, to the point of using narrative strategies to achieve it. For a learning model based on such a method, see Létourneau (2015).

14 This begs the question of the basis on which one can carve up an object of study called Canada, based on criteria that are neither political nor ideological nor arbitrary. My answer is as follows: It is possible to do so because the name Canada concretely refers to a bounded space of physical interaction, an instituted structure of political aggregation, and an articulated imagined community. Canada is also the contemporary outcome of a historical experience to which nearly 41 million people relate daily in order to insert themselves into the space/time of the world and, as such, exist on the planet in an identified location. One thing is certain: The history of Canada cannot be told without querying the object itself.

15 The image that can be associated with the intended form of the polythetic narrative could be that of a telescoped kaleidoscope of instances. The challenge of the polythetic narrative is to render and express, in an articulate narration that makes sense of things that appear to make none and while avoiding any unilateral, monosemic or deterministic schematization, the simultaneity of the complementary and contradictory processes in the dissonant interaction through which the structuring forms of society organize themselves and take shape.

16 This view is not so very distant from the position of John Ralston Saul, who decried the fact that the Canadian experience is assessed on the basis of different or

foreign national models – that of the United States, the United Kingdom, or France – and that the comparison results in holding out the Canadian journey as a failed example of a national route that succeeded elsewhere, a stance which denies the specificity or originality of Canada's case. See Saul (1998).

17 This is a delightful ethical quandary that cannot be dismissed: Is it appropriate, despite everything, to prolong the Canadian experiment (which does not mean perpetuate it as-is or as-was)? If the answer to this question is positive or basically positive, its incompleteness is an invitation to press on. Otherwise, it's better to stop, close the books, change everything, and start over.

18 As it is well known, the syntagm that is the root of the name Canada is most probably Kanata, an original Iroquois term meaning village or settlement.

19 The same is true of the history of the Acadians and Acadia.

20 Although the Constitution Act, 1982, is not favourable to the formal recognition of Quebec as a distinct society or the accommodation of the nationalist expression of the Québécois, the practice of Canadian federalism, sanctioned by the decisions of the Supreme Court, means that Quebec is a province whose government holds unique responsibilities concerning the society it promotes and directs and gives Quebec specific provisions and procurations in the form of administrative agreements and tax or financial compensations for equivalent programs. That this arrangement does not please independentists and Quebec nationalists is no surprise, but this *modus vivendi* contributes to the asymmetrical operation of the Canadian federation, deemed by many experts to be one of the most decentralized in the world.

21 Pierre Trudeau's pro-Canada crusade, beginning in 1968, can be seen as a means to protect the country, as best he could in the circumstances, from its inherent tendency towards disaggregation, accentuated in the 1960s and 1970s by a set of perils that included (1) the rise of Quebec nationalism, (2) the exacerbation of provincialism and regionalism throughout the country, (3) the identity-based and nationalist ferment of the First Peoples, (4) the agitation of ethnic minorities, and (5) the rapid "de-Britishization" of English Canada, creating, some believe, a void conducive to the dilution of the country's identity. Why did Trudeau do it? Perhaps because, motivated by fear disguised by arrogance, he truly believed in Canada as a physical and symbolic place of the metabolization of the insoluble problems of a fragile country, a country he believed held a promising future for its citizens and for the world. As the years passed and the risk of dismemberment increased for Canada, Trudeau flexed his approach into a "re-unification" plan, a plan of civic post-nationalism rooted in individualistic liberalism, democratic egalitarianism, federative centralism, personal bilingualism, and institutional multiculturalism. By establishing a constitutional framework that could "last for a thousand years," Trudeau hoped to exorcise the country, once and for all, of what he considered to be its recurring demons: ethnicism, nationalism, tribalism, provincialism, racism, separatism, regionalism, and identitism, all expressions of sectarianism in his eyes. Ultimately, the prime minister did not succeed in taking Canada out of its

historical course to project it into the hopes he cherished for it. Willy-nilly, the country continued to evolve along the path of an experience buffeted by sometimes tempestuous, sometimes milder, stress among its constituent parts. And thus, 157 years after the founding of the country, Canadian federalism, arising far more from pragmatism than idealism, is still a framework to hone and a project to develop. For an interesting discussion of the reasons explaining the former prime minister's approach, see Burelle (2005, Part I).

22 The idea that Quebec's journey is the product of a failed act of historical achievement – in this case, that of sovereignty – has been defended by some authors. For Gérard Bouchard, for example, Quebec and Puerto Rico are the two lone North American entities not to have ended in independence. In the eyes of Bouchard (2000/2008), Canada's trajectory reflects a different model, a belated and truncated miscarriage, a journey half achieved and half failed, disappointing in any regard.

23 Recall Jack Granatstein's castigations of social historians and other adepts of microstoria, whom he claims weakened Canada by compulsively crumbling the country into thousands of anecdotal vignettes instead of supporting the nation with a bracing portrait of its whole (Granatstein, 1998). Concern about the fragilization of Quebec through historical denationalization has also made itself felt in Quebec's public sphere. Mathieu Bock-Côté and Jacques Beauchemin, among other conservative nationalists including Éric Bédard, Serge Cantin and Robert Comeau, have rung that alarm.

24 The "beautiful loser" thesis does not suggest that the constituent parties of Kanadianity share an equality of "failure," the word failure being in any case inadequate to characterize the Canadian historical experience overall. Rather, it seeks to emphasize two points: that the Canadian historical experience has not crowned any final, decisive victor, and that within this historical experience, the "victors" often found themselves betrayed by passing time, while the "losers," on their knees, humiliated or obedient, often ruled and reigned within interstices not occupied by or known to their "masters."

25 Conversation and negotiation are not necessarily synonymous with dialogue and conciliation. Their opposite is not dissent or opposition but extremism and excess. Canada, whatever may be claimed and despite certain insurrectionist urges, republican leanings, and desires for a fresh start it harbours in its bosom, was weaned on the repudiation of the American revolution and the rejection of the French revolution. Of course, this does not mean that violence, brutality, and indeed raging fury are not also variables in the Canadian equation – we need only remember of the burning of the Canadian Parliament building in Montreal in April 1849. In general, though, the primacy of politics and the search for complex if not unconventional arrangements between opposing forces have taken precedence over the raw fury of power dynamics.

26 In an influential article, Ian McKay (2000) posited that the liberal order, in the mid-nineteenth century, had carried the day for the Canadian historical

experience, imprinting a fundamental direction on a country that was, at that time, under construction from coast to coast. While it is clear that liberalism has modelled the Canadian trajectory, it has always been in tension with other plans, ideologies, programs, or designs that tainted or disguised it to one degree or another: conservatism, cooperatism, reformism, clericalism, socialism, Keynesianism, social democratism, welfarism, and so on. Ultimately, minor ideologies metabolized the prime ambition into something else – a kind of tempered liberalism with a side of smooth socialism – that has, for some time now, moulded Canadian evolution.

27 Consider the Indian Act, residential schools and the sequestering of the First Nations on reservations; the federal government's bitter struggle against the territorial claims of the Métis in the West; the anglicization instituted in Canada outside Quebec; discrimination against Canadians of Asian origin; the creeping discrimination felt by French-speaking Canadians, including those in Quebec, for so long, which Gabrielle Roy (1984) expressed in a sentence as powerful as it is distressing for the reader: "When did I first realize that I was destined to be treated like an inferior in my own country?")

REFERENCES

Bouchard, G. (2008). *The making of nations and cultures of the new world: An essay in comparative history*. McGill-Queen's University Press. (Original work published 2000)

Bougie, É. (2005). The cultural narrative of Francophone and Anglophone Quebecers and their perception of temporal relative deprivation: Links with esteem and well-being. Ph.D. Thesis, McGill University.

Burelle, A. (2005). *Pierre Elliott Trudeau, l'intellectuel et le politique*. Fides.

Cohen, L. (1966). *Beautiful losers*. McLelland & Stewart.

Cormier, J.-M., & Savoie, H. (2011). De l'influence d'une visite au musée sur la conscience historique des élèves du primaire. *Canadian Journal for Social Research /Revue canadienne de recherche sociale*, 4(1), 42–72. https://www.umoncton.ca /umcm-hebdo-campus/impression.php?date=2012-12-13

Granatstein, J. (1998). *Who killed Canadian history?* Harper Collins.

Lantheaume, F., & Létourneau, J. (Eds.). (2016). *Le récit du commun. L'histoire nationale racontée par les élèves. Comparaisons internationales*. Presses universitaires de Lyon.

Létourneau, J. (2000). Die Selbst-Erzählung. Geschichtsbewußtsein und narrative Identität beim Kleinkind: Argumentationsversuche und Deutungshypothesen. In J. Rüsen (Ed.), *Psychologie des Geschichtsbewußtseins* (pp. 177–238). Böhlau Verlag.

– (2004). Mythistory. In G. Hallowell (Ed.), *Oxford companion to Canadian history* (p. 423). Oxford University Press.

– (2006). *Que veulent vraiment les Québécois? Regard sur l'intention nationale au Québec (français) d'hier à aujourd'hui*. Boréal.

– (2014). *Je me souviens? Le passé du Québec dans la conscience de sa jeunesse*. Fides.
– (2015, Août). Pour une pragmatique de l'enseignement de l'histoire. Leçons tirées d'une recherche. *À l'école de Clio, 1*. https://ecoleclio.hypotheses.org/212.
– (2017). A beautiful story: Canadians' attitudes towards their pasts. Seventeenth Distinguished Canadian Address, Bridgewater State University.
– (2020). *La Condition québécoise. Une histoire dépaysante*. Septentrion.
– (2024, ms). Les mots de la nation. Incursion au coeur du lexique de base de six communautés imaginées de communication (États-Unis, France, Angleterre, Écosse, Canada, Québec).
Lévesque, S., & Croteau, J.-P. (2020). *Beyond history: For historical consciousness*. University of Toronto Press.
Macdonald, W. A. (2020). *Might nature be Canadian? Essays on mutual accommodation*. McGill-Queen's University Press.
McKay, I. (2000). The Liberal order framework: A prospectus for a reconnaissance of Canadian history. *Canadian Historical Review, 81*(4), 616–45. https://doi.org/10.3138/chr.81.4.616
Peck, C., Poyntz, S., & Seixas, P. (2011). Agency in students' narratives of Canadian history. In D. Shemilt & L. Perikleous (Eds.), *The future of the past: Why history education matters* (pp. 253–80). Nicosia, Association for Historical Dialogue and Research.
Pollock, S. (2014). The poverty and possibility of historical thinking. An overview of recent research into history teacher education. In R. Sandwell & A. Von Heyking (Eds.), *Becoming a history teacher: Sustaining practices in historical thinking and knowing* (pp. 60–74). University of Toronto Press.
Robichaud, A. (2011). L'histoire de l'Acadie telle que racontée par les jeunes francophones du Nouveau-Brunswick: construction et déconstruction d'un récit historique. *Acadiensis, 40*(2), 33–69. https://id.erudit.org/iderudit/acad40_2art02
Roy, G. (1984). *La détresse et l'enchantement*. Boréal.
Russell, P. H. (2017). *Canada's Odyssey. A country based on incomplete conquests*. University of Toronto Press.
Saul, J. R. (1998). *Reflections of a Siamese twin. Canada at the beginning of the twenty-first century*. Penguin.
Seixas, P., & Morton, T. (2012). *The big six historical thinking concepts*. Nelson.
Wertsch, J. (2002). *Voices of collective remembering*. Cambridge University Press.
Wineburg, S. (2001). *Historical thinking and other unatural acts: Charting the future of teaching the past*. Temple University Press.
Wineburg, S., Mosborg, S., Porat, D., & Duncan, A. (2007). Forrest Gump and the structure of teaching the past. *Phi Delta Kappan, 89*(3), 168–77. https://doi.org/10.1177/003172170708900305

9 Unavoidable Middles: Dilatory Methods of Reading and Comics Creation in Teacher Education

DAVID LEWKOWICH

In her experimental autobiography of childhood, Nathalie Sarraute (1984) recounts a scene of being read to by her parents, where fear and anxiety paralyzed her in the face of unsettling imagery. "I have been given a big bound book," Sarraute recalls, "I enjoy listening when they read me what is written opposite the pictures ... but careful! – we're getting to that picture, it frightens me, it's horrible" (p. 37). Describing her dread as a young reader, Sarraute remembers encountering "a very thin man with a long, pointed nose … brandishing a pair of open scissors." "[H]e's going to cut into the flesh," she tells us, "blood is going to flow." As a young reader, not yet able to distinguish between the liquid world of thoughts and things, the threatening nature of this children's fable remains dangerously close to life as lived outside the text. As a response to their daughter's fear, Sarraute's parents playfully suggest a number of possible solutions: "Would you like us to tear out the page?" they ask. "That would be a pity, it's such a beautiful book." "Well, then," they decide, "we'll hide that picture ... We'll stick the pages together" (pp. 37–8), as if their daughter's knowledge of this fearful image would then suddenly subside.

Unsurprisingly, this creative solution does little to dispel the young reader's fears, for even if she no longer sees it, she cannot help but remember and anticipate the terrifying character now hidden within the page's folds, and though her parents may hope to rid the story of a middle that causes fear, the reader knows the middle is there, and perhaps even more threatening now that it is no longer visible: "I know that it's still there, shut in ... approaching, hidden here, where the page gets thicker" (p. 38). As most experienced readers know, when it comes to the work of narrative, "conditioned expectations of development," as Barthes (1985, p. 141) puts it, require more than a pasted page to be frustrated or seriously thrown into question. Most of the time, it seems, we read without actually reading at all, moving swiftly towards the end, reading what we expect rather than what we do.

In this chapter, I explore what it means to slow such forward movement down, discussing the presence of unavoidable – and at times unwanted, unsettling – middles in the narrative life of teacher education. I will also look at how turning to dilatory, digressive spaces may invite future teachers to play with speculative forms of articulation. For Brooks (1984), the "dilatory space" of narrative is "the space of retard, postponement, error, … partial revelation … [and] the place of transformation: where the problems posed to and by initiatory desire are worked out and worked through" (p. 92). Approaching something similar to Vasudevan's (2011) concept of "unknowing," as "an act of dwelling in the imaginative space between declarative acts of knowing and not knowing" (p. 1157), such speculative articulation may encourage imagination outside of the habitual language otherwise used to discipline lived experience. In reading, as in life, my conviction in this chapter is that it is up to us to shift our gaze to see the dilatory, desiring movements of what may otherwise remain unexpressed, "what is omitted yet exists in gestures between the words" (Taussig, 2011, p. 100).

In what follows, borrowing from Sarraute, I will first discuss an example of where "the page gets thicker" in teacher education, referring to a particularly ambiguous and evocative moment from Mariko and Jillian Tamaki's young adult graphic novel, *Skim*. While considering the questions posed by this tableau, I refer to conversations I had with preservice teachers about the intimate qualities of this scene, as well as what it means when intimacy – as a dilatory and digressive force – brushes closely against the life of students and teachers in school. As a way to foreground the uses of narrative pause and postponement in teacher education, I then describe a number of short comics created by preservice teachers, in which they narrate the enduring presence of adolescent emotional conflict. Thinking in terms of narrative meaning, which "concerns ends in relation to beginnings and the forces that animate the middle" (Brooks, 1984, p. 112), I understand such conflict as one of the permanent, unavoidable middles in the larger narrative plot of teacher education.

Intimacies, Partial and Incomprehensible

In my work with preservice ELA teachers, we sometimes deal with texts that offer a similar kind of anticipatory dread to that which Sarraute encountered as a young reader, where something untold and stubborn seems to bother, unsettle, and resist interpretive resolution. At times we may feel this resistance in relation to personal accounts of teaching; for example, in Sylvia Ashton-Warner's (1986) *Teacher*, we happen upon a story whose account in words feels painfully partial and incomprehensible. "I burnt most of my infant-room material on Friday," Ashton-Warner writes. "I say that the more material there is for a child, the less pull there is on his resources" (p. 118). And yet, as readers who are also teachers, we cannot help but sense that there is more to this act of burning than simple expediency and pedagogical design. There is also purification, hate, and violence, which leads to the question of how these desires, along with the author's frequent mention of love and student instinct, somehow inform the teacher's classroom life (in Ashton-Warner's case, we needn't look very far to see such desires intertwined). As most of my students are nearing the end of their undergraduate degrees, I find it important to consider how, when they read, they "address the work according to what [they] need" (Birkerts, 2007, p. 21), and that their desires and resistances tend to operate according to certain conjectured ends, "seeking the imaginative equivalents of closure that will confer significance on experience" (Brooks, 1984, p. 95). In the narrative structure of teacher education, such ends are typically presumed to be in the form of gainful employment, working as a classroom teacher, and given this, I consider desires and resistances in reading with this particular end in mind, recognizing that as desires shift, so may the reader's position towards the text. An interpretively open text may therefore offer readers a place to explore their own desires, and to pose questions that may have no final answers.

In particular, I have found that comics and graphic novels often appear to use methods of interpretive uncertainty as a means of amplifying the different kinds of readings that readers may pursue: "to allow for, encourage," as Baldwin (2016) argues in the context of dilatory experience, "multiple narratives and interpretations that bump up against each other, generating a continually changing narrative vitality" (p. 542). By pursuing a focus on "the movement, the slidings, the errors and partial recognitions of the middle" (Brooks, 1977, p. 282), we may note that comics work to trigger meaning through what is fragmentary and incomplete, where different layers of symbolization, including a "dance ... between words and pictures" (Mackey & McClay, 2005, p. 193), lead to values that do not always correspond or cohere. As Chute (2011) articulates this tendency of comics to amplify rather than simply reproduce, "The gaps in the story across which we are provoked to make connections are as much a part of the story as the frames themselves" (p. 285), including the knowledge of an unseen middle, perhaps frightening the reader in the face of what resists being understood. And on this point, I will turn my discussion to Mariko and Jillian Tamaki's (2008) *Skim*.

Defensive Positions in Dilatory Reading

As this graphic novel opens, 16-year-old Skim explores the spiritual practices of Wicca, tarot cards, and astrology, though the story soon takes a dark turn as we discover that one of Skim's peers has committed suicide. It is against this tragic backdrop that Skim develops a passionate crush on her English teacher, Ms. Archer. After being suspected of depression by her guidance counsellor, Skim heads down to a wooded area behind her school, and it is here that she first encounters Ms. Archer outside of the classroom environment. As they smoke cigarettes together and discuss *Romeo and Juliet*, bridging classroom activities with those that are not, Skim acknowledges that there is something undeniably peculiar about the way she feels around her teacher: "And suddenly," she narrates, "I'm talking like there's no tomorrow, which is weird, because I'm not a talker" (p. 26). As if to answer Skim's unasked question, Ms. Archer describes the story of Shakespeare's star-crossed lovers as one "of rebellion": "Maybe it's a story about two people who fall in love," she tells Skim, "when falling in love … is the one thing you're not supposed to do" (p. 27). While Ms. Archer's motivations remain unclear, since much of this novel is drawn and written to resemble Skim's diary, it is clear that she is falling deeply in love with her teacher, and soon enough we encounter a compelling limit-case of what may happen when spaces of dreaming and schooling, fantasy and reality, sexuality and pedagogy, collide.

Over a two-page spread, Skim and Ms. Archer share a kiss (figure 9.1) in the wooded area behind the school where they first discussed the prospect of love as a form of rebellion. Drawn as if in the foreground, this kiss appears as a rejection of what the faint and faded background image of the structure of school stands for, including a rejection of the expectations of distance between student and teacher that school habitually requires. In the context of this graphic novel as a whole, however, this scene is more than a straightforward repudiation of the norms governing student teacher relations, since nowhere else in the story is explicit mention made of this erotic encounter. As such, and as a dilatory moment outside of narrative's temporal flow, the question of whether this kiss should be read as reality or fantasy is actually left unclear. It is, as Chiu (2015) puts it, one of the novel's "curious moments out of time" (p. 35), where forward narrative movement is interrupted and the reader themselves steps momentarily out of plot to consider whether or not this episode is actually taking place. With a tension between the seen and unseen, the reader is asked to inhabit the story in a way that makes them curious and complicit; and as Kahn (2014) notes, any reading of this scene remains necessarily and productively unresolved: "Just as the linear progression of the reading is interrupted," she writes, "so is any definitive 'reading' of this encounter" (p. 341).

As such, while the uncertain boundaries of foreground and background may make the reader a culpable subject, we may also note that such culpability may be felt as a form of subversive pleasure, whose primary source is the fact that contexts and positions previously thought immovable and detached are soon shown to be in surprising states of relation and flexibility. For instance, even though the image appears to foreground the wooded area behind the school, the fact of the school is not forgotten, and as such, the image has no definitive centre. In philosophical terms, as Chambers (1999) argues, such ambivalent

9.1. Skim and Ms. Archer share a kiss. Pages 40–1 of Skim reproduced with permission from Groundwood Books Limited, Toronto. Text copyright © 2008 by Mariko Tamaki, illustrations copyright © 2008 by Jillian Tamaki. www.groundwoodbooks.com

borders illustrate an inescapable "permeability of contexts" (p. 12), whereby foreground and background (and the divergent cultural norms that such environments represent) cannot help but be part of the same picture, "neither fully discontinuous nor wholly continuous with each other" (p. 12). In this digressive framework, the image of a student and teacher kissing is invariably interconnected with that of school, and any attempt to separate these contexts prematurely represents a cultural effect of how we define the boundaries of pedagogical relations, as interactive or immobile.

In teacher education (and education writ large), such discursive order – governing what can and cannot be talked about, what is and is not thinkable – is often maintained at the expense of the kinds of curiosity that distraction, dilatoriness, and dreaming inevitably encourage. As Britzman (2009) tells us, “Straying dream thoughts hold no currency in daily classroom life” (p. x), where much of what happens is antithetical to unrestrained thought; on this point Britzman (1998) further speculates, “Education has that peculiar talent for rendering banal the uncertainties of the lived” (p. 55). For Taubman (2009), such tendencies to foreclosed and unremarkable enquiry is especially well established in the learning sciences, whose contemporary influence is felt across educational sites, including teacher education. “Learning,” in this perspective, “assumes a naïve correspondence between words and things, and intention and meaning,” and where an “answer or response is equivalent only to itself” (p. 193). In this point of view, and thinking back to Sarraute’s terrifying vision of childhood reading, pasting a page shut is clearly sufficient enough to ensure a disavowal of its contents. What cannot be seen – or rather, what is not desired to be seen – does not exist. Taubman, however, questions this impossibly acquiescent logic: “[W]hat if,” he asks, “real education happens when something doesn’t work? … What if there is no aim to education other than the brief coming together of teachers and students to question, explore, study, compose, create, and experience a kind of life that most will rarely experience again in our market-driven world?” (p. 195). What if, we may add – on the subjects of narrative, desire, and pleasure – education becomes a place to explore the uncertain detours of the middle, rather than a predetermined requirement to shut such exploration down?

As I now describe the various responses that preservice teachers offered to Skim and Ms. Archer’s kiss, I will emphasize the dilatory effects of reading between the permeable line of tolerable and intolerable, and how these readers articulated their trouble reconciling what they took as an ethical transgression with Ms. Archer’s status as teacher. Though these conversations emerged as part of a larger study, I will here focus only on how these readers (split into two groups) responded to this particular scene. I should also note that while I met most of these students in undergraduate-level classes, these group discussions were voluntary and not bound to any kind of formal curriculum, assessment practices, or disciplinary expectations. The first discussion group included four ELA students (Suzanne, Maria, Steve, and Simon, all pseudonyms) who were in the final year of their undergraduate degrees. They had each completed a five-week placement as student teachers, and often turned to this experience as a means of addressing the text.

As the first person to explicitly address the scene in question, Suzanne discussed the difficulty of reading about Skim and Ms. Archer’s relationship. As she noted, “It’s a complicated relationship to talk about since we’re preservice teachers.” Maria agreed, stating, “It made me pretty uncomfortable,” and “seeing it visualized was very shocking.” She then proceeded to discuss her discomfort in terms of an earlier conversation she remembered having with her mother. “I brought up a question to my mother,” Maria told us:

> … *do you think that teachers have crushes on students*? And before I could even clarify what I meant by that, she said: *Don't even say that, don't even think it, do not verbalize it, do not write it down*. And I was like, *Why? I'm not meaning it sexually*.

Maria then tried to clarify to her mother why she was asking this question: "Because," she continued:

> I experienced a child having a crush on me … and I was like *that's fine, whatever*. But I asked her if … it was the other way around sometimes, like I mean, academically. And she's like: *No, I don't want to hear it. Don't speak about it, nothing. Not even academically, not any way*.

There are two things here that I think especially worthy of conversation. First is the fact that Maria wonders whether attraction, or a "crush" – in this case, intergenerational and pedagogical – needs to be necessarily framed as sexual in nature, or whether there is also the possibility of a different kind of attraction, a cerebral and intellectual one that sidesteps sexuality altogether. In many ways, this is what Skim's relationship with her teacher looked like before they kiss, as they circle in the backwoods between a space of love and flora and one of institutional education. To think about this question in the context of Skim's story, it appears that Maria is actually wondering whether the characters were fated to kiss, or if it may have been possible to maintain their relationship as intellectual, more as friends and colleagues than lovers. Her mother, however, has absolutely no interest in entertaining this question, and even as a purely theoretical speculation, senses the very thought as a dangerous prospect. In this point of view, there is no such thing as ambivalence or curiosity when it comes to the notion of attraction in the classroom.

Following Maria's concern, Steve describes the story of Skim and Ms. Archer as "a cautionary tale of being a teacher," and a lesson regarding the necessity of "keeping a friendly but professional distance." In Steve's view, Ms. Archer's fault as a teacher is that she "lets her … whims guide her," rather than keeping the importance of professional distance "in mind." However, over the course of his group's conversation, Steve decides that this scene must actually be a fiction, that it's "imagined," that it's "a daydream," that "it's something [Skim's] fantasizing about." Given how Steve later admits, "I would like to teach it in schools, except for the whole teacher relationship thing," it seems that more so than his initial reading as "a cautionary tale," he actually needs to read this scene as Skim's fictional creation. In doing so, the transgression ends up being the student's *in fantasy*, rather than the teacher's *in reality*.

For these four readers, then, the fact of this scene is a tragedy, which is nowhere clearer than when Simon states, "I don't think I would teach it to a class, because of the teacher/student relationship." "It's a shame," he continues, hardly able to describe this shame at all, "that there's that one scene with *the thing.*" *The thing.* Not even nameable as a taboo attraction or fiction, this dilatory image has been relegated to the status of an object that, according to the OED, "one need not, cannot, or does not wish to give a specific name to." *The thing.* Sensing Simon's struggle, and a wish to protect his future students (which, if we take projection seriously, is a wish to protect himself), Suzanne makes the following suggestion, uncannily reminiscent to that of Sarraute's parents: "Just tape the pictures together."

Even if taped up, however, we should recall the insights of a young Sarraute, that the middle which is interfered with does not actually go away, but continues to bother and unsettle, even more so if it is ignored. To turn again to Taubman (2009), "Although teaching can be exhilarating, fulfilling, and enlightening, it is also terrifying," and no matter whether our fears are about the sexual nature of student/teacher attraction, the meaningless of teaching, or an out-of-control class, such fears "will always be with us" (p. 129). The question is what we do with our fears and whether or not we allow them to constitute a paranoid text. Nonetheless, and even if their only desire is to avoid this pasted page, these future teachers have here articulated some pretty complex ideas about what they value in educational spaces, values that will certainly continue to shift and mutate. More clearly, and as evidence of what can happen in a dilatory space, the above conversation illuminates the fear that preservice teachers have regarding appropriate pedagogical relationships, and the defensive impulses that the possibility of such relationships inspire.

In the second reading group, two readers in particular (Nicole and Ryan), felt drawn to this scene as an especially compelling example of the competing psychic demands placed on teachers (including themselves as future teachers). In his reading, Ryan focused explicitly on the interplay between foreground and background, seeing the image of the school as an intrusive and persistent force, impeding on the romantic feelings otherwise expressed in the foreground: "they can never actually be together," he said of Skim and Ms. Archer, "because the school is always looming there." Contrary to the first group, Ryan examines this scene without any hint of judgment or shame regarding Ms. Archer's behaviour, which is not to say that he approves of student/teacher relationships, but that he seems to suspend judgment, as an important value of interpretation. Since he reads the scene as "happening in Skim's mind," rather than as an actual encounter, Ryan also doesn't seem to draw a firm line between reality and fantasy, recognizing that what we experience in fantasy invariably forms a part of our reality – that the two are often in flux and conversation, and one does not always have to immediately decide which is one and which is the other. "Whether it actually happens or not," he noted, "it's real to Skim, [and that's] the most important thing." Rather than feeling the need to paste this page shut, Ryan senses the importance of the inessential and tangential, and that who we are is made up of so much more than only what we can see and transcribe.

In her reading of this scene, Nicole noted the difficulty of separating her interpretation from her developing teacher identity, that – as Ryan would probably also agree – our fantasy life informs our interpretation of reality (textual and otherwise), and since we are not typically in control of where our fantasy life leads, we may experience some conflict when reading a dilatory text, especially one whose meaning is ethically ambiguous. As Nicole described her first encounter with this scene, it "really messed me up." "There were," she said, "two halves of me in that moment," as an "internal struggle" compelled her to split her interpretive impulses into competing readers: one that was "personal and more emotional," and one that was "trying to be a professional." In the voice of her first reader, who she associated with herself at "fifteen or sixteen," Nicole argued, "you can't just say, *oh no, it's horrible*, because it's obviously really beautiful. … I was like, *yeah*. I was like, *they're really cute* … You definitely want it to be okay, because it's so romantic." Nicole's second reader, however, is closely aligned with how she imagines herself as a future teacher: "Almost graduating," she told us, "almost being a teacher … that's where the red flags come from." As this reader, concerned with "all the practical stuff," Nicole finds herself thinking, "No, Ms. Archer should know better. Why are they in this situation?" And though she actually finds it distracting, Nicole is unable to cancel out this second, more judgmental voice: "I can't," she noted, as if with a sense of regret, "back through my last four years. I can't unmake myself as a teacher."

Even when reading as a teacher, though, Nicole experiences a sense of deep confusion about Ms. Archer's status, and whether she should be read as "good" or "bad." "In a pedagogical sense," Nicole noted, "Ms. Archer seems to be the best teacher … [since] none of the other teachers seem to try and help [Skim] and engage her." "But," she continued, "when you think about it, no, she's not the best teacher. You're not allowed to kiss your students. That would make her the worst teacher in a way, too." Just as Nicole experiences a split in herself as reader, she also identifies a similar split in Ms. Archer, as an educator who may serve her students well, while at the same time, one who acts in a way that no "good" educator should. "I was left really confused by this," Nicole lamented. "Like, she's the best but the worst teacher. What does that mean?" she asked out loud, before responding with the only answer appropriate to this question: "I don't know what that means."

As an admission of ignorance in the face of a contradictory teacher, and a willingness to leave the question of this teacher's value unresolved, Nicole's approach to this scene stands in contrast to the earlier suggestion of pasting the pages shut. As a response to a dilatory text, however – which, we may recall, is characterized by delay, partial revelation, and error – both approaches seem to share a quality of frustration, since even if the graphic novel's central plot eventually ends, the digressive qualities of this scene ensure that something about Skim's story will always remain open and permanently in question. For the reader, it is certainly understandable that such a lack of resolve may lead to a feeling of frustration, especially if the story in question is one with which they personally identify. As Cixous (1993) states, "A text that presents itself but doesn't end questions the identity of what we are doing" (p. 99). However, what may first appear as frustration may also be read as a form of play, that in the face of a perpetually open text, one of "permanent deferral," as Brooks (1984) notes, the reader is "condemned to playing: to concocting endgames, playing in anticipation of a terminal structuring moment of revelation that never comes, creating the space of an as-if, a fiction of finality" (p. 313). For preservice teachers, this inclination to play in the face of indeterminacy might be a way to transform the anxieties of frustration into something more productive, even if such productivity paradoxically seems to resemble inefficiency. Similar to Manning's (2019) "pragmatics of the useless," such dilatory play is "skeptical of the very idea that we should know in advance where learning will take us" (p. 46), treating education as the indefinite structure that it is. Though we may wish it otherwise, lived experiences of education (Aoki, 2004) are unavoidably indeterminate and inconclusive, and while the school day may end, the time of learning is interminable, often belated, prone to revision, and despite the teacher's best efforts, sometimes never experienced at all. As such, learning to linger in the dilatory may be seen as an important way for preservice teachers to reckon with the emotional challenges of education itself. In the next section, I discuss the ways in which a teacher's adolescent past may serve as a dilatory text, as well as a prompt to alternative forms of speculative articulation.

Adolescence and Comics of Catastrophic Change

As "the conjugator of childhood and adulthood" (Kaplan, 1984, p. 14), adolescence is often defined as a space in between, a borderland connecting before and after, and in this way it functions as the principal dilatory period of the human life cycle. For preservice teachers, their position as not-yet-teachers is psychically similar to the adolescent's position as not-yet-adult, and in their teacher education their adolescence is often exposed in a number of unintended ways, including a defensive inclination to split things in terms of good and bad. If we recall Nicole's response to *Skim*, her idealization of teacher *as professional* is set against the more emotionally fraught and uncontrollable qualities of the adolescent, as if "only the adolescent has psychology and the teacher must manage that" (Britzman, 2012, p. 273).

As a reminder that adolescence and all it represents is not just something that exists in other people, I often ask my students to engage in autobiographical work that helps to reacquaint them with the emotional qualities of these years, while also recognizing that, as a series of psychic relations, adolescence never actually disappears. As a means of acknowledging the fallible nature of memory,

I also invite them to experiment with the kinds of stories they tell, using forms of expression that they may not initially feel that experienced or comfortable with. Especially when working with ELA teachers, a deliberate turn to relative incompetence helps to ensure that stories of self are made vulnerable, lacking the rhetorical consolations and orderly dispositions of scholarly expertise. For example, I recently asked my students to create a short comic about their adolescence, focusing on a particular difficulty – we called them "demons," after Barry (2017) – that like a spectre, continues to linger into adulthood. Turning to an especially dilatory period of life, I therefore asked my students to create dilatory texts, whose purpose was to amplify, symbolize, and illustrate, letting mysteries remain mysterious, rather than reproduce, explain, or overcome. In what follows, I refer to the work of four students, here named pseudonymously as Samantha, Meghan, Thalia, and Claire, turning to some especially curious moments of speculative narrative-making, which demonstrate the economy of pause and postponement that I try to encourage in teacher education. In my descriptions of these short comics, I attempt to provide enough detail for the reader to sufficiently visualize what is happening on the page.

At times, more important than the stories themselves are the minor details that students use in their comics, which often seem accidental in their capacity to reveal the emotional qualities of past experience, while simultaneously gesturing towards the author's current concerns, fears, and desires as pre-service teachers. While perhaps unnecessary to the larger plot, it is precisely the inconsequential nature of such gestures that allows them to "[make] felt the unsayable in the said" (Manning, 2016, p. 7), and to intuitively transport the reader back into the midst of dilatory adolescence.

For instance, in Samantha's comic about test anxiety, anxiety is illustrated as an actual demon, accompanying numerous other images where patterns of resemblance suggest the presence of unspoken relationships. As an example, the motion lines around a student's heart in one panel, indicating a racing heartbeat, are echoed in the next, in which her teeth are described as "get[ting] itchy," an itchiness indicated by motion lines emanating from the mouth. If we read these images as interconnected, the student's heart appears to be beating in her mouth, which she subsequently stops up with her hand. If the heart is a symbol for what the student loves and values, then one effect of anxiety experienced in school may be that the student is forced to silence this valuable part of themselves. As another example, in the story's frontispiece (an introductory page, announcing the story's theme through collage), Samantha has drawn two similarly shaped and similarly sized cracked objects: a chemistry test tube and a pencil. If we read these fractured objects as emotionally related, it seems that the demon of teenage test anxiety works to sabotage not only knowledge's expression (the pencil), but also knowledge itself (the test tube), while the student's anxiety is heightened by the fact that the test appears as the only place in school where knowledge is treated as legitimate and valuable. Though this story leaves such pedagogical implications unaddressed, the question that I see posed by these dilatory connections is how teachers may work to create spaces, outside the test, for students to express themselves and what they value, and how they may also share a variety of forms of knowledge, perhaps unrelated to what the test tube and the pencil represent.

In Meghan's comic, she shares a series of scenes from high school life, in which she felt compromised to change herself in the face of social pressure. There are two aesthetic choices that I find especially curious in these panels. First is the fact that the characters are drawn with absolutely blank faces, and while this may reflect Meghan's skillset as an illustrator, this choice also speaks to the feelings of anonymity that many secondary students experience, as well as the archetypal conflict between wanting to stand out and wanting to fit in. However, since this description points both backward and forward – to Meghan's adolescence and to her future classrooms – such blank faces may also describe Meghan's anxieties about teaching: perhaps, that she may not be able to "read" her students; perhaps, that her students may not be able to read her, and that across this divide of missed communication, that her pedagogy will fail. Curiously, there is also a dividing, jagged line that separates the panels on Meghan's page, which I interpret as not simply a temporal division, but also a metaphor for how ideas can never be fully or adequately communicated. In this sense, it is no coincidence that the speech and thought bubbles are just as blank as the character's faces. Faceless people and empty speech – as a series of nightmarish images, Meghan's comic communicates something about what keeps teachers up at night, similar to Taubman's (2009) recognition of "deadly silence" as one of the "fears [that] inhere in teaching" (p. 129).

After the first two pages of her comic, in which she shows herself as a young girl with a ball and chain attached to her feet, being told to "act like a lady," Thalia offers a heartbreaking description of resignation that, at the same time, is a recognition that things could and should be otherwise. Thalia's comic is a series of five simple panels. The first displays the upper torso of a human figure pictured from the back, facing down a long road, with an indiscernible object approaching in the distance. In the second panel, the approaching object (which now resembles a boulder) is larger, and thus threateningly closer to the motionless human figure. Attached to these two first panels are the words: "Just because it's normal, doesn't mean it's right." In the third panel, the figure appears as if shaded by a dark circle, indicating that they are likely now at risk of being smothered by the boulder. In the fourth panel, the figure's body is flipped and completely shaded, now expressing a pair of closed eyes and mouth. Accompanying the third and fourth panel are the words: "But what choice do we have." In the final panel, the figure is splayed out on the road, with the boulder on top of them, with the word "resilience," in quotation marks, appearing on the boulder itself.

The first conspicuous detail in Thalia's comic is the fact that, unlike the rest of the words on these pages, "BUT WHAT CHOICE" is written on a separate piece of paper pasted over the first. Though we are here far removed from Sarraute's story, as well as *Skim*'s illustration of student/teacher romance, Thalia's choice of including a pasted text cannot help but remind me of "where the page gets thicker." And, just as with the desire to paste over a controversial scene, we should recall that a pasted page always indicates the presence of something underneath, perhaps an alternative to the scene otherwise described. Are there other choices, I'm led to ask, held in reserve, living in the shadows? Can the pasted page be removed?

Though a little hard to make out, the boulder rolling towards Thalia's nameless character casts a long shadow, indicating a darkness eventually named "resilience." Though typically thought of as a sign of strength, as with Barry's (2017) story of the same name, resilience is here configured as a weight and burden, which runs the risk of crushing those who suffer under its pressure. However, we may also note that Thalia's version of resilience is in quotation marks, which compels the question: How actually resilient is this boulder of "resilience"? Is it hollow? Is it made of papier-mâché? Is it an expectation that can be thrown off, much like the pasted page? Does the word "resilience" mask another, with which it might nonetheless rhyme? Taking Thalia's act of comics creation as a dilatory gesture that brings the reader to an adolescent and emotional middle, "where the event is still welling" (Manning, 2016, p. 15), I suspect that her story is one that she will actively resist seeing reprised in her future role as teacher. To this end, I read "resilience" as rhyming with "resistance" and "recreance," the latter which indicates an unfaithfulness to duty.

In Claire's evocative comic, in which she struggles to pull the pasted pages of the past apart, while meditating on the influence of minutes and memories, she poses a question that frames the piece as a whole: "They said it only takes a minute to change your life … I guess my question is … how do you know which minutes are the ones that changed you? If there was a minute that changed me … I hope it changed me for the better." Over eight interconnected panels, we read a variety of distressing scenes of alienation, uncertainty, and retreat, some of which seem directly pulled from life, and others that read metaphorically, as hallucinations inspired by dreams and things half-seen. Both cases, though, describe moments of "catastrophic change" (Bion, 1977, p. 106), which Ogden (2010) sees as "a change in nothing less than everything" (p. 332). The issue here, however, is not the change itself, but whether or not we can see it, and whether or not we can even recognize that such changes have occurred. As we are living them, occupied in the present, we simply cannot know which thoughts and experiences will leave a lasting effect; it is only in retrospect, via the imperfect methods of memory, that we can hope to access and assess the cumulative impacts of past experience.

What I find especially intriguing about Claire's comic is her use of abstraction and dilatory perspective, whereby – as a reader – we only get an extremely limited view of these scenes, forced to invent our own order, to reach our own conclusions about the various relationships and representations on the page. I see a great white shark baring its teeth, and then what looks like human teeth on a dinner plate; and though I only see half her face, a woman is staring forward (perhaps into a mirror), next to a moment of crisis with words that literally drip, touched by a figure eaten by snakes, eyes hollowed out from the inside; a person lies alone in bed, still life plant life. The fact that Claire's stories are told in pieces reflects an overwhelmingly frustrating aspect of what it feels like to remember. However, while this limited perspective operates as a lack – like an overheard conversation between strangers, we never get the full story – such lacks are also gaps in which we may begin to tolerate the anxiety of not-knowing, and to recognize that certain stories, other's as well as our own, may fall forever outside our grasp. Admittedly, this is a difficult and undesirable task – it is a lot harder to accept and rest with narrative incoherence than to quickly fill a gap with our own stories, desires, and relations. Both for the subject of memory, as well as the reader of partial stories, Claire's comic therefore offers an aesthetic challenge: to not rush to judgment in the face of what we do not, and perhaps never will, know. Even though we may insert our own attempts at resolution, there will always be a surplus to the story that cannot be told, and which, as our expectations of completion are disappointed, brings us back repeatedly to the story's (any and every story's) unavoidable middle.

Conclusion – Middling as a Verb

Elsewhere, I have written about adolescence as "the non-place of human development" (Lewkowich, 2021, p. 45), borrowing from Augé's (1995) description of the "non-places" that travellers find themselves in when shuttling between more identifiable and governable locations. For such travellers, the psychic effect of being in a non-place encourages something different from life before and after, including a sense of momentary reprieve from the identities of everyday life: "a person entering the space of non-place," Augé writes, "is relieved of his usual determinants. … he tastes for a while … the passive joys of identity-loss, and the more active pleasure of role-playing" (p. 103). The experience of the non-place traveller is thus similar to Erikson's "psychosocial moratorium," where a space of developmental pause invites experimentation with different selves and social roles that need not necessarily be bound to lasting, real-world consequences. If understood as a piece of fantasy life, for instance, Skim's encounter with Ms. Archer may be read as a developmental experiment, and a dilatory moment, both for the reader and character alike. For readers, however, the difficulty arises in failing to grasp the ambivalent status of fantasy life, how this scene both could and could not be, at the same time, just as adolescence persists as a series of psychic relations into adulthood.

Building on the idea of adolescence and teacher education as non-places, where life is often lived in close relation to a different world (adulthood and the classroom, respectively) that is simultaneously ultra-real and theoretical, my concern in this chapter has been with the use and creation of literary non-places, as synthetic experiments that slow the forward movement of learning down, focusing less on teleological, satisfactory conclusions, than on what is speculative, fragmentary, and incomplete. In this chapter's illustrations of dilatory experience, where reading and comics creation appear to encourage middling as a verb, students learning to teach have been able to explore the defences and anxieties of being in a place where knowledge, both of self and others, is not always secure and dependable. As a preparation for classroom life, such digressive techniques insert an element of wonder in teacher education, which, as Burnett and Merchant (2016) note, "evokes an uncertainty or unknowing that is an important counterpoint to the certainties that undergird the rigid and unitary accounts" (p. 274) of knowledge creation and sense making in schools. Such acts of wonder also allow students to explore the artificiality of social conventions typically taken for granted as given in education; by making the real synthetic, we may thus work together to touch what is more transient and elusive about the inner worlds of teachers and students.

And yet … the question of the pasted page persists, where readers and teachers alike are often made to choose between ignoring the parts of a story that do not immediately satisfy, and continually labouring under the allied signs of fear and anxiety. Countering the knowledge of a young Sarraute, and adopting a dilatory position of wonder and unknowing, I will here speak counterintuitively, and propose that when the page is pasted shut, the middle continues to grow, in ways that we will always, necessarily, fail to comprehend. Teaching with the middle is thus equivalent to teaching with and through mystery – excessive, everchanging, persistent, invisible, unavoidable, and if we can bear being honest about not knowing, an important part of what seems to make us human. Speaking about dreams, Cixous (2006) describes this sense of mystery well, which also seems an appropriate place to – at least for a moment – suspend my thoughts: "Is that me? That's me. But maybe it is you as well. It is certainly an extremely inventive hell" (p. 5).

REFERENCES

Aoki, T. T. (2004). *Curriculum in a new key: The collected works of Ted T. Aoki* (W. F. Pinar & R. L. Irwin, Eds.). Lawrence Erlbaum Associates.

Ashton-Warner, S. (1986). *Teacher*. Simon & Schuster.

Augé, M. (1995). *Non-places: Introduction to an anthropology of supermodernity*. Verso.

Baldwin, C. (2016). Ethics and the tyranny of narrative. In I. Goodson (Ed.), *The Routledge international handbook of narrative and life history* (pp. 536–49). Routledge.

Barry, L. (2017). *One hundred demons*. Drawn and Quarterly.

Barthes, R. (1985). *The grain of the voice: Interviews 1962–1980* (L. Coverdale Trans.). Hill and Wang.

Bion, W.R. (1977). *Seven servants*. Aronson.

Birkerts, S. (2007). *Reading life: Books for the ages*. Graywolf Press.

Britzman, D. P. (1998). *Lost subjects, contested objects: Toward a psychoanalytic inquiry of learning*. State University of New York Press.

– (2009). Preface. In M. O'Loughlin (Ed.), *The subject of childhood* (pp. ix–xii). Peter Lang.

– (2012). The adolescent teacher: A psychoanalytic note on regression in the professions. *Journal of Infant, Child, and Adolescent Psychotherapy*, *11*(3), 272–83. https://doi.org/10.1080/15289168.2012.700818

Brooks, P. (1977). Freud's masterplot. *Yale French Studies, No.* 55/56, 280–300. https://doi.org/10.2307/2930440

– (1984). *Reading for the plot: Design and intention in narrative*. Harvard University Press.

Burnett, C., & Merchant, G. (2016). Boxes of poison: Baroque technique as antidote to simple views of literacy. *Journal of Literacy Research*, *48*(3), 258–79. https://doi.org/10.1177/1086296X16668625

Chambers, R. (1999). *Loiterature*. University of Nebraska Press.

Chiu, M. (2015). A moment outside of time: The visual life of homosexuality and race in Tamaki and Tamaki's *Skim*. In. M. Chiu (Ed.), *Drawing in color lines: Transnational Asian American graphic narratives* (pp. 27–48). Hong Kong UP.

Chute, H. L. (2011). Materializing memory: Lynda Barry's one hundred demons. In M. A. Chaney (Ed.), *Graphic subjects: Critical essays on autobiography and graphic novels* (pp. 282–309). University of Wisconsin Press.

Cixous, H. (1993). *Three steps on the ladder of writing* (S. Cornell & S. Sellers, Trans.). Columbia University Press.

– (2006). *Dream I tell you*. Columbia University Press.

Kahn, A. (2014). On being unique: Gender subversion in two graphic novels for young adults. *Journal of Graphic Novels and Comics*, *5*(3), 336–43. https://doi.org/10.1080/21504857.2014.908403

Kaplan, L. J. (1984). *Adolescence: The farewell to childhood*. Simon & Schuster.

Lewkowich, D. (2021). Adolescent memory beyond reflection: Hulu's *PEN15* and the emotional recapitulations of teacher education. *Review of Education, Pedagogy, and Cultural Studies*, *43*(1), 27–48. https://doi.org/10.1080/10714413.2020.1837603

MacKey, M. & McClay, J. K. (2000). Graphic routes to electronic literacy: Polysemy and picture books. *Changing English: Studies in Culture and Education*, *7*(2), 191–201. https://doi.org/10.1080/13586840050137955

Manning, E. (2016). *The minor gesture*. Duke University Press.

– (2019). Propositions for a radical pedagogy, or how to rethink value. In K. Leander and C. Ehret (Eds.), *Affect in literacy learning and teaching: Pedagogies, politics and coming to know* (pp. 43–9). Routledge.

Ogden, T. (2010). On three forms of thinking: Magical thinking, dream thinking, and transformative thinking. *The Psychoanalytic Quarterly*, *79*(2), 317–47. https://doi.org/10.1002/j.2167-4086.2010.tb00450.x. PMid:20496835

Sarraute, N. (1984). *Childhood.* (B. Wright, Trans.). George Braziller.

Tamaki, M., & Tamaki, J. (2008). *Skim*. Groundwood.

Taubman, P. M. (2009). *Teaching by numbers: Deconstructing the discourse of standards and accountability in education*. Routledge.

Taussig, M. (2011). *I swear I saw this: Drawings in fieldwork notebooks, namely my own.* University of Chicago Press.

Vasudevan, L. (2011). An invitation to unknowing. *Teachers College Record, 113*(6), 1154–74. https://doi.org/10.1177/016146811111300602

10 Reconstructing Curriculum Studies in Canada: Life Writing, Settler Colonialism, Truth, and Then Reconciliation

NICHOLAS NG-A-FOOK

#NarrativeSnapshot 1: Running a Course

Running. Struggling while running, to find a pace, one's place, as an uninvited guest along the shores of the Kichi Zibi, on the unceded and unsurrendered traditional territories of the Anishnàbeg. Pacing, to find one's breath, a rhythm, a coursing, a timing that momentarily forgets my body struggling, while moving, migrating, meditating about writing, researching, and teaching. Running along a gravel path. Running as mediation, meditation as running, running and meditation together as a praxis of curriculum theorizing. Pausing from a virulent world on fire, curriculum theorizing, while meditating, being, and running. Running to the past, and back again to this present moment, speculating towards a future horizon. I am running, a course, a coursing through time and space, recursive and iterative images come together, as a confluence of turbulent temporal movements, reactivating, reconstructing, juxtaposing, and restorying (restoring) a subject, subjected, in this chapter, and at this situated moment, to "life writing," "settler colonialism," "truth," and then "reconciliation."

I must have rewritten this chapter several times now … while running along the Kichi Zibi a major historical and contemporary artery for making, trading, and breaking relations here in, what most of us settler citizens call Canada. And, where our family was living at the time of Bill Pinar's and Anne Phelan's conceptualizations of *Curriculum Studies in Canada: Present Preoccupations* is quite different from the current contexts of living curriculum, *currere*, in relation to a global pandemic and its civic unrest. So, how might we start to restory a "reconstructing" of "Canadian" Curriculum Studies in relation to life writing, settler colonialism, truth, and then reconciliation? And why these curricular concepts, and not others?

What I proposed initially for this chapter was to retrace the intellectual studies that have shaped me as a curriculum theorist or, as Dwayne Donald (2020) suggests elsewhere, a student of curriculum studies. To do so today, I draw on life writing research to "reactivate" and "reconstruct" the international,

national, and provincialized curriculum studies scholarship which has shaped the situated particularities of this current moment of "curriculum theorizing." More specifically, I retrace the intellectual works that graduate students and I studied while running a course together called *EDU 6102: Curriculum Studies Seminar* (Ng-A-Fook, 2020).

In that course, we were called upon to attend to a "critical examination of research within the field of curriculum studies" (Ng-A-Fook, 2020, p. 1). During our weekly online conversations, I invited graduate students to reactivate, reconstruct, unlearn, and learn the different settler colonial conceptions of what might constitute "Canadian Curriculum Studies" in relation to Aoki's (1983/2004, 1992/2004, 1993/2004) concepts of the curriculum-as-planned, -implemented, and -lived (see also Baergen, 2021). Over the course of the term, and during our intellectual studies, our meditations, our conversations, we drew on *currere*, life writing research, to analyse and synthesize the juxtaposition of different narrative snapshots that seek, without promise, to reactivate the absent presence of "settler colonialism," "truth," and then "reconciliation" towards reconstructing our understandings of "curriculum," and perhaps even ourselves and our relations with others (Howell & Ng-A-Fook, 2023a). A micro-situated synthesis, if you will, of what Rocha (2020) calls elsewhere *The Syllabus as Curriculum*. Or here in this chapter, what we might contemplate as reconstructing a curriculum studies seminar, a complicated conversation, with and about the concepts of "Canadian" and "curriculum" in relation to restorying and (re)placing the intertextual narrative tapestries of our life histories.

In what follows then, I share a series of what I have called elsewhere narrative snapshots, always situated, and partial (Ng-A-Fook, 2014). Moreover, I draw on the recurring methodological movements of *currere* to address the following questions: What is the "isness" of "Canadian" curriculum studies? What are our relations to such "isness?" And yet, what I am asking here is not for the "business," or instrumentalized "busyness" of understanding "curriculum" in the making, but rather for a breaking, and a remaking, of our understandings of "Canadian," "curriculum," "settler colonialism," "truth" and then "reconciliation," in terms of the temporal dimensions of our public consciousness. Students often chuckle, or whisper to each other: "Is he really serious about the isness?" We often begin to address such curriculum inquiries through the life writing scholarship of Cynthia Chambers (1994, 1999). Together, we reconsider her four foundational questions in relation to our lived experiences with Aoki's (1986/1991/2004) conceptions of the curriculum-as-planned, -implemented, and -lived.

1. How are we experimenting with tools from different Canadian intellectual traditions and incorporating them into our theorizing?
2. What kinds of languages and interpretive tools have we created to study what we know and where we want to go?

3. In what ways have, and are, curriculum theorists writing in a detailed way the topos – the particular places and regions where we live and work?
4. How are these places inscribed in our theorizing, as either presence or absence, whether we want them there or not? (Chambers, 1999; and see also Ng-A-Fook, 2014)

As Dillon (2009) reminds us, the kinds of questions that have been asked of the "isness" of curriculum have not changed that much within our field of study, or the remaking of curriculum inquiries that take place within teacher education and/or within the K-12 schooling system. And yet, for several graduate students, it is a first invitation to experiment with life writing research methodologies, like *currere*, as they labour to break, reactivate, perhaps dreaming differently, towards reconstructing their understandings of being Canadian and as students of curriculum studies, in-deed, maybe even in terms of themselves. Together, we attempt to trouble the very settler colonial concept of (and of not) being Canadian, and its respective intellectual traditions, while seeking to reconstruct a field of dreams as truth and reconciliation education.

#NarrativeSnapshot 2: Life Writing Research as *Currere*

The undertones of my teachings, empirical research, life as a site of inquiry, and curriculum theorizing continue to be informed by Pinar's (2019a) concept of *currere*: regression, progression, analysis, and synthesis. "As a verb – *currere* – curriculum becomes," as Pinar suggests,

> a complicated, that is, multiply referenced, inspirited conversation in which interlocutors are speaking not only among themselves but to those not present, not only to historical figures (and unnamed peoples) and places they may be studying, but to politicians and parents alive and dead, not to mention to the selves they have been, are in the process of becoming, and someday may become. (p. 23)

Moreover, as I remind students, "the method of *currere* seeks to understand the contribution academic studies makes to one's life (and vice versa), and how both are embedded in society, politics, and culture" (Pinar, 2019, p. 25). And yet, studying our lived experiences, involves revisiting *currere* as a "recurring movement" (Aoki, 2004, p. 457).

For some time now, Pinar has revisited the concepts of allegory, juxtaposition, reactivation, reconstruction across his different scholarly works – what I would call intellectual pieces of art, of moving and juxtaposing historical and contemporary images, situated narrative snapshots, assembled in turn as complex temporal montages (Pinar, 2003a, 2011, 2019a, 2019b). In the third edition of *What Is Curriculum Theory*, for example, Pinar (2019a) explains,

> Through allegory one narrates a specific story that hints at a more general significance. Its characters are at once particular and symbolic, simultaneously historical and transcendent, even mythological or spiritual. Understanding curriculum allegorically self-consciously incorporates the past into the present, threaded through one's subjectivity. In speaking allegorically, we are not merely exchanging information. When we speak allegorically we do not do so for the sake of a future in which such information will, we imagine, become usable. Rather, we self-reflexively articulate what is at hand, reactivating the past so as to render the present, including ourselves, intelligible, in conversation with others. (pp. 27–8)

"Curriculum as *currere* emphasizes" then, as he makes clear, "temporal distinctions to encourage the preservation of the present through its reactivation" (p. 28). We can see Pinar leaning on these interpretative transdisciplinary concepts to analyse and synthesize different historical and contemporary societal movements and their respective macro and micro contexts such as, but not limited to the racialized and gendered violence of lynching in the American South, *No Child Left Behind*, *Race to the Top*, the nightmare that is the present, the Weimar Republic, Harlem Renaissance, or the cultural and psychic self-dissolution of our subjectivity into an enmeshment with distractions and our iPhone's digital screen. "Distraction, demands," as Pinar (2019b) warns, "self-dissolution," where "one runs fast to remain in place, updating to stay the same" (p. 2). And here we are, in Canada, studying during a global pandemic, where settler colonialism continues to update its hard drive and software, apologizing to remain in place, reconciling and replacing its future algorithmic ways, embracing economic dreams, breaking away, towards (re)settling to stay the same.

In *Moving Images of Eternity: George Grant's Critique of Time, Teaching, and Technology*, Pinar (2019b) reactivates the past, drawing our attention towards a Canadian philosopher, a teacher, and offers a reconstruction of how we might restory ourselves in relation to differing conceptions of "Canadian" and "curriculum" in our studies. "Even so," he tells us, "listening to Grant teach through studying the texts he composed – his conversation with "great thinkers" and with those in his midst – summons his subjective presence, requiring reactivation of the past that inhabits us, providing an opportunity for subjective reconstruction, perhaps even a portal to transcendence" (p. 15). Grant, like we students of curriculum, "struggled to decipher the meaning of 'what this is that we are'" (p. 17). Like Bill, I stress to students, to readers, that "reactivation" is a prerequisite towards reconstructing curriculum studies in Canada in relation to unlearning settler colonialism as "truth," and then, as "reconciliation." It is part, of what Pinar (2019b) calls

> a reformulation of the regressive phase of *currere*, a method of studying one's lived experience of curriculum that encourages not only the remembrance of things

> past from points of view in the present, but also a re-experiencing of their immediacy there, a temporal regression in the educational service of reconstructing one's subjective experience of the present. (p. 48)

"Reconstruction," is for Pinar (2019b), scholars, and students of *currere*

> a reformulation of the analytical phase of the method of ***currere***, wherein one attempts to learn from what reactivation of the past has disclosed, incorporating the knowledge revelation presents into a reconstructed understanding of who one was made to be, of what is at stake in the present moment, understanding that is now informed – experientially and intellectually. (p. 50)

So, for this chapter, this moment of curriculum theorizing, of life writing, of running and meditating, I am leaning on a method of *currere*, and Bill's concepts of reactivation and reconstruction to analyse and synthesize a settler colonial curriculum-as-planned, -implemented, and -lived inside and outside the temporal educational landscape of a curriculum studies seminar course.

#NarrativeSnapshot 3: Reactivating Settler Colonial Dominions towards Re/making an End

So how might we reactivate our past via life writing research towards a reconstructed understanding of who one was made to be? Our family now lives on the shores of the Kichi Zibi, a few kilometres downstream from our settler colonial Parliament of Canada. Prior to living on the ancestral unceded territories of the Kichi Zibi Anishnàbeg (McGregor, 2004), our family immigrated to Canada from Georgetown Guyana and Glasgow Scotland to Kapuskasing, a small rural logging town in northern Ontario (Ng-A-Fook, 2015, 2016). As a first-generation hyphenated bilingual – Hakka-Guyanese-Irish-Scottish – settler immigrant, I attended the Franco-Ontario Catholic schooling system, while learning to become a "good" bilingual settler colonial Canadian citizen (Ng-A-Fook, 2009). And yet, unlearning and learning about and with the First Nations communities whose territories we settled, Treaty 9, was not part of our family or school curriculum, nor our settler historical consciousness (Long, 2010). Such treaty citizenship education was certainly not part of the social studies or history curriculum.

During the 1970s, '80s, and '90s the Ontario public schooling system and its curriculum ensured that we would learn to forget while settling and becoming cohesive and prosperous Canadian citizens, in that place at that time. We learned the necessary settler colonial financial literacy to ensure (insure) that we could continue to profit from certain intergenerational settler colonial treaty benefits and exclusive privileges. Our family was able to purchase land, secure a mortgage, pay property taxes, and generate economic equity over time due to, among other things, the Indian and Lands Dominion Acts, Reserve and Pass Systems, numbered Treaties, and the Indian Residential and Indian Day Schooling Systems, the Métis Script, and the 1960s Scoop (Coulthard, 2014; Daschuk, 2013; Joseph, 2018). As Brant-Birioukov (2021) makes clear, "from the early sixteenth century onward, the colonization of North America inflicted violent, intentional, and aggressive tactics to remove Indigenous peoples from ancestral lands. The historical injustice of colonization was the original "apocalypse" of North America" (p. 4). Let us not forget, then, that such settler colonial violence, and the strategic apocalyptical removal of Anishnàbeg and other Indigenous Peoples from their ancestral lands, is what enables us the intergenerational privileges to study our relations with curriculum X at the University of Ottawa.

In turn, such intergenerational settler colonial economic "equity," wealth, and respective financial literacies, supported our university education as first-generation immigrants, which later translated into a professorship of curriculum theory at the University of Ottawa, with an annual income exceeding an annuity of four to five dollars a year,[1] buying land, sending our three boys to public school, and continuing to remake our intergenerational economic equity over time (Sharma, 2020). The Ontario school curriculum still teaches us to forget how old stock and first-generation immigrant Canadians, like myself and our family, become such "benevolent" beneficiaries who continue to profit from investing in settler futurities. It is, as Donald (2019) makes clear, part of the curricular perpetuation of *Homo economicus* and the great forgetting.

In 1906, Duncan Campbell Scott published in *Scribner's Magazine* an account of his canoe travels north to "negotiate" the parameters of Treaty 9 with different Cree and Ojibwe leaders and their communities. In it, he wrote,

> The territory contains much arable land, many million feet of pulpwood, untold wealth of minerals, and unharnessed water-powers sufficient to do the work of half the continent. Through the map of this unregarded region Sir Wilfrid Laurier, Premier of Canada, had drawn a long line, sweeping up from Quebec and curving down upon Winnipeg, marking the course of the eastern section of the new Transcontinental Railway. (p. 574)

Here I am attempting to reactivate the past in relation to my present intergenerational economic equity, and the future guarantees that came with the re/making of a settler colonial nation-state called Canada for some of its citizens, and an acknowledgment by Duncan himself, called a *making of an end* for First Nations families and their communities.

To do so, and at that time, Duncan Campbell Scott (1906) acknowledged the symbolic and psychological violent absent presence of a Dominion police force.

> I am bound to say the later (police force) outshone the members of the commission itself in the observance of the Indians. The glory of their uniforms and the wholesome fear of the white man's law which they inspired spread down the river in advance and reached James Bay. before the commission. (p. 574)

Policing was used to ensure the settler colonial parameters of negotiating Treaty 9. Policing continues to be used today against any First Nations, Inuit, and Métis communities seeking to protect what was promised by former and present settler colonial governments and its citizens. In our historical and moral justifications, all we are left with is a settler politician, public administrator, and poet's written interpretations of what Chief Missabay and others shared during their Treaty 9 negotiations.

> "Yes," said Missabay, "we know now that you are good men sent by our great father the King to bring us help and strength in our weakness. All that we have comes from the white man and we are willing to join with you and make promises which will last as the air above the water, as long as our children remain who come after us." (p. 578)

Such settler colonial "benevolent" and "paternalistic" historical and contemporary reinterpretations continue to persist in our public schooling history curriculum and policing its respective textbooks here in Canada. They persist in government policies directed at First Nations, Inuit, and Métis communities. It persists for several Canadian citizens, as the case of Senator Beyak illustrates, in our historical public settler consciousness (Carleton, 2021; Howell & Ng-A-Fook, 2022; Howell & Ng-A-Fook, 2023b). Duncan Campbell Scott (1906), a poet, a writer, a politician, a bureaucrat, a public intellectual, and "Canadian" citizen, put forth the following apocalyptical settler colonial futurity:

> But any forecast of Indian civilization which looks for final results in one generation or two is doomed to disappoint. Final results may be attained, say, in four centuries by the merging of the Indian race with the whites, and all these four things – treaties, teachers, missionaries, and traders – with whatever benefits or injuries they bring in their train, aid in making an end. (p. 582)

In response, how might we, then, reread such historical narrative accounts in ways that seek to reactivate, reconstruct, and restory the fetishization of such settler colonial "benevolence" in relation to how each of us has, and continues, to benefit from such broken treaty promises, harms, and injuries? How might we as a family live in relation with Kichi Zibi Anishnàbeg families, communities, and other First Nations who have yet to surrender their lands via any treaties? What are our responsibilities towards reactivating such past accounts and harms in relations to co-reconstructing a different kind of futurity?

#NarrativeSnapshot 4: A Canadian Curriculum Theory Project

Over 20 years ago, Bill invited me to join an amazing, thought-provoking group of curriculum scholars at Louisiana State University (William E. Doll Jr., Denise Egéa-Kuehne, Claudia Eppert, Petra Munro Hendry, and others). At that time, I, like many of the graduate students who now take the *Introduction to Curriculum Studies* course, were studying what constituted an international field of curriculum studies in terms of its histories and its discursive regimes. We analysed and synthesized its different situated particularities in relation to our curriculum-as-lived. Two of my first research assistantships involved copyediting the *International Handbook of Curriculum Research* (Pinar, 2003b), as well as *A Curriculum in A New Key* (a collection of Ted Aoki's intellectual work). At that time, I struggled to understand the different dimensions of studying, curriculum theorizing, reading different intellectual works on existentialism, phenomenology, post-structuralism, educational philosophy, Indigenous ways of knowing, life writing research methodologies, feminist and queer theory, internationalization, and so on, and so on. And all the while, not knowing, not necessarily understanding the relations among what I was studying in terms of who I was, am, and could be as a curriculum scholar, or even for that matter, a human being.

During the devastating and traumatic events of 9/11, in a course with Bill we read *The Gender of Racial Politics and Violence in America*. For me, within the contexts of public schooling, it was my first formal introduction to the historical and contemporary intersectional fluid confluences of gender, race, and sexuality, and to the narrative images of Black bodies, fellow human beings, hanging from southern magnolia trees. It was a "reactivation" and "reconstruction" for how I began to unlearn and relearn to look (back) at Canada, in terms of its historical harms perpetuated in the nation-state formation of a settler colonial democratic commonwealth confederacy. In its opening pages, drawing on Claudia Eppert's (1999) intellectual study on becoming a *historical witness*, Pinar (2001) reminds us,

> What is melancholic for me – or should I say what leaves me in mourning – is to live among and teach white people who remember nothing, who perceive "racisms" as merely attitudinal, and as common among black folks as among white, and, most surprisingly, having nothing to do with them. (p. 5)

"Such knowledge," he continues "may be traumatizing, threatening to shatter the narcissistic unity of the 'subject,' decentering and displacing it 'as ego' " (p. 5). Such calls for reactivating and reconstructing the unity of settler colonial violence is, as Pinar (2001) stressed then, "curriculum as *currere*, an excavation of the lived – including historical – relations among self, society, and subject matter" (p. 6). "This labor of excavation is made difficult," as he warned then, "by the various defenses in place against it." Such defences, or Socratic apologies, of "reconciliation" in the name of settler colonialism, in the name of neoliberal forms of democracy, are embedded in the very material and psychosocial bedrock of a Canadian society and its public consciousness (Henderson & Wakeham, 2013; Craft & Regan, 2020; Howell & Ng-A-Fook, 2023a).

Although I had several different intellectual opportunities to study the violent segregation and killing of black mothers, fathers, and children, such intellectual reactivations did not necessarily translate towards reconstructing (breaking from) my curriculum-as-lived in relation to anti-Black racisms outside of the gates of Louisiana State University (Munro Hendry & Edwards, 2009). Such psychic and institutional segregation, the present absence of the racial politics and violence in Canada continues to haunt my work as a curriculum scholar and university administrator today. Perhaps, what has been hopeful these past few years is to see different school administrators, teachers, and colleagues committed towards addressing the ongoing intergenerational violence of settler colonialism and unlearning its "syllabus as curriculum" (Rocha, 2020). And yet, I remain mired in frustration, even disheartened, with government institutions and their respective policies that continue to offer deferred broken promises as incremental equity. For many First Nations, Inuit, and Métis, settler Canadians continue to be *The Marrow Thieves* (Dimaline, 2017).

Creating *A Canadian Curriculum Theory Project* is an active response and a physical, intellectual, virtual curricular, and pedagogical place where our research team can draw on different life writing research methodologies – oral history, narrative inquiry, critical ethnography, autobiography, and more – to curriculum theorize and study, among other things, the macro and micro relational contexts and impacts of transnational migration, settler colonialism, truth and reconciliation education, teacher education, higher education leadership, systemic inequities, curriculum studies, ethical relationality, and anti-Black and anti-Indigenous racisms. Much like the *Curriculum Theory Project* at Louisiana State University, it provides a place, a communal ecosystem, for graduate students and me to study different intellectual histories in relation to present circumstances and future prospects (see www.curriculumtheoryproject.ca).

Part of our educational research, life writing, and curriculum theorizing, seeks to reactivate, reconstruct, juxtapose, and restory our past, present, and future relations with "settler colonialism," "truth," and then "reconciliation" and perhaps blaze another trail as a reconstructive intervention.

#NarrativeSnapshot 5: Changing Courses, a Coursing, in Relation to Global Pandemic

When I initially accepted to present this chapter as part of the University of British Columbia Faculty of Education *Curriculum Studies in Canada Seminar Series*, I was scheduled to teach during the 2020 spring/summer session. I hoped to spend the rest of July and August, taking some reprieve with family and focus on research and writing. I also planned to take a much needed sabbatical that January of 2021. Consequently, I thought it would be in my best interest to teach those two courses during the 2020 spring/summer sessions and then not teach again until the following September of 2021. One of those courses was EDU 5260: Introduction to Curriculum Studies, which I have taught online asynchronously on several occasions. The other course was the EDU 6102: Seminar in Curriculum Studies course, which I planned originally to teach on campus. At that time, it was unclear to me, and perhaps others, what the implications of a global pandemic might have for us here in the Ottawa region, let alone the rest of Canada (Ng-A-Fook et al., 2021; Brant-Birioukov, 2021; Donald, 2020). I remember driving in our black minivan as a family to Mount Sutton for March Break. Just as we crossed the Quebec provincial border, we received a phone call that Mont Sutton was closed for the foreseeable future. We scrambled to cancel our accommodations and travel plans. Shortly after, different federal, provincial, and municipal politicians quickly called on us to self-isolate and to physically distance from one another. Like others, we witnessed the exponential spread of COVID-19 first across Quebec, British Columbia, then Ontario, and the rest of Canada.

For the first two weeks we spent our days trying to support each other as a family and maintain some sort of routine. That routine, conducted from the security of our home, included creating an environment for our sons to do their schoolwork at a distance with their teachers. For some university professors, like me, we were also asked to "pivot" and teach our courses online via Zoom, Microsoft Teams, and Brightspace. At that time, I was teaching a synthesis course and a special topics course called Writing Toward Publication (Ng-A-Fook et al., 2021). My biggest pedagogical concern was to support each student's overall mental health and well-being. Being at home, in fear of the unknown, was mentally and emotionally difficult (Vaillancourt et al., 2021). It soon became clear that we would be remaining in self-isolation, teaching and learning at a virtual distance for the foreseeable future. At home with our family, I found myself becoming more and more frustrated, impatient, and even angry, jumping from Microsoft Teams to Teams meetings, zooming in and out, creating online course content, and starting up a podcast called *Fooknconversation* that would later be incorporated into the curriculum-as-planned, -implemented, and -lived for EDU 6102. Perhaps my biggest frustration, working from the security of our home, was the daily competition with my sons and other families in our neighbourhood, who were gaming for the limited internet bandwidth that connected us to a networked virtual world and its clouds. And yet, we were enormously privileged in terms of the lifestyle and access to economic capital that our family has been afforded through my work at a university and intergenerationally; that I can be paid to study, research, and teach from the safety and security of our settler colonial home, just up the ways a little from the banks of the Kichi Zibi.

On 17 April 2020, Laurie Anne decided to take our three boys to Wasaga Beach to finish their school year at a distance and to be closer to her aging parents. Once there, she and the boys self-isolated for two weeks, and then slowly integrated with her parents. There was no access to high-speed Internet, and hence limited access for the boys to plug into the digital gaming industry. Instead, the boys plugged in twice a day via their grandparents' Bell Digital Hub to check in with their teachers and submit assignments. I took advantage of the next 52 days to study and research the intellectual works of different Indigenous and non-Indigenous Canadian scholars, except for Hongyu Wang (2018, 2019) and William F. Pinar (2017, 2019a, 2019b), to produce the first 12 episodes of what now constitutes the *FooknConversation Podcast* and a tentative EDU 6102 course syllabus, a podcasting curriculum if you will, or what we might call curriculum-as-podcasting.

#NarrativeSnapshot 6: Podcasting a Canadian Curriculum Theory Project

The 12-week scope and sequencing of the curriculum studies courses I teach usually are framed through different questions and/or curriculum inquiries. For example, in EDU 5260 Introduction to Curriculum Studies, we might ask:

1. What "is" the "isness" of curriculum studies?
2. How might we understand our lived experiences in relation to the curriculum -as-planned, -implemented, and -lived?
3. What kinds of questions might we ask in relation to, and of, the very concept of "curriculum?"
4. How might we understand the differing intergenerational impacts of settler colonialism across the school curriculum?
5. How are different scholars seeking to disrupt the different curricular dynamics of settler historical consciousness?
6. How might we analyse the curriculum-as-planned, -implemented, -evaluated, and -lived as racializations, racisms, antiracisms, truth, and then reconciliation?
7. How might we critically analyse and synthesize the different (ideological) political perspectives put forth within the contexts of government curriculum policy and public schooling?

8. How might we learn to develop and theorize culturally responsive, relevant, and relational curriculum? What are its possibilities and limitations?
9. What are the possibilities and limitations of using social media curriculum to express public agency and calling attention to subverting and challenging systemic barriers?
10. How might we draw on and reconceptualize curriculum-as-planned, -implemented, and -lived in relation to the more-than-human world?
11. How might you narrate your lived experiences in relation to curriculum-as-planned and -implemented?
12. Why are we asking and/or not asking such questions in relation to curriculum X?
13. Where are we asking such curricular questions?
14. Who is, and is not, asking such questions?

In EDU 6102 Curriculum Studies Seminar, I framed the 12-week course in response to similar curriculum inquiries and as a life writing workshop. For several of us, such life writing, as *currere*, is epistemological. For others, it is ontological. And at times, maybe even relationally onto-epistemological, where study, theorizing, and writing about and with such concepts dissolve, as reactivations and reconstructions, into the temporal horizon of our conversations with ourselves and others. Drawing on Aoki's (1983/2004) theoretical works, we sought to deconstruct and reconstruct narrative interpretations of our realties. For the course, like Aoki and his students, we sought to understand the relations between the self and Curriculum X, where "we see the teacher as a person-who-acts, and thus as a creator of his [or her, their] own reality. As such, he [or she, they] interprets from within his [or her, their] horizon Curriculum X, and engages situationally in its transformation" (p. 120). Such relations among one's lived experiences during the COVID-19 Global Pandemic, academic study, and multiplicity of curricular "isnesses" informed the situated contexts of the ensuing *FooknConversation* podcast interviews with different curriculum studies scholars.

Prior to the start of the course, I began to invite different scholars to join me on the *FooknConversation* podcast. The first to accept was Dwayne Donald (2004, 2009, 2019). And over the course of 12 weeks, together we took up the intellectual works of other Indigenous and non-Indigenous scholars such as, but not limited to, Lindsay Gibson (2018, 2019), Hongyu Wang (2018, 2019), Aparna Mishra Tarc (2011, 2020a, 2020b), Vidya Shah (2018, 2019), Cathryn van Kessel (2018, 2020), Jennifer Tupper (2014, 2020), Theodore Christou (2013, 2015, 2016), Timothy Stanley (2019, 2020), Rita Irwin (Lasczik Cutcher & Irwin, 2017; Triggs & Irwin, 2019; Leblanc & Irwin, 2019), Kiera Brant-Birioukov (2019a, 2019b, 2019c), and William F. Pinar (2017, 2019a, 2019b). To create a curricular and pedagogical framework for each podcast, I invited each scholar to share some of their intellectual work prior to our scheduled conversation on the Zencastr podcast digital platform (see https://zencastr.com/). I then spent the next few weeks studying their work ahead of our conversation. During the podcast interview, I drew on the different concepts put forth in their scholarship to ask questions, free associatively, about their lived experiences during the COVID-19 pandemic, and what we might unlearn and learn together from such onto-epistemological relational reactivations and reconstructions. After our conversations, I downloaded our individual tracks and imported them into Garage Band. By myself at home, listening to our recorded conversation, I edited each episode as a narrative snapshot, which was later uploaded to Speaker (https://www.spreaker.com/), and then the FooknConversation website (see www.fooknconversation.com). I invited each scholar to send a photo, to which I applied different digital filters using Photoleap and Canva to create a unique cover for each podcast episode. The final podcasts are then shared on platforms such as Spotify, VoicEd Radio, and iTunes. The suggested scholarship that informed each podcast interview in turn became part of the weekly readings that we later took up together as part of the course scope and sequencing.

During our ensuing online conversational encounters with the readings and podcast interviews, we sought to "map and remap the ways in which" our "privileges are made possible through colonial structures and in relation to the land" (Tupper, 2020, p. 89). We drew on the different temporal, political, and psychological dimensions of *currere*, and such scholarship, to reactivate and reconstruct how a Canadian settler imaginary is constituted through the public education system and its respective provincialized and territorialized confederated nation-state curricular expectations. And in turn worked, as Tupper (2020) stresses, to maintain a "settler historical consciousness, a collective memory of Canada's part that in/forms a collective understanding of Canada's present" (p. 89). Such a public settler historical consciousness, as Donald (2019) reminds us, is committed to the re/making of a nation-state in relation to systematically ensuring, as memory thieves, a great forgetting. "One of the consequences of fervent faith and worship of consumerism and market capitalism is," as Donald (2019) warns, "a gradual forgetting of the entities that give us life and the stories that remind us of how we are all comprised of sunlight-inspired energy" (p. 114–15). Might we acknowledge, then, that to remember our past, reconstruct our present, and speculate future ethical sustainable relations as human beings with each other and the more-than-human world "calls for a break away from the [settler colonial] orientation that may blind us" (Aoki, 1992/2004, p. 190). For several students in the course, including myself, through studying and listening to these different scholars, as we reactivated the past, juxtaposed with our studies in the present, and worked to reconstruct the isness of "curriculum" via *currere*, we sought to experience and understand what "it" might mean, to be, and/or feel like pedagogically to break with the onto-epistemological temporal dimensions of a settler colonial historical public consciousness.

#NarrativeSnapshot 7: Reconstructing Curriculum Studies in Canada

On 2 June 2020, at 8:48 a.m., I sent the following email message to students, with the subject heading "checking-in":

> Hi everyone,
> I hope you are well. I know for some of you the past few days have been more difficult, perhaps even unbearable as you try to cope with what you have been living and witnessing on the news coverage of the USA and other parts of Canada.
>
> We cannot afford to let those in power silence us. So please, if expressing your pain, anger and/or outrage via writing provides an outlet, then I encourage you to rage in your posts, to share your pain. Dr. Vidya Shah, Dr. Mishra Tarc, Dr. van Kessel, and Dr. Timothy Stanley's podcasts really speak to this current moment of protesting systemic racisms. And, may we come together as a community to support one another.
>
> I was able to read over the posts in Module 4 Discussion Board. Thank you for sharing everyone.
>
> My song of the day: https://youtu.be/fIqi45D3B1E. Day 73!
>
> Until, Nicholas

Several students published narrative snapshots that sought to juxtapose their different lived experiences during a global pandemic in relation to the anti-Black racist killings and ensuing Black Lives Matter Movements in the United States, Canada, and elsewhere.

Drawing on van Kessel's (2018, 2020) scholarship and in his reader response, Drake (2020) wrote,

> *Annihilation is tragically the spark that ignited the flame with respect to the Black Lives Matter movement. In Canada, the list of names grows larger: Regis Korchinski-Paquet, Jason Collins, D'Andre Campbell, Olando Brown, Andrew Loku, Jermaine Carby, Kwasi Skene-Peters, Marc Ekamba-Boekwa, Sammy Yatim, Ian Pryce, Alain Magloire, Nicholas Thorne-Belance, Phuong Na (Tony) Du, René Gallant, Abdurahman Ibrahim Hassan, Bony Jean-Pierre, Abdirahman Abdi, Pierre Coriolan, Brydon Whitstone, Josephine Pelletier, Nicholas Gibbs, Jaskamal Singh Lail, Chad Williams, Greg Ritchie, Machuar Madut, Sean Thompson, Randy Cochrane, Eishia Husdon* (CPEP, 2020)*, are an unforgettable group of people who have lost their lives to police annihilation. It isn't hard to see the connections between these names and the actions that has been pushing this movement towards justice.* (https://www.fooknconversation.com/black-lives-matter-blm/)

Together we addressed such different theoretical concepts, societal issues, events, political movements, and conversations put forth in the readings and podcasts such as, but not limited to the school-to-prison pipeline, addressing the climate crisis, restorying settler colonialism as truth towards being unsettled, living an ethics of care, taking a pause, balance, treaty education, archetypes of consciousness, shadow work, psychic integration, revolt, reparation, unbearable feelings, genocide, assimilation, derogation, annihilation, tolerance, terror management theory, fetishizing fear, the grammar of settler colonial racisms, removing commemorative monuments, banning public expressions of certain faiths in Quebec, homelessness, pivoting, empathy, slow scholarship, new materialism, renderings of living artistic inquiries, seasonal knowledge, renewal, a returning to Elders' teachings, land, prophecies, educational estrangement, ethical relational spaces, transformational pops, systemic inequities, curriculum policy reforms, populist movements, instrumentalism, Black feminist autobiographical research and living curriculum as nonviolence.

Indeed, several students sought to "blaze another trail, one that is bent on a kind of creative, disruptive, reconstructive intervention on the curricular landscape, with no desire to clear or claim space, but only to act on it and change it" (Basile, 2021, p. 3). Together, we attempted to reactivate and reconstruct our lived experiences through life writing narrative snapshots, curriculum theorizing, as *currere*, in creative, ethical, and relational ways that hoped to be "life-giving and life-sustaining for all of us" (Donald, 2019, p. 121). Revisiting such counterpointed historical and contemporary social, political, and historical movements as juxtapositions of narrative snapshots reminds us that the very "isness" of curriculum studies here in Canada remains an opportunity for restorying the uncommon countenances of our differing lived experiences, intellectual histories, and respective interpretations (Ng-A-Fook, 2014). Coming back to Aoki (1983/2004), as part of the curriculum studies seminar, we sought to see ourselves as a person-who-acts, and is a creator of their own reality, where we can begin to reinterpret from within the temporal dimensions of Curriculum X (where X = a settler colonial historical public consciousness as one example), and engage it situationally, ethically, working through the potential transformational processes of *currere*.

Since beginning this chapter of my life, its situated narrative snapshot, we have now experienced four waves in response to the different COVID-19 variants. As we emerge from a global pandemic, might we take heed of Brant-Birioukov's (2021) curricular cautioning, for us "not rush this. Let us grieve for the loss of time, opportunity, relationships, and love" (p. 255). Several of us have been provoked to reconsider and reconstruct our understanding of "curriculum" in terms of our intellectual studies and lived experiences inside and outside the provincialized and territorial settler colonial intellectual and symbolic political borders of a commonwealth nation-state called Canada. We have been called on to reactivate and deconstruct our settler "Canadian" colonial past, put forth its reconstructions, its calls for truth, and then reconcilia(c)tion. Such reconstructions "demand," as Brant-Birioukov (2021) suggests, "greater Indigenous community engagement and required Indigenous education for students across K-12 and post-secondary institutions" (p. 253). Restorying our past, present, and future relations requires a great (re)membering of the kinds of stories, life writing, and narratives we seek to study, write, and share about and through our curriculum studies in relation to the unceded and unsurrendered traditional territories of the Anishnàbeg and other First Nations, Inuit, and Métis communities. Such reactivations and reconstructions invite Canadian educators, curriculum scholars, and citizens "to attend to the settler historical consciousness embedded in our current curricular landscape" (p. 256). And, in turn, reconsider "the implications of Indigenous resilience, innovation, and adaptation and how this informs or renews the curricular discourse" beyond rendering, extracting, mapping, or polic(y)ing it merely for its historical, anecdotal, or unregarded value (p. 256). Restorying curriculum studies calls on us to reactivate and reconstruct our imagination, as Donald (2019) reminds us, beyond "the cultural mythologies of individualism, progress, and anthropocentrism seen in the imagined person of *Homo economicus*" and a colonial mindset (p. 115). Life writing research then, as *currere*, for me, calls on us to continue troubling and re/making the grammar of settler colonialism, our coursings, reactivations, meditations, juxtapositions, running, and our reconstructions of curriculum studies.

NOTE

1 This was amount given per year to First Nations communities who agreed to sign a treaty agreement, set out in several numbered treaties, including Treaty 9.

REFERENCES

Aoki, T. T. (1983/2004). Curriculum Implementation as instrumental action and as situational praxis. In W. F. Pinar & R. L. Irwin (Eds). *Curriculum in a new key: The collected works of Ted. T. Aoki* (pp. 111–23). Lawrence Erlbaum.

– (1986/1991/2004). Teaching as in-dwelling between two curriculum worlds. In W. F. Pinar & R. L. Irwin (Eds). *Curriculum in a new key: The collected works of Ted. T. Aoki* (pp. 159–66). Lawrence Erlbaum.

– (1992/2004). Layered voices of teaching: The uncannily correct and the elusively true. In W. F. Pinar & R. L. Irwin (Eds). *Curriculum in a new key: The collected works of Ted. T. Aoki* (pp. 187–98). Lawrence Erlbaum.

– (1993/2004). Legitimating live curriculum: Toward a curricular landscape of multiplicity. In W. F. Pinar & R. L. Irwin (Eds). *Curriculum in a new key: The collected works of Ted. T. Aoki* (pp. 199–218). Lawrence Erlbaum.

Baergen, P. (2021). *Tracing Ted Tetsuo Aoki's intellectual formation: Historical, societal, and phenomenological influences*. Routledge.

Basile, T. D. (2021). Curriculum theorizing in a systematically antiblack world. M. A. Peters & R. Heraud (Eds.), *Encyclopedia of educational innovation* (pp. 1–5). Springer Nature Singapore Pte Ltd. https://doi.org/10.1007/978-981-13-2262-4_242-1

Brant-Birioukov, K. (2019a). *Mapping the borderlands of Indigenous narrative: An exploration of indigenous narrative inquiry* [Unpublished manuscript]. Faculty of Education,University of British Columbia.

– (2019b). *In pursuit of alterity: Oscillation between the familiar and strange* [Unpublished manuscript]. Faculty of Education, University of British Columbia.

– (2019c). *Towards praxis: Ethical Indigenous education in the practicum experience* [Unpublished manuscript]. Faculty of Education, University of British Columbia.

– (2021). Covid-19 and In(di)genuity: Lessons from Indigenous resilience, adaptation, and innovation in times of crisis. *Prospects, 51*, 247–59. https://doi.org/10.1007/s11125-021-09557-7. PMid:33941989

Carleton, S. (2021). "I don't need any more education": Senator Lynn Beyak, residential school denialism, and attacks on truth and reconciliation in Canada. *Settler Colonial Studies, 11*(4), 466–86. https://doi.org/10.1080/2201473X.2021.1935574

Chambers, C. (1994). Looking for home: A work in progress. *Frontier: A Journal of Women Studies, 15*(2), 23–50. https://doi.org/10.2307/3346760

– (1999). A topography for Canadian curriculum theory. *Canadian Journal of Education, 24*(2), 137–50. https://doi.org/10.2307/1585924

Christou, T. M. (2013). "Schools are no longer merely educational institutions": The rhetoric of social efficiency in Ontario education, 1931–1935. *History of Education, 42*(5), 566–77. https://doi.org/10.1080/0046760X.2013.832409

– (2015). "We find ourselves preoccupied with the world of the present": Humanist resistance to progressive education in Ontario. *History of Education Quarterly, 55*(3), 294–318. https://doi.org/10.1111/hoeq.12123

– (2016). "The task here before us is neither new nor easy": William Blatz and Progressive Education at the Institute for Child Study in Toronto. *The Journal of School & Society, 3*(2), 58–65. http://www.johndeweysociety.org/the-journal-of-school-and-society/current-issue/volume-3-issue-2-2016/.

Coulthard, G. S. (2014). *Red skin, white masks: Rejecting the colonial politics of recognition*. University of Minnesota Press.

Craft, A., & Regan, P. (Eds.), (2020). *Pathways of reconciliation: Indigenous and settler approaches to implementing the TRC's Calls to Action*. University of Manitoba Press.

Criminalization Protection Education Project. (2020, June 09). CPEP. Retrieved June 10, 2020, from https://cp-ep.org/

Daschuk, J. (2013). *Clearing the plains: Disease, politics of starvation, and the loss of Aboriginal life*. University of Regina Press.

Dillon, J. T. (2009). Questions of curriculum. *Journal of Curriculum Studies, 41*(3), 343–59. https://doi.org/10.1080/00220270802433261

Dimaline, C. (2017). *The Marrow Thieves*. Dancing Cat Books.
Donald, D. T. (2004). Edmonton pentimento re-reading history in the case of the Papaschase Cree. *Journal of the Canadian Association for Curriculum Studies*, *2*(1), 21–54. DOI: https://doi.org/10.25071/1916-4467.16868
Donald, D. (2009). Forts, curriculum, and Indigenous Métissage: Imagining decolonization of Aboriginal-Canadian relations in educational contexts. *First Nations Perspectives*, *2*(1), 1–24. https://galileo.org/pl/wp-content/uploads/004_Donald.pdf
– (2019). *Homo economicus* and forgetful curriculum. In H. Tomlins-Jahnke, & S. Styres, S. Lilley & D. Zinga (Eds.), *Indigenous education: New directions in theory and practice* (pp. 103–25). University of Alberta Press.
– (2020, March 29). Talking about "academicky" stuff with Dwayne Donald. https://www.fooknconversation.com/podcast/episode-1-dwayne-donald/
Drake, A. S. (2020, July 2). Black Lives Matter: A case against the defense of fragile beliefs. *FooknConversation Blogs*. https://www.fooknconversation.com/black-lives-matter-blm/
Eppert, C. (1999). *Learning responsivity/responsibility: Reading the literature of historical witness* [Unpublished doctoral dissertation]. University of Toronto.
Gibson, L. (2018). Ethical judgments about the difficult past: Observations from the classroom. In M. Gross & L. Terra (Eds.), *History and social studies education in a context of intolerance* (pp. 81–103). Routledge.
– (2019). Reshaping Canadian history education in support of reconciliation. *Canadian Journal of Education*, *42*(1), 251–84. https://www.jstor.org/stable/26756662
Henderson, J., & Wakeham, P. (2013). *Reconciling Canada: Critical perspectives on the culture of redress*. University of Toronto Press.
Howell, L. & Ng-A-Fook, N. (2022). Unsettling beneficiaries as curriculum inquiries: A case of Senator Lynn Beyak and anti-Indigenous systemic racisms in Canada. *Canadian Journal of Education*, *45*(1), pp. 1–34. https://doi.org/10.53967/cje-rce.v45i1.4787
– (2023a). Truth and then reconciliation research: An emerging field of educational studies. In Robert Tierney, Fazal Rizvi & Kadriye Ercikan (Eds.) *International Encyclopedia of Education* (pp. 272–82). Elsevier.
– (2023b). Just because we're small doesn't mean we can't stand tall: Reconciliation education in the elementary school classroom. *Studies in Social Justice*, *17*(1), pp. 112–35. https://doi.org/10.26522/ssj.v17i1.4044
Joseph, B. (2018). *21 things you may not know about the Indian Act: Helping Canadians make reconciliation with Indigenous peoples a reality*. Indigenous Relations Press.
Lasczik Cutcher, A., & Irwin, R. (2017). Walkings-through paint: A c/a/r/tography of slow. *Journal of Curriculum and Pedagogy*, *14*(2), 1–9. https://doi.org/10.1080/15505170.2017.1310680
Leblanc, N., & Irwin, R. (2019). A/r/tography. Oxford Research Encyclopedias of Education.

Long, J. (2010). *Treaty No. 9: Making the agreement to share the land in far northern Ontario in 1905*. McGill-Queen's University Press.

McGregor, S. (2004). *Since time immemorial: "Our story."* Anishinabe Printing.

Mishra Tarc, A. (2011). Reparative curriculum. *Curriculum Inquiry*, *41*(3), 350–72. https://doi.org/10.1111/j.1467-873X.2011.00554.x

– (2020a). *Pedagogy in the novels of J. M. Coetzee: The affect of literature* (intro). Routledge.

– (2020b). Engaging texts today or how to read a curriculum poem. *Journal of Curriculum Theorizing*, *35*(1), 32–45.

Munro Hendry, P., & Edwards, J. D. (2009). *Old south Baton Rouge: The roots of hope*. University of Louisiana at Lafayette Press.

Ng-A-Fook, N. (2009). Toward understanding a curriculum of being inhabited by the language of the other. *Transnational Curriculum Inquiry*, *6*(2), 3–20. https://doi.org/10.14288/tci.v6i2.32

– (2014). Provoking the very "idea" of Canadian curriculum studies as a counterpointed composition. *Journal of the Canadian Association for Curriculum Studies*, *12*(1), 10–69. https://doi.org/10.25071/1916-4467.37169

– (2015). Autobiography, intellectual topographies, and teacher education. In H. Zhang & W. F. Pinar (Eds.), *Autobiography and teacher development in China: Subjectivity and culture in curriculum reform* (pp. 121–50). Palgrave Macmillan.

– (2016). Becoming an international: Curriculum theory, currere, and subjectivity. In M. A. Doll & M. Morris (Eds.), *The reconceptualization of curriculum studies: A festschrift in honor of William F. Pinar* (pp. 121–9). Routledge.

– (2020). EDU 6102 *Curriculum research seminar syllabus*. University of Ottawa. https://curriculumtheoryproject.ca/wp-content/uploads/2021/08/EDU_6102_Curriculum_Studies_Seminar.pdf

Ng-A-Fook, N., Lee, C., Déri, C., Abat-Roy, V., Barette, J., Drake, A., S., Mya, N., & Luo, X. (2021). Life writing: A literary métissage during a global pandemic. *Transnational Curriculum Inquiry*, *18*(1), 1–23. https://doi.org/10.14288/tci.v18i1.195966

Pinar, W. F. (2001) *The gender of racial politics and violence in America: Lynching, prison rape, and crisis of masculinity*. Peter Lang.

– (2003a). *What is curriculum theory?* Routledge.

– (Ed.). (2003b). *The internationalization handbook of curriculum research*. Lawrence Erlbaum.

– (2011). *What is curriculum theory?* (2nd ed.). Routledge.

– (2017). Study: Concerning relationship in educational experience. In C. W. Ruitenberg (Ed.), *Reconceptualizing study in educational discourse and practice* (pp. 97–109). Routledge.

– (2019a). *What is curriculum theory?* (3rd ed.). Routledge.

– (2019b). *Moving images of eternity: George Grant's critique of time, teaching, and technology*. University of Ottawa Press.

Rocha, S. (2020). *The syllabus as curriculum: A reconceptualist approach*. Routledge.

Scott, D. C. (1906). The last of the Indian treaties. *Scribner' Magazine*, Vol. XL, no. 5, 573–83. https://treaty9diaries.ca/wp-content/uploads/2011/05/Last-of-the-Indian-Treaties.pdf

Shah, V. (2018). Leadership for social justice through the lens of self-identified, racially and other-privileged leaders. *Journal of Global Citizenship and Equity Education*, 6(1), 1–41.

– (2019). Calling in the self: Centering socially engaged Buddhism in critical pedagogy through personal narrative. *International Journal of Critical Pedagogy*, *10*(2), 45–68. https://libjournal.uncg.edu/ijcp/article/view/1898

Sharma, N. (2020). *Home rule: National sovereignty and the separation of Natives and migrants*. Duke University Press.

Stanley, T. (2019). Commemorating John A. Macdonald: Collective remembering and the structure of settler colonialism in British Columbia. *BC Studies*, *204*, 89–113. https://doi.org/10.14288/bcs.v0i204.191488

– (2020). Witnessing exclusion: Oral histories, historical provenance, and antiracism education. In K. Llewellyn & N. Ng-A-Fook (Eds.), *Oral history, education, and justice*. Routledge.

Triggs, V. & Irwin, R. (2019). Pedagogy and the A/r/tographic Invitation. In R. Hickman, J. Baldacchino, K. Freedman, E. Hall, & N. Meager (Eds.), *The international encyclopedia of art and design education* (pp. 1–16). John Wiley & Sons.

Tupper, J. A. (2014). The possibilities for reconciliation through difficult dialogues: Treaty education as peacebuilding. *Curriculum Inquiry*, *44*(4), 469–88. https://doi.org/10.1111/curi.12060

Tupper, J. A. (2020). Cracks in the foundations: (Re)storying settler Colonialism. In D. Llewellyn & N. Ng-A-Fook (Eds.), *Oral History, education, and justice* (pp. 88–104). Routledge.

Vaillancourt, T., & Beauchamp, M., & Brown, C. & Buffone, P., & Comeau, J. & Davies, S., & Figueiedo, M., & Finn, C., & Hargreaves, A., & McDougall, P., & McNamara, L., & Szatmari, P., & Waddell, C., & Westheimer, J., & Whitley, J. (2021). *Children and schools during COVID-19 and beyond: Engagement and connection through opportunity*. Royal Society of Canada.

van Kessel, C. (2018). Banal and fetishized evil: Implicating ordinary folk in genocide education. *Journal of International Social Studies*, *8*(2), pp. 160–71. http://orcid.org/0000-0002-7450-5963

– (2020). Teaching the climate crisis: Existential considerations. *Journal of Curriculum Studies Research*, *2*(1), 129–45. https://doi.org/10.46303/jcsr.02.01.8

Wang, H. (2018). Nonviolence as teacher education: A qualitative study in challenges and possibilities. *Journal of Peace Education*, *15*(2), 216–37. https://doi.org/10.1080/17400201.2018.1458294

– (2019). An integrative psychic life, nonviolent relations, and curriculum dynamics in teacher education. *Studies in Philosophy and Education*, *38*, 377–95. https://doi.org/10.1007/s11217-019-09661-4

11 Early Childhood Curriculum Studies: An Intellectual Engagement

VERONICA PACINI-KETCHABAW

This chapter is a kind of intervention. I have crafted it as a performance of my intellectual engagement in early childhood education curriculum. This performative piece, imbued with political and ethical demands for early education, both traces ways of living and organizing my scholarship into existence and creates worlds to come, through inquiries into what might be possible to pursue. As I trace, unevenly, my three decades of scholarship in early education, I do so to emphasize education as ethico-political and through this process to redress the instrumentalization of early childhood curriculum at a time when neoliberalism organizes most relations within the field (Vintimilla, 2014). Phelan and Rüsselbaek Hansen (2021) argue poignantly that, under neoliberalism, "ethics and politics are run into the ground because, we are told, there are no alternatives to consider, no other directions to look for" (p. 16). Although I do not think with alternatives in this chapter, my intention is to retrospectively create a tracing that reminds the reader that education should not be thought outside of ethico-political intentions.

As I narrate this early childhood journey, I walk with those who have already written extensively about the continuing degradation of the deeply ethical and political character of education (Biesta, 2014; Freire, 1968/1970; Meirieu, 2020; Phelan & Rüsselbaek Hansen, 2021). I am particularly inspired by feminist educator bell hooks's (1994) writings as I frame early education as a possibility for transforming the status quo, for inventing otherwise worlds, for reconfiguring what humanity might become. I write these stories to invoke hooks's idea that education can be a revolution, as she relates in the introductory quote, referring to her experience in an all-Black grade school. I also gesture towards her autobiographical methods to recount how my own relations to education have been intensified by the necessity and possibilities of reinvention.

Thinking about writing autobiographically (even when I do not consider this piece an autobiography) has been a difficult task. To tame my insecurities about producing a personal piece of writing, I have leaned towards the idea of performance – not as artistic practice but as organizational device. Rather than following traditional and logical forms of writing, I work through acts that highlight "the illogical and the fragment, seeking an anti-form" that in some way defies convention (Pather & Boulle, 2019, p. 2). The performative mode allows me not only to avoid setting out a chronology of my intellectual engagements but also to bring a political intention to the narrative that goes beyond the autobiographical.

Although this is a performance of my intellectual engagement, it is certainly not an individual journey: I have not walked, and I do not walk, alone. Engagements with my feminist colleagues in the Common Worlds Research Collective (https://commonworlds.net/) and the Early Childhood Pedagogies Collaboratory (n.d.) have enriched the ideas I share in this chapter. As I often say, it is impossible to speak without feeling that my thoughts are deeply entwined with the many insightful dialogues I have had with my colleagues over the years. Thus, I hope this performance is not read as seeking individual recognition nor as *the* exemplary trajectory for early childhood curriculum (in fact, my colleagues in the Collective and the Collaboratory speak of different journeys). My intention is to narrate *one story* of the configurations of power and the machinations that, for me, locate early education within political and ethical framings. Perhaps we might refer to this performance as a humble and incomplete *situated* story (Haraway, 1998) in education.

For the past 30 years I have been creating pedagogical spaces and conducting research that challenges the Canadian early childhood education status quo. Early education in Canada, steeped as it is in colonialism and capitalism through its adherence to child development theories (Burman, 2017; Taylor, 2013), is organized around a developing young child at the centre who is nested in contexts arranged according to the impact of each on the innocent child. In this arrangement, the central tenet of early education is to educate the child according to an ideal (optimum development) and in turn to build a (well-adjusted) society that is in full harmony with the needs and strengths of the child, which are predefined through neoliberal logics. As Phelan and Rüsselbaek Hansen (2021) write, "neoliberalism offers a sort of user manual that guides our thinking and living in certain directions" because it is "oriented toward uncontested endings and predetermined destinations" (p. 16). This vision of education is not only Cartesian and humancentric; it is propelled by an already defined colonial notion of humanity arranged around systems of production (Wynter, 2003). This is the context in which I write and to which the four acts of my performance piece speak back. Act 1, Pedagogical Commitments at a Time of Ecological Catastrophe, sets the stage. Act 2, An Education in the Midst of the Horrors of State Dictatorship, offers glimpses into my own early education – and my origins as an educator – in Argentina. Act 3, Migration and Engagements with Multicultural Education, glances at my encounter with Canadian multiculturalism when I migrated to Canada in the early 1990s. Act 4, A Curriculum Framework Within the Grasps of Neoliberalism gestures towards the challenges of translating scholarship to practice. Through each of these acts I think through my own relations with education – like hooks (1994), yet in very different contexts and circumstances – with the hope to open up, or simply interrupt, the current neoliberal thinking in early childhood education.

Act 1: Pedagogical Commitments at a Time of Ecological Catastrophe

As all readers know well enough today, we live in uncharted and challenging times: an ecological crisis is unfolding in front of our eyes that we are experiencing, although differentially, worldwide (Intergovernmental Panel on Climate Change, 2018). Education is responding to this catastrophe, yet its response, for the most part, is trapped within the neoliberal logics it breathes, and thus it aims at creating subjects who can better control the environment so that we can continue to take resources from the Earth. Haraway (2016) aptly refers to these responses as technofixes and suggests that they are inadequate to address the very problems that got us where we are in the first place. Relying on human ingenuity is not the answer. Echoing this suggestion, Stengers (2013) argues that "something may be "added" to the situation, something that could provide a line of escape from dilemmas that take us as hostages" (para. 5). She notes that critically engaging with our (human) place in the world might be a generative line of escape:

> Now those of us who were told stories since birth that there is something really special in being "human" are at a bifurcation point: either we furiously keep to that narrative, or we accept that if there is a post-Anthropocene worth living in, those who will live in it will need different stories, with no entity at the centre of the stage. (Stengers, 2013, para. 23)

For the past decade, with my colleagues in the Common Worlds Research Collective, I have been working with early childhood educators and young children to respond to the climate catastrophe (Taylor & Pacini-Ketchabaw, 2018; Taylor, Pacini-Ketchabaw & Blaise, 2021). These responses both attend to the profound challenges we face and engage with the paradoxes that the Anthropocene portends for the future of life on Earth as we know it. Using an actively inclusive more-than-human framework that reassembles worlds by countering the divisive distinction often drawn between sociocultural contexts and natural environments, our pedagogical work and research resist the epistemological division between society and/or culture as distinct from nature that underpins post-Enlightenment Western thinking in early childhood (Common Worlds Research Collective, 2020). Our common worlds research is interested in the creation of pedagogies that are concerned with the real-life worlds of twenty-first-century children and acknowledge that these lifeworlds are layered and complex, and that children are inheriting challenging legacies (Pacini-Ketchabaw & Taylor, 2016).

Working with educators and young children to think about the ways in which education (deeply rooted in humanist and anthropocentric traditions) is directly implicated in our current ecological crises, and our failure to imagine alternatives has not been an easy task. It is profoundly imperfect, incomplete, and tentative work. The Cartesian dualisms that structure the unswerving humanist belief that our supreme rationality and the exclusivity of our intentional agency set us apart from, and above, the rest of the living world (Plumwood, 1993) – alongside the associated belief that humans can endlessly act upon the rest of the world with impunity, either to exploit its resources or "improve" it at will – are deeply rooted at the centre of Euro-Western-human education, and they structure our curricula and pedagogies. Yet, it is time to recognize that education's foundational humanist epistemologies, its delusional humancentric and exceptionalist preoccupations, have become part of the problem, not the solution (Common Worlds Research Collective, 2020).

Like any educational project, common worlding pedagogies can become instruments of oppression when aligned with the aims of neoliberalism and neocolonialism. In Act 4, I outline some neoliberal tentacles that continually grasp and feed common worlding pedagogies in the twenty-first century. Thus, if there are principles attached to common worlding pedagogies, an important one is the ongoing interrogation and interruption (through creative acts) of the current conditions of power and the self-evidence of their status quo.

Act 2: An Education in the Midst of the Horrors of State Dictatorship

Any time I think about interrogating power arrangements, I am thrust back to my early education in Argentina during its last dictatorship, which lasted from 1976 to 1983. This was a time, as Vikki Bell (2014) describes, "when the military state was routinely kidnapping people from their places of work, from their homes, from the street, making no place safe, when meetings of more than two on public streets, or having the wrong hairstyle, or reading the wrong book, became sufficient causes of suspicion" (p. 17). The state held itself up as the moral institution; its goal was to restore order and the national values of morality, integrity, and efficiency that, according to the government, Argentinean society had lost (Bell, 2014; Dussel, 2001, 2005; Guitelman, 2006).

The educational system became the perfect space to enact and maintain these goals. The desire was to maintain a Western and Christian society through disciplinary and authoritarian means (including, among others, censoring texts, prohibiting "ideological" curricular content, and burning libraries).

Educational policy outlined everything that could not be accessed, everything that was excluded (Bell, 2014).

Schools were also about counterinsurgency, not only in terms of what was allowed to be taught but also a space for "suppression of all subversive infiltration" (Guitelman, 2006, p. 37). The notorious decree *Subversion in the Educational Sphere: Let's Meet Our Enemy* enlisted teachers to maintain national security, root out the causes of subversion (Avalos, 2018), and violently clean the educational system of all human and material elements that might prevent government from meeting its moral goals. Citing portions of the decree, Guitelman (2006) explains its purpose:

> It notes that the only way to combat enemy infiltration is with "crudeness and courage." The first objective of Marxism – according to the document – would be to "ideologically capture the young, the future leader of the Nation, which in successive generations will achieve and maintain the dominance of the State under Marxist ideology." It also points out that "a notorious Marxist offensive has been noted in the area of children's literature. Accordingly, it is proposed to issue a type of message that starts from the child and that allows him to "self-educate" on the basis of freedom and the alternative." The decree included identification elements to more clearly find teachers and students who upheld those principles in order to proceed towards their "eradication." (p. 38)

I don't remember hearing adults discussing these declarations, even though my mother was a practising teacher at the time. What I do remember are the hours I spent turning and reading the colourful pages of *Billiken*, my favourite childhood educational magazine. *Billiken* supported my schooling and connected me to the only world I knew at the time – a world I did not know was being carefully and pedagogically crafted to shape my generation (Guitelman, 2006). Initially published for the first time after the Second World War to reaffirm children's rights, *Billiken* not only ignored but also secured the dictatorship's ideas and practices. As Paula Guitelman (2006) writes:

> Instead of talking about bodies thrown into the water, it talks about dead fish, instead of referring to the fact that they were being killed people remember the birth of the founder of the magazine, instead of talking about the prevailing horror it talks about progress in space technology, instead of talking about transnational financial speculation, it talks about industrial development. (p. 59)

Most children did not have to be suppressed, but they had to be disciplined, transformed, and silenced (Guitelman, 2006). Fortunately, my experience did not entail suppression, incarceration, and extreme physical and emotional violence. Unfortunately, I was deeply engulfed in the dictatorship's other face:

going along (through education and its many technologies) with its maintenance of happiness and order.

It was not until I entered teachers' college in the late 1980s that I became aware of the kind of education I had participated in – even though during my high school years during the Malvinas War (1982) I had enthusiastically engaged in activist work demanding a democratic government. Becoming a teacher and an early childhood educator in the wake of a brutal dictatorship meant I was exposed to the strong movement towards community participation and democratization that pervaded education at that time. I am sure there were many crucial moments in my teacher education program that helped me think of the deeply ethico-political nature of education, but there is one I still remember after so many years: I was fortunate to spend an entire semester, in the course then entitled Theory of Education, thinking about Pink Floyd's analysis of education and schooling (Waters, 1979). As exhilarating as it was immersing myself in analyses of these powerful lyrics, it also still reminds me of the violence of education (Todd, 2001). And, indeed, as a teacher/professor it has become crucial for me to ask critical "questions about the non-neutrality of what is selected to be passed on to future generations" (Baker, 2009, p. x).

Act 3: Migration and Engagements with Multicultural Education

Migrating to Canada in 1990 right after completing my teaching education introduced me to a different mode of neoliberal education – not the blatant authoritarian education I had encountered during my childhood, nor the education that opened my eyes to its injustices in my early youth. Becoming an early childhood educator in Canada meant, as Phelan and Rüsselbaek Hansen (2021) write, engaging with the "neoliberal efforts to promote a utopian learning culture" and becoming "a skilled clinician stripped of an ethico-political form of life" (p. 16). Guiding young children to maintain their health and safety and using "evidence-based methods" that would "transform complex matters into ones that can be easily learned and compared" (p. 17) permeated my professional life. Yet, although I tried hard, as an immigrant I was never an adequate educator. My accent, my light brown skin, even my philosophical views always crushed my utopian dream of being a good educator. I could never be good enough. It was not until graduate school that I realized it did not matter how hard I tried, because it was not about my personal inadequacies. As an immigrant living and working in Canada, multiculturalism (shaped by a so-called progressive Multiculturalism Act) framed many of my relations with early childhood education.

Since the late 1990s, I have been interested in studying how early childhood education acts as a zone of governance for racialized young children. The zone is enacted through discourses of sensitivity, tolerance, flexibility, and acceptance of difference that characterize Canadian multiculturalism

(Pacini-Ketchabaw, 2007a, 2007b; Pacini-Ketchabaw et al., 2006; Pacini-Ketchabaw & Berikoff, 2008). Early childhood educators I interviewed in the early 2000s, for example, referred to all children needing and wanting the same basic experiences, not recognizing that these experiences have been normalized through discourses of whiteness (Pacini-Ketchabaw, 2007a). These discourses assume that racialized children do not have the "normal" opportunities that all young children should have. Racialized children are assumed to need strong attachment figures, routines, and exposure to a wide range of activities – as if these opportunities were not already available to them. They are assumed to be citizens in need of improvement, and this improvement is not imposed or coerced but achieved through the language of rights and democracy (every child is entitled to be happy and secure) and in the context of education (Pacini-Ketchabaw, 2007a).

There is also the illusion of the autonomous subject who has the choice to learn or not to learn. Hindness (2005) refers to this illusion as a new rationality of government that is deployed through "the civil and political rights of citizenship" (p. 256). Early childhood education serves the principles of multicultural national ideals, creating governable spaces for young racialized children. Within these spaces, racialized children and their families are reasoned to be incomplete, as deviations from the norm, and Western discourses provide the image of the good citizen to which young, racialized children and families are compared (Pacini-Ketchabaw, 2007a). Not questioned are the "normal" services that are modelled on normative and hegemonic whiteness.

The educators I interviewed as part of a study on racialization in early childhood education saw themselves as flexible, saw children as flexible and manageable citizens, and described themselves as flexible with families in order to help their children adjust in Canada (Pacini-Ketchabaw, 2007a). This idea of flexibility emerges as educators let children and parents adjust to early education environments at their own pace, accommodate the practices and routines of racialized children, and let children take their own time in learning English and "improving" their language development (Pacini-Ketchabaw, 2007a). Through the deployment of the discourse of flexibility, early childhood education is responding to the needs of global markets, becoming a zone with citizen-subjects with the potential to act in today's global spaces and compete and play the game of global capitalism (Ong, 2006). The educators who participated in the study embodied the latitudinal citizenship needed in a society of control (Pacini-Ketchabaw, 2007a). They were open to children's circumstances, were flexible in their approaches, continuously adjusted to the changing conditions of their environment, and tried to understand the conditions of racialized children (Pacini-Ketchabaw, 2007a). They brought a "set of flexible capacities, assets, and potentialities" to shape and mould the young racialized children in their care (Ong, 2006, p. 124).

There is also the possibility that racialized children are made flexible through the constant shaping educators perform. However, this is not to say that racialized children will have equal opportunities to compete in the global market, because the market creates and coordinates diverse possibilities and spaces for different populations – a process Aiwa Ong (2006) refers to as graduated citizenship. These spaces and populations are regulated according to their links to global production, often delineated by the interlocking social formations of gender, "race," ethnicity, language, and class (Ong, 2006).

Never good enough.

Act 4: A Curriculum Framework within the Grasps of Neoliberalism

In the late 2000s, I participated, with other early childhood colleagues, in creating the first British Columbia early learning curriculum framework (Government of British Columbia, 2008); more recently, I was peripherally involved in its revision (Government of British Columbia, 2018). Throughout the development of the framework, we wanted to politicize the field by emphasizing an alternative vision to the developmental one (as we wrote in a collaborative piece later on, Land et al., 2020). What we fought against through the creation of the framework were the normative discourses of child development so deeply embedded within early childhood education. We wanted to challenge early childhood education's aim (shaped within the child study movement of the early 1900s) to authoritatively "know," "predict," and "assess" children to guide them towards maturation and proper humanity (with predefined notions of what maturity and proper humanity are). We wanted to disentangle from the field the desire to guide children's development along a universalized and normalizing trajectory – and its related task of correcting and remediating. We wanted to ensure that educators understand that children who do not conform to Euro-Western developmental norms should not be automatically positioned as in need of intervention or support. We wanted to challenge the control and erasure of non-Euro-Western experiences of childhood. We wanted to question the production of the proper humanist subject who maintains the necessary conditions for ongoing settler colonialism. We wanted to open up spaces for other possibilities for existence, ways of living and conceiving childhood that do not ascribe to particular colonial universals. We wanted developmentalism not to be the only framework that educators are taught to engage with children (Land et al., 2020).

The revised early learning curriculum framework excludes all the right words: developmental principles, developmental domains, maturation, and so on. It includes many of the most progressive terms: pedagogy, postfoundational theories, dialogue, critical reflection, and pedagogical documentation. It even mentions the concept I and my colleagues in the Common Worlds Research Collective (2022) have been working with for the last 10 years: common worlds pedagogies. Some might say this is an accomplishment, that it reflects the impact of our scholarship on everyday practice. However, I think we need to be much more cautious of these moves in education policy. And here I am reminded of Michel Foucault's (1983) famous words:

> Everything is dangerous, which is not exactly the same as bad. If everything is dangerous, then we always have something to do. So my position leads not to apathy but to a hyper- and pessimistic activism. I think that the ethico-political choice we have to make every day is to determine which is the main danger. (pp. 231–2)

Despite efforts to promote early education as an ethico-political activity, early childhood centres and other educational institutions in Canada continue to prioritize workforce supply for economic growth. Humanist-inspired projects to achieve social justice and freedom have been hijacked by economic development and productivity agendas. Capitalist extraction, production, and consumption continue to be associated with human "progress" and "development." As I engage in conversations with early childhood educators and observe the ways in which common worlds pedagogies are being taken up in early childhood centres across British Columbia (see Early Childhood Pedagogy Network, 2022), I find myself facing the neoliberal tendency towards appropriation.

What concerns me is that common worlds pedagogies are becoming depoliticized. By that I mean they are becoming ***the solution*** to our problems. In the early learning curriculum framework, they give practitioners direction for managing and instructing children to be able to achieve predetermined ends. They are used to perpetuate "individualism, cynicism, and the frantic guarding of social privilege" (McCready, 2009, p. 163). They are thought interchangeably with nature education and stewardship programs. They are used to position children as investments for future economic productivity. Instead of being engaged in what bell hooks (1994) called "counter-hegemonic" (p. 2) ways (as we intended them to be), common worlds pedagogies are being politically engaged to maintain the status quo (i.e., the nature–culture divide). Children are not encouraged to "reinvent" (hooks, p. 3) themselves through carefully designed pedagogical processes. Common worlds pedagogies "merely strive to reinforce domination" (hooks, 1994, p. 4). Within the curriculum framework, common worlds pedagogies are not simply misunderstood. They have been appropriated, with neoliberal aims.

Clearly there remains more work to be done. There are courses of action I dream of. For instance, the progressively inspired curriculum framework has not yet opened up an enquiry that asks: *How might we think with these pedagogical projects to transgress the humanist project the early learning framework is trapped in?* I remain hopeful that we can compose more just worlds, that we can collectively create the conditions for different pedagogical projects than the one we are currently unravelling.

Concluding Thoughts

My intention in this chapter has been to trace my intellectual engagement in early childhood education to highlight the ethico-political nature of early childhood education. Without serving as an autobiographical piece, the chapter glanced at hooks's (1994) autobiographical methods, and I organized it around four acts that critically think with four crucial aspects of my life in early childhood education. I emphasized the urgency to think education beyond humanism, outlining my own experience with state-imposed education, my encounter with normative racist discourses of multiculturalism, and my observation of the inevitable grasp of neoliberal logics in education. We might read these four events as individual accomplishments or failures. Yet, such readings underestimate that every educational project is in fact a project of subject formation (Vintimilla & Pacini-Ketchabaw, 2020); thus, ethico-political engagements cannot be disentangled from any kind of education.

I end by returning to the writing of bell hooks, this time to her final chapter in *Teaching to Transgress*. She writes:

> The classroom, with all its limitations, remains a location of possibility. In that field of possibility we have the opportunity to labor for freedom, to demand of ourselves and our comrades an openness of mind and heart that allows us to face reality even as we collectively imagine ways to move beyond boundaries, to transgress. This is education as the practice of freedom. (p. 207)

hooks reminds us of the importance of not forgetting that how we organize educational activities matters for the kinds of worlds we hope to nurture and those we attempt to create. This is the hope I hold on to.

As I noted in the introduction, my purpose in this performative piece was not only to trace ways of living and organizing my scholarship into existence through an ethico-political intention, but to create worlds to come, through inquiries of what might be possible to pursue. As my colleagues and I argue (Vintimilla & Pacini-Ketchabaw, 2020; Vintimilla et al., 2021), we aim to open "alternative possibilities for pedagogy, curriculum, and education" and, in turn, enact "transformative relations that respond to, and (re)compose with, the times we live in" (Vintimilla et al., 2021, p. 6). Within the same lines, I offer this contribution as both an interruption for early education (as I challenge its neoliberal tendency towards instrumentality, standardization, and developmentalism) and an invitation to transform it by inventing and reinventing (as opposed to following or applying) otherwise modes of knowing and being, as well as worldly relations that are yet to come.

REFERENCES

Avalos, D. (2018, March 24). Dictadura y educación | Un folleto de 1977 muestra cómo se instruía a docentes para identificar «subversivos» en las escuelas de Salta. http://www.cuarto.com.ar/dictadura-y-educacion-un-folleto-de-1977-muestra-como-instruia-docentes-para-luchar-contra-la-subversion-en-las-escuelas/

Baker, B. (2009). *New curriculum education*. Sense.

Bell, V. (2014). *The art of post-dictatorship: Ethics and aesthetics in transitional Argentina*. Routledge.

Biesta. G. J. J. (2014). *The beautiful risk of education*. Paradigm.

Burman, E. (2017). *Deconstructing developmental psychology*. Routledge.

Common Worlds Research Collective. (2020). *Learning to become with the world: Education for future survival*. UNESCO background paper for the Futures of Education Initiative. https://unesdoc.unesco.org/ark:/48223/pf0000374032

Common Worlds Research Collective. (2022). Website. https://commonworlds.net/

Dussel, I. (2001). Repensando la crisis moral de la escuela: Hacia una historia del presente de la educación moral. In E. Antelo (Ed.), *La escuela más allá del bien y del mal: Ensayos sobre la transformación de los valores educativos* (pp. 31–54). AMSAFE.

Dussel, I. (2005). ¿Se renueva el orden disciplinario escolar? Una lectura de los reglamentos de convivencia en la argentina de la post-crisis1. *Revista Mexicana de Investigación Educativa, 10*(27), 1109–21. https://www.redalyc.org/pdf/140/14002708.pdf

Early Childhood Pedagogies Collaboratory. (n.d.). Website. https://www.earlychildhoodcollaboratory.net/

– (2022). Website. https://www.ecpn.ca/

Foucault, M. (1983). On the genealogy of ethics: An overview of work in progress. Afterword, in H. L. Dreyfus & P. Rabinow (Eds.), *Michel Foucault: Beyond structuralism and hermeneutics* (2nd ed.) The University of Chicago Press.

Freire, P. (1970). *Pedagogy of the oppressed* (M. Ramos, Trans). Continuum. (Original work published 1968)

Government of British Columbia. (2008). British Columbia early learning framework. Ministry of Health & Ministry of Children and Family Development.

– (2018). *British Columbia early learning framework* (2nd ed.). https://www2.gov.bc.ca/gov/content/education-training/early-learning/teach/early-learning-framework

Guitelman, P. (2006). *Infancia en dictadura: Modernidad y conservadurismo en el mundo de Billiken*. Prometeo.

Haraway, D. J. (1998). Situated knowledges: The science question in feminism and the privilege of partial perspective. *Feminist Studies, 14*(3), 575–99. https://doi.org/10.2307/3178066

– (2016). *Staying with the trouble: Making kin in the Chthulucene*. Duke University Press.

Hindness, B. (2005). Citizenship and Empire. In Thomas Blom Hansen and Finn Stepputat (Eds.) *Sovereign Bodies: Citizens, Migrants, and States in the Postcolonial World.* (pp. 241–56). Princeton University Press.

hooks, b. (1994). *Teaching to transgress: Education as the practice of freedom*. Routledge.

Intergovernmental Panel on Climate Change (IPCC). (2018). Global research and action agenda on cities and climate change science. https://www.ipcc.ch/event/cities-and-climate-change-science-conference/

Land, N., Vintimilla, C. D., Pacini-Ketchabaw, V., & Angus, L. (2020). Propositions toward educating pedagogists: Decentering the child. *Contemporary Issues in Early Childhood. 23*(2). https://doi.org/10.1177/1463949120953522

McCready, A. L. (2009). Redressing redress: The neoliberal appropriation of redress in the anti-Native backlash at Caledonia. *English Studies in Canada, 35*(1), 161–90. https://doi.org/10.1353/esc.0.0170

Meirieu, P. (2020). *Frankenstein educador* (E. Olcina, Trans.). Laertes Educación.

Ong, A. (2006). *Neoliberalism as exception: Mutations in citizenship and sovereignty*. Duke University Press.

Pacini-Ketchabaw, V. (2007a). Child care and multiculturalism: A site of governance marked by flexibility and openness. *Contemporary Issues in Early Childhood, 8*(3), 222–32. https://doi.org/10.2304/ciec.2007.8.3.222

– (2007b). Racialized migrant women's narratives on child care: An anti-racist, transnational feminist analysis. *International Journal of Equity and Innovation in Early Childhood Education, 5*(1), 69–88. https://static1.squarespace.com/static/55ab27f3e4b048cfac1c647a/t/55b5ee59e4b04e39fb61e491/1437986393952/Pacini-KetchabawIJEIECVol5No1.pdf

Pacini-Ketchabaw, V., White, J., & Armstrong de Almeida, A.-E. (2006). Racialization in early childhood: A critical analysis of discourses in policies. *International Journal of Educational Policy, Research, & Practice: Reconceptualizing Childhood Studies,* (7)1, 95–113.

Pacini-Ketchabaw, V., & Berikoff, A. (2008). The politics of difference and diversity: From young children's violence to creative power expressions. *Contemporary Issues in Early Childhood, 9*(3), 256–64. https://doi.org/10.2304/ciec.2008.9.3.256

Pacini-Ketchabaw, V., & Taylor, A. (2016). Common world childhoods. *Oxford Bibliographies in Childhood Studies*. https://doi:10.1093/OBO/9780199791231-0174

Pather, J., & Boulle, C. (2019). *Acts of transgression: Contemporary live art in South Africa*. Wits University Press.

Phelan, A., & Rüsselbaek Hansen, D. (2021). Toward a "thoughtful lightness": Education in viral times. *Prospects, 51*, 15–27. https://doi.org/10.1007/s11125-020-09536-4

Plumwood, V. (1993). *Feminism and the mastery of nature*. Routledge.

Stengers, I. (2013). Matters of cosmopolitics: On the provocations of Gaïa. Isabelle Stengers in conversation with Heather Davis and Etienne Turpin. In E. Turpin (Ed.) *Architecture in the anthropocene: Encounters among design, deep Time, science and philosophy*. Open Humanities Press. https://quod.lib.umich.edu/o/ohp/12527215.0001.001

Taylor, A. (2013). *Reconfiguring the natures of childhood*. Routledge.

Taylor, A., & Pacini-Ketchabaw, V. (2018). *The common worlds of children and animals: Relational ethics for entangled lives*. Routledge.

Taylor, A., Pacini-Ketchabaw, V., & Blaise, M. (2021, January 6). What is our pedagogical response-ability in the face of climate and pandemic crises? *Common Worlds Research Collective*. https://commonworlds.net/what-is-our-pedagogical-response-ability-in-the-face-of-climate-and-pandemic-crises/

Todd, S. (2001). "Bringing more than I contain": Ethics, curriculum, and the pedagogical demand for altered egos. *Journal of Curriculum Studies, 33*(4), 431–50. https://doi.org/10.1080/002202701300200911

Vintimilla, C. D. (2014). Neoliberal fun and happiness in early childhood education. *Journal of Childhood Studies, 39*(1), 79–87. https://doi.org/10.18357/jcs.v39i1.15246

Vintimilla, C. D., & Pacini-Ketchabaw, V. (2020). Weaving pedagogy in early childhood education: on openings and their foreclosure. *European Early Childhood Education Research Journal, 28*(5), 628–641. https://doi.org/10.1080/1350293X.2020.1817235

Vintimilla, C. D., Pacini-Ketchabaw, V., & Land, N. (2021). Manifesting living knowledges: A pedagogists' working manifesto. *Journal of Curriculum and Pedagogy, 20*(1), 1–10. https://doi.org/10.1080/15505170.2021.1955051

Waters, R. (Writer). (1979). Another brick in the wall [Pink Floyd studio album: *The Wall*]. Harvest & Columbia Records.

Wynter, S. (2003). Unsettling the coloniality of being/power/truth/freedom: Towards the human, after man, its overrepresentation – An argument. *The New Centennial Review, 3*(3), 257–337. http://www.jstor.org/stable/41949874

12 The Radical Pedagogy of Climate Striking in a Petroculture

JACKIE SEIDEL, SIDRAH ANEES, EMILY BLACKMORE, AND KELSEY MACKENZIE

We compose ourselves and this piece as settlers in a colonial state. We learn together in *Moh'kins'tsis*, the Blackfoot name of the City of Calgary where the snow-melt and glacier-fed Bow and Elbow Rivers meet. It was at the convergence of these waters that Treaty 7 was signed in 1877 between Indigenous people and the Crown/Canada. Treaty 7 comprises the territories of the Blackfoot Confederacy, the Tsuut'ina Nation, the Stoney Nakoda Nation, and the Métis Nation of Alberta Region 3. We commit ourselves to learning about the ongoing colonial history of Canada and what it means to be "treaty people" (McKenzie-Jones, 2019). Our participation in the Fridays for Future youth climate strike movement is part of this commitment, as teachers, to facing the colonial, racist, misogynistic, and extractivist histories (and present) of the schooling project.

This chapter seeks to make existential and pedagogical sense of our experiences participating in climate strikes in Calgary in 2019 and 2020 as Bachelor of Education students (Sidrah, Emily, and Kelsey) and an associate professor (Jackie). Climate striking in a petroculture[1] and a settler-colonial state presents specific challenges including encountering and confronting climate change denialism, racism, and misogyny. Contemporary compulsory education emerged during the industrial period fuelled by petro-fossil combustion, thus, schooling and curriculum are deeply and historically entangled and implicated in a cultural system that now portends an existential and catastrophic threat to life itself.

In August 2018, Greta Thunberg began striking from school every Friday. Sitting alone outside Sweden's Parliament with her iconic "School Strike for Climate" sign, she captured the attention of other youth globally. The first global youth strike was in March 2019, with 2,200 strikes and more than a million participants in 125 nations (Glenza et al., 2019). A second global strike followed in May (BBC News, 2019). More than four million people participated in the strike in the fall of 2019 (Laville & Watts, 2019). Globally, millions of climate striking children are expressing their desire for a livable future with diverse life, breathable air, and social, ecological, and economic justice for all beings. They are asking adults to take responsibility for this world *now*.

This chapter stories our efforts to join climate-striking children in mutuality, love, and reciprocity. We begin by contextualizing the contemporary political climate in Alberta including the government's hostility towards teachers and curriculum. This is followed by a series of stories that weave together our collective and personal memories of climate striking and serve as a form of teacher theorizing in these important times. We conclude with some thoughts about what our experiences mean for our work.

Contexts

In spring 2019, the right-wing United Conservative Party (UCP) was elected to a four-year term in Alberta. Their election platform was: "Jobs. Economy. Pipelines." They immediately cancelled the carbon tax and created a $30 million per year tax-funded private corporation, the Canadian Energy Centre (CEC, n.d.) with a mandate "to promote Canada as the supplier of choice for the world's growing demand for responsibly produced energy" (n.p.). They initiated a "Public Inquiry into Anti-Alberta Energy Campaigns" (Alberta Inquiry, 2019.) for the purpose of investigating "anti-Alberta energy campaigns that are supported by foreign organizations" (n.p.). The inquiry's final report, overdue and over budget, was released in fall 2021. It found no evidence of wrongdoing by any environmental organizations. Scholars and lawyers describe the inquiry as an attempt to intimidate organizations and individuals who stand up to the "rampant development of Alberta's oil and gas resources" (Anderson, 2021, n.p.) in the face of the existential threats posed by climate change.

During this time, the Fridays for Future climate strikes and Extinction Rebellion movements were growing globally, and across Canada there was a resurgence of Indigenous resistance and protest that included court challenges and unprecedented simultaneous blockades of pipelines, roads, and railways by Indigenous peoples and settler supporters (Lindeman, 2020; Montenegro, 2020; Muskrat Magazine, 2013; Palmater, 2020). In June 2020, the Alberta government responded to the growing protest movements by passing Bill 1: The Critical Infrastructure Defense Act (Government of Alberta, 2020), which criminalizes protests that block "critical infrastructure" with hefty fines and possible prison time. While what constitutes "critical infrastructure" remains unclear, it is possible that it refers to any public space (Conacher, 2020). This Bill is unlikely to survive a federal court challenge as it violates the Canadian Charter of Rights and Freedoms (Koshan et al., 2020).

Education has become a regular target of the Alberta government's hostile disdain. Education Minister Adriana LaGrange, some MLAs, their press secretaries, and issues managers, have repeatedly vowed to get "ideology," "politics," and "radical activists" out of the curriculum and classrooms (Aitchison, 2020; Goodridge, 2019; LaGrange, 2019; UCP Caucus, 2020). A new grades K–4 curriculum developed collaboratively by an unprecedented number of teachers, professors, and other experts under the two previous Conservative and New Democratic governments was to be implemented in the fall of 2019. During their election campaign, the UCP claimed this curriculum was "ideological." Upon election, they appointed a new curriculum review panel. Following a secretive process, a draft K-6 curriculum was released in early 2021. The draft was met with immediate and harsh public, expert, and school district criticism. Within weeks, more than 40,000 citizens joined a Facebook group discussing and critiquing the document. Shortly after, a website supported by the Association of Alberta Deans of Education began compiling an ever-growing number of expert critiques (Alberta Curriculum Analysis, n.d.). Nearly all school districts in the province refused to pilot the draft. The result was unprecedented public engagement about the purposes of education and curriculum. It is unlikely, however, that any of the critique will be attended to by the government.

Laurie Adkin (2016a) has observed that "Alberta provides a case study of a first-world petro-state governed politically by neoliberal ideologues for more than two decades" (p.19). The editors of *Petrocultures* (Wilson et al., 2017) commented that "(t)he importance of fossil fuels in defining modernity has stood in inverse relationship to their presence in our cultural and social imaginaries" (p. 5). Modern education itself emerged during the industrial period fuelled by petro-fossil combustion. While the Alberta government claims its new curriculum is non-ideological and non-political, the Guiding Framework (Alberta Education, 2020b) and the draft do not take the climate emergency seriously. Even while defining characteristics of the coming decades will feature climate change and energy transitions, the Alberta curriculum framework and draft offer no acknowledgment of ecological crisis, the threats to more-than-human kin, food and water security, or the growing global displacement of human beings due to climate change and fossil-fuelled conflicts. When a draft of the Social Studies curriculum was leaked to the press in late 2020 (French, 2020), Indigenous curriculum studies scholar Dwayne Donald (2020) observed that the draft is "(r)eviving colonial myths" and "provide[s] little guidance on how to proceed differently. What is urgently required instead are stories that teach young people to be good relatives to their human and more-than-human kin" (n.p.).

Cara Dagget (2018) has described the rise of authoritarian movements in the West as characterized by a combination of "climate denial, racism and misogyny" (p. 25). Shortly after Greta Thunberg attended the October 18, 2019, climate strike at the Alberta Legislature in Edmonton (CBC, 2019), employees of X-Site Energy, a central Alberta energy company, distributed stickers portraying images of her being raped (Beattie, 2020). Greta Thunberg tweeted, "They are starting to get more and more desperate ... This shows that we're winning" (Mitchell, 2020). Overt displays of toxic masculinity, its relationship to petro-politics and extractivism, and the dangers it presents to women, children, Indigenous, racialized, and other vulnerable people are both visible and invisible in Alberta politics and government policies. The Greta sticker, the targeting of Indigenous protestors and land defenders, and the threats towards teachers (and therefore children) have made the racist and misogynistic impulses of this government (and the culture that elected them) increasingly visible.

Climate strikes in Calgary generally take place at City Hall, next to the skyscrapers of numerous fossil fuel corporations, just blocks away from the confluence of the Bow and Elbow Rivers where Treaty 7 was signed and near the site of The Calgary Stampede.[2] The Stampede is an annual event drawing over a million visitors that Kimberly Williams (2021) describes as a "block party" for the "dozens of multinational oil and gas extraction corporations headquartered in Calgary" (p. 1). She argues that the Stampede is "at its core, a misogynistic, white supremacist institution that is both product and active purveyor of Canada's ongoing settler colonial project" (p. 2). Climate striking in Calgary places participants at a critical nexus of the ongoing extractivist, settler-colonial project and legacy that the strikes inherently challenge.

Bachelor of Education students in the Werklund School of Education specialize in a curriculum discipline. In the final two years of the degree, students take two sequential courses in their chosen discipline. By the time we attended our first strike together, we had known each other for eight months and were in our second Social Studies curriculum specialization course together. As the climate strike movement grew, we witnessed children planting the seeds for enhanced opportunities for self-determination and autonomy for themselves and their futures. The strikes provoked serious questions for us about teacher education/preparation and school curriculum. We started attending strikes, individually and collectively, to witness what was happening, to talk with the children, to put our bodies in the streets with their bodies. Attending our first climate strike together was a spontaneous decision during a Friday morning class. None of us can quite remember the details but it was during September 2019 as we carefully followed the rapidly growing strike movements. What we do remember is our after-class rush to create signs and running to catch the train for the 15-minute train ride from campus to Calgary City Hall. Attending later strikes together was always planned ahead of time. The following reflections on our climate strike experiences were composed through many collaborative conversations over months by Zoom, telephone, and email. This was challenging work during the COVID-19 pandemic. Not only were we coping with the implications of the pandemic and the politics of health and education in Alberta, several of us were surviving as new teachers. Our intention was to enquire into our shared experiences to remember, document, slow down, and theorize the existential and pedagogical meanings of this moment, in this context and time. Our process including writing, reading our stories aloud, and editing together. Where we thought it mattered that incidents or reactions were amplified across stories, we left them in. We refined our narratives to capture as much of the experiences as we could.

These eight autobiographical pieces reflect our shared and divergent experiences and learning through witnessing and participating in climate strikes. To guide our reflections, we posed three questions: *What are we learning from participating in the strikes? What does it mean to be a teacher in this time and place? What are our pedagogical responsibilities to children and the future?* Following our names, we have indicated our birth years as parts-per-million CO2 in the atmosphere as a reminder of the pace of climate change during our own lifetimes (the monthly average CO2 concentration for 2021 is now 419 ppm) and the necessity of acting in every way possible, as fast as possible, to provide children with the livable future they are begging for.

Climate Strike Stories

Sidrah (born @ 363 ppm)

I was first drawn to the climate strikes after seeing the student-led nature of the Fridays for Future movement. While I have always been concerned about climate change, as a preservice teacher I felt a new sense of responsibility towards my students. I began attending the strikes regularly, often rushing to City Hall in between education classes at the university. The vibrant energy of the climate strikes – children, families, elders, all together and working towards the inherently loving and optimistic work of reclaiming and saving our natural world – was starkly contrasted by the return to campus. The quiet halls, lined with plaques naming the businessman who paid for the building, quickly brought us back to the reality of this place – entire institutions (of learning and progress, no less) that seemed untouched by the disaster slowly unfolding around us.

As a preservice teacher actively involved in climate activism, I feel a palpable sense of career anxiety. During our time at various climate strikes, concerns about repercussions from our attendance echoing into our professional and personal lives were ever prevalent. These concerns came to life for me during an academic showcase in 2019, while sharing a project with a school board representative. This showcase was the culmination of several months of work with a small group of my peers, developing a detailed unit plan across several subjects on the topic of climate change and human migration. We examined this topic through several subjects in the Alberta Education grade 9 curriculum, covering units in Social Studies, Science, English Language Arts, and more. We chose climate change and human migration as our area of focus as climate-change-driven human migration is one of the most pressing issues facing our world today and is relevant to our diverse Alberta classrooms, as Alberta experiences the impacts of climate change in the form of floods, fires, and superstorms.

Despite the rigorous grounding in curriculum and scientific fact, the school board representative was less than thrilled with our project. We were immediately asked how parents would react. I was taken by surprise – why would parents take issue with an engaging interdisciplinary project that was developed to meet curriculum requirements and had grounding in the most up-to-date science? The representative continued to assert that this project would alienate families who work in the oil and gas sector. As I continued to listen to his concerns, my initial surprise wore off as I realized that his trepidation was likely rooted in experience. This representative did not ask any further questions about the project, their immediate and only concern being parental and community backlash. This experience left me with a troubling thought: if a unit plan project elicited this sort of reaction, what would the response be to my actual climate activism? What will be the response to *this* writing? Does practising pedagogy that responds to the interests of children – particularly when this interest is the sensitive topic of peer-reviewed climate science – make me a liability to hire in Alberta?

I carried this experience with me through the remainder of my time as a preservice teacher. While our courses taught us the importance of engaging with real-life issues and creating lesson plans that respond to student interests and lived realities, I was always aware that this may not be possible in certain Alberta classrooms, as made clear to me by the individuals responsible for hiring classroom teachers. The fear of repercussions for climate activism, or any teaching that may be perceived as such in the classroom, has restricted my ability to engage with this important topic as an educator. What impact does this atmosphere of censorship have on Alberta teachers' ability to meaningfully engage their students and prepare them for the great challenge of our times?

Kelsey (born @ 355.61 ppm)

Growing up in Calgary, a city driven by an oil economy, I never understood the importance of caring for the environment or considering global relationships. I was never taught in-depth about climate change or the impacts that our species has had on the planet. I never learned about social issues, and I had the view that the world was as it was, and I was comfortable with the status quo. It wasn't until university that I started to consider the scope of the world beyond the borders of Alberta, the only home I've always known.

My undergraduate degree in anthropology was my pathway to self-discovery and understanding of the global community. I learned about social injustices, environmental crises, and the need for a more realistic education for the youth of tomorrow. In 2018, I began my formal teacher training and quickly learned that the true role of a classroom teacher is to do more than facilitate curriculum. We were encouraged to foster effective relationships with our students, seek out their interests, and facilitate learning through those pathways.

In early 2019, I learned of the Fridays for Future (FFF) movement and was thrilled to hear about youth taking their future into their own hands. Students from all over the world were gathering en masse and orchestrating a call towards societal change. The idea was simple: on Friday afternoons school-aged students would strike from classes as a call for environmental action and change. I knew I wanted to be an ally to this movement. I attended my first climate strike in March 2019. Seeing children gathering in solidarity moved me to tears, and I have been following the movement ever since.

Our social studies specialization class took a new direction as we followed the movement. Our focus of discussion turned towards how our role as future educators was evolving to a role as allies, and how we could support and stand alongside students. I felt driven to use my platform as a teacher to encourage the youth movement. Prior to the March 15th strike, I had posted a link to FFF's website on social media. In the post, I talked about the movement and the climate strikes that were happening around the world. My post served as declaration of my support and a call to action, asking adults to be allies of this movement. This was the first time I had publicly posted about my personal and educational commitments and was excited to engage in the conversations around climate change.

This enthusiasm came crashing to a halt in the fall of 2019 after attending another Fridays for Future strike. Globally, an estimated four million participants came out in support of the cause, garnering a significant media presence (Barkley & Resnick, 2019). To attend this event many of us had to skip class, another conflict in itself. I felt obligated to have permission to attend granted by my professor. On September 20, we marched to City Hall. I made a sign that read "YOUR TEACHERS SUPPORT YOU."

I didn't consider the impacts of my sign or the attention that it garnered, until the days that followed. People I knew contacted me saying they had seen my face and sign in the news. I saw photos of myself posted online. At first, I was elated but then quickly began to fear that my activism could negatively affect my potential to obtain work. I was afraid that my participation would create "waves" in a province and economy that is not quite ready for change – a province whose backbone was built on the petroleum industry. This is when the reality of our dilemma set in, a moral debate between standing for what I believe in and the fear of tarnishing my professional reputation in the future. As the FFF movement grew larger, so did the political backlash.

During our final semester's interdisciplinary showcase for all B.Ed. students, there was a panel of representatives from the major school boards from our region. A professor got up to ask a question regarding their opinion of teachers and student teachers actively participating in climate strikes and whether their involvement could harm their chances of obtaining a position within their school division. The district officials tip-toed around this question, giving generic non-answers. It became obvious that the boards did not support activism within the classroom. It became very obvious that school boards would not want to hire someone like me.

Emily (born @ 363.48 ppm)

During my B.Ed. I specialized in social studies. I had always loved social studies for history, learning about people and their ways of knowing, and learning about past events. However, I learned that this discipline is not only about past events, but how we create history in the present, through social justice and by being active citizens. It all started when Jackie came into class with news about a young Swedish girl, Greta Thunberg, and the large movement of students who were protesting all over the world. I was shocked that students were walking out of school to protest something that they were so passionate about. From our four-walled classroom, with no windows, we watched protests unfolding and news of students standing up for justice all over the world. This is when I learned that education is not learning what the curriculum says or what the teacher wants. It is about what the students want to learn about, what are they passionate about. Their curiosity should be leading the classroom.

One day, five of us attended a climate strike. It was a gloomy Friday, but spirits were bright. We hurried to make posters out of recycled paper – nothing like attending a protest last minute! I was excited to go. But in the back of my mind I was worried about getting into trouble, worried about what people would think if they saw me or a photo of me.

The energy in the air was exciting. We hopped on the train with other protestors and even other professors from the university. We chatted about the climate, about the kids all over the world, and about change.

Gathering at City Hall, I was shocked by how many students were there and inspired to see so many kids, teens, and parents. However, mostly middle school students were in attendance. They were making the conscious decision to leave their classes to participate in protest. This showed dedication to change and concern for their futures.

I was anxious and worried about how school boards might view me and what a school board might do if they saw a picture of me on the internet or the news. Would I get a job?

The protest was run completely by students – students reading poems about the environment, sharing artwork. Students organizing the protest walked across the street, in front of cars, and I felt a sense of responsibility, protectiveness, to make sure that they were safe. I was inspired but, at the same time, overwhelmed and anxious. I had to walk away. It might have been the size of the crowd or my selfish thoughts of "do not do anything that you will be seen doing because no one will hire you." There was not much media when we first arrived at City Hall, but by the time students were voicing their protests on the stage and marching across the street the media was everywhere. As I was leaving, listening to the students chanting in the background, I noticed a funeral procession coming towards the protest – a funeral procession for a tree. The procession walked slowly towards City Hall as passers-by stared in wonder at their gas masks. The ring of their bell echoed through the street from a block away. It was moving, and I wondered what would happen once they got to City Hall … to see those kids and youth faces ... I wish I had never left.

Jackie (born 322.18 ppm)

In grade 10 science (1982), we were assigned to present on a science issue in the media. I chose "the greenhouse effect/global warming." That project ignited my ecological awareness. During my undergraduate degree and early teaching years, urgent environmental issues were constantly in the media including the clearcutting of old-growth rainforests on Canada's west coast, acid rain, and the hole in the ozone layer. My PhD (Seidel, 2007) focused on how teachers can face ecological crisis, on what it means for our pedagogy, for how teachers can "be" with children in this time of so much grief and loss. While working on my dissertation, increasing numbers of species were going extinct, the climate kept warming, horrific wars were being waged over oil, and immeasurable suffering was being inflicted on humans and our more-than-human kin. I was also teaching elementary school during this time. The deeply felt urgency of my scholarship was often in tension with day-to-day institutional goals, structures, and processes.

During my PhD, several professors told me that my focus was "not a topic for education" and warned that I would "never get a job." Today I am often labelled by colleagues and administrators as an "environmentalist." I have learned to receive such comments with a sense of humour and scholarly curiosity. Why are energy politics, mass extinctions, or ecological awareness viewed as controversial or taboo when talking about education? Why is researching or teaching about them viewed as environmentalism or activism? Returning to campus after attending a strike was a jarring experience. The strikes were bursting with the energy of diverse young people, those we as educators claim to serve and support. The strikes were deeply moving. I witnessed grief, rage, and passion in the faces and bodies of young people. Back on campus, the quiet education building felt frozen in time. Something momentous had just happened a short train ride away. A colleague once commented to me that our university is "coated in oil." Our campus has benefitted immensely from fossil fuel wealth. I was reminded that as scholars we have the responsibility to analyse and face the complexities of the times and places in which we are entangled and implicated.

When exiting the train at the global climate strike in September 2019, I was shocked by the crowd of young people and the absence of adults. I felt a sense of pedagogical responsibility not only to participate alongside the children but to watch over their well-being. I recall the moment an enraged man emerged from a large black pick-up truck in the middle of several lanes of traffic to initiate an altercation with some young people on the sidewalk. The presence of these youth with their bold signs and loud chanting is a direct challenge to the petro-soaked identities that have long defined this place. These young people are transgressing boundaries including compulsory school attendance and here, in Alberta, openly critiquing the oil and gas industry while marching under the towering headquarters of Husky, TC, Imperial Oil, Enbridge, Repsol, Shell, and Canadian Natural Resources, among many others.

In the fall of 2018, I began bringing news stories of the climate strikes into education courses – that children all over the world were practising civil disobedience by walking out of school seemed like something teachers should be paying attention to. That children were using social media to teach one another about political activism, create their own curriculum, and demand that adults take action, seemed to be a critical moment for pedagogical relations between generations. How might teachers and faculties of education respond? Over the past two years, an increasing number of students in my courses have been focusing their projects on ecological issues, as well as related social, political, and economic issues. In the past, many pre-service teachers asked if these topics were too controversial for their projects but now that question is rare. The rising courage and conviction among young people to demand urgent political and socially just action for a livable future inspires me to overcome my own hesitation at speaking out in our context where it can feel easiest to stay silent.

Sidrah (born @ 363 ppm)

One afternoon following a climate change rally, as Jackie and I were walking to the train station, a man confronted us on the street. He had seen us leaving the protest and started questioning the mini flags we were carrying ("tell the truth"). After some back and forth, he shouted that during his post-secondary studies in the '80s, he had learned that we, as a society, could not engage in climate change work without first prioritizing the economy. This statement struck me profoundly. The false dichotomy of economy vs. climate action was so deeply ingrained in this man's mind that he was literally shouting in the street about it. What kind of education had he received? Who wrote that curriculum? Despite the fact that the economy does not exist without a livable planet, healthy humans, and viable resources, this man insisted that climate action must come secondary to this notion of "economy." The fact that this bias was directly rooted in the post-secondary education he had received over 25 years ago, helped me to see for the first time an example of the long-term, real-life impact of education on shaping an individual's (and a society's) worldview. This was a concept often discussed in our courses, but to see it out in the streets of my own city, causing divisions where there should be unity, was alarming and enlightening. The climate strikes, and the public backlash to these strikes, have helped me to understand that our Albertan petro-based culture, and the governments that prop up these unsustainable industries and ideas, simply make education worse.

If educators are cautioned, whether overtly or implicitly, from the time they are preservice teachers, against meaningfully engaging in climate-change-related education, their professional practice is diminished. We know climate change is real, and the Fridays for Future movement makes it clear that students are deeply concerned about it. So, why are we made to feel afraid of broaching this subject in our classrooms? Meanwhile, decades of pro-oil-and-gas agendas have been allowed to infiltrate our school systems, leading to the types of confrontations outlined above. Climate change is an important, relevant, and complex challenge – the kind perfectly suited to brilliant classroom projects. Needlessly politicizing a global and all-encompassing issue like climate change, to the point that it becomes a contentious topic within education, is harmful to Alberta students and educators. Leadership that bows to the desires of industry at the expense of engaging, robust, and ethical education practices harms us all. Cowardly leadership undermines the brilliance of Alberta teachers and preservice educators. This culture of fear extends well beyond the education sector. From non-profit CEOs being "repositioned" following calls for climate action (Abdel-Nabi, 2020) to an Alberta company creating misogynistic and pedophilic stickers of Greta Thunberg, the message is clear that climate activism, especially if you're a woman, is not a consequence-free endeavour in Alberta.

Kelsey (born @ 355.61 ppm)

I am currently in my first year of teaching as a substitute within the Calgary area. I was hired despite my name being out in the public sphere. Since the last climate strike I attended, in March 2020, I have graduated with my B.Ed., there has been a global pandemic, and the climate strikes have been put on the backburner. Over the course of writing these reflections, which were often difficult to express, I have learned that my "radical" ideologies may never jibe with what is expected of teachers. I have also learned that the path towards what is right and just may never be clearly defined or achieved. I have learned that a lot needs to be unlearned. What I know now, for sure, is that the key to success lies in following your heart. So, what does this mean for me as a new teacher? It means that I continue on my path as a social activist, that I continue to do the (hard) work, and I continue to challenge the norms of expectation. I have learned that it is okay to make waves, as long as I am prepared to ride them with dignity and self-assuredness.

Fortunately for us in Alberta, teachers are governed by the province's Teaching Quality Standard (Alberta Education, 2020a). Teachers are required by law to follow the guidelines and competencies outlined in the TQS and use them to meet the holistic needs of our students in our implementation of the curriculum. These include, but are not limited to, "planning and designing learning activities that consider relevant local, provincial, national and international contexts and issues" and "using instructional strategies to engage students in meaningful learning activities, based on an understanding of students' backgrounds, prior knowledge and experiences" (p. 5).

Knowing I am governed by competencies like these, I feel confident in my professional ability to help students pursue topics of their interest and interpret the content of the curriculum to fit the context of the classroom that I am in. My hope as a teacher is to provide my students with the opportunity to challenge the status quo, to ask the hard questions, and to extend the scope of their learning beyond the walls of the classroom. I will provide my students with the education I wish I had received.

Emily (born @ 363.48 ppm)

Currently I am a teacher in a small Alberta town, where family livelihoods depend on oil and gas. Parents and grandparents work front-line rigging jobs to make sure their children have food and shelter, and my students know that this is their future. Oil and gas is all they have ever known.

The climate strikes have lit a fire under not only me but many children, youth, teachers, parents, and grandparents. People in the '60s, '70s, and '80s were protesting for change, and now public displays of activism have surfaced again, wanting change – and not always positive change. The Fridays for Future strikes are protests by youth concerned for future youth. Meanwhile, there were pro-oil-and-gas counter protests at the climate strike at the Alberta Legislature in 2019. The Black Lives Matter protests are supporting widespread social justice and human rights. The anti-mask protests, during a health crisis, involve people who do not want to wear a mask because it curtails their freedoms. As an educator, I am interested in further understanding the concept of protests. Also, I want to consider other ways of knowing. In the Alberta grade 6 curriculum, students explore the Iroquois Confederacy as part of the learning journey through democracy and learn about the Seventh Generation, a philosophy found in many Indigenous communities in addition to the Iroquois. A guiding principle in this philosophy encourages people to consider how their decisions might impact the seven generations to come. As a white settler woman, I am not an expert in Indigenous knowledge, but I want to bring to the forefront that the Fridays for Future youth are protesting for the seventh generation – compared to the adults at the anti-mask protests who care only about their personal freedoms. I look forward to learning about the intertwining of activism, protests, education, and Indigenous ways of knowing.

Jackie (born @ 322.18 ppm)

When a young person at the 2019 global strike announced through their megaphone that we were going to do a "die in" and lay down in silence for seven minutes I felt a moment of uncomfortable hesitation. It felt vulnerable to lay down in public. It was a sunny fall day. The concrete beneath my body was warm. The chanting went silent as people settled, and our view changed from seeing hundreds of other people and the corporate office towers to seeing only the iconic Alberta blue sky. As I lay there, a thought burst into my mind: *We are not dying, we are resting.*

A preoccupation of my scholarly work has been to meditate on the existential meanings of time in education. What could education be if we thought beyond and away from industrial(ized) time? As I lay there, I noticed how tired I was, how good it felt to lay down. I reflected on how industrial time is exhausting humans and exhausting the planet. In his poem *Things to Think*, Robert Bly (1997) wrote, "… it's/ Been decided that if you lie down no one will die" (p. 20). I lay there thinking about this line. I thought about it again a year later, during another climate strike die-in in front of the provincial government building in Calgary. Many months into the COVID-19 pandemic, laying on the prickly grass, gravity grounding me to the earth, I breathed the musty fall air alongside so many mask-wearing others. I thought again how we were not dying; *we are seeds*. This global striking community is preparing the soil, germinating the ecologically, socially, economically just world that children are asking for. I thought about the meanings of the climate strike movement, about the regressive new curriculum draft and its dire implications for children's learning and the future. I thought about this government calling teachers "radicals" and how this is actually true. The word radical means "roots" (Latin: *radix*). The only life-serving way through this time might be to radically root ourselves in our places and communities in such a way that liberates schools, cultures, and economies from the industrial timeline. It's getting late. The climate striking children have shown the way by simply walking out the door.

Closing Thoughts

We were not unaware of the risks writing this chapter could pose in the current political climate in Alberta, Canada – not so much for Jackie as a tenured associate professor, but for Kelsey, Sidrah, and Emily as new teachers. We understand that our collective and individual fear and anxiety is localized, yet also materially and contextually very real. We understand that our political situation is not the situation everywhere and that our obligation to children, as teachers, extends beyond the borders of this place and time. We understand that our local atmosphere of oppression, fear, and threat, including Bill 1, is a situation that could become *not local* – that the opportunities for oppression, right-wing populism, and fascism are everywhere (in some places more than others), and that our participation and support as teachers signals commitments to the present and future beyond our own place, work, and lives. Climate strikes are part of "triggering transition in the present" (Petrocultures Research Group, 2016, p. 13). Our experiences and the current political situation with curriculum, schools, and government threats remind us of the ways education is often invisibly entangled in the "historical conditions of a fossil fuel culture" (Wilson et al., 2017, p. 10) and that "cultural and social values" also need to be transformed. Indeed, journalists Mary Annaïse Heglar and Amy Westervelt (2021) recently observed, "what we see in internal documents from oil companies is that the youth climate movement is the first thing that's ever really made them worry about losing their social license" (n.p.).

Much has happened in the short time since we attended the (mostly pre-pandemic) strikes together. Across Canada and globally, immeasurable and unjust suffering from climate and ecological disruption unfolds. Several recent studies have highlighted the extreme impacts that ecological crisis is and will have on young people. These imply a need for urgent action and reflection from educators in how to relate to and with young people and how to interpret curriculum and learning in current contexts. In August 2021, UNICEF (2021) released a report documenting that one billion children are currently at *extreme risk* from the impacts of climate change. Meanwhile, researchers surveyed 10,000 young people (16–25) across ten countries to collect their thoughts and feelings about climate change and concluded: "Climate change and inadequate governmental responses are associated with climate anxiety and distress in many children and young people globally. These psychological stressors threaten health and well-being, and could be construed as morally injurious and unjust" (Marks et al., 2021, n.p.). During the lead up to COP26, a large group of scientists published an article concluding that climate change is a severe threat to children's futures (Thiery et al., 2021).

We strike for all children in the present, for all future generations, and all future time. Striking for the future means that we acknowledge that the place where we live, its economy and culture, have had and will continue to have an outsized impact on climate warming. These impacts are unequally felt by people and other creatures in places where our fellow humans who have contributed very little to this crisis are experiencing the impacts in significant and life-threatening ways. Our participation in strikes, and in writing this paper, also signal our commitments to Indigenous-settler reconciliation and decolonization, to moving forward in a good way. And finally, our participation signals our commitment to ways of learning and being together that create livable and socially just futures including for our more-than-human kin. The climate striking children have invited us to join in their powerful gesture of leaving the school, of practising civil disobedience, walking out of the industrial-colonial entangled spacetime, into the world, in love and community and imagination for what is to come.

ACKNOWLEDGMENTS

Thank you to Lesley Tait (PhD student and RA) for providing support in locating references, and to Stephanie Westlund (PhD) for manuscript editing support.

NOTES

1 Several terms in this chapter may be new to some readers. These include petrocultures, petrostate, and extractivism.

Petrocultures: In *After Oil* (2016), The Petrocultures Research Group (University of Alberta), wrote: "We use this term to emphasize the ways in which post-industrial society today is an oil society through and through. It is shaped by oil in physical and material ways, from the automobiles and highways we use to the plastics that permeate our food supply and built environments. Even more significantly, fossil fuels have also shaped our values, practices, habits, beliefs, and feelings" (p. 9).

Petrostate: Andrew Nikiforuk (2010) observed that in Alberta, "Oil hinders democracy and corrupts the political process through the absence of transparent reporting and clear fiscal accounting. Alberta, a classic petrostate, has one of the least accountable governments in Canada as well as the lowest voter turnout" (p. 4). For comprehensive discussions about why Alberta may be described as a petrostate, we recommend Laurie Adkin's (2016a) edited collection *First World Petro-Politics: The Political Ecology and Governance of Alberta,* and Angela Carter's (2020) *Fossilized: Environmental Policy in Canada's Petro-Provinces*. The defining feature of a petrostate is "high dependence on oil, typically defined as oil representing one-third of exports, GDP, or government revenues" (Carter, 2020). Importantly, petrostates share political, historical, social, and governance qualities that are observed (and experienced) in the Alberta context, including "deleterious economic, social and political effects" (p. 13), "democratic deterioration" (p. 14), and a trend "towards authoritarianism" (Adkin, 2016b, p. 567).

Extractivism: A term often used in relation to Latin American economies, extractivism takes different forms in different places. In Alberta, it is characterized predominantly by oil and gas extraction/export, but also includes logging, mining, and monoculture crops (e.g., canola). Acosta (2013) defines extractivism as "a mode of accumulation that started to be established on a massive scale 500 years ago. The world economy – the capitalist system – began to be structured with the conquest and colonisation of the Americas, Africa and Asia. This extractivist mode of accumulation has been determined ever since by the demands of the metropolitan centres of nascent capitalism. Some regions specialized in the extraction and production of raw materials – primary commodities – while others took on the role of producing manufactured goods. The former export Nature, the latter import it" (p. 62). The UCP government's obsessive focus on pipelines, the use of public money to fund the anti-oil enquiry and an energy "war room" (Canadian Energy Centre), anti-democratic attacks on teachers as "radical activists" and other attempts to undermine public education are clear examples of the province's extractivist petrostate status.

2 *Calgary Stampede*: Originally the Calgary Exhibition (founded in 1884) brands itself as "The Greatest Outdoor Show on Earth." Williams (2021) describes it as "Canada's oldest and largest festival celebrating the mythical Wild West of the late nineteenth century" (p. 1). More than a million visitors attend the annual 10-day festival in July. Events include rodeos, chuckwagon races, a parade, agriculture shows, midway, food, concerts, daily fireworks, city-wide pancake breakfasts hosted by politicians and corporations, and Indigenous Treaty 7 Nations' participation and presence at the Elbow River Camp (Calgary Stampede, n.d.).

REFERENCES

Abdel-Nabi, Hadeel (2020). What Sandip Lalli's departure says about Alberta. *The Sprawl.* Retrieved from https://www.sprawlcalgary.com/sandip-lalli-leaves-calgary-chamber.

Acosta, A. (2013). Extractivism and neo-extractivism: two sides of the same curse. In M. Lang & D. Mokrani (Eds.), *Beyond development: Alternative visions from Latin America* (pp. 61–87). Transnational Institute/Rosa Luxemburg Foundation. https://www.researchgate.net/publication/303543079_Beyond_Development_Alternative_visions_from_Latin_America

Adkin, L. E. (Ed.). (2016a). *First world petro-politics: The political ecology and governance of Alberta.* University of Toronto Press.

– (2016b). Democracy and the Albertan petro-state. In L. E. Adkin (Ed.), *First world petro-politics: The political ecology and governance of Alberta* (pp. 560–99). University of Toronto Press.

Aitchison, C. [@ColinAitchison]. (2020, August 6). *The NDP are angry that Alberta schools will focus on reading, writing and arithmetic, and that curriculum will focus on basics and keep out political bias.* [Tweet]. Twitter. https://twitter.com/ColinAitchison

Alberta Curriculum Analysis. (n.d.). *Alberta curriculum analysis.* https://alberta-curriculum-analysis.ca/general

Alberta Education. (2020a). *Teaching quality standard*. https://open.alberta.ca/dataset/14d92858-fec0-449b-a9ad-52c05000b4de/resource/afc2aa25-ea83-4d23-a105-d1d45af9ffad/download/edc-teaching-quality-standard-english-2020.pdfTRC

– (2020b). *The guiding framework for the design and development of Kindergarten to Grade 12 provincial curriculum*. https://open.alberta.ca/dataset/f3fb3059-fdec-4c62-89b7-a34eb9d33c3c/resource/0a51ffa3-76bf-4f8b-a31c-7481eb2fba5c/download/edc-guiding-framework-curriculum-development-2020.pdf

Alberta Inquiry. (2019). *Public inquiry into anti-Alberta energy campaigns*. https://albertainquiry.ca

Anderson, D. (2021, October 21). *"Anti-Alberta" inquiry points finger at media and environmentalists but finds no wrongdoing*. The Narwhal. https://thenarwhal.ca/alberta-public-inquiry-energy-findings/

Barkley, E., & Resnick, B. (2019, September 22). *How big was the global climate strike? 4 million people, activists estimate*. Vox News. https://www.vox.com/energy-and-environment/2019/9/20/20876143/climate-strike-2019-september-20-crowd-estimate

BBC News. (2019, May 24). *Students walk out in global climate strike*. https://www.bbc.com/news/world-48392551

Beattie, S. (2020, Feb 27). *Disgusting sticker of "Greta Thunberg" linked to Alberta oil company shocks Canadians*. Huffington Post Canada. https://www.huffpost.com/archive/ca/entry/greta-thunberg-alberta-oil_ca_5e58175fc5b60102210e12ff

Bly, R. (1997). *Morning poems*. HarperCollins Publishers Ltd.

Calgary Stampede. (n.d.). https://www.calgarystampede.com

Carter, A.V. (2020). *Fossilized: Environmental policy in Canada's petro-provinces*. UBC Press.

CBC. (2019, October 18). *"Our future is at stake": Greta Thunberg tells climate rally in Edmonton*. CBC News. https://www.cbc.ca/news/canada/edmonton/greta-thunberg-edmonton-climate-rally-1.5325030

CEC (Canadian Energy Centre). (n.d.). Canadian Energy Centre. https://www.canadianenergycentre.ca/about-us/

Conacher, D. (2020, December 16). *Abuse of power: Jason Kenney's many violations of democratic norms*. Alberta Views. https://albertaviews.ca/abuse-of-power/

Daggett, C. (2018). Petro-masculinity: Fossil fuels and authoritarian desire. *Millennium: Journal of International Studies*, *47*(1), 25–44. https://doi.org/10.1177/0305829818775817

Donald, D. (2020, November 3). *Leaked Alberta school curriculum in urgent need of guidance from Indigenous wisdom teachings*. The Conversation. https://theconversation.com/leaked-alberta-school-curriculum-in-urgent-need-of-guidance-from-indigenous-wisdom-teachings-148611

French, J. (2020, October 21). *Education experts slam leaked Alberta curriculum proposals*. CBC News. https://www.cbc.ca/news/canada/edmonton/education-experts-slam-leaked-alberta-curriculum-proposals-1.5766570

Glenza, J., Evans, A., Ellis-Petersen, H., & Zhou, N. (2019, March 15). *Climate strikes held around the world – as it happened.* The Guardian. https://www.theguardian.com/environment/live/2019/mar/15/climate-strikes-2019-live-latest-climate-change-global-warming

Goodridge, L. (2019, January 29). *Radical activists in the classroom.* https://ucpcaucus.ca/tag/laila-goodridge/ [article is web archived as: 29-01-2020_radical_activists_in_the_classroom-1.docx]

Government of Alberta. (2020). *Protecting critical infrastructure.* https://www.alberta.ca/protecting-critical-infrastructure.aspx

Heglar, M.A., and Westervelt, A. (2021, November 10*). "Nice" isn't going to save the planet.* The Nation. https://www.thenation.com/article/environment/climate-cop26-civility/

Koshan, J., Silver, L., & Watson Hamilton, J. (2020, June 9). *Protests matter: A Charter critique of Alberta's Bill 1.* ABlawg. http://ablawg.ca/wp-content/uploads/2020/06/Blog_JK_LAS_JWH_Bill1.pdf

LaGrange, A. [@AdrianaLaGrange]. (2019, November 28). "It is concerning that anybody would think that these were appropriate questions for a Gr.10 Social Studies test." [Tweet]. Twitter. https://twitter.com/adrianalagrange/status/1200176719761510401?lang=en

Laville, S., & Watts, J. (2019, September 21). *Across the globe, millions join biggest climate protest ever.* The Guardian. https://www.theguardian.com/environment/2019/sep/21/across-the-globe-millions-join-biggest-climate-protest-ever

Lindeman, T. (2020, February 28). *"Revolution is alive": Canada protests spawn climate and Indigenous rights movement.* The Guardian. https://www.theguardian.com/world/2020/feb/28/canada-pipeline-protests-climate-indigenous-rights

Marks, E., Hickman, C., Pihkala, P., Clayton, S., Lewandowski, E. R., Mayall, E. E., Wray, B., Mellor, C., & van Susteren, L. (2021). Young people's voices on climate anxiety, government betrayal and moral injury: A global phenomenon. *The Lancet.* Prepint article at https://doi.org/10.2139/ssrn.3918955

McKenzie-Jones, P. (2019, August 29). *What does "We are all treaty people" mean and who speaks for Indigenous students on campus?* The Conversation. https://theconversation.com/what-does-we-are-all-treaty-people-mean-and-who-speaks-for-indigenous-students-on-campus-119060

Mitchell, L. (2020, Feb 29). *Greta Thunberg responds to graphic decal bearing Alta. oilfield company logo.* CTV News Edmonton. https://edmonton.ctvnews.ca/greta-thunberg-responds-to-graphic-decal-bearing-alta-oilfield-company-logo-1.4833281

Montenegro, Y. (2020, March 6). *Wet'suwet'en action timeline.* The Leveller. https://leveller.ca/2020/03/wetsuweten-action-timeline/

Muskrat Magazine. (2013, June 14). *Indigenous peoples' resistance timeline.* http://muskratmagazine.com/indigenous-peoples-resistance-timeline/

Nikiforuk, A. (2010). *Tar sands: Dirty oil and the future of a continent.* Greystone Books.

Palmater, P. (2020). *Warrior life: Indigenous resistance and resurgence*. Fernwood Publishing.

Petrocultures Research Group. (2016). *After oil*. Petrocultures Research Group.

Seidel, J. (2007). *Unknowing the future: Meditations on the time of teaching* [Unpublished doctoral dissertation]. University of Alberta.

Thiery, W., Lange, S., Rogelj, J., Schleussner, C., Gudmundsson, L., Seneviratne, S. I., Andrijevic, M., Frieler, K., Emanuel, K., Geiger, T., Bresch, D.N., Zhao, F., Willner, S. N., Büchner, M., Volkholz, J., Bauer, N., Chang, J., Ciais, P., Dury, M., … Wada, Y. (2021). Intergenerational inequities in exposure to climate extremes. *Science, 374*(6564), 158–60. https://doi.org/10.1126/science.abi7339

UCP Caucus [@UCPcaucus]. (2020, Nov 17). "#ExtinctionRebellion – the extremist group that shut down the Walterdale in #YEG – is back at it. This time, they're blocking a rail line in B.C. in an effort to cancel #TMX." [Tweet]. Twitter. https://twitter.com/UCPCaucus/status/1328792850683752448

UNICEF. (2021, August 19). *One billion children at 'extremely high risk' of the impacts of the climate crisis – UNICEF*. https://www.unicef.org/press-releases/one-billion-children-extremely-high-risk-impacts-climate-crisis-unicef

Williams, K. (2021). *Stampede: Misogyny, white supremacy and settler colonialism*. Fernwood Publishing.

Wilson, S., Carlson, A., & Szeman, I. (Eds.) (2017). *Petrocultures: Oil, politics, culture*. McGill-Queen's University Press..

13 Disquieting Returns

TERESA STRONG-WILSON

During my sabbatical leave, I wrote a book based on a research project that I had been working on with teachers.[1] The book was based on my thinking over the past five or so years, a central part of which concerned my meditations on disquiet. As I was writing the book, I was analysing data from time spent in two secondary-school teachers' classrooms. At the same time, I had embarked on entering one of the elementary-school teacher's classrooms. The classroom data took time to transcribe; indeed, it was not completed until the following year. All of this is by way of preamble to explain the subject of this chapter, which is on disquieting returns. W. G. Sebald (1996) intimates that "time … is nothing but the disquiet of the soul" (p. 181).

The fact is that working with this elementary-school teacher in her classroom gave rise to new questions. The book enquired into teachers' teaching to social injustice using counter-stories and how teachers became not simply implicated subjects but concerned, disquieted ones and where autobiography was both a lens as well as a method (Strong-Wilson, 2021). During this time, I was also reading Amarou Yoder's dissertation on ambiguity and violence in the teaching of language arts; Amarou was a doctoral student of mine (now PhDEd) as well as someone with whom I have often co-authored and who was a research assistant on this project.[2] The questions informing her dissertation hovered in the back of my mind, questions having to do with the intimate relations between teaching to violence (via social justice narrative texts) and one's narrative identity as a classroom teacher, an identity that is partially reflected back to us through our students. At the heart of engagement with social justice texts is language, especially classroom talk (Strong-Wilson & Huang, 2023). Part of my purpose in writing is to work through the question of the potential violence *of* teachers' words even as we (as teachers) are teaching *to* violence and where I have elected to do so through juxtaposing my research with teachers (one in particular) with my own autobiographical memories, as student and teacher. Yoder (2020), as a secondary English teacher, perceptively asks: "Can

I be certain whether or not I am foisting a narrative on those around me, attempting to control discourse so that I might feel less vulnerable, and less fragile in answering the question, 'Who am I?' " (p. 97). Throughout, I deliberately refer to the teacher as she/her or simply as "the teacher," this to suggest the relationship between the subject of this chapter – violence and social justice teaching – and ourselves as teachers in teaching to social justice. The chapter juxtaposes and relates reflections on myself (as student, as teacher) with what I noticed and felt in being in the teacher's classroom – this in the same school where I was an elementary student.

Beginnings

During my university leave, I had the opportunity to return to the place in which I grew up and went to public school and to conduct research in a classroom outwardly identical to the very one that I had once sat in. I recall snippets of my younger school self. My younger school self was shy and withdrawn, almost to a vanishing point. I loved school, literature especially, and loved to handle books. I also loved blackboards and the smell of chalk and generally the furniture of a classroom, which perhaps presaged my idea that a career in education was something I could do. But such could not have been foreseen at the time.

I went through my elementary school years being, and feeling being, largely inconspicuous, which was fortunate in a way. I wasn't bullied, for instance, or even teased, which I easily could have been, as after grade 4 I was also visibly overweight. Teachers noticed me, obliquely, conscientious being a word that appeared often on my report card. As far I could tell, the word was tantamount to being unproblematic; I did what I was told, and I did it in such a way that I didn't need or demand any help. I sat quietly in my wooden desk, one in a sea of rows of like wooden desks, and that spot was my little fiefdom – the desk containing all of my books, exercise books, pencils, erasers. The deep and rich world of reading was an experience I lived largely outside of the classroom – in libraries and at home. As far I can recall, my presence only attracted the attention of four classroom teachers. I earned a $25 gift certificate for a book in an end-of-the year assembly, so the grade 1 teacher must have noticed the reader in me. In grade 3, a teacher commonly referred to as Miss Hippo informed my parents, looking through her crystal ball: "Teresa will never make anything of herself." Quietness took on another hue; I felt *visibly* quiet. *Abnormally* shy.

In grade 5, I had a teacher whom I greatly admired. She was passionate about teaching, which was exuberantly mirrored in her patterned dresses and stylized shoes. She pinned one of my compositions on the bulletin board. I remember its general contours, a story informed by the myths and fairy tales that comprised my reading diet. She was the same teacher who pinned me to a corner, facing the wall; it had something to do with being out of my seat, something connected to a bathroom visit, as I dimly recall. I was never so mortified.

As a researcher, I have entered countless public schools, and as Alan Block remarks (and Philip Jackson before him), schools tend to look and feel and even smell much the same. However, there was a particular poignancy in coming back here. Given my history and especially my terror at any public attention (except of a positive nature – the reading award, the composition tacked to the bulletin board), it is a mystery as to how I became a teacher at all. Brodsky (1995) notes: "in the final analysis, a human being doesn't so much obtain knowledge from the outside as secrete it from within" (p. 308) – their True Self.

The shunning of the public light can be a disguised desire to be noticed. Miss Hippo was right in one way: my efforts at showing – or sharing – any talents or gifts I might possess were lackluster. In Allan Block's (2020) words, though, I may have been nurturing my True Self – my true and private self, a notion that he borrows from Winnicott (1986, as cited in Block, p. 47). A true self, by definition, does not appear; it is mainly known through its defences, or its False Self. On this account, my invisibility *was* my way of appearing, falsely, this so as to take care of my True Self. When during my master's research, I interviewed an Indigenous teacher and elder in the First Nations school where I had taught, she explained that, traditionally, people used to identify and help nurture a child's gifts. She gave the example of public speaking. If a child showed inclinations in this direction, they were encouraged. As far as I can tell, the main gift I possess is writing and the scholarship and study that has gone with it – and I *was* encouraged in this, by various teachers, by my parents. Although there can be a very public, even "star," quality to being a scholar, those are two activities that are also legitimately carried on quietly, away from the public eye. Later, whenever I would tell people that I wanted to be a lawyer (as I aspired to be at one point), there was often polite silence as I was not known for being outwardly anything; rather, the opposite. In recent years, and remarkably especially during this pandemic, I have finally figured out that another gift of mine might be teaching, although I never would have thought so. Neither, presumably, would Miss Hippo. Teaching is very much a public vocation. Receipt of the gift was, shall we say, delayed, but I also believe consciousness of teaching's gift came in its own time, in my time.

I start with this leg of my intellectual journey because for the longest time, and especially since I have become a researcher, I have sought out the classrooms of teachers dedicated to teaching and doing so thoughtfully and critically – teachers who perhaps I thought I could become, even emulate: this as I sat in the corners of classrooms, quietly observing. In research, I have been privileged to conduct research in the classrooms of many such teachers.

My elementary teachers were quite ordinary; however, the teaching of some, I suspect, may be tied to memories I have suppressed. The only reason I know about Miss Hippo's remark is that it became the focus of one of those stories that are told and re-told during one's childhood. For my parents, it was a story of outrage with a *teacher* – how dare she say such a thing! For me, it was like an image in a crystal ball; it became a defining moment, one that I have spent the better part of my life trying to surpass. During my first teaching practicum, which was a long, drawn-out incubation of weekly visits over eight months, I was paired with a grade 5–6 teacher close to retirement, whom I will call Mrs T., who was nice enough to me but alternately callous and raging towards students who, from my vantage point at the back of the room, very much needed the opposite. I learned (or perhaps, re-learned) from her how not to be. As Britzman (2009) notes (and Block reiterates), teachers' reasons for entering teacher education are often based on negative rationales: the determination to be other than their, or students,' destroyers.

To pick up my thread again, encountering this teacher in a classroom of my old school was a bit like coming face to face with a ghost, to recognize in her a certain part of myself, even though we are quite different, she and I. She is the very opposite of shy, not afraid to speak her mind: a quality that can set her at odds with others, including, at times, her students. What was the same, though, was a certain vulnerability, an element I well recognize in becoming – and being – a teacher.

Teacher as Autobiographical Subject

The most exhilarating – or terrifying – thing about teaching, depending on one's point of view, is the prospect of students. Real students. Britzman's (2004) first extended unit as a student teacher was on monsters, beginning with the reading of *Frankenstein*. Students were not interested in the *critical* readings of the monster – the Other – as Britzman was. Instead, the students positioned themselves more as the monsters sent to undermine Britzman's curricular intentions, she mused. Reflecting further, she meditated on a teacher's *furor* to teach, the phrase coming from the work of Robert Gardner (1994/2012) where he describes teachers as being impelled, even "goaded," by their theory of teaching as well as their character (as cited in Britzman, 2004, p. 257). "How can this be otherwise given the teacher's subjectivity?" Britzman asks (p. 257). She elaborates: "However one might try to disguise it, deny it, or even shed its more scaly qualities, the teacher's subjectivity is exaggerated, animated, and projected into these various objects that then become the teacher's proxy, made to communicate the teacher's desire." Britzman then reflects: "But it may also be the case that the curriculum, too, was used as terrific defence against not knowing what it will be to learn to teach *as* one is teaching" (p. 258, emphasis added) and where one of the greatest fears is "of losing control of everything," including of oneself (p. 258).

We know stories like these. There is the fictionalized yet highly recognizable Miss Maple in Leah Fowler's (2002) storied teacher who, highly frustrated, indeed enraged (for reasons unknown to the reader yet tied to teaching), drags a table across the classroom door and then empties the contents of her desk along with the students' assignments into the wastepaper basket, setting it on fire. Students are aghast, horrified. Then there is the very real Janet Frame (1989), who wrote in *Angel at My Table* about how she left the profession. Instead of locking herself in with the students (as had done Miss Maple), she simply walked out the door. I can remember how I longed for that ferry that took me away on weekends, away from my classroom during my first year of teaching, and especially, away from my students. I recall too how deeply I dreaded the return. Our dread can even approximate hatred – "mentalized … aggression," as Block (2020) calls it (p. 81) – this as I remember imagining students must feel much the same dread about me.

A Teacher's Furor: Travelling Somewhere …

Yoder (2020) points out that: "it is this story – this difficult story – that is the story that matters" (p. 51).

The fact is that I hadn't really thought too much about what it would feel like to actually travel back to a place I know, this for the purposes of research.

I take the bus. It makes a detour into a new development on the other side of the highway before heading up the boulevard I know well, wending its way by familiar landmarks before I get off at the stop closest to the school. I am entering from a different direction than the route on which I would travel on my bike, but I nevertheless recognize the houses as of the same sort I would have called on while selling Girl Guide cookies or the chocolate rabbits sponsored by the local Lion's Club, of which my father was a devoted member.

In my first visit to a school not seen in decades, I find myself somewhat at a loss. Where is the field? Where is the hill on the side of the school? The surroundings are tamed. There is a landscaped park and a small playground. I sit down on one of the benches and look at the school, recognizing the entrances on far left and far right. I survey the part of the school that was, and must still be, the gym and recall the phys ed classes that I hated, like dodge ball, which could be exciting but brutal. I still remember the sting of the ball against my bare thigh. My reverie is interrupted by some mildly curious stares from a grandparent in the park with his grandchild, and I move to enter the school.

The teacher's classroom is on the top floor. I try to recall if I was a student in this particular room. I preferred classrooms on this treed side. It is June so there are boxes about. Things are being put away for the summer. Students are gone. She shows me some of her favourite social-justice picture books. The book she wants to do with her students is called *Fatty Legs*; it is written by a residential school survivor, Olemaun Pokiak-Fenton, in collaboration with her daughter-in-law, Christy. The teacher explains: "For me it was something very personal because a lot of stories that I read about or that I've heard about is really at the age when I went to school." Olemaun was eight when she left her community to attend residential school. The teacher was seven when she emigrated to Canada and started grade 1. She also senses in Olemaun the same drive to learn, which is how the novel begins, with Olemaun bothering her father to let her go to learn how to read until finally, exasperated, he lets her, this against his better judgment, having attended himself. "I'm a very curious person and always have been," the teacher says – and so was Olemaun, she comments, who was pulled in by the story of Alice (in Wonderland) that her elder half-sister would read to her.

I return in the early fall. There is something Sebaldian about her reiteration to me of being struck by the fact that as she was enjoying a happy childhood, others were undergoing very difficult experiences in residential school. German author W. G. Sebald says the same in his writing: as his pram was being pushed in a meadow with snowy mountains in the background, Kafka's sisters were being killed in a concentration camp (see Strong-Wilson, 2021). The teacher says, "I feel ashamed that I'm part of the generation that did this," that is, the residential school system. She opens her first class on *Fatty Legs* by sharing with students that she always wanted to gain a broader outlook on the world. *Fatty Legs* is a book that opened my mind, she says. I hope it will open yours.

From now on, twice a week, I am privy to seeing her teach the "same" lesson, with different students. One group of students is her homeroom. The other class has Language Arts with her and at a certain hour there is a flurry of activity as the students switch places, her home room students crossing the hall. Students are predominantly French-speaking; circumventing Quebec's Bill 101, they are managing to attend an English school because their parent or grandparent did.

I learn about how different these two groups of students are for her. Because one group is her home group, they feel more like her "real" students, the others like "visitors," this even though she clearly cares for all of them. She knows their families and may have taught one of their older siblings. A greater elasticity around time obtains in her home group, though, which can lead to digressions and the need to rein in. They are perpetually in catch-up mode with the other group, her visitors, who she only has for one hour; she is more disciplined about how their time unfolds.

What did you notice? What did you feel? These are the questions she repeats often, "popping" back and forth between readers; she uses a popcorn method of sharing responsibility for reading aloud with students. I become sensitive to how her teaching shifts from one group to the other, even if only through small nuances, and I find myself taking note of it again when analysing the transcripts.

The routine on this day in October departs from what will be the norm. She has her home group first, then her visiting students. Both classes were fascinated to hear her story of how much she wanted to learn English. It was a story she told more than once: "I wanted to speak like my grade 1 teacher. I would speak to the mirror. Mirror, mirror on the wall, who can speak the best English of all?" (Field notes, Oct. 11, 2018). Each class spent at least two periods on this question of desire – it was fundamental to Olemaun's motivation in wanting to attend residential school, or thinking that she did – but why did she want so much to learn to read, the teacher asked? At one point in the book, the author recounts how, as her parents brought her to the school, her father laid a hand on her shoulder, giving her a last opportunity to change her mind: "You will not be able to return for a very long time." Olemaun recounted: "I said I know, but I didn't" (Jordan-Fenton & Pokiak-Fenton, 2020, p. 26).

I move to looking at her class with the visitors and compare the discussion there. She does not tell her mirror, mirror story right away. Instead, she hints at it by the words she chooses to describe Olemaun: Olemaun has a "big, bright attitude" (Class discussion, Visiting class, October 4, 2018). This undercurrent of her affinity with Olemaun opens the door wider to another set of memories, ones related to parental opposition. Paramount in her teaching is, as she continually reiterates, the "feeling of the story" (Class discussion, Visiting class, Oct. 4, 2018). We may think we get "the sense of the story, but we won't get the feeling of the story" if we don't notice carefully. Noticing is helped through class discussion, part of which depends on recalling one's own experiences and associated feelings. I compare how she develops the same discussion in the two classes. We are at the part in the book when Olemaun and her family, having travelled to town for the purpose of bringing Olemaun to the residential school, see a boat arrive with crying children on board. Her mother points out the children, saying they will be Olemaun's classmates. Olemaun asks why they are crying. Because they do not want to go to school, her mother responds. Don't they know they will learn to read? Olemaun asks. Her mother replies: "They would rather be with their families" – on which follows (as Olemaun discloses her mind): "Her words stung" (Jordan-Fenton & Pokiak-Fenton, 2020, p. 24). In both classes, she asks, "What does it mean, 'her words stung'?" "How many of you have been stung by a bee?"

Her visiting students (whom she teaches after the home group that day) rally to the side of the mother. They sense what is coming – despite Olemaun's great desire to go to school, there will be great disappointment. The scales need to drop from Olemaun's eyes. Students no doubt peeked ahead, too, seeing the image of girls working in the fields outside of the school – not reading *in* classrooms. "I can see where you get that," the teacher says, with the direction of the responses verging on regret. She wants the students to go elsewhere, though. More responses surface, one of which she says gets "warmer." The delay becomes too protracted, leading her to perhaps believe the students will not arrive at the response she is thinking of – and that her earlier, home class arrived at sooner, so she tells them: "Okay, we're getting warmer. The reason why I asked this question is because when I read this with another group, one kid said to me, "Oh Miss, I know why it hurts. It's because her mom is making her feel guilty that she wants to read more than she wants to be with her family.' " A student blurts out, "The truth hurts," which provides a further opening. She uses it to step inside when she asks: "Why is that the truth? Whose truth is that?" "So then, do we know what guilty is?" She rephrases as "What does guilty mean?" These are two potentially different questions; the second asks what a word means; the first what we, in our minds and bodies, know. One student proffers a mild example – feeling guilty when homework is not done – however, for the teacher, guilt has a powerful association with memories of her mother. She shares with students: "My mom was the queen of guilt … That student making that comment reminded me that I used to get that from my mom … You're twelve years old, you want to be with your friends" (Class discussion, October 4, 2018). The question of whose truth is being told is at the very heart of this residential school story, but not only there, as teachers work with these counter-stories in the context of their teaching, bringing their own histories.

In the home class, she had also asked this question of what it means when Olemaun says that her mother's words stung. "What do you think, what is she feeling?" The students' responses were "warmer" from the start, as when a student said: "It hit her." Another posits regret – the line that the other class will fruitlessly pursue – before a student returns to the initial idea of hit: "Can I say something about the word 'stung'?" Yes, she says. "The word like, frappé." Exactly, she says. In French, *frapper* means to hit. This violence gets more to what "stung" feels like – like the violence of a bee sting, which a student vocalizes, "Ouch! It hurts!" She then asks a student, one on whom she relies for insightful comments: What is he thinking? "That she cares more about reading than going with her family, and that she's not that close with her family?" He ends on a question mark – as if unsure – but this is the point or a great part of it. She follows up with: "And what does that make a kid feel?" (Class Discussion, Home class, October 4, 2018).

Here is quite a powerful example of a teacher's furor – which can be potentially any teacher's, I emphasize. Such teaching may not appear as furor initially because personal connections are a very legitimate way of deepening understanding, this by drawing attention to feelings – in the character, in one's own life. However, at a certain point, it is apparent that the teacher is harbouring deeper resonances as tied to *guilt* associated with a remembered relation with one's mother and a lived context – that of the Catholic church, which the book also invokes. It is somewhat ironic, though, that guilt is being put over onto Olemaun's mother, who is Inuvialuk; her culture is neither European nor

Catholic. The guilt may be there, insinuated by the author (who underwent the school's brainwashing). Students no doubt know about guilt. The point is that the teacher knows it *more*; it is part of this teacher's furor in teaching to this counter-story, pulling as it does on a counter-story of her own. She would not have become a teacher had she not resisted her parents, especially her mom, who may have had other visions for her daughter than becoming a teacher.

A Teacher's Furor: ... From Somewhere

Victimhood is a political category, LaCapra (2014) suggests; "not everyone traumatized by events is a victim" (p. 79). Olemaun saw herself as resilient. The teacher, too, was adamant about her own resilience, which is one of the reasons (she explained) why she gravitated towards *Fatty Legs*. No matter how real and true her story, Olemaun's loss could not represent a loss to her, though. This is one limitation of the use of counter-stories (which often have a truth basis) in teaching to social justice even as it is also the very thing that provides an opening to go somewhere, a place of unsettlement, to which they – teacher and students – might otherwise not travel.

Being in the teacher's classroom brought these complexities home more.

Traumatic materials are hot and combustible (Fowler, 2002) – as are teachers themselves. Teachers *will* bring themselves and their emotions and experiences to the text, to teaching, and to their interactions with students, who also bring their own.

When I engaged a transcriber – an undergraduate student in political science – to transcribe the classroom data, I warned her that sometimes she might hear the teacher lecture a student, or the class, on a particular misbehaviour, and that she did not need to transcribe these; there were a few of them, I knew, and transcribing them might take up unnecessary time. She didn't; however, she must have felt it was important to note their occurrence, as she did, in square brackets:

[slight reprimanding]

[some reprimanding]

[reprimanding]

I am glad she did because her notes were a validation to me that even if the reprimands seemed tangential to the teaching of *Fatty Legs*, they occurred and were heard by more than one person. The transcriber must have reasoned that their occurrence was perhaps important to note, even as (as per my instructions) she avoided their transcription.

My purpose here is not to pass judgment but, like Yoder as well as Britzman and (to come) Block, to reflect on the larger issues and questions arising from the potential violence *of* our words and actions, as teachers, even as we are teaching *to* violence.

Yoder suggests, quoting Ricoeur, that "It is for a being who speaks, who in speaking pursues meaning, who has already entered the discussion and who knows something about rationality that violence is or becomes a problem" (1974, p. 89, as cited in Yoder, 2020, p. 28). Teaching is not always a rational discourse; in fact, there is much going on that lies on and below the surface of what is said and is not said or, more appositely, felt. I am aware of not wanting to throw a stone at a glass house, one in which I can detect my own reflection. Was I not there myself at times, when the class had become unruly and to settle things, as an elementary teacher, I sometimes turned off the lights and the students lay their heads down quietly, subdued, "listening" as I talked about the kind of behaviour that was expected versus not expected. Even as a university professor, there have been times – rare but occasional and fresh in my mind – when if students are talking while I am talking and I have noticed and it is beginning to irritate as well as embarrass me, this among budding teachers who know a thing or two about classroom management, that the students have left me no choice. I slowly become quieter – I give them a chance and then if nothing changes, I become deadly silent and we are all frozen – this elaborate performance so that only their voices can be heard trailing off, all so that I can look their way, meaningfully. I only want to do this (excessive gesture) once. "Please don't talk when others are." After class, as the last three hours replay in various ways in my mind, as they always do at a conscious or unconscious level, I feel that slightly bitter aftertaste, which is of: Those students may hate me for what I did to them today. And then it's gone, and I carry on because I also tell myself, experienced teacher that I now am, I should not agonize over judgments that in the moment called for action, and where I acted for the benefit of all.

It is in this light that I appreciate the reminders about the reprimands. I also take note of the heavy irony as a reprimanding occurs almost immediately after the teacher has asked the class what the word in the story, "chastise," means. And there my disquiet settles in more. I remember how shocked I felt when I heard the first reprimand, which was on the occasion of my first visit to the teacher's class, when I was, again ironically, sitting at the teacher's desk. For it was as if I was an elementary student again. I found myself mentally and emotionally back in my *student* desk, feeling powerless to escape from this room that suddenly had all the air sucked out of it and where all my fibres were telling me to run, fast. An unbearable tension exists, on the one hand, between who the teacher believes she is and believes about what she is doing, and on the other, who she ardently wishes to be (as a social justice teacher warrior) and the experiences of others – her students, me as I slip into my student skin. As teachers, at one time or another, we have all found ourselves in some version of this place: a place that produces an untimely blush or hackles at the back of one's neck, in short, a sense of profound discomfort in one's own skin.

Disquiet and A Violent Subject

My disquiet, I have concluded, rests on a doubt about the degree to which the teacher – potentially, any teacher – can see herself seeing (Grumet, 2006, p.112, as cited in Yoder, 2020, p. 191). Could she see the contradictions between her fairly regular reprimanding and the subject of the counter-story, at the heart of which was Olemaun refusing to be intimidated by the Raven, the nun who is determined to make her life hell on earth? No, she could not; she was not the Raven. She was Olemaun and when not Olemaun, she was the Swan who was a kind and loving teacher that had the students' best interests at heart; this story too was true. Students were attached to the teacher, by her own account and from what I could clearly see. Still. How could she not notice the power of words to sting, as she had once been stung?

Yoder returns more than once to a point raised by one of her Mennonite aunts, Yoder's family being part of the Mennonite community, which prides itself on being peace-loving and non-violent. Her aunt pointed out that Mennonites can be "skilfully violent" with words (p. 161). Sometimes, her aunt explained, we need to be violent and not nice: this to bring an end to something that needs ending, or to start something that needs starting. We can do this to others; we can also do it to ourselves, as a form of self-discipline, she elaborated. In such contexts, she suggested, violence is akin to surgery. It constitutes a necessary cut. Even as the aunt said so, she went on to wonder whether "cut[ting] loose on somebody with words" doesn't reveal "just an awful lot of violence" in her heart (p. 162). Yoder comes back to this in the context of her teaching: times when she felt this way towards a student, having used language to cut. I know I have been guilty of the same.

"Perhaps we are all neurotic," Block (2020, p. 89) suggests. We are all coping in one way or another with our upbringings, what we have learned and not learned and where "Winnicott says that home is from where we start" (p. 89). The classroom is also like a home. We spend countless hours there, teachers and students alike; it becomes "a holding environment" (p. 91), another term Block borrows from Winnicott to convey how we learn about the world and how to behave in it. We also learn about different feelings, and where one of them is hate. Hate is such a strong word, and it strikes me as such an odd one to use in the context of teaching and learning (even as I acknowledge that hatred is and has been often manifest in classrooms, especially with racism). Teachers, Block says, tell themselves stories about teaching and its rewards even if those stories represent "idealizations" (p. 92). Hate, he suggests, stems from anger – at feeling frustrated, thwarted or otherwise "interfered with" (p. 83).

Block (further pulling on Winnicott) distinguishes between hate and managed hate. Managed hate marks an interval between hating and acting. Winnicott tells the story of a teenage boy that he and his wife took in. His behaviour disrupted the household. Did he want to hit him? Yes, said Winnicott. Did he hate the boy for all the trouble he was causing? Yes. Had he not known about his hate, Winnicott says, he would have lashed out at the boy. Instead, he devised a routine. In moments of crisis, Winnicott would use his "bodily strength" to remove the boy and put him outside the door; he did so "without anger or blame" and no matter the weather. Outside there was a "special bell." If the boy rang it, he "would be readmitted and no word said about the past" (Winnicott cited in Block, p. 85). Winnicott added that "the important thing" was that every time he put him outside, he would tell the boy "that what had happened had made me hate him" – the wording draws attention to the behaviour and events following from it rather than the boy himself – and that it was only by acknowledging his feelings that he avoided murdering the boy "now and again" (Winnicott in Block, p. 85). In other words, it was by managing his hate – and releasing those feelings in a physically non-violent way – that love also became possible. The hate was transitory; it was allowed to be a passing thing, even as it was allowed to be.

One goal that hate accomplishes, Block points out, is that it allows "us to recognize the Other as separate and to have existence not merely as my subjective creation" (p. 85). Block goes on: "Hate eventually makes empathy possible: Empathy might be defined *not* as the ability to *feel* the other's feeling (this is impossible) but as the ability to have enough control of ourselves and our feelings *to listen* with attentiveness to another person" (p. 86; emphasis in the original). Winnicott's managed hate was a highly deliberate response to a situation that would have otherwise become highly unpleasant for the parties concerned.

What about in the classroom, when strong emotions – hate – can also lash out, eliciting resistance in the other party, if not openly at the time, then later? The same obtains. Hate's unpredictable aspects can "*spoil the professional attitude*" (Winnicott in Block, p. 88; emphasis in the original). Block insists: "Teachers must bear the strain of the work [of teaching] and that means to recognize that the student might not know what the teacher is doing at any one time, and therefore, *the teacher* must be aware of her own fear and her hate" (p. 93; emphasis added). The teacher needs to be aware of what she is capable of feeling *and* doing, which entails being able to perceive her hate and capacity to hate, if the situation seems to warrant it.

Backshadowing and Sideshadowing

At a certain point, I stopped trying to be loved by students. Especially when I came to university teaching, I could see teachers around me – professors or faculty lecturers – who were loved by students, to whom students would flock like bees to honey. When I stopped worrying about being loved, and instead focused on my love of the subject, I also began to see better how students perceived the subject and what was easy and what was harder for them, as well as how to try to move them towards what was harder, of their own accord. It was as if students began to love me then, when there were no expectations on my part that they would. Gardner (1994/2012), in his study *On Trying to Teach* – who tied teaching to a teacher's furor – keeps returning to the question: "How can a teacher 'have so much knowledge of another as is necessary to make instruction useful'?" (p. 14). His point is that a teacher can't. Perhaps all they can know, really, is the subject and based on past experience of teaching and of students, ways conducive to access it.

Our teacher openly acknowledged that she was a learner. She had taught to the Holocaust. She had taught to the struggle for civil rights on the part of Black Americans. However, she seemed fundamentally unprepared for Olemaun. Olemaun was the one who really drew her into the subject of residential schooling as one that concerned her and those of her generation who had looked away while residential schooling carried on.

So much of social justice education happens in the idiom of backshadowing. In a book on the different idioms of narrative time and their implications, Morson (1994) considers three: foreshadowing, sideshadowing, and backshadowing. Tongue-in-cheek, he sets up the impossible conditions under which backshadowing operates: "Backshadowing may be defined as foreshadowing after the fact. The past is viewed as having contained signs pointing to what happened later, to events known to the backshadowing observer. Visible now, those signs could have been seen then" (p. 234). He then explains the consequences of seeing time through a lens of backshadowing: "Those who failed to foresee are therefore typically regarded as blind or self-blinded" (p. 234). They are as Oedipus who, we all know, came to a tragic end, sleeping with his mother and killing his father. Morson (1994) comments on the "tone of superiority" that informs a backshadower: You should have known. You should have read the signs right. Most social justice education (aptly or inaptly) is framed within a narrative construction of backshadowing. Shame on me!, the teacher once declared, as she slapped her hand, hard (Teacher Research Workshop, April 26, 2018). From one perspective, she was only saying what we all felt, implicitly, as "implicated subjects" (Rothberg, 2019). One of her gifts, I had started to recognize, was her artlessness: saying what others might be thinking but didn't dare to.

Gardner's book is called *On Trying to Teach*. When do teachers ever stop trying? If they stopped, Gardner (1994/2012) implies, they wouldn't be teachers. This teacher was approaching the end of her teaching career; she said that she would retire soon. Like the other teachers in the project (Strong-Wilson, 2021), she was a settler teacher, driven by the same sense of urgency we all feel with respect to this important subject to which we often come belatedly. Gardner (1994/2012) explains:

> Each furor to teach is goaded and guided by each teacher's theory of what is essential to teach. And each furor is heightened by conditions specific to the teacher's

> character, persuasion, and current preoccupations. The true teacher, however, of whatever character, persuasion, or preoccupation, finds it particularly hard to temper the furor to teach when confronted with a student whom that teacher judges in urgent need of learning what that teacher is in urgent need of teaching. And temperance is made still more difficult when that teacher judges that what the student needs to learn is something the student should have been taught long ago. Little can fan the furor to teach more furiously than the true teacher's perception that time is running out. (p. 8)

The teacher's reprimands tended to occur in one of two contexts: there was a burr in her side – a student whose behaviour was inappropriate, or there was a general sliding away from the subject, whether in a more focused way (an interesting distraction) or an unfocused way (a descending of the discussion into multiple side-conversations). "We keep getting off track," one student wryly observed (Classroom discussion, Home classroom, Oct. 4, 2018).

Sideshadowing (rather than backshadowing) offers the greatest latitude for something "qualitatively new" having a "chance" to come about (Brodsky, 1995, p. 301). Sideshadowing allows for grasping what else *might have* happened and where for the teacher, as she continuously reiterated, the project represented an important alternative. With her less deliberate way of teaching, the teacher resembled Dostovesky's Dmitri (another example from Morson) who does not know why he picked up the pestle or what to do with it once picked up – "What does one pick things up for at some moments? I don't know what for. I snatched it up and ran – that's all" (as cited in Morson, p. 145). She picked up the project and along with it, *Fatty Legs*, and ran with it. And yet, any thoughtfulness in her on-the-spot, heart-on-her-sleeve teaching to the text (for example, noticing how we are feeling as we read) was being systematically undercut by her reprimanding – a violence with words that, however outraged the teacher felt, it would falsify things to say that students did not notice. They grew visibly quieter, looked down or away, as if caught in a place that, by their body language, they preferred not to be or were waiting to blow over.

Sideshadowing draws our attention to contiguity: the placing of a teacher in relation to her students, this in relation to the place and very school where I once was, dimly entertaining thoughts of the teacher might become, each of us finding ourselves here in relation to Olemaun's counter-story about the violence of (residential) schooling. I cannot regret being in her classroom, which opened up to me in a highly visceral way the subject of violent words in relation to teaching with texts that depict violence. In keeping with Morson, Winnicott, and Block, though, I see this problem of a teacher's violence with words as acting on the teacher like "an astronomical black hole" making "escape increasingly difficult" (Morson, p. 164). Speeding up as it carries on, that internal vortex careens towards catastrophe, this as long as we fail to confront ourselves in teaching – to see ourselves feeling and doing. As Block points out (inspired by Winnicott), the hate needs to be allowed to be; however, its expression needs to be thought through in such a way as to maintain the integrity and dignity of all in the presence of this subject (violence and difficult knowledge) of which we all share our part.

NOTES

1 The book was Strong-Wilson, T. (2021), *Teachers' ethical self-encounters with counter-stories in the classroom: From implicated to concerned subjects*, Routledge. The research project was "Developing a pedagogy of social justice in the classroom through post-colonial literature," which was funded through SSHRC [Social Sciences and Humanities Research Council] 435-2014-1225 and led by Principal Investigator Ingrid Johnston, working in collaboration with colleagues at six other universities across Canada. I gratefully acknowledge SSHRC's support for the research project.
2 I thank Amarou for her astute readings of different versions of this text.

REFERENCES

Block, A. (2020). *Finding hope in the turbulent classroom: Curriculum theory, psychoanalysis, and school-based practice*. Routledge.

Britzman, D. (2004). Monsters in literature. *Changing English, 11*(2), 253–65. https://doi.org/10.1080/09540250042000252703

– (2009). *The very thought of education: Psychoanalysis and the impossible professions*. State University of New York.

Brodsky, J. (1995). *On grief and reason: Essays*. Farrar, Straus & Giroux.

Fowler, L. (2002). A curriculum of difficulty and 'The anger in our Miss Maple': The story and the commentary. *Language and Literacy, 3*(2), 1–20. https://doi.org/10.20360/G2VC82

Frame, J. (1989). *An angel at my table: The complete autobiography*. Counterpoint.

Gardner, M. R. (2012). *On trying to teach: The mind in correspondence*. Routledge. (Original work published 1994).

Grumet, M. (2006). Toward a poor curriculum. In W. F. Pinar & M. R. Grumet (Eds.), *Toward a poor curriculum* (pp. 67–88). Educator's International Press.

Jordan-Fenton, C., & Pokiak-Fenton, M. (2020). *Fatty legs: A true story*. Annick Press.

LaCapra, D. (2014). *Writing history, writing trauma*. Johns Hopkins University Press.

Morson, G. S. (1994). *Narrative and freedom: The shadows of time*. Yale University Press.

Ricoeur, P. (1974). *Political and social essays*. Ohio University Press.

Rothberg, M. (2019). *The implicated subject: Beyond victims and perpetrators*. Standford University Press.

Sebald, W. G. (1996). *The emigrants*. New Directions.

Strong-Wilson, T. (2021). *Teachers' ethical self-encounters with counter-stories in the classroom: From implicated to concerned subjects*. Routledge.

Strong-Wilson, T. & Huang, Y. (2023). "I don't know what they think until they talk": Exploring the place of talk in engaging students in difficult conversations. In G. Balzer, T. Strong-Wilson & A. Burke (Eds.), *Teaching social justice using postcolonial texts: Encountering pedagogies of discomfort in practice* (pp. 127–39). Springer.

Winnicott, D. (1986). *Home is where we start from: Essays by a psychoanalyst*. Norton.

Yoder, A. (2020). *A necessary ambivalence: Narratives of violence in life and language arts*. [Unpublished doctoral dissertation]. McGill University.

Epilogue: Curriculum Studies in the Shadowlands

ANNE M. PHELAN

What is an "epilogue"? What does an "epilogue" do? These were the questions that preoccupied me as I began this writing task. Do I repeat those concepts gathered in the pages of these chapters? Do I reaffirm the authors' respective contributions? Do I run the risk of overscoring, drawing a line through their words so as to cancel or obliterate them? Or might the risk of underscoring, misplacing emphasis on what has been said, be equally problematic?

Written in the midst of a pandemic, this collection of essays presents not simply a gathering of ideas but a gathering of experience – the visceral sense of newly lived spaces and temporalities of home-working, home-schooling, and home-caring; running a different course than usual; seeking release from the unrelenting rhythms of COVID-19 restrictions and recordings of infection rates, hospital admissions, and deaths. How does one write during such times? Ghosts, William Doll (2002) writes, can cripple our imagination. In times like these we cling to those "expired stories" of modernity[1] – humanism, reason, science, progress, and technology – that offer a sense of "security, purpose, and direction – precisely because they seem stable and solid" (Machedo de Oliveira, 2021, p. 15). And yet, the evidence of those universal fictions emerge time and time again as unmarked mass graves continue to be located at residential school sites across Canada, revealing the remains of hundreds of Indigenous children. To know that the worst can happen, because it already has, casts a particular shadow over a scholarly life.

Shades and shadows populate the pages in this volume conjuring hidden realms of darkness and light, horror and wonder, melancholy and mourning. Dion writes of how "the shadow of colonialism" eclipsed the "warmth of her "parents' love of their children and of one another." Eppert invokes Shakespeare's insight that "life's but a walking shadow … full of sound and fury, signifying nothing," illustrating the English Bard's "poeticizing [of] dualistic selfing while also gesturing to witness/ing nothing/emptiness." Blades illustrates how "lingering in shadows is productive precisely by avoiding the temptation to move out of the shadows or destroy the shadows by creating a new, bright light." He draws our attention to the "blends of light and shadow" that add "texture and depth" because they "press us toward nuance and complexity." Lewkovich wonders if there are "other choices ... held in reserve, living in the shadows?" So too Strong-Wilson as she reflects on "sideshadowing," a literary technique which "allows for grasping what else might have happened...." Something "qualitatively new" might have "a small chance of coming about," she ponders. Perhaps.

Each chapter reflects the attempt to study, teach, and write while appreciating that our habits of knowing and being and the ways in which we experience reality are at once blinded by "the shiny side of modernity associated with seamless progress, industrialization, secularization, humanism, individualism, scientific reasoning, and nation-states" (Machado de Oliveira, 2021, p. 24) *and* implicated in "the shadow side of modernity associated with colonialism, imperialism, slavery, militarization, genocides, and ecocides" (p. 24). Modernity/coloniality (Machado de Oliveira's term) is full of contradictions; in Canada we breathe the air of ongoing colonialism *and* reconciliation, of neo-liberal imperialism *and* public education, of exponential growth *and* sustainability, of freedom *and* responsibility.

Living in the midst of educational institutions that shore up the pillars of modernity/coloniality – erasure of history; formal rationality; and certainty (Hartley, 2000) – means a scholarly life full of tensionality. Feeling at once complicit and resistant can quickly lead to melancholic attachments to what could be or a depressive anxiety about what might never be. How then do the writers in this volume face up to the systemic horrors and seductions of modernity/coloniality? How do they help the system "die with grace" (Machado de Oliveira, 2021)? In this chapter I reflect on the "arts of getting by"[2] in the shadowlands, that indeterminate borderland replete with unrealities, uncertainties, and the unimaginable. How do they think, live, and dream? How do these scholars "work through, and get stuck in" (Britzman, 1998, p. 23) the tension that results from all the conflictive representations and theories of education bequeathed by modernity/coloniality? Turning both inward and outward, looking backwards and forwards, these scholars write in the shadows of the dominant order and consider what might be thought, unthought, imagined, and enacted. Their "arts of getting by" constitute scholarly practices – returning; lingering; complicating – that draw law and life together, disappointments and resolve, hesitation and action.

The Art of Returning

Re – back; *tornare* – to turn; to turn back ...

Modernity loves the new; hence, "the widespread use of the prefix "re-" in contemporary life" (Hartley, 2000, p. 120). The new is associated here with the possibility of a clean slate and the alluring belief that we can indeed "set aside history and cast ourselves anew" (p. 120). While the prefix *re-* is ever present in this collection, its prevalence and significance are quite different. The small syllable or "prefix *re-* meaning "again" or "back" – as in reconceptualization or revisioning" is important because "it implies shift, movement, action" (Aswell Doll, 2017, p. 50). The art of return, evident in so many of these writings, implies that "what is situated in the present must be visited again, entered imaginally again, so as to see anew what was once accepted, repressed, or overlooked" (p. 50). Far from cleaning the slate, the authors return again and again to the entanglements of personal, professional, and national histories:

> The again-ness of this move requires a necessary regress, back into the buried material of memory, shame, and suffering. Concomitantly, the "again" quality of regression propels another set of re-actions with such words as *recast, reactivate, recover*, and – importantly – *reconstruct*. These actions … are steps the intellect must take in order to recover and reactivate an essence of the self that has been colonized … by the identities placed on us by others. Revisiting the past requires an unveiling. (pp. 50–1)

While the art of returning may be haunted by a desire to make amends and to loosen the grip of harmful histories, it begins with an acknowledgment (not an erasure) of one's historical situatedness, the play of the past in the present.

Létourneau asks: "How do Canadians or Quebecers write themselves, collectively, into scripts of the past?" He observes his children "crafting themselves into human beings, incorporating the notion of time in their Self and mastering the principles of narration, leading them to conceive of and perceive themselves as stories enmeshed in other, larger and more complex stories." But what narratives are available to Canadians? He argues that acritical narratives – "Victimhood and Duality for French Canada, and Diversity and Peace for English Canada" – while harbouring an element of the factual, provide little more than over-simplified stories that "twist the dense matter of the past."

Conscious of the challenges of unlearning closely held narratives about the past – bequeathed by beloved grandparents, for example – Létourneau is clear that if Canadians are to appreciate their complex history, they will need some "reference points" against which to evaluate "appealing, effective, and 'handy' resources for making sense of the past." The challenge for curriculum studies, he continues, is not simply to foster intellectual skills such as "criticism, verification, analysis, and interpretation" but also to offer students "a historical narrative that allows them to construct an idea about what was."

Dion appreciates firsthand the epistemic injustice visited upon Indigenous students who have been offered limited knowledge of their history, language, and culture – ultimately impacting Indigenous peoples' rights to self-determination. In Létourneau's lexicon, they have not been offered any "reference points." Indigenous students, she writes, "need and want access to the history of settler colonialism." Without it, they cannot make sense of their lives. She is also aware, however, of "the complicated perpetrator-victim entanglement that serves to reproduce resistance from both settler teachers and Indigenous students." It may be in the preparation and enactment of teaching Indigenous history that settler teachers experience a break, a disruption of the grand narrative of Canadian benevolence and peacefulness. She is generously resolute that the only option is to begin from the position that settler teachers are committed to act in the best interest of their students. The hope is that settler teachers will begin to understand our implication in settler colonialism and that we will be willing to live with and do the emotional labour it takes to create necessary conditions for learning a difficult history.

Ng-A-Fook also hopes for an awakening, a moment of non-identification with inherited narratives of nation state that have shaped settler consciousness, and "for a breaking, and a remaking, of understandings of "Canadian," "curriculum," "settler colonialism," "truth" and then "reconciliation." His struggle to find a comfortable pace while jogging along the Kichi Zibi river runs parallel to his struggle to "live in relation with Kichi Zibi Anishnàbeg families, communities, and other First Nations who have yet to surrender their lands via any treaties." "What are our responsibilities toward reconstructing a different kind of futurity?"

Ng-A-Fook is haunted by the unforgettable trauma visited upon Indigenous peoples in Canada, a trauma from which he and his family continue to benefit. Haunting is a phenomenon whereby "organized forces and systemic structures that appear removed from us make their impact felt in everyday life" (Gordon, 2008, p. 19). To be haunted is to be tugged by a thread that links us to unresolved histories, calling on us to give an account for "what has been done and what is to be done otherwise" (p. 18). Ng-A-Fook responds to the call in his teaching wherein he and his students seek "to experience and understand what 'it' might mean, to be, and/or feel like pedagogically to break with the onto-epistemological temporal dimensions of a settler colonial historical public consciousness." Exemplifying a notion of the present as a site of return, Ng-A-Fook's now-time is transient and incomplete, reflected in his "snapshots," and captured in his life-writing. Therein he attempts "to reactivate and reconstruct lived experiences … in creative, ethical, and relational ways."

But there are few if any guarantees. Strong-Wilson's "disquieting return" to her own elementary school in Ontario illustrates the entanglement of past and present, professional and personal, in mundane classroom moments. As personal histories haunt, she confronts us with "the potential violence *of* our words and actions, as teachers, even as we are teaching *to* violence." Reflecting on the practice of a classroom teacher, teaching "Fatty Legs," a story about an Indigenous child's experiences of residential school, Strong-Wilson wonders whether the teacher could in fact "see the contradictions between her fairly regular reprimanding and the subject of the counter-story, at the heart of which was Olemaun refusing to be intimidated by the Raven, the nun who is determined to make her life hell on earth?" She writes:

> An unbearable tension exists, on the one hand, between who the teacher believes she is and believes about what she is doing, and on the other, who she ardently wishes to be (as a social justice teacher warrior) and the experiences of others – her students, me as I slip into my student skin.

While it is likely, she acknowledges, that we have each found ourselves disturbed and ashamed when confronted with the contradictions of our own practice, denying our complicity in violence, or declaring our innocence does not erase the harm we habitually enact, albeit often unconsciously, because of the systems within which we work and/or the families that raised us. The ways in which personal histories, affects, and meanings are played out in the classroom exceed institutionally defined roles (Todd, 2003). As such, teaching social justice literature to children raises enough questions to last a lifetime, but this is committed reflection, something teachers engage in because they care so deeply about their work *as* teachers. This is not to say, however, that as teachers we will not defend against "the threatening and difficult truths of ordinary fragilities" (Britzman, 1998, p. 36). One may never get it right in teaching; there will always be something missed, overlooked, forgotten, perpetrated.

The realization that what we need to, or be made to, forget in the interest of modernity/coloniality is very much part of Eppert's art of returning. Not unlike Dion, Ng-A-Fook and Strong-Wilson, Eppert invites us to wonder about which forms of forgetting – the assumed benevolence of education perhaps – might we want to use to imagine a future. She admits that despite the grounding of her intellectual life "in questions of ethical living," she had overlooked "species extinction" and now wishes "to bring this absence into presence." "[B]usy chasings, aversion, and delusion that comprise selfing are so loud and centre stage, so replete with clinging," she writes, that "presence of abiding awareness, of witness/ing capacities, often remains obscured." Eppert is adamant that the planet cannot sustain exponential growth, consumption, extraction, and exploitation indefinitely, and this is evident in the vast numbers of species that have become extinct since her own birth. She is also clear that "capacities for human and nonhuman flourishing depend upon generative sociopolitical conditions," but also, significantly, our capacity to remain "dynamically open," vulnerable to alterity's touch. She is compelled by the potential of witnessing as *anagnorisis*, that is, "embodied and critical insight that disrupts certitudes, unsettles narrow worldviews, and opens us more fully to responsibilities we bear for each other and the world." Citing Camus, Eppert's hope is to become "more attuned to ethical obligation to attend to the nonhuman world, to stay with the trouble rather than look away." Here I am reminded of Ted Aoki's description of his return to a Japanese garden he had visited as a youngster in 1934.

> I lingered, facing one memorialized tree, no longer a tree – stark, twisted, black remnant of a tree, without foliage, with only a few twisted limbs. A memorial to what? Man's capacity for inhumanity. (Aoki, 2005, p. 37)

Like Eppert, Aoki invites us not to turn away from history but to linger intimately in conjunctive spaces that require thoughtful listening (Lee, Wong & Ursino, 2022).

The Art of Lingering

To dwell; to stay; to delay....

"To run is not to race" (Aswell Doll, 2017, p. 57). Inspired by Pinar's conception of curriculum as *currere*, or "running the course" (Pinar & Grumet, 1976/2006), she writes that reconstructing oneself and one's relation to the world in light of academic study and reflection on experience, is "slow work, like excavation" (p. 57).

Lewkovich favours slow work. He embraces the emotional quality of adolescence as an allegory for a middle, or non-place to linger, where it is possible "to slow the forward movement of learning down, focusing less on teleological, satisfactory conclusions, than on what is speculative, fragmentary, and incomplete." Literary works can provide such "dilatory digressive spaces" where intimacy "brushes closely against the life of students and teachers in school"; and indeed, where wonder can re-enter teacher education programs evoking "an uncertainty or unknowing" that are a crucial counterpoint to the certainty, rigidity, and unitary accounts of knowledge creation and sense making in schools." The dilatory space of narrative, a "space of retard, postponement, error, ... partial revelation ... [and] transformation," could offer the conditions wherein problems related to initiatory desire are worked through. Dwelling in the imaginative space between declarative acts of knowing and not knowing can generate thoughts beyond the "habitual language otherwise used to discipline lived experience." Lewkovich asks provocatively: "What if education becomes a place to explore the uncertain detours of the middle [narrative, desire, pleasure], rather than a predetermined requirement to shut such exploration down?"

Increasingly, however, schools are "regulated by proliferating bureaucratic protocols, institutionalizations of Western (mis)conceptions of 'individualism' and 'competence' " (Pinar, 2005, p. 77). The pervasiveness of formal rationality in systemic education results in the suppression of affect – which Lewkovich wishes to evoke – and a generalized disenchantment (Hartley, 2000).

Gauthier traces the emergence of the "school form" to "the establishment of a new urban order." Giving form to what was previously "improvised, more or less organized, unstructured and not yet institutionalized," schools imposed "order" on the "multiples." The invention of the school form is accomplished, in part, by the production of school subjects, "the codification of the method of teaching" those school subjects, and organization of space, time, and participants (controlling the "posture" of students and teacher) so that transmission can take place. Gauthier explains: "The old process of the impulsive teacher who unceremoniously strikes his pupils or embraces them has been replaced by that of a graduated scale of punishments and rewards administered by a serious master, who intervenes in full control of his emotions." While there have been many, many attempts to unite school with life, Gauthier explains, the concept of school form and "the system of subjugation that it puts in place" including "obedience to impersonal rules" persists. The school has, he writes "digested innovations" by means of Cuban's (2013) "dynamic conservatism." Indeed, Gauthier argues that "far from disappearing … the school form will unfold even more in the reign of the digital." He muses that we may be witnessing "the completion of the transition from a disciplinary society to a control society … with the emergence of algorithmic societies with the Big Data." His conclusion that the "need to meet the other face-to-face is the essence of the school form and is absolutely necessary to a quality mass education."

Gauthier's emphasis on the face-to-face quality of school is borne out in Beck's vivid depiction of teaching English to carpenters, recent immigrants to Canada. Relinquishing the instruction manual, her classroom

> transformed into a noisy, busy, lively group of 16 men and a woman, connected through our common experiences of being here; we listened to each other's unique life stories, witnessed one another's vulnerabilities without judgement and with empathy, listened to Peter Gzowski on CBC, and took turns to facilitate conversations on such topics as "what I hate about Canada" and "how to defeat stupid English." They wrote, they composed, sang original tunes, taught one another how to read the trades manual, and they laughed.

Recalling Aoki (2005), Beck concludes: "[M]ultiplicity is not a noun" (p. 269)! Laughter and song interrupt the formal rationality – of Gauthier's "school form" – that thinks only in terms of requirements and regulations. In the midst of laughter, subjectivity emerges in a "dense entanglement of affect, attention, the senses, and matter" (Stewart, 2010, p. 340). As she and her students share and mine material from their personal and professional lives, their senses of self and of Canada are playfully unthought and rethought.

Beck celebrates "the distinctive localness, the complex histories, contexts, and identities that make up knowledge, [and] are overlooked and even erased" when "Western knowledge systems are assigned the highest value, [and] disseminated as a universal standard." She argues that "the general direction of the internationalization of higher education continues to be neocolonial and market-driven in spite of critiques generated in critical internationalization studies." The upshot is an instrumental C&I landscape (Aoki, 2005) and a neo-Tylerian approach to curriculum, "with lists of skills, competencies, and content that result in freezing the very notions of international-ness, culture, nation, and local-ness"; impoverished theoretical foundations, and a "worldwide *and* uniform, simplistic set of practices." In "a new form of economic expansion," universities embark on a mission to recruit and school "a new category of 'others,' the international student." Internationalization becomes the next bright object to blind us to the "complexities and contradictions" of education.

Indeed, there is much to dazzle in modern education policy and practice. Writing autobiographically of his participation in the creation of the new British Columbia science curriculum, Blades advises that "lingering *within* shadows" of national and international efforts to reform science curriculum can "reveal creativity, complexity and the beauty of possibilities." He illustrates how in "places of dappled light and shifting shadows formed by bright light" the vision of the curriculum is "less distinct." It was this very "lack of clarity," he suggests, that encouraged novel patterns of thinking and imagining the new BC science curriculum; a curriculum that might have otherwise been "overtaken by bright illumination" of post-Sputnik reforms or "the continuing darkness of using science education for social engineering for military or economic advantage." In the shadows, the "game of progress" as "a single, defined movement" was abandoned and in its stead "an on-going dialogue with teachers and students without a specific plan for the outcome of the dialogue" was embraced. "This 'post-modern' approach to curriculum," he writes, "recasts the notion of "development" into a continual, circular conversation of suggestion and advice by those charged with coming up with ideas and those realizing these ideas with students." Such curriculum conversations evade instrumentalism and gesture towards Lewkovich's "uncertain detours of the middle."

The Art of Complicating

-plicare: folded; *-com*: together; intertwine; entangle

Modernity rejects complication; the belief is "through theory and empirical research, we can come to know the world; and, having understood it, we can then change it for the better" (Hartley, 2000, p. 119). Why give up on the fantasy of progress, of linear development? Why complicate matters by emphasizing ethical-political and historical entanglements? If "science gives us faith in the future" (p. 119), why fight it? The point of course is that while science can inform our judgments, it cannot make them for us; judgment and action require conversations across difference.

"Difference is a social asset," writes Bickmore, and "it does not necessarily imply conflict." And, while conflict may be inevitable, they argue, violence is not: "its underlying conflictual causes can be satisfied, redirected, ended, or mended." Bickmore recognizes dissonance in democracy and the importance of facing difference and conflict in a spirit of pluralizing, of agonism rather than antagonism. Their questions revolve around what Canadians, as "citizen actors," need in order to live *with* difference and conflict. Here, they underscore the manner in which school and society are intertwined. Recognizing that the curriculum "tends to be skewed by the unjust social structures and oppressive cultural beliefs and practices that permeate schooling," Bickmore believes that school curriculum can encourage "continuing expression of difference, surfacing and facing contrasting perspectives on the causes and consequences of un-peace." Their scholarship is devoted to showing how "meaningful peacebuilding education is challenging but demonstrably possible in public schools." As Gauthier reminds us, it is after all in public schools that "meeting the other face-to-face" remains possible.

"Peace*building* involves multidimensional ongoing efforts to "transform" the systemic political-participatory, economic-equity, and cultural-inclusion factors that cause and exacerbate destructive conflicts, to redress and repair their disproportionate harm to the most vulnerable."

> Multidimensional learning opportunities – engaging diverse students in encountering and expressing themselves about social-structural equity, cultural inclusion, and political participation action options – can happen in ordinary public schools. Such curriculum practices can widen space for young people to develop hope and capabilities, to build just peace in their own and others' lives.

Curriculum lived as the kind of complicated, and complicating, conversation about equity, inclusion and diversity, envisaged by Bickmore, involves the reciprocal construction of academic knowledge, subjectivity, and society (Pinar, 2015). Students and teachers are confronted by "the immediacy of the historical moment, the particularity of place, and the singularity of one's own individuality" (p. 32) as articulated through subject matter such as history, science, and literature. It is through study that we learn to appreciate how different domains in society at large – art, science, politics – offer different arguments that can be represented and translated for one another (Adams & Cousins, 1996). Put simply, "a democratic society does not add up. It is a society of the discontinuous" (p. 57). The degree to which a society tolerates or crushes the difference between domains is a measure of its freedom or tyranny.

Gilbert acknowledges that curriculum as a complicated conversation about lived experience is not easily achieved after decades of educational practices that "reduce the curriculum to a knowledge delivery system." While "the sex education curriculum may outline a comprehensive list of skills and knowledge," they inform us, "the volatile, capricious, and elusive nature of a sexuality" cannot be neatly "bound to categories or identities." Rejecting "curriculum-as-checklist," Gilbert invokes Janet Miller's "queer curriculum practice," inviting educators to embrace "the messiness of sexuality and gender as itself a place of learning, not something that could be cleaned up through a revised set of [curriculum] guidelines." However, there is no escaping that whatever a teacher does will arouse "complaints that it is both too much and not enough, too soon and too late." Ultimately, teachers and students find themselves caught in the middle of the planned and the lived curriculum of sex education. Not an easy place to dwell when "progressive sex education" is "closely tied to the legitimizing discourses of health and well-being." Gilbert asks that adults consider "our own ambivalent desires towards sexuality and gender – that is, the curriculum doesn't just outline what we want children to learn, it also archives the adult's desires for the child." A "return to our own history of desire" is necessary if we are to appreciate that any set of curriculum guidelines will point not only to "some established set of knowledge, skills, and attitudes (no matter how exhaustive) we want to impart to youth but to our own hope and fears for ourselves and for young people."

Educators' faith in "foundational humanist epistemologies, its delusional humancentric and exceptionalist preoccupations" is at the core of Pacini-Ketchabaw's concerns about how we inject difference into the educational conversation. She rejects universalized and normalizing theories of child development and challenges "the control and erasure of non-Euro-Western experiences of childhood." Directing our attention to children who "do not conform to Euro-Western developmental norms" and are "automatically positioned as in need of intervention or support," she argues that we must open up "spaces for other possibilities for existence, ways of living and conceiving childhood that do not ascribe to particular colonial universals." Translation across domains of research and policy are challenging, she acknowledges: early childhood policies seem to use "all the right language" but amount to little more than an appropriation of concepts at the surface level with no effort towards in-depth understanding and thoughtful implementation. While Blades bears witness to the possibilities of doing science curriculum differently – as a complicated conversation – Pacini-Ketchabaw's experience in the field of early childhood makes her less sanguine. Still, the author is resolute, as she argues: the introduction of alternative frameworks to teacher education would at the very least enable teachers "to question the production of the proper humanist subject who maintains the necessary conditions for ongoing settler colonialism."

Seidel, Anees, Blackmore, and Mackenzie write "as settlers in a colonial state" and as educators who appreciate the historical entanglements of schooling "in a cultural system that now portends an existential and catastrophic threat to life itself." Modern education itself emerged during the industrial period fueled by petro-fossil combustion. Yet, they write, the most recent iteration of the Alberta curriculum does not even acknowledge the ecological crisis. While the domains of politics and science are at odds, reflecting antagonistic rather than agonistic relations, elementary and secondary students take the curriculum into their own hands, as it were, by joining "the Friday for Future youth climate strikes" in 2019 and 2020, in the hope of stalling the ceaseless processes of "petro-politics and extractivism."

"Feeling pedagogically responsible" for their students, the authors join the strikes but worry that their environmental activism may be perceived by school boards as at odds with their professional obligations. When difference is read as indifference to norms it may not be seen as "a social asset," in Bickmore's terms. In their chapter, Seidel et al. explore the following questions: "What are we learning from participating in the strikes? What does it mean to be a teacher in this time and place? What are our pedagogical responsibilities to children and the future?" What indeed are our responsibilities when the promises of an imagined future – a future conjured from an idealized past – seem no longer legitimate?

At the time of writing, Canadian society is slowly emerging from the COVID-19 global pandemic with the relaxing of restrictions at the provincial level. During past weeks we have witnessed "freedom convoys" protesting federally imposed vaccine mandates in Ottawa, Quebec City, and Toronto. The Liberal government has invoked the Emergencies Act to enable police to remove protestors and their blockades, now deemed illegal, from the streets. It is difficult to assess whether what we are witnessing relates only to the pandemic restrictions or whether this is a form of populism come North. Protests in Canada, whether Freedom Convoys, Friday for Future youth climate strikes, Black Lives Matter rallies, and Indigenous pipeline protests, are clearly distinct in origin and concern. Yet, one wonders if they are indicative of a kind of anomie whereby parts of the Canadian population feel normatively alienated from today's social and institutional structures (Beckert, 2020). The only perceived options are deviance or resignation. Culture and social structure are no longer aligned for many. Beckert explains: "When the light at the end of the tunnel cannot be seen, people must still believe that the tunnel will eventually come to an end. Imagined futures fulfill this role. Social crises ensue when such imaginaries are exhausted …" (p. 327). As a student interviewed by Denise Ryan, reporter with the *Vancouver Sun* newspaper, explained it: "Everything is so uncertain. It would be nice if school would be the one thing that is certain" (2022).

Conclusion

The authors in this collection speak of situations, in school and out, that seem to have spun wildly out of control: extinction; expansionism; and extraction. In the shadowlands of modernity/coloniality they stage their "disquieting returns" as "implicated" and "concerned subjects" (Strong-Wilson). Their scholarship illustrates how we might attempt "to do less harm in uncertainty" (Britzman,

1998, p. 43) and to imagine education as "something different than repression and normalization, something that is capable of surprising itself, something interested in risking itself" (p. 58).

The scholarly critiques and imaginings in this volume confirm what Létourneau intimates of (what he terms) the "Kanadian experience" more generally:

> that power does not always manage to crush prospects, that the rationale of systems does not always quash the potential of lifeworlds, and that the omnipotence of conformity does not always suppress the possibilities of interstices from which arise discreet movements and slender vitalities, vectors of emergence, crucibles of thought and action, and even potentialities of transformation …

Returning, lingering, and complicating constitute the chosen arts of getting by, marking each scholar's resolve not only to survive but to respond. "Nameable clarities" (Stewart, 2010, p. 344) such as peace, school form, climate, history, protest, violence, curriculum, childhood, or literature are forms of attending to what has happened and what is happening – the differences and indifferences of our time. Each preoccupation is a worlding, "an attunement to a singular world's texture and shine" (p. 341), revealing vital spurts of intentionality, moments of encounter, glimpses of history, and "slender vitalities" of insight in the shadowlands.

NOTES

1 Machado de Oliveira (2021) uses the term "modernity/coloniality," signalling "historical, systemic, and ongoing processes that are inherently violent and unsustainable" (p. 18). As a constellation of movements, she writes, modernity cannot exist without "expropriation, extraction, exploitation, militarization, dispossession, destitution, genocides, and ecocides" that connote coloniality (p. 18).

2 I first encountered the notion of the "arts of getting by" in Deborah Britzman's (1998) *Lost Subjects, Contested Objects: Toward a Psychoanalytic Inquiry of Learning*. Attributing the phrase to Parveen Adams in the *The Emptiness of the Image*, Britzman proceeds to characterize "the arts of getting by" as "a fugitive moment … something quite elusive" (p. 23).

REFERENCES

Adams, P., & Cousins, M. (1996). The truth on assault. In P. Adams (Ed.), *The emptiness of the image: Psychoanalysis and sexual difference* (pp. 57–70). Routledge.

Aoki, T. (2005). Teaching as indwelling between two curriculum worlds (1986/1991). In W. F. Pinar & R. L. Irwin (Eds.), *Curriculum in a new key: The collected works of Ted Aoki* (pp. 159–65). Lawrence Erlbaum Associates.

Aswell Doll, M. (2017). Excavating the self: The archaeologies of Pinar and Hillman. In M. Aswell Doll (Ed.), *The reconceptualization of curriculum studies: A Festschrift in honor of William F. Pinar* (pp. 50–8). Routledge.

Beckert, J. (2020). The exhausted futures of neoliberalism: From promissory legitimacy to social anomy. *Journal of Cultural Economy*, *13*(3), 318–30. https://doi.org/10.1080/17530350.2019.1574867

Britzman, D. (1998). *Lost subjects, contested objects: Toward a psychoanalytic inquiry of learning*. State University of New York Press.

Cuban, L. (2013). *Inside the black box of classroom practice. Change without reform in American education*. Harvard Education Press.

Doll, W. E., Jr., (2002). Ghosts and the curriculum. In W. E. Doll, Jr. & N. Gough (Eds.), *Curriculum visions* (pp. 23–70). Peter Lang.

Gordon, A. F. (2008). *Ghostly matters: Haunting and the sociological imagination*. University of Minnesota Press.

Hartley, D. (2000). Shoring up the pillars of modernity: Teacher education and the quest for certainty. *International Studies in Sociology of Education*, *10*(2), 113–31. https://doi.org/10.1080/09620210000200058

Lee, N. Y. S., Wong, L. E., & Ursino, J. M. (Eds.). (2022). *Lingering with the works of Ted T. Aoki: Historical and contemporary significance for curriculum research and practice*. Routledge.

Machado de Oliveira, V. (2021). *Hospicing modernity: Facing humanity's wrongs and the implications for social activism*. North Atlantic Books.

Pinar, W. F. (2005). "A lingering note": An introduction to the collected works of Ted T. Aoki. In W. F. Pinar & R. L. Irwin (Eds.), *Curriculum in a new key: The collected works of Ted Aoki* (pp. 1–85). Lawrence Erlbaum Associates.

– (2015). *Educational experience as lived: Knowledge, history, alterity: The selected works of William F. Pinar*. Routledge.

Pinar, W. F., & Grumet, M. R. (2006). *Toward a poor curriculum*. Educator's International Press. (Original work published 1976)

Ryan, D. (2022, January 25). The kids are not alright: B.C. students face learning losses and uncertainty due to COVID-19. *Vancouver Sun*. https://vancouversun.com/news/local-news/the-kids-are-not-alright-students-face-learning-losses-and-uncertainty

Stewart, K. (2010). Afterward: Worlding refrain. In M. Gregg & G. J. Seigworth (Eds.), *The affect theory reader* (pp. 339–53). Duke University Press.

Todd, S. (2003). *Learning from the other: Levinas, psychoanalysis, and ethical possibilities*. State University of New York Press.

Contributors

Sidrah Anees is an independent scholar, with a Bachelor of Arts in Sociology with a concentration in Criminology, Deviance and Social Control; and a Bachelor of Education with a specialization in Social Studies. She enjoys reading and hiking. Sidrah currently works in the non-profit sector.

Kumari Beck is Associate Professor, Co-Director for the Centre for Research on International Education, and co-academic coordinator of the Equity Studies in Education master's program in the Faculty of Education at Simon Fraser University, British Columbia in Canada. Her research interests span internationalization of higher education, international education, internationalization of curriculum, equity issues in education, and international development. The courses she teaches reflect these inter-related interests: intercultural and international education, critical multiculturalism and anti-racist education, the politics of difference, contemporary issues in curriculum, teaching for social justice, and issues in development and education.

Kathy Bickmore is Professor in Curriculum and Pedagogy and Comparative International and Development Education at OISE, University of Toronto. She studies young people's school learning opportunities for building and making peace, gender equity, and democratic justice in comparative transnational and local perspectives. She co-edited *Comparative and International Education: Issues for Teachers* (2017 Canadian Scholars Press), and edited *Peace-building (in) Education: Democratic Approaches to Conflict in Schools and Classrooms* (2014 *Curriculum Inquiry*). Recent chapters appear in *Contestations of Citizenship: Children and Youth, Democracy, and Education in an Era of Global Change* (Routledge) and *International Handbook on Critical Theories of Education* (Palgrave).

Emily Blackmore has her Bachelor of Education with a specialization in Social Studies. Currently, Emily teaches in a small northern Alberta community. She is passionate about learning more about Reconciliation and about Indigenous ways of knowing. Emily enjoys reading, knitting, and being outdoors with her dog.

David Blades is Professor of Science Education and Curriculum Studies at the University of Victoria in Victoria, British Columbia Canada. He is a former Associate Dean, Teacher Education and award-winning teacher, including a 2016 3M National Teaching Fellowship. David is also a Killam scholar and holds a Ted Aoki Award for his research on curriculum change. His research examines the practice and philosophy of science education, curriculum change, ethics and aesthetics in science teacher education. David loves playing guitar, hiking, snowshoeing, and exploring with family and friends the bays and marinas of the Pacific Northwest aboard their sail boat, *Almirena.*

Susan Dion is a Potawatomi-Lenapé scholar with Irish/French ancestry who has been working in the field of education for more than thirty years. She is the inaugural Associate Vice President Indigenous Initiatives at York University and Professor in the Faculty of Education. Her research focuses on Indigenizing, decolonizing, and realizing urban Indigenous education. Dion works in collaboration with the Toronto District School Board Indigenous Education Centre on research and program development. She is widely consulted by diverse community groups, workplaces, and institutions on developing methods for building more equitable, respectful relationships between Indigenous and non-Indigenous people.

Claudia Eppert is Associate Professor in the Department of Secondary Education at the University of Alberta, where she teaches undergraduate and graduate courses in Curriculum Studies and English Language Arts Education. Her research focuses on the ethical and pedagogical complexities of witnessing social/environmental suffering and trauma through literary, aesthetic, and contemplative engagements, and on the possibilities for psycho-social and ecological transformation. She is co-editor (with Roger I. Simon and Sharon Rosenberg) of *Between Hope and Despair: Pedagogy and the Remembrance of Historical Trauma,* which received an AESA Critics Choice Book Award. She is also co-editor (with Hongyu Wang) of *Cross-Cultural Studies in Curriculum: Eastern Thought, Educational Insights,* which received *AERA Outstanding Book Recognition* and an *AESA Critics Choice Book Award.* In addition to numerous book chapters, she has published in such peer reviewed journals as *New German Critique, Journal of Philosophy of Education, The Review of Education/Pedagogy/Cultural Studies, Studies in Philosophy and Education, JCT: Journal of Curriculum Theorizing,* and *Changing English: Studies in Reading and Culture.*

Clermont Gauthier has published several works on the theme of pedagogy, its origins, its foundations, and teacher training. He held the Canada Research Chair in the Study of Teacher Education (2000–2014). He is co-founder and researcher emeritus of the Centre for Interuniversity Research on Teacher Education and the Teaching Profession (CRIFPE). Now retired from Université Laval, Quebec, he continues to publish on the theme of teaching.

Jen Gilbert is Professor of Education at York University. Gilbert is author of *Sexuality in School: The Limits of Education* (University of Minnesota Press, 2014) and collaborator on The Beyond Bullying Project, an LGBTQ+ storytelling and research study in high schools. Gilbert's research focuses on LGBTQ+ students, teachers, and families; sex education; and youth studies.

Jocelyn Létourneau, FRSC, is Professor of Canadian History, Université Laval, Quebec City, where he held a Canada Research Chair for 14 years. During his career, he has been twice a Fulbright Fellow, first at Berkeley/Stanford and then at Yale. He received fellowships from the Institute for Advanced Study (Princeton), the Collegium de Lyon, the Zentrum für interdisziplinäre forschung (U. Bielefeld), and the Trudeau Foundation; he has been visiting scholar at UCL-Institute of Education. Author of numerous publications, Prof. Létourneau was awarded in 2018 the ACFAS André-Laurendeau Prize for his excellence in research and influence in humanities.

David Lewkowich is Associate Professor in the Department of Secondary Education at the University of Alberta with a research background in literacy education, reading experience, psychoanalytic theory, and comics literature. In his teaching he invites indeterminate curiosity into the classroom, and encourages all kinds of experimentation on the way to building and dwelling with knowledge. Current interests and passions include ASMR, noise-making, old toys, and the cultural history of teachers in comics.

Kelsey MacKenzie has her Bachelor of Education specializing in Social Studies. She is currently working as an elementary school teacher in Calgary, Alberta Canada. Having a background in Social Sciences (Bachelor of Arts in Anthropology), she aims to find connections between the two fields. Kelsey has a passion for outdoor education and project-based learning. In her free time she enjoys hiking, backcountry camping, and gardening.

Nicholas Ng-A-Fook is Professor of Curriculum Theory and Vice-Dean of Graduate Studies at the University of Ottawa. He is the former Director of the Teacher Education and Indigenous Teacher Education Programs at the

Faculty of Education. His teaching and research are situated within the wider international field of curriculum studies, history education, and life writing research. Dr. Ng-A-Fook is currently part of several SSHRC grants that seek to disrupt settler colonialism, systemic racisms, and inequities across the K-12 school and university curriculum. He recently created the FooknConversation podcast to address these challenges with colleagues, community activists, artists, educational leaders, and teachers. Dr. Ng-A-Fook has co-published several award-winning books such as, but not limited to, *Oral History and Education: Theories, Dilemmas, and Practices*; and *Provoking Curriculum Studies: Strong Poetry and Arts of the Possible in Education*.

Veronica Pacini-Ketchabaw is Professor of Early Childhood Education in the Faculty of Education and Director of the Interdisciplinary Centre for Research in Curriculum at Western University in Ontario, Canada. Her writing and research contribute to the *Common Worlds Research Collective* and the *Early Childhood Pedagogies Collaboratory*.

Anne M. Phelan is Professor in the Department of Curriculum and Pedagogy at the University of British Columbia and Honorary Professor at The Education University of Hong Kong. Her research focuses on teachers' intellectual and political freedom and responsibility, and on the creation of teacher education programs and policies that support those ends. Dr. Phelan is the author of *Curriculum Theorizing and Teacher Education: Complicating Conjunctions* (2015, Routledge), and with Matthew Clarke, *The Power of Negative Thinking: Teacher Education and the Political* (2017, Routledge). With William F. Pinar, Nicholas Ng-A-Fook, and Ruth Kane, she is co-editor of *Reconceptualizing Teacher Education: A Canadian Response to a Global Challenge* (2020, University of Ottawa Press); and with Jennifer Sumsion, *Critical Readings in Teacher Education: Provoking Absences* (2008, Sense Publishers).

William F. Pinar is the Tetsuo Aoki Professor in curriculum studies at the University of British Columbia in Vancouver. Pinar is the author of *Moving Images of Eternity: George Grant's Critique of Time, Teaching and Technology* (2019, University of Ottawa Press) and of the forthcoming *A Praxis of Presence in Curriculum Theory: Advancing Currere against Cultural Crises in Education* (Routledge). With Anne Phelan, Nicholas Ng-A-Fook, and Ruth Kane, he is co-editor of *Reconceptualizing Teacher Education: A Canadian Contribution to a Global Challenge* (2020, University of Ottawa Press).

Jackie Seidel is Associate Professor (Curriculum and Learning) in the Werklund School of Learning at the University of Calgary. She is passionate about exploring the existential and pedagogical meanings of ecological and social justice with teachers, including what it means for curriculum and pedagogy to face biodiversity loss and climate change. She enjoys writing poetry, knitting socks, and cycling. Several colonies of honeybees occupy her yard, and she enjoys their sweet buzz, earthy scent, and putting her bare hands in the hives.

Teresa Strong-Wilson is Associate Professor in the Faculty of Education at McGill University and Editor-in-Chief of the *McGill Journal of Education*. Her research has primarily been with teachers on critical use of stories in social justice education. She has published extensively in autobiography, curriculum, early childhood, memory studies and social justice education, in such peer-reviewed journals as *Changing English, Children's Literature in Education, Educational Theory, Journal of Curriculum Studies, Journal of Curriculum Theorizing, Teachers and Teaching,* and *Theory into Practice*. Her most recently published book is called *Teachers' Ethical Self-Encounters with Counter-Stories in the Classroom: From Implicated to Concerned Subjects* (Routledge, 2021).

Index